FINGERS

The Man who Brought Down Irish Nationwide
and Cost Us €5.4bn

ABOUT THE AUTHORS

Tom Lyons is deputy business editor with *The Sunday Independent*. He is an award-winning journalist and was joint National Newspapers of Ireland Business and Economics journalist of the year 2011. He is co-author of *The FitzPatrick Tapes*.

Richard Curran is a business journalist and broadcaster. A former deputy editor of *The Sunday Business Post*, he has also been business editor of the *Irish Independent* and business correspondent with RTE News. He has made several documentaries for RTE Television including 'Future Shock: Property Crash' in 2007. He is the presenter on RTE Television's highly successful 'Dragon's Den'.

FINGERS

The Man who Brought Down Irish Nationwide and Cost Us €5.4bn

**TOM LYONS AND
RICHARD CURRAN** ～

Gill & Macmillan

Gill & Macmillan
Hume Avenue, Park West, Dublin 12
with associated companies throughout the world
www.gillmacmillanbooks.ie

© Tom Lyons and Richard Curran 2013
978 07171 5583 5

Typography design by Make Communication
Print origination by Carole Lynch
Printed and bound by CPI Group (UK) Ltd,
Croydon, CRO 4YY

This book is typeset in Linotype Minion and
Neue Helvetica.

The paper used in this book comes from the
wood pulp of managed forests. For every tree
felled, at least one tree is planted, thereby
renewing natural resources.

A CIP catalogue record for this book is available
from the British Library.

5 4 3 2 1

CONTENTS

ACKNOWLEDGEMENTS

The authors would like to thank Fergal Tobin, publishing director at Gill & Macmillan. He both commissioned this book and provided invaluable support along the way. We would also like to thank his team in G&M, including Deirdre Rennison Kunz, managing editor, and Teresa Daly, publicist.

We are grateful to all the people who provided source material and answered our questions regarding the Irish Nationwide story. Many of the people who contributed to this book must remain anonymous, but we would like to offer them our heartfelt thanks. We could not have written this book without you.

In putting together a project of this kind we drew upon newspaper and broadcast reports from many journalists over the decades. The publications used are named in the text, but we would like to acknowledge some of the great journalists whose work or recollections helped us complete this book. In no particular order, they include Brian Carey, Simon Carswell, David Murphy, Matt Cooper, Ted Harding, Frank Fitzgibbon, Aine Coffey, Damien Kiberd, Miriam O'Callaghan, 'Prime Time', John McManus, Liam Collins, Shane Ross, Ronald Quinlan, Seán O'Rourke, Brendan Keenan, Paul Drury, Siobhán Creaton, Frank Connolly, Colm Keena and Dearbháil McDonald.

The authors would also like to draw attention to Bill Tyson, a fine journalist, who was prepared to challenge Irish Nationwide before anybody else dared to do so.

The authors would also like to thank all at Animo and RTE who worked on the Fingleton documentary.

Richard Curran would like to thank his parents, Noel and Betty, along with his brothers and sisters, Margaret, Eugene, John, Noel, David and Bridget, for their help and support throughout his career (especially Noel, who encouraged him to become a journalist in the first place). Most of all he would like to thank his wife, Kathy, for her incredible patience taking care of their sons, Dallan and Oirghiall, while countless late nights and weekends were spent putting this book together, and also her parents, Terence and Philomena Donaghy, who gave tireless support at home while he was away working on this project. He would also like to thank Cliff Taylor, editor of the *Sunday Business Post*, for his continued understanding of the demands of a project like this, and the entire editorial team at the *Sunday Business Post*, with whom he enjoyed working for six years. He would also like to thank Brendan Doherty from Drung in Inishowen, Co. Donegal, who provided a badly needed fax machine in emergencies!

Tom Lyons would like to thank Lynne for her love and support while putting this book together. He would like to thank his parents, Lorcan and Frances; his three brothers, Eoin, Lorcan and Vincent; all the Lyons and Foley clan; and his friends from school, university and elsewhere. Tom would like to thank all his colleagues at the *Sunday Independent*, including Anne Harris, Nick Webb, Shane Fitzsimons, Róisín Burke, Louise McBride, Daniel McConnell, Niamh Horan, Jerome Reilly, Brendan O'Connor, Maeve Sheehan, Willie Kealy, Jody Corcoran and Campbell Spray. He would also like to acknowledge his friends at the *Sunday Times*, 'Newstalk', the *Irish Independent* and other media, including Ian Kehoe, Chris Donoghue, Niall Brady, Conor Brophy, Paddy McDonnell, Charlie Weston, John Mooney, Mark Tighe, Niamh Lyons, Gavin Sheridan, Mark Paul, Vinnie O'Dowd, Ian Guider, Neil Callanan, Douglas Thompson and Bryan Meade.

PROLOGUE

Fingers and the Prince

P rince Albert of Monaco and his fiancée, Charlene Wittstock, were used to turning heads. Wittstock, a stunning South African former Olympic swimmer, would have attracted attention anywhere, even if she was not accompanied by a minor European royal who was the son of the late American actor Grace Kelly.

However, at a private dinner in the K Club at Straffan, Co. Kildare, on the night of Sunday 3 April 2011 it wasn't the soon-to-be-royal who caused eyebrows to be raised: instead it was the sight of a neatly dressed 73-year-old gentleman who sat down with her for a jovial dinner. This was Michael Fingleton, the old boss of Irish Nationwide Building Society, who regaled the prince and his glamorous bride-to-be as if his society had never collapsed at a cost of €5.4 billion to the taxpayer.

The dinner, on the first floor of the Palmer Smurfit Clubhouse, was in the elegant surroundings of the Kwam Suk-Royal Thai and oriental restaurant, which was celebrating its opening weekend. The owner of the resort, the multi-millionaire paper and packaging tycoon Michael Smurfit, was hosting the soirée.

Fingleton, known as 'Fingers', was among the twenty or so guests invited to the exclusive gathering. For four decades he had ruled his small building society with an iron fist. His nickname reflected his shrewdness, his love of power and his immense greed. Unlike Smurfit, whose father had been a successful businessman, Fingleton was an entirely self-made man. He was a gossip, who could be good company, but he was also a man with a controlling and even vindictive side to his character, which was capable of keeping many secrets.

Fingleton prided himself on always having the inside track. This allowed him to mix with minor European royalty as easily as he had with the elite of boom-time Ireland, who had got ahead sometimes by what they knew but other times only by who they knew.

By 2011, however, this was no longer enough. The tide of public opinion had turned against men like Fingers. He was no longer an influential figure, someone to be feared, but was instead being hunted by the media, which blamed him—not entirely unreasonably—for being one of those who caused Ireland's economic collapse.

The fall of Fingleton's beloved building society came after Ireland's property bubble burst spectacularly. The taxpayer has had to foot the bill of €5.4 billion, at the cost of drastic cut-backs in public services.

From the wreckage of his fiefdom Fingleton had walked away with a bonus of €1 million and a pension fund worth at its peak €27 million. He had received more than €11 million in pay, bonuses and benefits in the six years before he left the society. He had helped impoverish a nation, but he still enjoyed a life of holidays abroad, giving him a slight tan behind his trademark goatee beard.

Sitting near Fingleton was Michael Lowry, the scandal-dogged Tipperary politician who still managed to top the poll. Only the previous month Lowry had been accused by a tribunal of inquiry of having a 'profoundly corrupt' relationship with Ben Dunne, scion of the wealthy retail family. On top of that, the tribunal concluded that he had improperly 'delivered' a valuable mobile phone licence to a young entrepreneur, Denis O'Brien, who later became Ireland's richest man.

None of the twenty guests at the dinner cared a jot about either Fingleton's or Lowry's fall into disgrace but were happy to dine with both men. The meal was a pleasant and cordial affair, preceding an official visit by Prince Albert to Ireland, a country that had once been compared to his wealthy principality. Now, however, Ireland had fallen a long way from being considered one of the wealthiest countries in the world. Instead it was lumped in with Greece, deemed a disaster area and a beggar reliant on hand-outs from its wealthier euro-zone partners, such as Germany and France.

News of the dinner caused a minor diplomatic incident, with the Tánaiste and Minister for Foreign Affairs, Éamon Gilmore, insisting that 'we had nothing to do with it. It was a private dinner.' Both Fingleton and Lowry refused to comment or even confirm that they had been in attendance.

Smurfit, Ireland's honorary consul for life in Monaco, was a vastly wealthy man who had done it all in business. He didn't give a fig about public opinion when it came to old friends. Later, in October 2011, an indignant Smurfit would tell Justine McCarthy in the *Sunday Times* that he believed both Fingleton and Lowry were innocent men. Fingleton, he suggested, was simply a scapegoat for others eager to assign blame for Ireland's loss of economic sovereignty when its banking collapse forced it to seek a joint EU-IMF bail-out. 'People will always look for somebody to hang because of what's happened. That, of course, is way over-exaggerated and totally unjustified in relation to Fingleton, as far as I'm concerned,' Smurfit said.

The truth, as uncovered in forensic detail in this book, is that when it comes to Fingleton, his rise and fall, along with his toxic building society, in a sense Smurfit is right. The twisted tale of unchecked personal ambition and greed that is Fingleton's story could never have happened for so many decades without many willing, and some unwitting, accomplices.

Irish Nationwide is the second-largest corporate failure in Irish history, after Anglo Irish Bank. Despite the scale of its losses, relatively little is known about its inner workings. This is the tale of the men in suits, in banking, politics, the bond market and regulation, who allowed Fingleton to run so recklessly that he cost every citizen dearly. He could not have done it alone.

Irish Nationwide, relative to its size, is the worst bank in the country, with hidden secrets that even five years into financial crisis remain unknown to a public who have nonetheless been forced to pick up the enormous bill for its collapse.

This book looks at both Fingers the man and the financial institution he created. It examines the reasons for the society's failure and Fingleton's direct and indirect role in it and brings the situation regarding both the banker and his society up to the present.

It exposes for the first time the way in which Fingleton was allowed to operate at will around the board table at Irish Nationwide, despite the society being chaired by an eminent professor of banking and being regularly micro-managed by the state's banking watchdog. It shows how the Financial Regulator knew about colossal failings in the society from 2000 but failed to really do anything about it. It publishes for the first time the details of the Ernst and Young report, commissioned by the Central Bank to examine what was going on in the society in regard to failings of corporate governance.

It names the clients of Irish Nationwide who ended up as beneficiaries of those failings, and it examines their relationship with Fingleton.

It divulges what life was like inside Irish Nationwide for those working under Michael Fingleton.

It delves into the culture of the company and the management style of the man who brought it down.

It examines the role of Fingleton's family: his son Michael junior, who helped run the British and European lending operations, and the British law firm at which his daughter works, which acted on both sides of property deals (for the society and the client). It also raises the issue of his other son's mysterious Chinese property venture, into which funds from Irish Nationwide's biggest borrower were paid.

The book looks at Fingleton's appetite for financing lavish projects, such as the €50 million renovation of the yacht *Christina O*, Updown Court (the most expensive house in Britain), the Kilternan Hotel (loans of €150 million for a hotel project Fingleton never even went to see), and the Provençal Hotel renovation in the French Riviera that has never been finished, among many other deals.

It also looks at the life of Michael Fingleton, from early beginnings working for charity in Nigeria to his social life, his friends, his lavish expenses, and how in the end he blew his fortune and ended up as part of a small group of pariah figures, blamed for costing Irish citizens billions.

Fingleton's closeness to politicians—usually as a lender but also as a business partner—is also analysed. We look at the extraordinary deal he believed he had struck with the government as he walked out of the ruins of his building society. We also uncover the top borrowers from the society near the peak of the boom and reveal some of the many well-known names from politics, business and the media who he favoured. And we report on how the taxpayer was forced into paying the bill when the music stopped.

The book also reveals the mistakes made by the Irish Nationwide board, the government and the regulator in allowing this failure to happen over many decades. And it looks forward to what is likely to happen now in follow-up legal actions against Fingleton and other board members.

Fingleton had many contradictions, and he often had two sides. He was capable of being generous but could also be a bully. He knew everybody but was in many ways a loner. He had huge appetites for the high life but was obsessed with driving down costs. He was a perfectionist but with huge personal flaws. His character is more intriguing and complex than that of other bankers.

In the end, what was it within him that drove him to ultimately give two fingers to the Irish people, despite the horrendous cost of his greed and lust for power?

Michael Fingleton's survival for decades as a rogue banker in charge of a toxic building society goes to the heart of the dark side of the 'Celtic Tiger', which would eventually kill it. The implosion of Irish Nationwide was not an isolated incident among Irish lenders: others collapsed, or would have collapsed if not for the intervention of the state. But Irish Nationwide was not quite like the others. This was a building society dominated by one man for more than thirty-seven years. Its mistakes were his mistakes. Its failings were his failings.

The Central Bank had the information and the powers needed to force the society to change direction. It knew what was going on but failed to take real action. The other banks were a calamity that would always have happened when the property bubble burst; Irish Nationwide was a financial disaster waiting to happen. For many years in plain view.

Chapter 1 ∿

FINGLETON: CHAMPION OF LAW AND ORDER

On 5 July 1983 Michael Fingleton took the stand in Dublin's daunting Circuit Criminal Court. Outside, the dark River Liffey flowed on a bright Tuesday afternoon. Smartly dressed, with his trademark dark goatee neatly clipped, Fingleton cut a dapper figure. The respected boss of Irish Nationwide—the up-and-coming building society beloved of the media—was comfortable as he slid into the witness box.

He was the first witness in what promised to be the explosive trial of Alex Tarbett, former chief executive of Concern, the country's biggest overseas aid agency. Fingleton had the rather delicate task of outlining the evidence in the criminal prosecution of a former friend who faced both ruin and imprisonment.

In the confined space of the courtroom Fingleton could see Tarbett, only yards from him. Their eyes met. Tarbett, a smooth-talking and accomplished businessman who lived in an expensive suburb of south Co. Dublin, was not the court's typical accused. He looked a sorry sight. Despite his wealthy background he had suffered the indignity of having his assets frozen by the court, so he could not afford his own lawyers. The only concession made to his former position in the establishment was that Judge John Gleeson granted leave for his distraught wife, Mary, to sit beside him throughout the trial.

A 54-year old father of six children, Tarbett was a friend of cardinals and bishops. He had mixed in the highest levels of Irish business, even working for a time as lieutenant of Michael Smurfit, the packaging tycoon and one of the country's richest men. Now he was far from high society and was instead facing ten charges of embezzling £240,000. This was a colossal sum, equivalent to more than €1 million today. The money that was allegedly taken had been collected from the public and the Church to help the poorest of the poor in Africa and Asia over a period of three years, up to the time he left the charity in 1981. All the alleged fraud had taken place under Fingleton's nose as chairman of the charity from the end of 1977. It was embarrassing for Fingleton, who prided himself on his canniness and ability to judge people. Now the newspapers were all over the story, and Concern's hard-earned reputation was threatened.

Maurice Gaffney, senior counsel for the prosecution, began his questioning. He had already described to the jury how the prosecution's case was that Tarbett had repeatedly moved large sums out of Concern's bank accounts into his personal account and how he had managed to siphon off big cheques made out to Concern for his own benefit.

It was up to Fingleton—a trained barrister and accountant—who had personally led Concern's internal investigation into the affair, to fill in the damning detail.

Fingleton was a credible and steely witness, who showed little sentiment for Tarbett's predicament. He began his evidence by describing how Concern's main bank account in 1978 was in the College Green branch of Bank of Ireland, but it also had several other accounts, including one with AIB in Baggot Street. At that time, Fingleton said, everybody trusted Tarbett and nobody suspected him of wrongdoing.

As chief executive of Concern, Tarbett earned a modest salary of £4,000 a year, but he appeared to be independently wealthy, as he also ran his own publishing company. There was no reason to believe he would need to top up his earnings by stealing from Concern.

Unknown to Concern, however, Fingleton stated that in 1978 Tarbett had set up a new bank account in AIB, Baggot Street, in his own name. He told the court that two signatures were required for withdrawing any money from Concern's accounts, but somehow Tarbett had got around this and managed to move money around on the strength of his sole signature.

Tarbett had explained his actions to AIB by saying it was to cover his personal expenses as he jetted around the world's disaster zones and went on epic fund-raising drives. As a result he had managed to use Concern's bank account as his personal piggy-bank, to be tapped into at will.

Fingleton told the court that Concern had found out what was really going on only after Tarbett left the charity when his contract expired in September 1981. In November 1981, he said, questions suddenly emerged about where large sums of money from donors had gone. The Bishop of Orange County, California, Dr William Johnson, had set alarm bells ringing by asking how his donation had been spent. He said his parish had given a donation of $85,500 to Concern that nobody in Concern knew about. About the same time Concern also found out that a cheque for £20,000 from its Cork branch had gone missing.

The organisation quickly began a review, led by Fingleton, into what began to look like fraud on a grand scale. Fingleton summoned Tarbett to explain himself at a specially called meeting of the executive committee in Dublin. 'I interviewed him and put it to him that the auditors had discovered that cheques sent to Concern seemed to have been lodged in his account,' Fingleton said. Tarbett seemed surprised at this news. He promised Fingleton that he would investigate it immediately and return that afternoon with a full explanation.

Later that day Tarbett rang back. He said he'd been delayed and asked for the meeting to be deferred until the following day.

Under questioning from a now deeply suspicious Fingleton, Tarbett admitted that he'd found two missing cheques for smaller sums in his bank account. He also said he'd uncovered a cheque to Concern for £4,000 that he had forgotten about. As for the cheque for £20,000 from the Cork branch of Concern, he said he had no idea where it was now.

Under pressure from Fingleton, Tarbett admitted that the money must somehow have ended up in his personal bank account. This was an 'error', he insisted.

Fingleton then raised the issue of the $85,500 from the bishop in California—a huge donation at the time. Tarbett admitted he had got the cheque but said he'd decided to hang on to it while he waited for a better exchange rate between the American dollar and the Irish pound. When he finally got around to cashing it he said he'd noticed for the first time that the cheque was not signed. 'He said he'd sent it back to the Bishop of Orange for signature,' Fingleton said. Somehow the cheque had then got lost, Tarbett suggested rather implausibly.

Fingleton openly disbelieved him. He told Tarbett he needed to come up with a much better explanation to account for the missing cheques. He demanded that Tarbett give Concern a letter authorising him to look inside his bank accounts. Under pressure, Tarbett had little choice but to give his consent.

Once the bank details were handed over, Fingleton could see big sums intended for the charity somehow ending up with Tarbett, who was spending large sums every month. Fingleton told the court that he was satisfied that none of these movements were legitimate.

Concern had hoped not to be forced to pursue Tarbett, and it had first invited him to repay all the disputed money. Tarbett had readily agreed, and the date of 21 November 1981 was set. It was a stalling tactic; and Fingleton told the court that in fact he had 'no knowledge' of any money being repaid. When the deadline passed, Fingleton called in the authorities.

On Saturday 19 December 1981 Detective-Sergeant John Carty of the Fraud Squad arrested Tarbett for questioning. Tarbett's plan to fly on Christmas Day to Australia for a holiday with his family had to be abruptly cancelled. He had a visitor's visa for a year, further arousing Fingleton's suspicions.

Fingleton finished his testimony and allowed others to fill in more gaps for the prosecution.

John Millett, Cork area organiser for Concern, said that a cheque for £20,000 dated 7 November 1978 and one for £7,500 dated 8 October 1980 had been sent to Concern. But, he said, he now knew they had made it only as far as Tarbett.

Seán Duffy, secretary of the Agency for Personal Service Overseas, said he had sent Concern a cheque for £4,164 in July 1981, but this too had stopped at Tarbett.

Ronald Smiley, chairperson of the Disaster Appeals Committee of Ireland, said he had sent a cheque for £84,000 to Concern in March 1980. The cheque had been paid out all right, on 14 April, but it had been done on the signature of Tarbett alone, and yet again the money had ended up in his bank account.

As the evidence against him mounted that Wednesday afternoon, Tarbett, acting in his own defence, recalled Fingleton to the stand. He had some questions to ask of his former friend who, in Tarbett's eyes, had turned against him.

Fingleton had shown that when it came to wrongdoing or treating an organisation's money as one's own he was fully prepared to step up, investigate and try to ensure that the money was at least given back. When this didn't happen Fingleton would not shirk his responsibilities in dealing with the matter.

Fingleton's own interest in Africa began in the late 1960s. Unmarried and without ties, he had travelled to Nigeria in 1968. Using his accountancy expertise, he had helped to administer the Catholic Bishops' Fund in Nigeria. There he had got to know most of the significant personalities in Concern and overseas development.

Based in the teeming capital of Lagos, he was part of an extended network of hundreds of Irish missionaries and lay people working there when a secessionist movement among the Igbo people in south-eastern Nigeria broke away and established the state of Biafra. The young Fingleton was part of a group of Irish people energised into action by the war and its consequent famine to begin helping not only on the ground but by embarking on a huge fund-raising drive in Ireland. It was an exciting time.

'Biafra was the first famine on television,' Tom Arnold, chief executive of Concern, recalled in an article in the *Irish Times* on 2 February 2008. 'But stories coming home from Irish missionaries, into almost every parish in the country, also contributed to the massive response.'

Among the Irish missionaries working in Biafra was the charismatic Father Raymond Kennedy of the Holy Ghost order. With his brother John O'Loughlin Kennedy and the latter's wife, Kay, he set up Africa Concern in March 1968, which later became simply Concern. By the close of 1968 they had raised £3½ million for Biafra—equivalent to €64 million today—as the public responded emotionally to television and press reports of devastating famine.

Michael Fingleton, while never based in Biafra during the war, still managed to play a part in the relief effort as well as helping with existing good works in Nigeria. The extent of his bravery is not clear. In an interview with the business magazine *Strategy* in July 1988 he described the experience as

unreal, interesting, exciting and a great adventure. You're not frightened when you're involved and you were much more likely to get killed in a car crash than in the war. They drove on the wrong side of the road and if there was a gap, there was a car.

In a profile of Fingleton in the *Sunday Business Post* in 1994 the journalist Ted Harding described what he called a 'celebrated' incident involving Fingleton as a sort of Indiana Jones figure. 'Irish clergy were rounded up and imprisoned in the country's Port Harcourt jail. Fingleton managed to cajole a pilot with government ties to fly him into the area. Coming off the plane, he was asked to open his case by security forces. The soldiers were stunned to see around £100,000 of bail money for the priests.'

Contemporaries of Fingleton in Concern don't recall him ever telling this story during the time they knew him—the 1970s to early 80s—so maybe it grew legs in the telling. Fingleton certainly never denied it: he was happy to foster the image of an adventurous, anti-establishment spirit. He regularly recalled Africa fondly in interviews about Irish Nationwide. For *Strategy* he described the Igbo people in awed terms. 'They're gracious, dignified, cultured and they're both fatalistic and ambitious. They've an extraordinary attitude to life—they don't worry about tomorrow and yet they've a voracious appetite for knowledge and they are highly educated. You'd see kids of 13 and 14 with a gun in one hand and an algebra in the other.' This attitude, combining knowledge with power, fascinated Fingleton.

Together with absorbing Nigerian culture Fingleton did a lot of growing up and left his three-year spell in a seminary firmly behind him. He tasted alcohol not only for the first time but also out of necessity, as canned beer was often a safer option when no clean water was available.

The Nigerian sojourn left one other lasting mark on Fingleton: his trademark beard, of which he merrily quipped, 'All imitators beware.'

When he returned to Ireland in 1970 to embark on his banking and business career with Irish Nationwide he was eager to continue helping out with Concern. On 19 June 2002 Tony Farmar interviewed Fingleton in a meeting room on the top floor of Irish Nationwide when he was researching for the official history of Concern, *Believing in Action*. Farmar said he was still clearly proud of his involvement. 'He obviously had contacts with Concern and Concern people because he became a member and later joined the board,' Farmar recalled. He was one of the ring-leaders pushing for the charity to change in response to its rapid growth in what Farmar called a 'fundamental conflict between the inspired enthusiast and the cool professional.'

As time went on, Fingleton, always impatient, became an increasingly harsh critic of the Kennedy brothers, who had put the charity on the map but were far from management experts.

By 1971 Concern was expanding from its base in Africa into East Pakistan, now Bangladesh, which was trying to break away from West Pakistan. A gigantic cyclone had hit the region, killing at least 300,000 people. This created a huge housing and sanitation problem, combined with a human tragedy. Concern, buoyed by its success in Nigeria, decided to help. It had substantial reserves, including £800,000 originally collected for Biafra, and a fund-raising network in Ireland. But there was disagreement about how effectively it was spending it.

John O'Loughlin Kennedy, according to *Believing in Action*, engaged in 'wild talk' and was prepared to consider everything from a Biafra-style airlift to sending Concern's ship, the *Columcille*, half way around the world to bring supplies. Deciding what to do created tensions within the board, and Fingleton and others were particularly angered by the proposed use of the *Columcille*, which they thought of as a needless and wasteful expense. Farmar recalled:

> They were all over the place. In one sense you have to think that Fingleton was smack right in wanting to tidy up Concern. Control it and discipline it and what have you. There is no question that the Kennedy brothers were very charismatic but with a slight tendency to trust in God. They had a slight tendency to just say let's do it.

By February 1972 feeling was so bad that Michael Doheny, a Holy Ghost priest, was forced to speak out in favour of the Kennedy brothers. '[Concern's] whole concept and history is based on big thinking, daring decisions, adventurous action . . . It seems to me there is no shortage of "prudent" people in the world, but a famine of courageous thinking.' The comment was a critique of the Fingleton faction, who took a rather different view.

On 10 May 1972 Fingleton and three others put their criticisms in writing. *Believing in Action* describes the letter, now buried in Concern's archives, in a telling way. 'The letter was aggressive beyond the heat typically generated in voluntary organisations,' it concluded. Farmar, recalling reading the letter, said he couldn't be certain that Fingleton was the principal mover behind it, but he suspected he was. The letter placed great emphasis on the high cost of administration at the time, which sucked up 35p of every pound raised.

> Fingleton was quite aggressive but I don't know if he wrote it . . .
> It was a very awkward time when Concern didn't know whether

it was coming or going. It was a strong letter repeating criticisms about accounting stewardship. It was about the 35 per cent. Basically the business people were complaining bitterly about the amount of expenditure relative to cost, and the boat was part of it.

Soon after the letter was written, Michael Doheny, fresh from the field, rode again to the Kennedys' side. 'I came back ten days ago full of the glory of Concern,' he told a meeting of Concern's executive. 'I came home full of the joy of it and I see this letter. In God's name we are spending energy and worry on negative things, let's get together, let's back up our team in Bangladesh.'

The rows, however, did not end; and gradually the Fingleton faction gained more influence in Concern. 'He felt the Kennedys had lost the plot,' Farmar said. '[Fingleton] wanted to declericise the organisation and broaden it into a more secular thing with proper plans and financial base.'

In 1974 Fingleton was among twenty-two people selected from the ranks of the clergy, former volunteers and business to join the council of Concern at its annual general meeting in Dublin. 'The council of Concern when he came in were people who had worked overseas,' Farmar said.

> They knew from their personal experience what was required but they weren't necessarily businesslike and quite a lot of them at that time were priests or religious. They felt—and this was how Fingleton put it to me—they slightly felt the lay people had a duty to supply the cash for them to do the good. That was the deal. That was how he put it to me.

Concern, as a result, saw its income rise and fall in response to particular crises. Fingleton wanted to make its funds more stable.

> His idea was to create a reserve and stop the boom and bust nature of the income. He wanted a three month reserve of expenditure in the kitty as it were. That was his plan.

Éanna Johnson, the then chairman, said:

> I had to manage the transition from highly charismatic, sometimes erratic founders into an organisation with goals and achievements.

That transition was made in the mid-70s. Organisations who don't make that transition don't survive.

There was some friction. Around that time an article appeared in Hibernia magazine that was highly critical of Concern. Michael would have been one of the ones who agreed with that article. It was part of my job to steer things away from personalities.

Fingleton's push for a more businesslike approach was reinforced when, in 1977, Alex Tarbett, a respected businessman and publisher, became chief executive of Concern. 'Tarbett was the one who refocused the thing,' Farmar said. 'Concern had become less effective. There was a sort of disillusion, and Tarbett provided it with a new drive and direction. Fingleton supported that.'

Tarbett was a marked departure from what went before. He had trustworthy credentials as a former student priest who studied in Maynooth in the 1940s, where he befriended the late Cardinal William Conway and many other members of the clergy. He had spent six years with the publishing house of C. J. Fallon and later joined the London publishers Geoffrey Chapman. His biggest coup, with the help of his friend Cardinal Conway, was to secure the rights to publish missals and other religious books in numerous international markets. He was feted in business and very much a friend of the Church.

His record in business also included running the retail, office equipment and publishing division of the Smurfit Group, then one of Ireland's most dynamic businesses. He left after 'personality differences', which was not that unusual among the employees of Michael Smurfit, who was a brilliant businessman but a hard taskmaster.

'Alex was very well connected and a smooth man. He was going to, and clearly did, change the scale of the thing,' Farmar said. At his first annual general meeting as chief executive, in 1977, Tarbett described passionately his vision for the charity, which was then nine years old. Back from a visit to Bangladesh, where Concern had forty-four volunteers working in the field, he said: 'If the public at large could see what I have seen in my very short visit, it would have no hesitation in saying "we must do more for Concern".' He described in vivid detail the scale of the catastrophe they were facing. 'Our engineers and agriculturists are today fighting a battle against time to ensure that vital crops will not be washed away in the next monsoon, to ensure that communication by road is possible from one stricken area to the other, to ensure that our nurses and doctors are dealing with malnutrition and helping to eradicate disease.'

It was powerful stuff, and the Irish people, including Fingleton, reacted to it. Despite his determination to expand Irish Nationwide, Fingleton decided to become even more involved in charity work.

Towards the end of 1977 he took over as chairman from Éanna Johnson. '[Fingleton] was very interested, very committed and very outspoken. I like people who speak their minds,' Johnson recalled in 2012.

Fingleton found in Tarbett a kindred spirit who was interested in expanding Concern in a more professional way. The Kennedy brothers were now far less influential—but, according to John O'Loughlin Kennedy in 2012, they did not bear Fingleton any ill will for squeezing them out.

[Fingleton] was chairman of Concern during a very difficult period and he was good. He could be very demanding. That was the Michael Fingleton I knew. He was a little bit gruff at times but behind the crusty exterior he wasn't as crusty inside as he appeared outside. He could have a short way of answering but apart from that he was a splendid person.

As Tarbett and Fingleton worked together, Concern's income tripled, to £2.3 million, while spending on non-field work was reduced to below 20 per cent.

The two men liked each other. They got to know each other on trips abroad, including a visit to Tanzania in 1978 to meet its first president, Julius Nyerere. At the time Nyerere was widely seen as a progressive African leader, a vocal opponent of colonialism and apartheid who helped found the Organisation of African Unity. (His reputation, like that of his visitors, would in time be tarnished as he turned to brutal prison camps that were used to quell dissent.)

As Concern grew rapidly under Tarbett, Fingleton hit on the idea of introducing tax relief to encourage more giving—an idea he would later promote in the 1990s and onwards for property in Ireland. In January 1981 Fingleton called for tax breaks in the *Irish Times* and suggested that the state should give more money to Concern, rather than to governments in the developing world or non-Irish aid agencies. 'My personal view is that if the same money was given to voluntary organisations such as Concern, we would spend it to greater advantage. We have greater flexibility, greater experience and expertise.' They were words that within less than a year would prove questionable.

With Tarbett's alleged fraud uncovered and in the process of being investigated, Fingleton faced a difficult task preparing his chairman's report for 1981. As ever, he didn't shirk from presenting the hard facts.

Last year has been the most difficult that Concern has ever seen. There has been a change in top management and in addition we are now in the midst of a depression the worst in 30 years.

Finally we have suffered the effects of the publicity from the impending court case which in itself has caused a great deal of work and worry for all members of Concern staff, the executive committee and council. It is evident that from here on it will be much more difficult to obtain local funding in Ireland. This should only encourage us to redouble our efforts.

We are advised that we will be able to recover funds if it can be established [that] they were misdirected. Members will be aware that the delay in calling the AGM was due to the necessity of calling the auditors to investigate these alleged irregularities.

Together with Father Aengus Finucane, Concern's brilliant and charismatic new chief executive, Fingleton now had to hold the charity together and to weather the coming storm of bad publicity. On 3 August 1983 the *Irish Times* reported that fears had been expressed at the July council meeting that its reputation had been damaged badly.

In a statement to the paper, the council, chaired by Fingleton, sought to assure the public that its problems were firmly in the past. 'Concern has always considered itself to be fully accountable to the public for all funds donated and entrusted to it for its work in the Third World,' it said. It assured the public that it had an accounts policy that, apart from its own personnel, was backed up by professional accountants who provided regular and detailed financial institutions.

Ironically, as we will see in relation to his own stewardship of Irish Nationwide in later years, Fingleton was keen to stress that the correct procedures now existed for ensuring that an isolated incident could never be repeated.

Meanwhile Father Finucane embarked on a national campaign in parishes and communities throughout the country to assure its supporters that Concern was still a charity they could trust. 'Alex did a lot of good work while he was there. He had vision,' Johnson recalled. 'It was a serious shock, a very serious shock when money went missing.'

As a result of his years of preparation, Fingleton proved a formidable witness when Tarbett called him back to the stand in 1983. He was on top of his brief, having worked hard to get to the bottom of what had happened. Johnson recalled: 'He did extremely well handling the situation. Michael Fingleton called me into a mini war cabinet to help handle the situation. He was firm, tough and absolutely resolute that it all would be done in the open. There would be no cover-up of anything.' Johnson said while Fingleton was tough he was 'not unreasonable. For example on two occasions I asked him to help people who didn't meet the usual loan criteria for mortgages. They were people of great personal integrity. On both occasions he did speak to them and he gave them both mortgages. Neither of them let him down.'

Tony Farmar recalled:

[Fingleton] reckons it took him two years to sort out the mess. Eventually he put together a package and in effect forced the bank to repay. One of the points the bank had failed to do was insist on second signatures. They had made mistakes.

He felt put out that on his watch it had happened. He had been the promoter of a sort of business like Concern and to have this happen with a businessman . . . he felt a bit miffed and a bit put out that the person he had promoted and was in favour of had done this. There was an element of feeling responsible to get it right again.

Not everybody agreed that Tarbett should be pursued legally, Farmar said.

There was some pressure. As in all of these things there was a big temptation to hush it up. There was a lot of pressure to sweep it under the carpet. There was another point . . . 'If we started opening the sea cocks God knows what we will find.' He said, 'We didn't know quite what else was there. We knew what we could see but maybe there was other stuff.' He took the view that it was actually the responsible thing to do to take the case.

Tarbett was extremely well connected to the clergy and what have you. And of course you know the Irish way: it is always assumed the individual is right and the organisation is wrong. There is always an assumption that there is a nasty organisation beating up the unfortunate individual.

Facing his former friend in the courtroom, Fingleton showed little sign of strain or emotion. 'I don't think Michael had any difficulty. He was fair-minded but tough,' Éanna Johnson said. 'He would have had a personal liking for the guy but he was in no doubt [that he needed to be prosecuted].'

By questioning Fingleton on the matter, Tarbett hoped to show that it was not unusual for Concern to be lax with its bank accounts. Fingleton was having none of it. 'Nothing improper', he stated categorically, had ever happened in relation to overseas spending by Concern as long as he was there. He added that disciplinary action had never been required against anybody until now.

Tarbett put it to Fingleton that he had brought to his attention various problems with overseas accounts, and 'nothing much had been done about it.' Fingleton said he could not recall such complaints. He did admit there had been occasional problems overseas, but these were of an honest nature.

Tarbett made little headway against Fingleton. Instead the evidence against Tarbett kept mounting as a series of bank managers, Concern employees and donors gave their testimony.

On 13 July, Tarbett finally convinced the court to unfreeze a sum 'not greater than £2,000' to allow him mount a proper legal defence. Bill Shipsey, then an up-and-coming senior counsel, agreed to take on the case. Tarbett's defence now began to call witnesses.

Its first was Charles McCarthy of the Blackrock branch of Bank of Ireland, where Tarbett had borrowings. Tarbett knew there were rumours that he had stolen money from Concern to plough into a mansion in Co. Kerry worth £150,000 and he was anxious for McCarthy to clear the matter up. McCarthy told the court that Tarbett and his wife had only a 20 per cent stake in the property.

Shipsey then questioned Aengus Finucane on financial practices in the charity. Despite tough questioning, Finucane proved a reliable witness, and little headway was gained.

Father Michael Doheny, a founding member of Concern, did admit under questioning that Concern sometimes had 'loose arrangements' when it came to monitoring its many bank accounts. But he was definite that money had never gone missing before.

As Tarbett struggled to convince the jury, he finally decided on Thursday 16 July to address them directly. The next day's *Irish Independent* reported:

He said that the jury might have been confused by the picture painted of Concern by witnesses for the prosecution. It was implied that it was a tightly run organisation rather similar to a normal business and there was a chain of command from the council downwards, Tarbett said. There was also evidence given that there was a tight system to handle all expenditure with strict budgetary controls. This was not the case, Tarbett insisted.

He told the jury he was prepared to draw back a veil and reveal what Concern was about, but that he would not do this in any spirit of bitter or rancour despite what happened to him. 'When you are at the bottom of the barrel, as I have been for the past few months, not many people want you, but when you become successful, you start out as someone important or as someone who should not be questioned.'

Tarbett then described travelling to Tanzania, Yemen, America, England, Brussels, Geneva, Bangladesh, Calcutta and Singapore. He repeated Concern's admission that it had overseas bank accounts, not all of which were audited. He said he had questioned this 'from time to time,' and he maintained that it was not unusual for huge sums to be in the control of a small number of individuals. 'At times there was confusion and money was misspent or the budget exceeded, but on no occasion was I pointing any fingers at anybody,' he said, in a pointed reference to Fingleton and other senior figures in Concern.

In the early years the 'cupboard was bare,' he said, and he had covered many of his own expenses. There was an agreement in his contract that he would be reimbursed; and this was the reason, he argued—rather unconvincingly—that large sums of money had ended up in his bank account.

Essentially, the *Irish Independent* concluded, 'Mr Tarbett maintained that the factors which he might be found guilty of were carelessness, extravagance, and not to have kept a miser-like account of his expenses and outgoings.'

———

On Friday 15 July 1983 arguments concluded. Judge Gleeson told the jury they had been asked to consider a 'very disagreeable case.' Tarbett was highly educated and successful but they must not allow either sympathy or vindictiveness to cloud their judgement. He told them to 'take a good look at the defendant,' who he described as 'an impressive man, well cultured, good mannered and polite, and find out whether underneath that he was a clever exploiter of the bonanza that came his way.'

The jury should consider that Tarbett blamed the committee and council of Concern for his situation. 'You might think he, as chief executive, could have rectified any looseness.' They should also think about whether the looseness was of his own making, to allow a 'dishonest mentality to play ducks and drakes with Concern money and to live well.'

After one hour the jury returned. Tarbett was found guilty of all ten charges relating to the embezzlement of £240,000 between September 1978 and August 1981.

He asked for sentencing to be adjourned so that he could be allowed to plead mitigating circumstances. His counsel asked for bail, but this was refused. 'Honestly, I think in the long run it would be more merciful for you to remain in custody,' the judge told him. In response to Michael McDowell, counsel for the state, who suggested that a week's adjournment might be appropriate, the judge said: 'The sooner this poor fellow is put out of pain and knows what's facing him the better.' Tarbett's wife broke down when she heard that he was to be held in custody until sentencing. His family embraced him and clung to him as he was handcuffed and led out to a prison van. The nine-day trial, attended on most days by Fingleton, was finally over.

Afterwards an unnamed former colleague told the *Irish Independent* that Tarbett was a 'Walter Mitty, who liked everything to be as he wanted. I think he was afraid of being a failure. He probably used the money to influence people to like him. He gave the impression of being a big spender and a genial host . . . but in reality he was a lonely and insecure man.'

The following Thursday at 10 a.m. sentence was delivered. In his favour, Tarbett had no previous convictions and had never been before the courts before. But character references from Cardinal Tomás Ó Fiaich and Father Austin Flannery, a friend of Tarbett's for twenty-five years, among others, were not enough to save him. Father Flannery said, 'I could never see Tarbett as a crook or a person who would put personal gain before his duty to his employer. He took his role in life very seriously and had a missionary zeal.'

Dr Tom Walsh also testified in his friend's defence. 'He had a tremendous interest in the Third World and was a man of the highest possible integrity. His life-style was absolutely modest. He was probably overworked in this period . . .'

The most emotional moment came when Mary Tarbett described how her husband had taken on the job only on a part-time basis but that gradually it had taken up more and more of his time. 'My view of my husband will never change, and my respect for him is unique.'

In pronouncing sentence, Judge Gleeson said: 'I believe that the accused had locked himself into a world of belief where he was the philanthropic Sir Bountiful, not subject to his employers . . . I am not made of stone,' he said, 'and I pity you.' Tarbett was sentenced to three years' imprisonment.

Afterwards it was hard to understand why Tarbett had felt compelled to take so much money. 'There was no evidence that he spent the money on women or drink or that he was a heavy gambler,' the *Irish Independent* concluded. Yes, he had enjoyed a 'jet-set' life and drove a 'flashy' car, but he had also helped transform Concern from a small organisation into a major agency for overseas development.

Whatever his reasons, Tarbett's reputation was ruined. The former seminary student and successful publisher was finished. His reputation and his career never recovered.

A hard lesson had been learnt also by Concern. It kept growing and is now the biggest and most professional development agency in the country. Michael Fingleton too went on to greater success. Whether he learnt from Alex Tarbett's experience, however, is more debatable.

As the years went by, Fingleton was certainly happy with the acknowledgement of his role in the prosecution of his former friend and in ultimately forcing AIB to accept that it was negligent and should repay the missing money in full. A flattering profile in *Irish Business* in

July 1985 concluded: 'It may be assumed that Fingleton played a role in persuading AIB to make this handsome gesture.'

The lack of greater acknowledgement in *Believing in Action* seemed to rankle with Fingleton, a sign of his ego. Tony Farmar recalled a chilliness at the launch of the book in 2002 by the former Taoiseach Garret FitzGerald.

I suspect that he did feel quite personal about it and that's why he hammered at it so hard. Maybe he felt it was too cool an assessment of all that hard work. We all feel that we are insufficiently praised. I don't think he thought I gave him enough credit for AIB. He wasn't particularly happy about the way I expressed this.

Farmar read from the relevant page of his book.

Michael Fingleton devoted himself to forcing the bank to repay the money. He was so successful that Concern was very quickly able to announce [that] the bank had already repaid £200,000 in funds and would make sure the rest was recovered. After some shadow boxing the bank behaved well and the money was paid.

As he looked up from his book he remarked: 'There was a certain amount of disgruntlement that I didn't give him enough credit. He got back everything that was stolen. He got it all. He was very proud of that. He was like, "Yeah, I did it!" to me with slightly clenched teeth.'

Chapter 2

FROM TOBERCURRY TO THE TOP FLOOR

A layer of dust covered Michael Fingleton's old desk on the top floor of Nationwide House at Grand Parade, Dublin 6.

It was September 2012, and on all six floors helmeted workers were ripping out the building's innards. Within six weeks they were to have it ready for the Irish Bank Resolution Corporation, the state's bank set up to manage the winding down of the society and its toxic sister Anglo Irish Bank.

The shiny raised lettering of Irish Nationwide's name across the front of the building had been ripped down two years earlier. Only the untouched top floor and the handles of its grand entrance, which still bore the society's initials, remained of the institution Fingleton had ruled like a feudal lord, doling out billions to developers while ruling his staff and smaller borrowers with an iron rod.

Fingleton's green leather chair had deep creases from his years in charge. In front of him had sat politicians, sports stars, journalists and developers who had come to get a loan, ask a favour or beg a dig-out in their time of need. For more detailed conversation, whether on how to rezone a field for housing or how to borrow money to buy an extravagant holiday home, there was a round table at the front of his office. At this table, with its four chairs, Fingleton would pore over plans and numbers as he worked out where the society should lend, lend, lend.

Along the wall was an inlaid wooden bookcase with lockable drawers in which he kept his most sensitive files as well as room for a large television, where he could view video presentations from developers. The door to the left of his desk opened into his secretary's office, where big borrowers or cronies were left waiting on a long green sofa. To his right was the society's impressive boardroom, where the decisions Fingleton had already made were rubberstamped.

Fingleton had bought the premises in 1994 when he successfully bid for the former offices of P. J. Carroll, the cigarette manufacturers, and had converted the building, which had also once contained a cinema, into his headquarters. Under his supervision the society combined functions not unlike those of the previous occupants: spewing out toxicity and indulging in fantasy.

Fingleton's office was messy when he was there, but he had stripped it clean of every piece of paper when he finally left it in 2009 as the extent of his catastrophic rule began to emerge.

It was hard to imagine in the autumn of 2012. The office was full of light. At each end of the room it had panoramic views of Dublin city and county. His love of property had shown itself in the way so many buildings in view of his office had been financed by his decisions at Irish Nationwide. He could watch the city progress, like a real-life monopoly board.

Behind his desk Fingleton could see up towards the Dublin Mountains and Sandyford, while in front of him stretched the heart of the south city. Bang in the middle of his viewpoint when he was sitting at his desk was the distinctive outline of the Central Bank building in Dame Street. With its twelve steel trusses running down its façade to hold up each floor, it was an imposing building that was hard to miss. For Fingleton during the four decades he was in charge, however, it might as well have been invisible.

Michael Patrick Fingleton was born on 26 January 1938. His father was a garda, and Michael was second-youngest in a family of two brothers and two sisters. He grew up on the Mountain Road in Tobercurry, Co. Sligo.

The young Fingleton attended Holy Family Primary School between 1942 and 1946 before going on to St Joseph's Boys' School. At the age of thirteen he was sent to boarding school, St Nathy's College in Ballaghaderreen, the cathedral town on the Mayo-Roscommon border. Classmates included the greyhound trainers Charlie Faul and Luke Kilcoyne.

St Nathy's was a fee-paying school, but it was no holiday camp. More than two hundred boarders attended the school, which was in a former military barracks and had similarly strict rules. Fingleton recalled in his interview in *Strategy* in July 1998: 'It was a tough school, with no frills. It taught me to stand on my own two feet and I benefited from the discipline. If you'd notions or affectations they were belted out of you. After school I spent three years in All Hallows.'

The frugal life of the seminary in Drumcondra, Dublin, Fingleton realised was not for him. When asked decades later by a journalist, Patricia O'Reilly, why he dropped out, he murmured something about 'being another Bishop Casey,' in reference to the Bishop of Galway who resigned in 1992 after it emerged that he had fathered a child. 'Strangely, it's as a Bishop you'd see him, never as a priest,' O'Reilly noted in her flattering profile in *Strategy*, which concluded: 'Michael Fingleton is a basic man with in-built confidence, a golden tongue and an aura of success.'

Money as well as the flesh, it seems, was already tempting Fingleton. 'The whole set-up was so antediluvian, or maybe I was just too commercial to take to it,' Fingleton recalled.

In 1961 he got his first taste of banking by joining a small outfit called Allied Irish Finance. This gave him the money to start a bachelor of commerce course at night in UCD. In 1966 he joined the Dairy Disposal Company, which was charged by the government with taking over and rationalising ailing creameries in the west of Ireland.

In 1967 Fingleton completed his degree and in rapid succession gained a first place in his chartered secretary exams and qualified as a certified accountant. The Dairy Disposal Company ran creameries, cattle stations and cheese factories, and as Fingleton travelled around them he became familiar with the fields he would later come to feel were development land worth millions of pounds. It also introduced him to the culture of 'strokes' and favours that dominates Irish politics. He later recalled in interviews that a politician once recommended seven different candidates for the position of manager in a creamery. Each recommendation was acknowledged, and seven families' votes were won. That taught him, he said, about Irish politics.

Ever restless, after a few years Fingleton was ready for a more radical change of direction as the Dairy Disposal Company slowed down. The organisation controlled a third of the dairy industry and employed about two thousand people. 'I anticipated its inevitable end,' said Fingleton. 'So it proved, and I left on a wing and a prayer to Nigeria.'

It was 1969, and the conflict in Biafra was two years old. Nigerian politics and the system of short-cuts and favours required to get things done was not unlike that in Ireland. Fingleton used his financial expertise to do the books for Irish missionaries while gaining a reputation as a 'doer'.

In 1971 he came home, determined to get stuck into business. 'By the time I had come back things had run their course in Nigeria and it gave me a quiet satisfaction to know that I'd contributed all I could,' he mused in his *Strategy* interview.

But Fingleton told the *Irish Press* journalist Eoghan Corry that his time in Nigeria acted against him when he tried to get back into the often insular and conservative world of Irish business in the 1970s. 'Fingleton swears that one prominent businessman told him in an interview that he could not have any business ethic,' Corry wrote, 'as he was now a Communist Third World groupie.'

He managed to get a job with the electrical firm ACEC, a subsidiary of Westinghouse Group, a giant transnational corporation. While he worked with the company as a management and corporate accountant in Waterford he hankered after a return to Dublin. An advertisement in the *Irish Times* that read 'Commercial organisation seeks secretary' was to change everything.

In 1972 Fingleton got the job, in a tiny organisation called the Irish Industrial Building Society, previously the Irish Industrial Benefit Building Society. Fingleton was not even a home-owner, and his knowledge of building societies, he admitted, was only 'peripheral', but the job offered an opportunity to return to Dublin.

When he joined it the society had assets of £2½ million and employed five people. In Fingleton's first year a profit of £12,000 was recorded. In the 1960s he delighted in recalling that he had applied for a mortgage from a rival firm, the Educational Building Society, but had been turned down by its stuffy officials as he had no record of deposits with them.

In 1973 Fingleton married Eileen McCarroll, who he had met before he went to Nigeria. She was a secondary school teacher and, Fingleton told *Strategy*, 'a traditionalist.' In interviews he would stress his credentials as a family man. 'Despite my fairly high profile, five nights out of seven I'm at home.'

He added to his qualifications by being called to the bar in the same year as his marriage. The following year he bought his first house, in Leopardstown, Co. Dublin, with a mortgage from his new employer.

Fingleton became a relentless worker in the hitherto sleepy society. He appeared to have few vices—they would mainly come later—and was known only to enjoy a game of golf in Woodbrook Golf Club at Bray, where he played off a handicap of fifteen. His powerful character quickly began to influence the small society, which held meetings every Tuesday evening to discuss strategy. Steadily, his determined character took control. At one of these meetings he convinced the society to expand outside Dublin city and county for the first time. Until 1969 statutory restrictions had prevented it from doing so, but in early 1974 Fingleton gave the society the confidence to think bigger.

A clever marketer, he realised that the society needed to change its name to reflect its ambitions. At his second attempt he managed to convince the members, by a margin of three votes, to support a change, and in 1975 Irish Nationwide Building Society was born.

The choice of name was not only linked to the company's geographical ambitions but also perhaps gave the impression that it was connected to the Nationwide Building Society in Britain, a much bigger and more credible organisation. Later, when it did expand into Britain, Nationwide would become annoyed at the similarity of the Irish society's name— and at its radically different business model of lending to developers.

These objections were shrugged off by Fingleton. 'They certainly tried to stop us, but we felt it was a good strong name and that it reflected us,' he said. The similar name he would in later years dismiss as just a coincidence. In 1983 the society bought the Garda Building Society, the first in a series of small acquisitions.

Fingleton and his wife had two sons and two daughters. 'The books balanced on that,' he said. Their father's wealth ensured that they all went to the best private schools, though he was anxious to make sure they received their early education in ordinary schools. 'I'm a great believer in national schools—they give a broader education and the children mix with all classes,' he told Strategy. Would his younger daughter, Eileen, go on to a private school? 'I'm not sure,' he said. 'Eileen's extremely independent, and I'm certain she'll have a say as to where she goes.'

A snapshot of his children's education given by the banker in 1988 reveals a family on the way up, living in a nice house in Leopardstown and mixing with the upper echelons of Co. Dublin society. Ann, the eldest, was a fifteen-year-old in Holy Child Convent School, while William, a year younger, went to Gonzaga College, a progressive Jesuit school whose famous past pupils include Michael McDowell, the former Minister for Justice, and Peter Sutherland, chairman of Goldman Sachs and a former Attorney-General. Eileen, aged ten, and Michael junior, aged six, were at the time in Foxrock National School.

Fingleton was keen to position Irish Nationwide as a contender. When the prestigious number 1 O'Connell Street came on the market he stopped at nothing to get it. The building, on the corner of O'Connell Street and Eden Quay, had little architectural merit. The original building was that of Hopkins and Hopkins, watchmakers and jewellers, which was destroyed in the 1916 Rising. The building that replaced it in 1922, however, had one great potential benefit: signage on the city's main thoroughfare.

Fingleton bought the building from under the nose of Ulster Bank by not letting them know he planned to bid for it. Four hours of haggling with the trustees of Hopkins and Hopkins, ensured Fingleton had the keys of the building for £160,000. He erected a big Irish Nationwide sign with individually mounted back-lit letters, ugly but impossible to miss.

The society began to open branches around the country, but it also used agents—usually local businessmen, retired sports people or auctioneers—who acted as feeders for the society. The branches and agencies, often sharing premises with auctioneers, extended the society's reach nationally while keeping costs down. By 1984 it had twenty full branches and 110 agencies.

Fingleton set about raising the profile of the society to reflect its new outward focus. He hadn't the money to compete directly against the bigger banks, so he began strategically sponsoring sports events. He was always careful to stand in the centre of photographs, so that there was little chance of being cut out of the picture if it was trimmed.

On the day he opened the O'Connell Street branch Fingleton grandly announced that men and women would be treated equally when they applied for mortgages. He was lauded as a result by the media as a radical. He courted journalists and senior newspaper executives by offering them mortgages at a time when working in the media was looked down upon by lenders. The veteran journalist and editor Paul Drury, who now works with the *Irish Daily Mail*, recalls that when he started as a junior reporter in the *Irish Independent* in the early 1970s the pubs used to close early on Christmas Eve, but there were was an open door for journalists to attend Fingleton's head office Christmas party.

'We used to head up a back stairs and into Fingleton's office. There were loads of journalists there and we were sitting on crates of beer. Fingleton didn't really participate or engage, he would just sit at his desk, a big oval-shaped business desk, and watch everything.'

At that time journalists attending a drinks party in the office of a bank's chief executive was completely unheard of. As Drury says, 'you would never even get a bank chief executive down the end of a phone, never mind have a drink in his office.' Fingleton made himself available directly to journalists. He would take a call even from junior reporters and give them a comment if they wished. They loved him for it.

At the same time Fingleton had a tremendous ability to pick up secrets and to attract confidences from all sorts of characters. He would occasionally leak one of these to a favourite journalist, further ingratiating himself. By 1980 he had become the 'go-to' person for Ireland's building society industry any time there was a cut in interest rates or any development that might affect them. The late Des Crowley recalled in the *Sunday Business Post* in 2002 that 'one Christmas during the 1980s when Irish Nationwide's Michael Fingleton was at the height of his popularity with the media, he sent journalists a Christmas card portraying himself as Santa Claus.'

Fingleton told the *Irish Times* in 1991:

In the days when other financial institutions refused to talk to the press, I saw it as part of my role. We were a small society which wanted to grow and we felt PR and publicity could play an important part in increasing the public's awareness of us. I didn't mind being quoted by name. I made myself available for comment when others did not and I have always been forthright in my views about our industry.

'Always ready with a quote' was how Ted Harding described him in an article in the *Sunday Business Post* in 1994. 'He became the self-appointed spokesperson for a stuffy sector in which the society bosses did not condescend to address reporters.'

Damien Kiberd, founding editor of the *Sunday Business Post*, recalls regularly bumping into Fingleton about town or at GAA matches.

He was well got, everybody knew him. He was a friendly devil. He took me to lunch in the Shelbourne once . . . We went to the dining room and it was all very posh. Very nice. He went up to pay the bill.

There was a woman there. He shook her by the cheek and said, 'How are you, girlie?' I was just shocked. I thought, You can't do that, but he did!

At this time Fingleton claimed that building societies were democratic and that members were free to be elected to their board, unlike, say, state boards or PLCs, which were much more difficult to get onto. 'Just because people don't get enough votes to get elected to the board they shouldn't blame the societies,' he said, a remark that years later, when the society faced regular rebellions, would prove prescient.

As unofficial spokesperson for the building societies, Fingleton campaigned hard for them to be allowed to compete with banks: lending to builders, offering mortgage services, and selling insurance, shares and foreign exchange. 'Most building societies are losing money on mortgages, the margins are too tight. They have to pay more for their money. They have to generate income by other activities in the money markets. The government should release us from bondage.'

At the same time that Fingleton called for more freedom for his society, he had already developed a harsh reputation for pursing borrowers who fell into arrears. He told Eoghan Corry:

We protect people from themselves. Very often people are afraid to come in to discuss their problems with you. Very often it can all be settled amicably and they can get themselves out of a situation, whereas if they fall four months behind they tend to say, ah, sure I have come this far, there's no getting out of it now.

Brazenly, he said it often worked out for the best that borrowers lost their home, as the society sometimes returned money to them, even if they had been forced to emigrate, when it sold the house later for more than their debts.

Chapter 3

A GLIMPSE OF THE BIG MONEY

The 1990s kicked off in a very inglorious way for Irish business. The corporate world was plunged into a series of financial scandals and grubby business deals. The early 1990s saw the Beef Tribunal, following the collapse of Larry Goodman and Goodman International and allegations of malpractice against the beef industry. The privatisation of Greencore had seen secret share dealings going on behind the scenes, linked to a senior executive of the group.

John Glackin, a Dublin solicitor, was appointed High Court inspector to get to the bottom of a complex series of transactions surrounding the sale of the Johnston, Mooney and O'Brien site in Ballsbridge, Dublin. The controversy saw Michael Smurfit step aside as chairman of Telecom Éireann and the financier Dermot Desmond face heavy criticism in the inspector's final report for his part in the controversy.

There were few reasons, however, to think that the small world of building societies would be completely turned upside-down in the years ahead. As the new decade began it would have seemed to most people involved in Dublin's relatively small financial services scene that building societies would find the next ten years slightly more exciting than the dull decade that was ending.

This could not have been further from the truth. The 1990s would see the end of the family dynasties behind some of the building societies. It would also see a major expansion of financial institutions as international financial services became more integrated. Several building societies would disappear, while two of the biggest, Irish Permanent and First National, would be floated on the stock market.

The 1990s would also see the first phase of Ireland's economic boom and the beginning of one of Europe's biggest post-war property bubbles. All this presented a huge opportunity for building societies, which would ride the Celtic Tiger till it dropped.

But the Ireland of the opening years of the 1990s was quite different from the country that greeted the new millennium ten years later. Corporate scandals and corporate collapses, such as Guinness Peat Aviation and Goodman International, were not the only financial action of the early 1990s. The currency crisis in late 1992 had caused havoc on international markets and threatened the country's entire economic stability.

For building societies the 1980s hadn't been too bad. In general, the little club of building societies had grown its share of the mortgage market and tried to beat the banks where it could. The decade had seen massive interest rates, high unemployment and an exchequer crisis. But despite these setbacks, building societies used their nimble size, flexibility and at times aggressive commercialism to rub the banks up the wrong way.

The building societies used to sit down informally together to discuss interest rates. Then they would troop down to the office of the Minister for the Environment, who had responsibility for building societies, and have a more formal meeting with him. If a decision was made to lower rates, the press would have been tipped off in advance and the minister would emerge from the meeting and inform the assembled journalists that he was delighted to announce that building society mortgage rates were going to be cut.

Fingleton had brought a shrewd commercial and consumer head to the building society sector. He was ambitious for the society and kept publicly complaining about the disadvantages the societies faced when competing with the banks. The banks in turn complained bitterly that the building societies benefited from special tax treatment.

Spats between the banks and the societies over commercial advantage or disadvantage dominated the mortgage landscape in the 1980s. Fingleton led the charge for the mutual societies. Banks complained that deposit customers of building societies were not paying enough tax; building societies complained that legislation allowed the banks to subsidise their mortgage rates from other profitable activities. The building societies argued that under section 28 of the Finance Act (1976) the banks had a tax advantage, which allowed them to subsidise their mortgage rate by a few percentage points. In return the banks argued that they paid 50 per cent corporation tax, compared with the societies' 35 per cent.

The societies did not have to disclose individual accounts but paid a composite rate of tax on their total deposits; this meant that deposits in building societies were taxed at a lower rate than in banks. In the early 1980s the government decided to pursue some of the 'hot money' hidden in building societies. In 1982 Fingleton said that 'we should recognise the national paranoia and suspicion about taxation. It's better that this money should pay some tax than leave the country.'

Fingleton complained at every opportunity that mutuals needed to be given greater commercial freedom, including the ability to offer more services to customers, such as chequebooks and insurance products.

The banks were clearly rattled. The societies were doing well. It prompted Bank of Ireland to make a bid for the ICS Building Society in the mid-1980s. This had the unique status of being a mutual listed on the stock exchange. Fingleton was very critical of this deal being allowed to go ahead, but it did.

Shortly before the 1987 general election, which saw Fianna Fáil returned to power, its leader, Charles Haughey, announced that if elected he would ensure that all financial institutions competed freely, and that building societies could expand their operations.

Meanwhile Fingleton was determined to close the gap any way he could. In 1987 he reintroduced what were known as tiered mortgages, under a different guise, which the government had outlawed the previous year. Fingleton had cleverly found a new way of getting around the ban. The Minister for the Environment, Pádraig Flynn, summed up the attitude at the time. 'It is clearly an attempt to circumvent Section 4 of the 1986 Building Societies Act . . . I have to admire the skill with which these people can drive a coach and four through hastily passed legislation: the 1986 legislation had the right idea but it was riddled with loopholes.'

Eventually, at the end of the decade, the new Building Societies Act (1989) was supposed to deal with the anomalies between banks and mutuals. It was a comprehensive piece of legislation aimed at enabling the societies to grow and thrive while updating and consolidating a lot of older, scattered pieces of legislation. But the act contained one clause that would prove to be a massive thorn in the side of Michael Fingleton. While it enabled building societies to 'demutualise', it placed a restriction on what could happen afterwards. Where a building society demutualised by, for example, floating on the stock exchange, a single shareholder could not own more than 15 per cent of the company for five years. It essentially meant that, once demutualised, building societies could not be taken over or controlled by another company or financial institution for five years.

In 1989 such a rule would not have appeared too restrictive to Michael Fingleton. After all, he didn't even begin talking publicly about the possibility of demutualising until about 1995, and he never fully committed himself publicly to the idea until well into the 2000s.

By 1990 Fingleton was a well-known figure in financial and media circles. He would not have been a household name by any means but he had attracted the attention, and respect, of many executives in rival building societies. Fingleton was by now enjoying running Irish Nationwide. He told the *Irish Times* in 1991: 'Stress means nothing to me. I never get over excited and I don't take myself too seriously and I have never believed in the cult of my own personality. I am very practical and down to earth in my approach to running my business.'

> When you are handling other people's money you have to be conservative. But that doesn't mean you have to stand still. For me the most important thing is to have a flexible approach to business and an awareness of what's going on at all levels. From what I can see large organisations, weighed down with theory, often lose their way.

For a business not 'weighed down with theory,' by 1991 the society was pretty big. It had opened fifty branches, had 160 agents and a staff of two hundred, operated on a cost base that was a small fraction of that of its competitors. 'No organisation should be overstaffed. It is counterproductive. Our staff are not overworked, but they are stretched and challenged a little. I tend to reach decisions swiftly and it helps if one is in touch with things.'

Fingleton was a leading figure in the Irish Building Societies Association. His stint as chairman of the association during the currency crisis of late 1992 and early 1993 brought him in close proximity to Bertie Ahern, then Minister for Finance.

As the value of the Irish pound continued to rise on the back of wider European currency speculation in 1992, Irish building societies found that the cost of securing inter-bank finance to lend to customers was rising rapidly. By the end of 1992, only weeks before Ahern's government devalued the Irish pound by 10 per cent, inter-bank borrowing rates had hit 17 per cent. This in turn was putting enormous pressure on building societies to push up their mortgage rates to well above that.

The Department of Finance had a series of meetings with representatives of the building societies, largely through the association chaired by Fingleton. The government was close to agreeing a £650 million financing package for the societies when the decision was made to devalue the currency.

The crisis placed Fingleton at the centre of his sector's negotiations, and the public eye, as anxious mortgage-holders watched to see what would happen their borrowing rates. Fingleton had become the public face of mortgage lending, even though Irish Nationwide was only the fifth-largest society by value of assets.

1992 was a landmark year in the creation of the single market in Europe and the loosening up in European money markets. In time it would lead to French and German banks recklessly pumping tens of billions into Irish banking, which in turn would lend this money on for property. It would prove an addictive and dangerous concoction for Irish bankers.

Just as the currency crisis came to an end in 1993, the small world of Irish building societies was about to be turned upside-down.

There was something about building societies back then. They tended to be run by individuals with strong personalities for very long periods. They could sometimes be dominated by colourful, larger-than-life characters, who were heavily associated with the society. It might have been the virtually non-existent regulation under the Registrar of Friendly Societies that contributed to this phenomenon; it may equally have been their tendency to attract lots of deposits made up of 'hot money' that made them seem a bit like mavericks. But they tended to get drawn into scandals, and when one hit it hit hard.

Two of the biggest building societies were Irish Permanent and First National. Just as Fingleton dominated Irish Nationwide, the Irish Permanent was controlled by Edmund Farrell. For years First National had been run by members of the Skehan family, but in 1993 its boss was Joe Treacy.

Following the introduction of the Building Societies Act (1989), Irish Permanent had begun to consider demutualising. It would be possible for the society to become a private company and then be floated on the stock exchange. Edmund Farrell, its long-time chief executive, felt he was the man to lead the move. But floating a company on the stock exchange brings its own challenges. One of them is transparency.

When investors are considering buying shares in a company that is about to be listed on the stock exchange they have to be given a prospectus. This is a very detailed document describing every financial aspect of the company. Its financial performance, its potential conflicts of interest, its directors' salaries and all other financial dealings that might be relevant are laid bare.

In the preparation of the Irish Permanent's prospectus it emerged that Edmund Farrell had sold his house in Foxrock, Co. Dublin, to the society in 1987. The society spent £440,000 in renovating the house and then sold it back to Farrell in 1991 for £275,000. In addition, when Farrell became executive chairman in 1991 he was paid approximately £300,000 for agreeing not to work for any other financial institution as part of a restrictive clause in his employment contract.

The controversy led to a massive row within the society, and Farrell was removed. The society later sought the return of the £440,000 through the courts. Farrell denied any wrongdoing and counter-sued Irish Permanent for unfair dismissal. Eventually the actions were settled out of court.

As it turned out, 1993 also saw another bombshell go off. The chief executive of First National, Joe Treacy, was accused by an employee of sexual harassment. Treacy denied the claim but was effectually removed from the job. He later sued the society and reached a settlement that resulted in his receiving a lump sum of £140,000 and his full pension.

It had been an extraordinary year for building societies and one that left much for Fingleton to ponder. It is not clear how he felt about early exits of the chief executives of two of his biggest rivals, but he certainly would not have wanted a repeat performance. He may have felt sorry for both of them, or perhaps he took a purely commercial view in which controversy and uncertainty in a competitor was good for Irish Nationwide. In two competitors it is even better. However, the nature of both departures would have left much for Fingleton to weigh up.

It was clear to him that floating a building society on the stock exchange would bring significant financial disclosures, and if there were any financial skeletons in the cupboard they would most certainly jump out, with potentially explosive repercussions. In Joe Treacy's case the incident showed how even an allegation of impropriety in relation to an employee can lead to scandal and an early exit from the job.

Whatever his thoughts were, in his following sixteen years in charge he never once contemplated in a serious way floating the society on the stock exchange. And in fact many years later he was named in an employment appeals case taken by a senior executive who had had an affair with him.

And 1993 wasn't over yet. The political correspondent of the *Irish Times*, Geraldine Kennedy, uncovered a story about the sale of a complex of 299 apartments near the Burlington Hotel in Ballsbridge, Dublin. Known as Mespil Flats, it was home to mainly retired tenants who had been living there for a long time.

The complex was sold by Irish Life, a company in which the state was still a major shareholder. The buyer was a group of approximately twenty investors put together by the businessmen Brendan Gilmore and Michael Holland. The investors included two daughters of the Taoiseach, Albert Reynolds, the attorney-general, Harry Whelehan, the former managing director of First National Building Society, Joe Treacy, the broadcaster Marian Finucane, the barristers Patrick MacEntee and Kevin Haugh, the well-known publican Dessie Hynes, and Michael Fingleton.

The tenants were not invited to buy their flats, despite the fact that many of them envisaged spending the rest of their days there. As long-term property-fund investors, Irish Life would not have sought to remove any of the tenants, but a set of new owners might have a different approach.

The Mespil Flats controversy became an enormous national story. It played out badly for Irish Life, and news coverage also did not reflect well on the buyers. 'People thought that if there were household names, politicians and private investors involved something must be wrong,' Michael Holland told the *Sunday Times* in August 2004. He admitted that some tenants were entitled to feel aggrieved but argued that half way through the deal the currency crisis erupted. Some of the venture's original backers pulled out, forcing Gilmore and Holland to broaden the net of potential investors to include anyone known personally to them who might have the money required to come into the deal. This is how so many well-known people ended up as investors, and part of the reason why public interest in the venture was so intense.

Eventually Irish Life set up a trust fund to compensate the tenants for any hardship or losses incurred as a result of the sale.

It was the kind of negative personal publicity that Fingleton hated. This was compounded when it emerged that he had taken out a mortgage loan from the society that had not been included in the Central Bank file, as required. The mortgage was for £100,000. Fingleton dismissed the oversight on the grounds that the auditors and the society's compliance officer were of the view that because it was granted on normal commercial terms it was not required to report it under their reading of the relevant section of the 1989 act.

With hindsight, Fingleton's involvement in the Mespil Flats controversy and the non-disclosure of this loan reflect two things: a keen eye for a good property deal, and a liberal approach to interpreting corporate governance rules.

However, neither story would have been too damaging to Fingleton's general reputation. Many business people would have felt that the Mespil Flats deal was perfectly acceptable, and might have wished they could have been in on it themselves. But the non-disclosure of the loan should have been taken as a real warning by the Central Bank as regulator, though it would not have been regarded as a big deal by others, given the culture of the time.

Something that particularly irked Fingleton during the 1990s, and beyond, was the question of public disclosure of how much he earned. The salaries of directors of building societies were traditionally never disclosed. However, when the Central Bank took over regulation of the sector in 1989, total salaries for all directors were disclosed to it.

In the early 1990s journalists began to realise that they could go to the Central Bank and ask to see these returns. The first newspaper story about Fingleton's salary appeared in April 1994 and disclosed how much he had earned in salary, pension and other benefits in 1993. It included a comparison for 1992. It showed that he had received salary, pension and other benefits totalling £249,000 in 1993, up from £201,000 in 1992. This was an enormous sum at the time. For example, the chief executive of ICS Building Society, Tony O'Connell, earned £103,000 that year.

Building societies did not have to provide a breakdown of the individual earnings of each director but only the total for executive directors. But Fingleton was caught out by the fact that he was the only executive director, as was O'Connell at ICS.

So it was not very surprising that, after the story of his salary appeared, one Irish Nationwide executive, Stan Purcell, was elevated to the board in time for the next year's report. Every year after that a total figure was given for Fingleton and Purcell together, which meant that people could only guess at how much of it had gone to Fingleton and how much to Purcell.

Fingleton and Purcell shared total pay of £357,000 in 1995 and pension contributions of £322,000. When questioned about the figures at the annual general meeting that year, Fingleton refused to disclose individual pay packets, saying the society was not required to break down individual payments to its directors. 'Financial institutions can't be run like charities,' he said. And anyway, their contracts were performance-related. The substantial pension contributions in 1995 were because in earlier years 'we forgot about our own pensions,' he said.

TAKING A PUNT

It's extraordinary to think that a small mutual residential mortgage lender could end up losing more than €5.4 billion. It is even more incredible given that most of the losses came from commercial property loans to developers, builders and speculators. Relative to its size, the collapse and subsequent cost to the taxpayer of €5.4 billion is one of the most expensive in the world. Losses of over €5.4 billion on a loan book of just €12 billion are relatively greater than those at Anglo Irish Bank.

Why the society slid away from its raison d'être of providing small mortgages to members of the public to massive developer loans is a complex question. It is even more difficult to trace when Fingleton first turned down this road.

In the final few years before Irish Nationwide imploded it had become more and more apparent that it was lending large sums to commercial property investors. But throughout the 1990s there were barely any references to commercial property lending in any of the media coverage of the society. In fact Fingleton makes only a couple of public references to it at all.

Yet it is clear that he was lending money for commercial property deals as far back as the early 1990s. Many of these were never made public. Details emerge in the report compiled by KPMG in 2007 as a sales brochure and 'vendor due diligence' statement when Irish Nationwide was being sold. That document is disclosed here for the first time.

It shows that 1993 was the year Dermot Desmond's company, IFSC South Block Ltd, did business with Irish Nationwide. The society bought three floors of IFSC House, Desmond's big office block. The floors were already leased to tenants such as Barings and Danisco. Irish Nationwide bought a lease of 199 years and 362 days for £12.9 million. In March 1995 the society took up a leasehold interest of the same duration in part of the ground floor of IFSC House, which was subject to a lease agreement with Citibank. This cost £3.3 million.

There were tax benefits to the deals. A lease that was three days less than the leasehold held by Desmond's company meant that this deal qualified for full capital allowances on tax, which was confirmed in writing by the Revenue Commissioners. The cost of these transactions was considered to be expenditure on a relevant interest in the building, which was an industrial building for tax purposes and therefore subject to accelerated allowance claims at a rate of 54 per cent of the qualifying expenditure in the year it was incurred. A further 4 per cent per year straight-line claim applied after that, until 97.4 per cent of the cost was claimed in full.

Two separate, specially established companies, known as special-purpose vehicles (SPVs), granted options to Irish Nationwide on the deals. This meant that the society could sell its interest in the building to the SPV for specified amounts. The price of exercising this option was secured by deposits placed with Irish Nationwide in Dublin on the first deal and Irish Nationwide in the Isle of Man on the second. These are reflected in charges and liens against IFSC South Block Ltd and in favour of the society, registered with the Companies Registration Office at the time. The options Desmond held to buy back its interest from Irish Nationwide at these set prices ran out in 2007 and 2008. They were designed like that to avoid a tax claw-back on the thirteen-year tax allowances that Irish Nationwide had enjoyed from the purchase. Both charges were fully satisfied by Desmond's company in 1997.

Fingleton had an appetite for doing all kinds of unusual deals for a building society. In the late 1990s the society purchased plant and equipment with a view to leasing it to Intel, the transnational microchip manufacturer. The amounts involved are enormous, totalling €175 million. In the mid-2000s the company transferred these assets to special-purpose companies, which were then transferred to Intel. This was done for a nominal sum, described in one confidential document as 'tax written down value.' These are all perfectly legitimate tax-efficient types of business but certainly reflect how far Irish Nationwide was moving away from bread-and-butter lending to ordinary people for buying a house.

Even if little was known about these non-residential mortgage deals, there were some clues about the effect Fingleton's love of commercial deals was having on the financial success of Irish Nationwide as early as the 1990s. An analysis of the accounts of the society shows that whenever Fingleton faced tough times in the residential mortgage market he was able to boost profits significantly by making what were referred to as 'exceptional investment gains.' This often related to the sale of financial instruments such as government bonds or other assets. Fingleton's early success in boosting profits when he needed to from avenues other than mortgages showed he had an eye for a deal, and usually a good sense of timing, when deciding when to buy and when to sell.

As far back as 1984 Irish Nationwide reported an 88 per cent increase in profits, from £4.5 million to £8.4 million, on the back of a £3 million gain from the sale of investments. Then in 1993 profits shot up by 53 per cent, from £16 million to £24½ million, on the strength of a £10 million gain on the sale of gilts. Taking out the investment gain, profit rose by a more modest 11 per cent.

There were several years when exceptional investment gains seriously lifted the net profit. But there was virtually no mention of lending to property developers. 'I always admired Fingleton in the way he ran his operation,' said a senior executive in a rival building society. 'He always seemed to be able to generate good profits from a fairly small business. We were baffled for a long time how he was doing it.'

'There was no animosity towards Fingleton among building societies,' said a former senior executive in another society. 'He seemed to run a good operation, and if anything there was some degree of envy as to how he was getting so much out of it.'

But by the end of the 1990s and early 2000s rival building societies and mortgage lenders no longer saw Irish Nationwide as competition at all. 'It was clear that Fingleton was going for the commercial property end of things,' one former building society executive said. 'He was just ticking over with mortgages, but by that stage they weren't really what he was at. We no longer even saw him as a competitor. This was because we were selling mortgages and that was no longer the INBS [Irish Nationwide] focus.'

'He had gone down the Anglo road,' said another. 'He wanted to be a mini-Anglo. We didn't even see ourselves as competing against him any more.'

Fingleton himself mentioned what he called 'commercial lending' in March 1994. When talking about the society's financial results for 1993, he said that provision for bad debt amounted to £4 million, the same level as in 1992. This was 'not indicative of any deterioration' in the quality of the loan book, he said; 'we are going into more commercial lending,' and he felt he wanted to take a more prudent view of this activity.

It is ironic that the first time he talks about getting into commercial lending it is in the context of being more prudent by allowing for bigger potential bad debt. It was as if he was aware even then of the risks, and his instincts were to be cautious. But all that had gone within seven or eight years.

So too had the view of rival building societies that he was going down a different road. Eithne Tinney, a non-executive director of EBS Building Society for eight years, said that undoubtedly executives in EBS were envious of Fingleton's salary, apparent financial success and contacts when it came to property developers in the 2000s. 'There was a view by about 2005 that Irish Nationwide was leaving us behind. The view had become very much, if Irish Nationwide can do it, we should be able to do it.' Ultimately it proved a massive mistake for EBS—not only to get into commercial property lending but to do it so late in the boom. 'We were getting involved in the tail end of it all. I have no doubt that Michael Fingleton inadvertently led EBS astray. We should have stuck to the knitting.'

EBS ended up losing its independence and requiring approximately €1 billion in capital injections from the state to cover losses primarily on commercial property deals.

But just as Fingleton was deciding to increase his lending to developers in the 1990s, he also began to make bigger and more ambitious plans. He made a bid for TSB in 1994. This was a mutual mortgage and personal banking operation, formerly the Trustee Savings Bank. Its sale was being handled by the Minister for Finance, Bertie Ahern. Fingleton went up against National Irish Bank by making an offer of £102 million. It may have been as much about stating his ambition as seriously making an offer. He hadn't bid as much as National Irish Bank but justified it by saying that Ahern suggested that price would not be the only factor. In the end the sale did not go ahead at that time, though TSB was sold a few years later.

In 1995 Fingleton said he was interested in buying the Agricultural Credit Corporation or Industrial Credit Corporation from the state, both of which were due to be privatised. A successful acquisition here would have brought a banking licence and with ICC a business and commercial property loan book.

Fingleton may simply have been thinking in PR terms by stating his interest, but equally he may have been half-serious. In any event both ICC and ACC were sold off to others a few years later, and Irish Nationwide didn't buy either.

THE FEELING IS MUTUAL

One of the most influential factors in the apparent failure of regulation from outside Irish Nationwide, and the failure of corporate governance within it, was the fact that Fingleton toyed for years with the idea of demutualising the society. Without coming out and saying he wanted to sell the society, from the mid-1990s onwards he began talking about the restrictive and 'unfair' nature of the Building Societies Act (1989). This meant that if the society was demutualised it could not be taken over for at least five years.

By the mid-1990s one building society, Irish Permanent, had already converted to a PLC and was listed on the stock exchange. In Britain building societies were being snapped up by large banks or were rushing head-first towards the stock exchange themselves. By 1996 there were only three large building societies in Britain still wedded to the mutual concept. It began with the flotation of Abbey in 1989. Later came the takeover of Cheltenham and Gloucester by Lloyds Bank, and the takeover by Halifax of Leeds Permanent before a fresh float. A year later Abbey National had taken over National and Provincial.

At home, Fingleton watched Irish Permanent demutualise and float on the stock exchange in 1994. But he had also seen how the preparatory work for that process had cost Edmund Farrell his job. For the chief executive of Irish Permanent, Roy Douglas, and other executives the flotation had proved to be incredibly rewarding. Irish Permanent was floated in October 1994; within a year Douglas, who was being paid a fortune, had shares in the company worth close to £1 million. Irish Permanent had access to capital, growth potential and a very lucrative share option scheme. And it seemed inevitable that it would be taken over once the five years were up.

This was a case study in how a flotation can be very enriching, as long as you don't have too many skeletons in the cupboard. Publicly listed companies tend not to be prone to the development of personal fiefdoms. It is possible to run a PLC with a dominant chief executive, but it can go very wrong, as so many things have to be fully transparent and disclosed.

In 1998 First National, having changed its name to First Active, was also floated. This was a somewhat different experience. Before the flotation, stock markets began to weaken. There was an expectation that the issue price of the shares would be no lower than £2.65 and could be as high as £3.80 per share. Former members were being given free shares as a sweetener for agreeing to the privatisation. This also suited carpetbaggers who had put money on deposit just to get some free shares.

But as D-Day approached, the promoters were forced to cut the flotation price down to £2.25 as a result of market nerves and weak demand. Some commentators felt the board should have pulled the float altogether and tried again when the market recovered. But the board decided to press ahead with it at a knock-down price to ensure success.

But, unlike the Irish Permanent flotation, the timing was not so good, and trading and operational issues dogged the early period of the float. The society, now a PLC, still had outstanding cost issues and felt compelled to sack 175 employees and close 25 of its 76 branches. 'It simply wasn't ready to compete for mortgages on the tighter profit margins that were now coming in,' said one former building society executive. 'The mortgage market had got very competitive. The only way to make money was to have lower running costs, drive up volumes by selling more and more mortgages, or by cutting your costs.' Pressure mounted on the chief executive of First Active, John Smyth, and he stepped down in February 2000.

Here was another lesson staring Michael Fingleton in the face. He was not carrying heavy costs, but it was clear that floating on the stock exchange could be an arduous and risky business.

Fingleton's real attitude to demutualising was not at all clear at first in the 1990s when he began to talk about it. The five-year rule obviously annoyed him, as did other restrictions on the commercial activities he could get up to as a mutual building society and not a bank.

Speculation began to mount that Irish Nationwide would demutualise. The speculation prompted a flood of deposits from carpetbaggers, who wanted to collect whatever free shares might become available. But Fingleton made it clear that he did not want the five-year rule. This prompted a lot of media analysis at the time, suggesting that Fingleton felt he should be able to float the company and then have it taken over fairly quickly. The obvious interpretation was that Fingleton would be given free shares in the demutualisation and would not have to wait five years for his shares to be sold off in a takeover bid.

But this was far too simplistic an interpretation, and it missed several crucial points. There was nothing wrong with the five-year rule in one sense. If Fingleton really wanted to float the company he could have done so, been well paid, and got free shares and share options. It shouldn't have mattered whether the company was then taken over in one year, five years, or ten years. On the face of it there was nothing stopping Fingleton from floating the society and doing exactly what Irish Permanent and First Active had done. Yet there is no evidence that he seriously contemplated that course. Instead he spent years lobbying successive governments for a change in the law, which only one building society wanted, enabling him to demutualise and immediately sell the company in a private trade sale.

Just because Irish Permanent had been floated once it demutualised did not mean that Fingleton wanted to float at all. Sources close to the society say that all he wanted to do was demutualise the society and at the same time sell it, without floating it on the stock exchange.

This sequence of events would have placed him in the driving seat. A private buyer would mean there would be no public disclosure of pay, connected party transactions, corporate governance practices or due diligence; there wouldn't be an Edmund Farrell moment for Fingleton in the event that there were aspects of how he ran the society that he wanted to keep private. He could do a private deal with a buyer behind closed doors.

Members would get a large pay-day. A mechanism would have to be found by which Fingleton would get a large pay-day too. As a mutual he didn't own any more of it than anyone else; but if a deal was done in private he could be granted a nice new job by the new owner and a large one-off payment in gratitude for all the work he had done in building up the society. An allocation of the proceeds of the sale would have been earmarked for the executives and staff. There were suggestions that it could have been as much as 10 per cent of the proceeds. If Irish Nationwide went for €1.3 billion, approximately €130 million would be divided up. The person with the biggest influence in deciding who would get what was Michael Fingleton.

Another valid point was that Fingleton was running the society as though he were indispensable. In a way he was. He had the personal contacts for the growing loans to developers. He decided who got what. He knew about the structure of deals and how much the society charged in interest.

The alternative, under the then rules, was running a gauntlet of due diligence that would result in a publicly issued prospectus. The society's systems, board structure, pay structure, board committee structure and lots more would all come under public scrutiny.

A PLC would require a new board, with independent directors and an independent chairman. Fingleton could even be ousted by a new PLC board. He could have been ousted in a hostile takeover after flotation.

Attempts by Fingleton to have the legislation changed were misinterpreted in some quarters and linked to an unexplained desire to have the company floated and then taken over. It seems far more likely that Fingleton believed a quiet trade sale, immediately switching the society from a mutual to a subsidiary of something else, suited him, the board and the members a lot better.

But he didn't directly and openly talk about selling the society at all in the 1990s. He suggested creating a third banking force by acquiring TSB or ACC. In 1995 he was openly talking about buying TSB and then floating the merged entity within a couple of years. He also suggested that a change in the law would allow Irish Nationwide to form a partnership with a bigger international bank. At one stage he even suggested creating a mutual bank, in other words to stay as a mutual but become a full bank with a banking licence.

Fingleton began to lobby politicians to have the legislation changed to abolish the five-year rule and allow for a straight trade sale. He had first really raised the issue in public in 1995, a year after the Irish Permanent flotation. In 1996 he said the society was not necessarily committed to maintaining its mutual status. 'Mutuality is a concept which is still relevant,' he said, 'but not to the exclusion of other options, and the board of Irish Nationwide would not presume on behalf of its members to exclude any such options.'

He began to step up his lobbying campaign. He had one major obstacle: EBS. How could a government change the law to suit one building society and do so in a way that would leave the other vulnerable to takeover? EBS wanted to stay mutual and be protected by the existing rules.

Apart from Irish Nationwide itself, EBS was the last remaining genuine mutual society by the late 1990s. First Active had already announced its intention of floating and did so in 1998. EBS had decided that with the flow of exits from mutual status, remaining as a building society should be its point of difference. It also believed that a change in the legislation such as Fingleton sought would undermine its mutual status.

Fingleton felt differently about it. He felt that the building society structure was too restrictive for his ambitions for the society. But because EBS didn't want the law changed, a change in the law would look as if it was being introduced specifically for Michael Fingleton and Irish Nationwide. This made it all more politically sensitive. EBS's opposition to a change in the legislation left Fingleton alone on the issue and facing active opposition from a rival building society.

But introducing legislative changes to suit a single company was hardly new for Fianna Fáil governments. And it looked like an open-and-shut case when just before the 1997 general election Charlie McCreevy backed the idea. He was opposition spokesman on finance and expected to become the next Minister for Finance.

In February 1997 a Dáil committee discussed joint amendments by Fianna Fáil and the Progressive Democrats to the Central Bank Bill that would have cleared the way for building societies to quickly enter a joint venture or agree to a takeover after flotation. The 'rainbow' coalition government was opposed to the amendments.

While Fingleton continued to insist that no decision had been taken, he had nevertheless advanced his political lobbying pretty far. 'We haven't decided to go public,' he said. 'We always have to consider our options. It would be negligent of us not to have all possible options available.' This seemed like a reasonable approach, except that forming such a joint venture or being bought out was not an option. It was simply not allowed in the legislation.

The amendments had been proposed by Charlie McCreevy of Fianna Fáil and Michael McDowell of the Progressive Democrats. The PDs would have seen it as simply opening up financial services to greater competition and creating a more level playing field. McCreevy, who had similar views on the free market, agreed. He appeared to be quite close to Fingleton. (A few years later he would receive a fast-tracked loan from Irish Nationwide of €1.6 million to buy a house at the K Club that at the time was valued at €1.5 million.)

At the time of the Dáil committee debate Fingleton said he had been lobbying for such a change to the legislation for the 'last five years,' suggesting that he had been trying to influence politicians on the issue since 1992. 'We are in a free market now. We are all facing competition. All we want is to have the same options as other financial institutions.'

But the coalition government of Fine Gael, the Labour Party and Democratic Left was having none of it. Both the Department of Finance, headed by Ruairí Quinn, and the Department of the Environment, headed by Brendan Howlin, were opposed to the idea. If the legislation changed in the way Fingleton wanted it, what was left of the mutual sector could simply evaporate. If enough members supported a move by the directors of any institution they could simply put themselves up for sale. EBS argued that the existing legislation allowed building societies to float if they wanted, but the safeguards that existed discouraged boards from just opting for a quick sale.

McCreevy may have liked the idea before the 1997 general election, but once he got into government he didn't move on it. Nearly two years later Fingleton had to tell the members at the annual general meeting in April 1999 that there was still no change. It is not clear whether McCreevy could not get the backing of his government colleagues, especially in the Department of the Environment, or whether he went off the idea. Alternatively, he may just have moved his focus elsewhere.

EBS had been very quiet about its lobbying efforts during this period, but clearly it was winning the behind-the-scenes battle.

The 1990s drew to a close with Fingleton presiding over an Irish Nationwide that perhaps had not changed very much in the decade. He was still the dominant, all-powerful figure. The society was run in pretty much the same way as it had been ten years earlier. But all around him the entire banking landscape had changed. The European Union was heading towards a single currency. Most of the mutuals were gone. The economy had taken off, and property was becoming a bigger part of it. House prices were rising as young couples and investors snapped up houses on the market. Lower interest rates had become the norm, leaving mortgages a lot more affordable as wages began to rise sharply.

But there were problems on the horizon too. On the one hand the ready availability of cash from other banks in Europe left Irish lenders with lots of money to lend; but the arrival of new competitors in the mortgage market, such as Bank of Scotland (Ireland), was savaging the profit margins that lenders could make on mortgages.

Fingleton had grown the Irish Nationwide mortgage book as the property market had taken off. But it wasn't such a hugely profitable business to be in. There was money in it, but it was extremely competitive.

Fingleton had found another way of keeping up profit margins. A core group of property developers were making a fortune on the strength of the property boom and rising prices for development land. Fingleton had built up relations with them and had discovered whole new ways of making money from his dealings with them.

By the end of the 1990s Fingleton was, in banking terms, in first, or perhaps second to Anglo Irish, with a whole raft of developers who were in a hurry to get rich. His commercial property lending was growing. Just as selling mortgages was a growing but low-margin business, Fingleton was dealing with those further up the food chain, where the big money was being made.

And, given that he was always interested in property anyway, he was loving it.

Chapter 4

SEEING OFF THE REGULATORS AND THE REBELS

On Tuesday 21 March 2000 Con Power entered the boardroom on the seventh floor of Nationwide House. Below, the water of the Grand Canal moved sedately as Power took his seat and waited with his fellow-members for the main event.

It was exactly 11 a.m. when he arrived: Michael Fingleton; the man. The sharply dressed banker slipped through his personal door that linked his paper-strewn office with the more refined boardroom. The two rooms were the only ones used by the society for meeting its biggest customers, who already included Ireland's newest class of multimillionaire: the property developer.

Fingleton's successor, Gerry McGinn, would later remark on the close proximity of the two rooms. 'What does that tell you? One guy made the decisions here—the layout of the building reflects that.'

Nodding and greeting everybody that Tuesday morning, Fingleton had the air of a busy and successful man granting his board a short amount of his precious time between deal-making.

Peter Donal O'Connor, the long-standing 69-year-old chairman of the society who had taken over the position from his father, smiled broadly at the man who had put it on the banking map. He put his two elbows on the table and tucked both his thumbs under his chin. 'Well, Michael, what have you got for us today?' he asked.

Con Power, a chartered secretary, chartered certified accountant, economist and specialist in ethics for professionals was taken aback. Attending his first board meeting of one of the fastest-growing lenders in Ireland as a non-executive director, he had expected that the meeting would at least have had an agenda. Instead there were not even minutes available to record what had happened at the society's last meeting, let alone what it intended to discuss at this one.

It was all very casual while O'Connor and the rest of the board listened in awe as Fingleton recounted tales of big lending and rapid growth.

The only hiccup in the adulation was when mention of the Central Bank came up. Watchdogs in the bank were very concerned about how fast the society was growing and whether the appropriate checks and balances were in place. But the issue was only discussed briefly and light-heartedly. A meeting was set up afterwards for the three-person audit committee of the board to discuss it in more detail with the society's auditors, KPMG, so little time was wasted on the matter.

As O'Connor ran through the meeting, barely questioning Fingleton, Power thought to himself, 'This is even worse than I expected.' When the meeting ended, he faced Fingleton privately, in the first of many such encounters. 'We can't have board meetings without an agenda and supporting documents being circulated in advance. Never again, Michael.'

Fingleton smiled. 'Ah, Connie, sure we're all friends here,' he said. Power was not amused. From then on the company secretary, Stan Purcell, circulated both agenda and minutes to directors in advance, and it must be admitted that the quality of documents and records improved somewhat over time.

Power then, in his other new role on the audit committee, went straight into a meeting with KPMG.

———

Chris Cullen and Darina Barrett, two senior accountants with KPMG, didn't pull their punches. The Central Bank was worried about the speed with which Irish Nationwide was growing. In 1999 alone its loan book had grown by 34 per cent, or £462 million, to £1,806 million. The Central Bank was pushing hard for the society to review its 'credit function', or how it was lending to make sure things were not expanding out of control.

On 4 January 1999 the euro had been launched in financial and investment markets. A momentous event, much of Europe united under one currency for the first time since Charlemagne's reign in the ninth century. This suddenly opened up a whole new set of opportunities for even a small building society on the edge of Europe. In this climate, Ireland's small banking industry experienced a mini-wave of consolidation as banks sought to become bigger so as to tap into a wall of money in Europe that suddenly became available.

On 25 January 1999 Anglo Irish Bank bought Smurfit Paribas Bank for €38 million, bringing to its client list for the first time the industrialist Seán Quinn, while a few months later Irish Life Assurance merged with Irish Permanent to form Irish Life and Permanent in a £2.8 billion mega-merger, creating a third force in Irish banking behind AIB and Bank of Ireland.

More consolidation was seen as inevitable. Irish Nationwide, once it could get the necessary demutualisation legislation passed, was seen as unlikely to remain independent for longer than a few years. In the meantime Fingleton was determined to expand and take on the big boys of banking. He knew, however, that getting the legislation required to demutualise the society would be a complicated process. Inviting Con Power onto its small board was part of his strategy for achieving this. The two men barely knew each other beforehand.

Fingleton realised that he needed someone with Power's legislative expertise and experience. Power was director of economic policy at the Confederation of Irish Industry (now IBEC). He had previously been seconded to work for the state in both the Department of the Environment and Local Government and the Department of the Taoiseach; he knew how the civil service worked and what was required to change legislation.

Power was not at first convinced. He rang a friend in the Department of Finance to ask him if it was 'safe' to join Irish Nationwide's board. His friend said he would make enquiries and come back to him. 'He came back and said Michael Fingleton will push it to the limit but he is too cute to go beyond the limit. That's what came back from the Department of Finance.' Power agreed to join the board, with the principal objective of paving the way for the society to be sold.

This sense that the society's independence would be short-lived was exploited by Fingleton. Publicly he began to dangle the prospect of a windfall from demutualisation to lure in more deposits. Behind the scenes he kept an iron grip on the controls.

Just as Fingleton wanted to fatten the society for sale, the emergence of the euro provided the steroids of the European money markets to allow it to do so. It was an intoxicating cocktail for a man as egotistical as Fingleton, who felt that his small society could compete with anybody.

Europe was awash with cash, and careless French and German money managers were happy to back the little society that believed it could.

Fingleton, not the most diligent man for paperwork, was cutting corners, and the Central Bank suspected it. Perhaps he felt that, once the society was sold, any unpaid loans would ultimately be someone else's problem. Yet right up to the end he acted like someone who genuinely believed the boom would continue, or at least there would be a soft landing. He was far from alone in that view. This combination of more deposits from greedy carpetbaggers and access to the overseas money markets allowed Irish Nationwide to expand rapidly.

The beginnings of Ireland's property bubble were becoming evident as house prices rose by 17 per cent and commercial property shot up by 31 per cent. It was against this background that the Central Bank was concerned that Irish Nationwide might be over-stretching itself. It wanted Fingleton reined in; but at the same time it seemed to admire the building society boss's ability to always have the inside track on any deal.

The day before the meeting of its audit committee, Irish Nationwide had agreed to pay its auditors to conduct a review, for a fee of £25,000 plus VAT. Nobody on the society's board raised any concerns about its auditors having a potential conflict of interest in carrying out such a sensitive review. Con Power, for one, was impressed by KPMG, who seemed up to speed on what needed to be done. They seemed more anxious, he felt, than either Fingleton or O'Connor to bring the society into the new millennium.

Afterwards he was surprised that the directors and senior executives did not go for a meal or even for a sandwich together, as would be usual on other boards on which he had served. 'I thought it odd, as a lunch was a good way to discuss things away from the formality of the boardroom,' he recalled. 'But in Irish Nationwide there was never any socialising between board members that I was aware of.'

On 9 May 2000 there was another board meeting. This time Power was absent. Purcell now updated his board with the information that KPMG had met the Central Bank. It had told KPMG it wanted a review of the society that would take a hard look under its bonnet. Things were inching further on the regulatory front even as Fingleton continued to lend tens of millions every week relatively unchecked.

On 23 May 2000 KPMG wrote to Irish Nationwide outlining the terms of reference for its review, which had now been agreed with the Central

Bank. At first it had four objectives, according to its letter. It was asked to look at 'the appropriateness of the society's lending policies and approval procedures,' the 'appropriateness of arrangements for management of non-performing loans,' the adequacy of the society's provisions, and the adequacy of supervision of the credit function by its board.

As the review was going on, its terms of reference were expanded. This happened in September after more discussions with the Central Bank. Now it also planned to look at the society's arrears and reporting of non-performing assets to both the Central Bank and the society's board, both of which were woefully inadequate.

KPMG had to push the society hard to get all the information required, which kept delaying the completion of its review. On 10 October, Con Power was so frustrated that he rang Purcell to find out if the report would ever be finished. Purcell coolly assured him that it was all going well. The report, he said, would find nothing much out of the ordinary and was just part and parcel of the 'normal course of the bank's supervisory function.'

Finally, on 12 October 2000, KPMG completed its 44-page report plus eleven appendixes. It was far from normal.

Even after months of preparation, KPMG was careful to heavily qualify its conclusion in a section entitled 'Information sources.' This stated that 'no detailed substantive audit work was performed to independently verify either the accuracy or the completeness of the explanations or information obtained from senior management.' In other words, in something that was a constant theme with the society, there was a reliance on the senior management—namely Fingleton—to take the accountants into the bowels of the society. (Within five years this reliance on managements for information would become a source of regret for all Ireland's banking auditors, who failed to warn shareholders or the public of the catastrophic risk of allowing banks to get out of control. But none of them offered to return their fees, nor were they asked to by the state.)

Digging down into the society, KPMG found that Fingleton funnelled customers into the society in four different ways.

Firstly, the society offered loans indirectly through between twenty and twenty-five mortgage brokers. Then it had eighty-five so-called agents, who could be anybody from estate agents to local GAA luminaries, who drummed up yet more business in towns and villages around the country. The society dealt directly too through its fifty-one branches, including offices in Belfast, London, and the Isle of Man. The final route was by way of head office. This meant in effect dealing directly with Fingleton and his tiny team of lieutenants. A staff of thirty oversaw the granting of home loans, which gradually ran to billions under its department head, John Byrne, while another thirty-five reported to Kiera Mansfield, who managed administration.

Meanwhile the society's already rapidly expanding multi-billion commercial loan book was managed by an even smaller team. A mere nine people looked after commercial lending at head office, headed by a senior underwriter, Mick Leonard.

John Byrne reported to Fiona Couse, the society's operations manager. Unusually, he reported to her only on administrative matters; when it came to the important stuff—making the decision to lend, for instance—he bypassed her. Instead everything had to be routed through Fingleton, ensuring that only a very tight team really understood how and on what terms the society was lending to developers.

This report of 2000 is illuminating in the way it describes how the board on occasion generated business for the society. It states that 'an element of new business, particularly commercial is referrals from the board.' According to sources in the society, this note explains why some of the society's directors at least became involved with the society despite its many shortfalls. Of course board members were paid, but membership of the board also gave access to Fingleton, who at the stroke of a pen could lend tens of millions within hours.

He was a powerful man to have the ear of just as the economy began to take off. Sitting around the boardroom table gave directors access too to the inside track of Irish business. The benefits of being a director could easily extend to doing better in their other businesses.

The report states clearly that the directors approved all loans greater than £500,000 as well as looking at monthly reports on arrears, an arrears trend report, and 'any significant recoverability issues.' Both the internal audit and Fingleton, the report said, always brought 'any significant items' to its board.

At least on paper, and according to Fingleton and his cronies, the board was fully in touch with what was going on. The reality was that board meetings were largely rubberstamping exercises, where numerous deals were run through in a couple of hours in meetings that never ran beyond lunchtime. Con Power would later recall that at his first loan approvals meeting dozens of loans went before the board in the space of a morning. 'At every step along the way we were always assured by Michael Fingleton that Irish Nationwide not only obeyed the letter of the law but also its spirit,' he said.

The KPMG report entitled 'Irish Nationwide Building Society: Review of the Credit Function,' described an array of serious problems. KPMG said these went from the boardroom down. It found that the level of information available to directors simply was not good enough. Irish Nationwide claimed that 'any significant issues' about problem loans went to its board, which then made their recommendations. The reality, KPMG found, was that 'the Board minutes do not document the conclusions arising from this review.'

> During its fortnightly meetings, the Board, as well as reviewing all new proposed credit facilities also discuss any significant loans in the pipeline, market developments which may have an impact on the societies credit strategy and recoverability issues, including their potential impact on provisioning levels. The board minutes do not document these discussions.
>
> The board's oversight of the risks inherent in the credit portfolio would be aided by an improved level of portfolio summary reports, e.g. as at 31 December 1999 there was no analysis of the Society's credit portfolio by product, by maturity, by vintage, by size, by loan to value, by interest rate, by geographical concentration or by number of customers was available. In addition no exception reports, e.g. loans in excess of a certain maturity or loan to value etc., were available.
>
> There is no formal documentation to support the key assumptions and components of the underlying credit strategy formulated by the board.

In short, Irish Nationwide's board was operating somewhat in the dark, just as Fingleton was ramping up its lending to ever greater levels.

At the same time, at the executive level the society was operating in an ad hoc way. It was simply making things up as it went along, rather than adopting the correct procedures and processes for a financial institution of its size. Irish Nationwide, KPMG said, had not even a documented policy for working out its provisions for bad loans. Instead it relied on the instinct of its senior management.

Residential lending policy, the report concluded, was very poor. 'There are no specific concentration limits imposed in respect of the composition of the residential portfolio, eg geographical, by product etc.' The society did not create 'exception reports,' making it hard to 'identify any peculiarities or trends within the existing residential portfolio.' This meant it could not easily find out how many of its mortgages had 'unusual interest rates,' or were highly leveraged.

Commercial lending to developers, which Fingleton prided himself on, was even worse. The society was lending hundreds of millions to property speculators without the proper checks. Among KPMG's findings were:

There are no concentration limits applied to the components of the commercial portfolio in its entirety, e.g. sectoral limits, risk categorisation limits.

The level of reports analysing key aspects of the commercial lending portfolio, at either a detailed or summary level, does not facilitate an oversight of this portfolio.

The society's policy is that all commercial loans should be reviewed on an annual basis. There was no documentation to support that this review had been performed during 1999. Management have indicated that an informal review was conducted and that a more formalised review will be performed for the year ended 31 December 2000.

The ongoing monitoring process of commercial loan facilities is not formalised and not documented ... There are no formal checks to ensure that regular information e.g. monthly management accounts and any other key documentation, is received from all commercial customers on a timely basis, or that on site visits are made of larger commercial customers on a regular basis. The society does not have a credit watchlist mechanism, ie to record all commercial loans which although still performing are considered to have potential recoverability issues in the future.

This report should have had serious implications for Irish Nationwide. It explicitly warned the society that it was overexposing itself, not only to individual borrowers but also to particular segments of the market, including development land. As the society prepared to go on a massive lending binge, the Central Bank knew that it was ill prepared to cope if anything went wrong.

Irish Nationwide was a black box, into and out of which billions flowed while only its chieftain, Fingleton, and a small number of others fully knew what was going on. Yet for some reason, no effective action was taken by the Central Bank. The KPMG report was instead allowed to gather dust on the shelves of the society and the Central Bank. Nobody followed through on it, even though year after year KPMG, when preparing the society's end-of-year report, would submit yet more memos to the Central Bank pointing out that essentially the same flaws identified in the 2000 report were only half-heartedly being rectified.

The report was a crucial document given to Michael Walsh for his personal review in the months before he moved from being only a director to becoming chairman of the society in May 2001. Walsh, as we shall see, failed to fully act on the report.

———

As the KPMG report was being prepared for the Central Bank there were other public signs that the society was not working as well as it should.

One day in 2000 a Cork businessman and property dealer, Denis 'Starry' O'Brien, rang Frank Connolly in his office in the *Sunday Business Post*. Connolly was on a formidable roll of stories at the time. He had brilliantly exposed the Fianna Fáil minister Ray Burke as being on the take from builders in return for getting them planning permission. The clamour created by this and other stories led to the setting up of the Flood Tribunal, a full state inquiry into such matters.

Out of the blue, O'Brien told Connolly that he had made a payment of £50,000 to Bertie Ahern, then Minister for Labour. The payment, O'Brien said, involved him lodging £100,000 from a Cork developer, Owen O'Callaghan, in his account in Irish Nationwide's Cork branch. He then withdrew half the money in the form of a cheque for £50,000. He gave this cheque to Ahern, he claimed, in the car park of the Burlington Hotel in Dublin in or around September 1989. He alleged that he made a second payment of £50,000 to an unnamed politician in a similar manner, using his account in Irish Nationwide.

The money, so O'Brien's story went, was paid over to help O'Callaghan secure planning permission for a large shopping centre he was building at Quarryvale, near Lucan, Co. Dublin.

Connolly waited months before publishing the story. Critically, O'Brien had documents describing the movements of money in his Irish Nationwide account in Cork to support his claim.

Eventually, on Sunday 23 April 2000, Connolly published an article that said the tribunal was investigating an alleged payment of £50,000 to an unnamed senior Fianna Fáil figure. It was explosive stuff, and swiftly Ahern's name emerged as the man accused of taking an illicit payment after a senior Fianna Fáil figure assured a rival journalist that they would not be sued for making such a link. O'Callaghan immediately denied the story, as did Ahern, who sued O'Brien for defamation. He did not, however, sue the *Sunday Business Post*.

While the facts of Connolly's story were later proved to be untrue, he was right that the tribunal was taking O'Brien's allegations seriously. How Michael Fingleton responded to the tribunal says much about his attitude towards authority.

In February 2000 the Flood Tribunal wrote to Irish Nationwide seeking all records of deposits and withdrawals made at the St Patrick Street branch of the society in Cork. It wanted to look at files from 15 March 1987 to 15 April 1989 and from 1 June to 30 September 1989, dates that encompassed O'Brien's allegations.

Irish Nationwide struggled to come up with what it was ordered to produce. In the witness box, Fingleton said that statements and cheque counterfoils for the period concerned had been destroyed. 'We have a policy to destroy certain things after six years,' he said. 'There is no guarantee that everything will be destroyed in any organisation, it can be haphazard from time to time, but I am satisfied that we have nothing, no bank statements relating to this period.'

Irish Nationwide had even lost its back-up records for its Cork branch, Fingleton said, after a flood in its Grafton Street office in Dublin. It was all very unfortunate.

In frustration, senior counsel for the tribunal, Patrick Hanratty, said he found Fingleton's attitude 'cavalier in the extreme.' Fingleton rejected this. 'I refute any inference that we're avoiding giving the information,' he said.

Eventually the society did manage to dig up a few documents, but they were incomplete. By then it was clear that O'Brien was back-pedalling on his story, and the matter was dropped by the tribunal. Questioned afterwards by a member of the society over the tribunal's criticism of his attitude, Fingleton was disdainful. There were 'no skeletons' in Irish Nationwide, he insisted.

Meanwhile Bertie Ahern's legal action against O'Brien went ahead in the Circuit Court in July 2001. O'Brien threw in the towel before the case began by admitting that his story was false. 'There is nothing in it for me,' he said. 'I was sucked into this, and I am now unsucking myself.' Nonetheless Ahern pressed ahead with the case. Among the evidence he produced was an affidavit by Fingleton swearing that the Irish Nationwide documents O'Brien had produced were forgeries. The Circuit Court backed Ahern, and in July 2001 he was awarded £30,000 in damages, the maximum then possible in the Circuit Court. 'I am delighted that my character has been utterly, completely and absolutely vindicated,' Ahern told the press afterwards. 'These things were fairly devastating. It said I was a fraud. It said I was a gangster. It said I was corrupt.'

Later Ahern would be found by the Mahon Tribunal to have in fact received large amounts of cash from businessmen, other than O'Callaghan, in the form of a 'dig-out' when his personal finances were in trouble. In his final report the chairperson of the Tribunal said he did not find Ahern's evidence in relation to various payments a 'truthful account.'

But for Frank Connolly, publishing O'Brien's false claims left his reputation in tatters, and he resigned from the *Sunday Business Post*. Writing after the publication of the report in 2012, he reflected on the O'Brien affair. 'No defence was put up; no reason ever given for O'Brien's coming forward with his detailed cock-and-bull story,' he wrote.

In his book *Bertie: Power and Money* (2011) the reporter Colm Keena concluded: 'The case had the effect of dampening media interest in any rumours about payments to Ahern out of fear that they might again be sold a pup. What was motivating O'Brien in all this was never disclosed.'

From a banking point of view, despite a public dressing-down by a statutory tribunal, nobody in Irish Nationwide or the Central Bank moved to ensure that from then on the society kept its files better. Another problem was left stored up for the future.

———

Irish Nationwide would also play a cameo role in other tribunals. In 2008 the Mahon Tribunal investigated what was called the B/T account in the Irish Permanent branch in Drumcondra, Dublin. The account, according to Bertie Ahern and his friend Tim Collins, was set up to hold funds for a building trust associated with a house in Drumcondra used by Ahern to manage his constituency business. The tribunal concluded that this was not true and that the account was used to hold funds for the benefit of Ahern and Collins.

It also discovered that Ahern's then partner, Celia Larkin, had bought a house in Phibsborough, Dublin, in 1993 using money from the B/T account. When the Mahon Tribunal began investigating this matter, Fingleton personally fast-tracked a loan to Larkin of €40,000 in a matter of hours to allow her to repay the money she had taken from the B/T account.

In the Moriarty Tribunal also Fingleton played a role. Here Michael Lowry gave evidence about going to Fingleton when he was a government minister in August 1996. He was instantly approved for a 100 per cent loan to buy a house in Blackrock, Co. Dublin. Lowry also held an offshore bank account in Irish Nationwide in the Isle of Man, into which £147,000 was paid in October 1996. The tribunal believed this money had been paid to him by Denis O'Brien in return for making sure he obtained a valuable mobile phone licence.

Lowry, however, maintains that the account was set up for him by the late David Austin, a Fine Gael fund-raiser. He told the tribunal that the money was a loan from Austin to pay for the renovation of his new house in Blackrock. The tribunal again faced difficulty in extracting information from Irish Nationwide on this affair.

Fingleton's regular appearances or mentions at the tribunals never damaged him. He was, after all, in the excellent company of powerful politicians and wealthy developers who then called the shots in Ireland. Reflecting on these matters today, the broadcaster Matt Cooper concludes:

> Michael Fingleton was almost like Forrest Gump in the way that he turns up at the side of all of the major figures of the major business and political scandals of the last twenty-five years.
>
> The planning tribunal where he was central to Bertie Ahern's partner Celia Larkin, he was very involved with Michael Lowry in various things along the way as well. He was secretive, unwilling to answer the questions that are legitimately asked of him, having excuses not to provide the answers. That's exactly what you often

want in a building society boss who just happened to have an off-shore bank on the Isle of Man. You want someone you can rely on to be discreet, provide the money and who won't tell tales.

REBELLION

But the sleepy world of the Central Bank that Irish Nationwide so easily danced around was about to be shaken up by an unlikely source: a small group of members who had the skill and the doggedness to take it on.

As 2001 began, Peter Donal O'Connor finally retired after reaching the age of seventy, as he was required to do under the rules of the society. Along with his father, he had allowed Fingleton to strengthen his control of the society over the previous decades.

'He was gently-spoken and a nice guy,' Con Power recalled. 'But he never took on Michael Fingleton. It was the absolute opposite. He held Michael Fingleton in absolute awe.'

At O'Connor's last AGM as chairman, on 18 April 2001, fewer than a hundred members showed up. Fingleton gave his usual upbeat assessment of the outlook for the society.

The society announced also that it was going to appoint Terry Cooney, an accountant, to its board. Cooney shared his practice, which was founded in the early 1990s, with Paschal Taggart, a notably gregarious deal-maker. Taggart was a serious hitter in Irish corporate life, having joined a consortium including Noel Smyth, the solicitor, and Dermot Desmond, then an up-and-coming financier, in taking advantage of the collapse of the H. Williams supermarket chain to buy it for a song in 1987. Before that he had also worked for a time with Brendan Gilmore, a corporate adviser, who would later play a role in the Mespil Flats affair.

Cooney, on the other hand, was a former inspector of taxes who preferred to keep a much lower profile than his partner. While he had considerable accountancy expertise, he was a deferential character who was unlikely ever to challenge Fingleton.

There were only two real questions from the floor for the assured Fingleton. One member, Derek Collins, asked if the society could try to avoid any negative publicity in the future in relation to repossessions, a long-running sore point for the society. Fingleton assured him that the society always tried to avoid confrontation, before showing his steely side. 'Inevitably these things happen, because individuals won't pay you anything. You can write it off or go for the asset, and we can't adopt the first option.'

Another member questioned the society's historically low pay rates and whether this meant that its staff were only second-rate and received inadequate training. Fingleton was again dismissive: the staff were getting the market rate of pay, he said.

Entirely unquestioned was Fingleton's own salary, which was the market rate and much more besides. In one of its many quirks designed to protect Fingleton, the society did not give a breakdown of its chief executive's pay; instead it lumped Purcell's and Fingleton's pay under the same heading. In 2000 Fingleton and Purcell were paid a combined €962,000, made up of salaries and bonuses of €737,000 and pension contributions of €225,000. Asked by journalists afterwards if he would give a breakdown of his salary, Fingleton laughed. He had 'no plans' to do so, he said.

The society's board members, by contrast, received a salary of €25,000—not bad money, but nothing to write home about.

On 1 May 2001 a new chairman took over, Dr Michael Walsh. Unlike O'Connor, this time the society's chairman was steeped in formal banking and financial qualifications. A former professor of banking and finance at UCD, Walsh was a close lieutenant of Dermot Desmond, then a multi-millionaire financier who within a decade would become a multi-billionaire. In his role as a director of Desmond's investment vehicle International Investment and Underwriting, Walsh was instrumental in helping Desmond become a very wealthy man. Along the way Walsh himself had made a small fortune. He had no need of the modest salary that went with the job of chairman of Irish Nationwide; nor was he short of something to do as the restless Desmond pushed into ever new areas, from owning London City Airport to successfully riding the technology bubble.

Why someone so qualified became involved in such a banking disaster area remains unclear. Former employees of the society believe Walsh may have taken the job reluctantly after Dermot Desmond turned down an offer to be a director. Equally, being close to Fingleton and chairman of a building society was seen at the time as prestigious and influential as the society continued year after year to report record profits. Other sources suggest that Walsh may have believed he could help the society by using his expertise to clean up its act before a sale.

Whatever his reasoning, Walsh would later tell friends that getting involved with the toxic society was his greatest regret in an otherwise distinguished career.

————

Brendan Burgess, a chartered accountant, was sitting at his desk in his office in Baggot Street, Dublin, in early 2002 when he received an unexpected phone call. Burgess ran an accountancy recruitment company, but this call related to his sideline as a media commentator on consumer affairs for the personal finance pages of the *Irish Independent*. On the line was James Morrissey, joint founder of the *Sunday Business Post*, now a PR man, who was ringing Burgess to complain about a throwaway remark he had made about Irish Nationwide's high interest rates. The society was Morrissey's client.

'[Morrissey] rang me one day to say that the Irish Nationwide was very annoyed,' Burgess recalled. He could barely remember the article, as the comment on Irish Nationwide had been a small one in answer to a reader's question that remarked that the society could on occasion vary the interest rates it charged 'at will.'

'James Morrissey got on to me and roared and screamed at me down the phone,' Burgess said. It was the first time the two men had ever spoken. Until then Burgess had thought little about the society, although he was aware that the personal finance editor of the *Irish Independent*, Bill Tyson, had written several articles criticising the society's treatment of some borrowers. Tyson was a very experienced finance correspondent. He had edited the business section of the *Evening Herald* for years and was bringing the personal finance pages of the *Independent* to a new level. He was giving more and more coverage to the real experiences of readers, relying on the letters he received from readers about their financial experiences. It was a far cry from the more traditional soft-focus stuff on investment products.

Recalling recently how he began writing about Irish Nationwide, Tyson said that in many ways typical borrowers were similar to typical readers of the *Irish Independent*. 'They represented middle Ireland, ordinary people who wanted to pay their way,' he said. He didn't get a lot of letters from readers about overcharging or overpayments, but almost all of them were to do with Irish Nationwide.

Tyson had been plugging away by writing about the experiences people had at the hands of Irish Nationwide. The society was deeply unhappy about this. One of the problems was that Tyson was perfectly entitled to write about the experiences of borrowers who got into trouble, after a close examination of their financial statements, while the society was not allowed to comment publicly on individual cases, as this would have been a breach of confidentiality. Fully cognisant of this, Tyson was meticulous in verifying facts and navigating the potential legal difficulties.

At times things got nasty. 'I remember one time Irish Nationwide contacted a woman who had written to me, and they told her it was a breach of confidentiality for her to have contacted me.' The society's application of penalty interest payments, which in one case Tyson found to be running at a de facto 36 per cent, featured strongly in his articles. 'Irish Nationwide would go much further than other institutions. It is difficult enough to pay a mortgage, but when all of this penalty interest was heaped on, one person compared it to throwing water on a drowning man.'

There were even more basic problems with how the society dealt with some borrowers. Some of them seem unthinkable now, yet it was only ten years ago. Tyson found that Irish Nationwide was not telling borrowers what interest it was charging them. In their statements they received a list of what they owed and how it was shooting up, under various penalty rates, if they fell into arrears. But it never said what the rates were. 'There was a Clare schoolteacher who was clearly paying far too much. He just wanted to find out his interest rate. Next thing there was a memo went around telling managers not to tell anyone what their rate was. They had to contact head office in Dublin and enquire there.'

Meanwhile Burgess's curiosity was piqued by the tone of Morrissey's criticism of his own article. Morrissey had a long association with Fingleton, which meant he felt the need to fight the fight for his client. In 1992 he had left journalism to go into business with the boutique deal-makers Gilmore and Associates. One of his first ventures was to help sell the Mespil estate in Dublin which had turned into a minor scandal for Fingleton and all involved. It had not damaged the gregarious Morrissey's relationship with Fingleton, and they enjoyed a mutual love of gossip about the rich and powerful.

The fondness for secrets was a side of Fingleton that allowed him to build bridges to journalists by dropping an occasional dazzling story, sometimes to score a point against a rival or merely for his own amusement. Fingleton hired Morrissey to handle the society's dealings with the media when he drifted away from business by joining Murray Consultants in 1995. By 2002 Morrissey was essentially out on his own, but his list of clients, including developers like Bernard McNamara and Seán Dunne, overlapped somewhat with the society's customers.

Morrissey tended to become so close to his clients that he sometimes felt more passionate about any slight towards them than they did themselves. He was not afraid to play hard-ball with anybody who challenged his masters, as Burgess was finding out.

'I told him, Look, if I have written something incorrect I will apologise,' Burgess recalled. 'I'm talking to a PR guy, so I'm expecting the guy to be reasonable or whatever. I said, Look, I'll meet your client. He said you won't meet my client, this will be resolved in another venue.'

Burgess interpreted this as a legal threat. Afterwards he was 'a bit shook.' He took a note of the phone call for his files as a cautionary measure, just in case the society followed through on the threat. As Burgess wrote it all down he made up his mind that, rather than backing off Irish Nationwide, he would take it on. 'I don't owe them any money, they have nothing over me, and yet I was a bit upset. It was unpleasant to have someone screaming down the phone. I said, Could you imagine if I was one of those borrowers who Bill Tyson was covering and they can't make their payments, and these guys are shouting and roaring that we're going to repossess your house? I just resolved there and then that I would actually campaign on those guys' behalf and sort out the issues in the Irish Nationwide.'

Although he did not realise it, for the first time Fingleton was about to face a serious external challenge. A rebellion had begun.

————

On Wednesday 24 April 2002 some three hundred members of Irish Nationwide Building Society showed up in the five-star Conrad Hotel for its AGM.

For decades the meetings had been rather sedate affairs, with members more concerned about free tea and sandwiches than about asking hard questions of Fingleton. A former *Irish Times* finance correspondent, Siobhán Creaton, recalls one of the first times she went to cover an AGM of Irish Nationwide. She says she distinctly remembers one elderly person sitting beside her snoring throughout the proceedings.

The format was usually the same. The members every year were promised a windfall when the society finally demutualised, and in the meantime Fingleton should be congratulated for yet again posting a record profit. There was little dissent, as members of the society typically only held deposits there. Their interests were not aligned with borrowers who had fallen into arrears.

This time, however, the mood was different. A campaign was about to begin. Outside the Conrad, Brendan Burgess and his twenty-year-old nephew, on a day off from university, handed out leaflets to members outlining his criticisms of the society's punitive interest charges on borrowers who went into arrears and on its repeated failure to pass on cuts in interest rates to them. The leaflet said that borrowers who went into arrears could pay a surcharge as high as 5 per cent per quarter, which, when combined with the society's standard interest, could push the cost of borrowing as high as 27 per cent APR. This made it impossible for some borrowers ever to repay their mounting debts to the society.

The leaflet also criticised the society for its lack of transparency about how much exactly it paid Fingleton. This amount had never been broken down but instead was hidden within the category of 'directors' emoluments.'

Hotel employees moved in on Burgess and his nephew, telling them to leave as they were committing an 'offence against the Litter Act.' By then it didn't matter, as most members had been given a leaflet.

A small number of disgruntled borrowers followed Burgess through the revolving doors of the hotel. They hoped to be allowed in to the meeting to confront Fingleton and his board, but as they were only borrowers and not registered members of the society they were not sure if they would be allowed. Chief among this group was Gerry Mullin, a Co. Monaghan garage-owner who had spent years paying off ultra-high interest bills to the society. Security men headed them off and told them they would have to wait in the lobby and would not be allowed into the meeting.

Burgess, however, had to be allowed in. He was a full member of the society for many years, after depositing £1,000 in the hope of getting a windfall if it ever demutualised. Taking his seat in the room, he glanced around him. Dotted around he knew was a hard core group of rebels who had met in his office earlier that day. From the corner of his eye he could see Shane Hogan, a 37-year-old information technology project manager and a fellow-ringleader, take his seat. Hogan was a seasoned AGM campaigner who had spoken out for members or shareholders of First Active and Eircom. He was primarily concerned with hastening the society's demutualisation so that its members could finally get their hands on a windfall. But he was also conscious of borrowers' concerns and believed that the best way of getting them better treatment was for Fingleton to sell, a move that would surely trigger his departure.

Also scattered around the hall were various borrowers who were also members of the society. They had all fallen on hard times under the weight of the society's vertiginous penalty interest charges. Some of them made contact with Burgess and Hogan after Tyson published an article in the *Irish Independent* on 20 April calling for them to make contact with the rebels. They planned to air their grievances as soon as questions were allowed from the floor.

First, however, the ordinary business of the society had to be dealt with. Between two great bunches of golden flowers was the society's recently expanded board of directors: Con Power; Michael Fingleton; Michael Walsh, a long-time director making his debut as chairman; the secretary, Stan Purcell; the accountant, Terry Cooney; and a new addition, Maurice Harte.

An experienced accountant and banker with the merchant bank Hill Samuel and AIB Investment Managers, Harte had been appointed chief general manager of the society in January. He also knew how to work with developers after becoming chief executive of Johnny Ronan and Richard Barrett's Treasury Holdings in 2000, where he had laid the groundwork for the National Convention Centre at Spencer Dock, Dublin, and helped develop the €43 million Westin Hotel in the city centre and the sprawling Central Park office complex in Leopardstown.

Harte had been headhunted as a successor to Fingleton by Walsh. 'Michael Walsh was extremely anxious that an appropriate successor could be found,' Con Power recalled. 'After I met with Maurice Harte, I agreed. I saw him as the ideal replacement.'

Harte was tipped by the media as a successor to Fingleton, to the latter's chagrin. Below the board, former employees said they recalled that everybody doubted that the boss was ready to let go of his life's work just yet. Harte would find this out in time, to his cost.

Walsh began with the society's finances, which, as usual, appeared to be spectacular. In its most recent results, to the end of December 2001, the society told members it had increased its pre-tax profit by 19 per cent, to €77 million. Its assets had increased by 16 per cent, to €4.7 billion, as the society trebled in size within five years.

For the first time, lending passed the €1 billion mark, an increase of 8 per cent on the previous year. The society's total loan book was up 20 per cent, to €3.2 billion. 'The society has increased its lending book by a remarkable 94% in the past three years,' the directors' report for members said.

The results were greeted warmly, and nobody questioned the sustainability or possible dangers of such growth. Instead the board sought to assure the meeting that the outlook was rosy. Low interest rates and strong employment levels were 'extremely positive' for the society. There was no chance that it would ever get carried away, was the message.

The society continues to refine and update its systems of control together with the introduction of risk management techniques. The society has, as part of its conservative traditions, adopted a very strong provisioning policy, which reflects the relatively high level of house prices and our increasing exposure to the commercial markets.

This is also of course a reflection of the increasing concerns of the Central Bank for caution to be at the forefront of all lending and credit policies.

Having spun its members again through the results, Walsh sought to pre-emptively take the sting out of the rebels' criticisms by announcing a series of changes. He had been on the board of the society since 1995, but despite his refined understanding of banking he had never pushed for these changes in public before. Now, in his first meeting as chairman, suddenly he was magnanimous. In future, he said, Irish Nationwide would include details of the interest rate charged in all annual mortgage statements issued to borrowers. It was an incredible admission that the society had until then failed to do so. Already the rebels were making an impact.

As a result of not knowing what interest they were paying, tens of thousands of borrowers were simply unaware that many of them were paying above market rates as the society jacked them up. Even when the society cut its rates—after the Central Bank or European Central Bank did—they were in the dark about how much of a given reduction was passed on to them.

In another remarkable concession, Walsh said that in future Irish Nationwide would credit interest payments to mortgage holders' accounts monthly from 1 June. Up to then the society had applied an 'annual rest' on mortgage payments, which meant the full year's interest was calculated at the beginning of the year, ignoring payments throughout the year. This had made the society more money, at the expense of its borrowers.

But there was still no pleasing the protesters, who were anxious to make their points. A chaotic meeting ensued, with elderly members who couldn't hear questions shouting out, 'I can't hear a thing!' 'This is a meeting—we should all be able to hear,' 'Why aren't there two microphones?' and so on.

In fact microphones were passed around the floor, leading at one point to some confusion as one member questioned a DIRT settlement of €5.64 million with the Revenue Commissioners on the years 1986–99 in the accounts ('Did the auditors realise this was illegal?') while another objected to the reappointment of its auditors, KPMG, because it was time for 'fresh eyes.'

Amid questioning from the floor on Fingleton's salary, Walsh again sought to calm things down. For the first time in its history, he announced, Irish Nationwide next year would break down Michael Fingleton's remuneration as part of a plan to improve communication with its members. He was not prepared, however, to reveal it before then.

The two executive directors, Fingleton and Purcell, were paid €1.1 million between them in 2001, Walsh explained. This was made up of €854,000 in pay and €258,000 in pension contributions. Walsh quipped, to laughter, that 'you can ask Stan later how much he got.'

Burgess then stood up to challenge Walsh. Neither man realised that this would be the first of many such tussles. Burgess said that Irish Nationwide's mortgage rate was 'the most expensive of any institution, excluding moneylenders.' He claimed that the average rate was 7.2 per cent, significantly more expensive than others in the market. The society, he said, would have to 'buck up' with the appointment of the new Irish Financial Services Regulatory Authority (Financial Regulator), which he predicted 'will have great interest in Irish Nationwide.'

Walsh responded coolly that the society had 'no problem' with the new regulator. Anybody, he said, who felt they were being unfairly treated was already free to complain to the Central Bank.

Burgess welcomed Walsh's moves to finally allow its borrowers to know what their interest rate was, before going back on the attack. The society, he said, was 'coming the heavy immediately' on any borrower who fell into arrears. Deliberately, he finished his attack by asking Walsh what the society's policy was on jailing its members.

Fingleton grabbed the microphone from Walsh, his fury palpable. 'The courts may—but we never, ever sought to put anybody in jail,' he angrily declared. He called on Burgess to apologise and to retract the remark.

Burgess's response was to sit down, further infuriating Fingleton. This cleared the way for the orchestrated appearance of another speaker from the floor. Joseph Nulty, a carpenter from Barna, Co. Galway, stood up. He had been locked in a dispute for years with the society, which claimed he owed it £65,500 in arrears on £113,000 he borrowed in 1993, to build his dream home in Barna. When he was a child in school he even drew some outline plans of the house that one day he wanted to build. It also had his carpenter's workshop attached. Because Nulty was self-employed and his income was sometimes erratic, he wanted a mortgage with a difference. He got his broker to negotiate a special deal with Irish Nationwide whereby his interest rate would not fluctuate above a certain level in relation to the general inter-bank rate.

'In a sense, I got the first tracker mortgage in Ireland,' Nulty said recently, recounting his experiences. He put his heart and soul into the house, designing and making all the furniture. When he ran into difficulties with his mortgage he noticed that the repayments and interest levels did not appear to correspond to the mortgage contract he had. Things got worse for him as he fell deeper into arrears under punitive penalty interest.

He had got someone to take an independent view of what, under his contract, his repayments should have been. His arrears, he believed, should have been about €25,000. This was a lot less than he was told he owed. He decided to take legal action against the society.

The situation became really nasty when his electricity and phone were cut off. He says this was not as a result of his not paying the bills but that it happened after Irish Nationwide contacted the ESB and Telecom Éireann to say that his house was no longer insured and for this reason he was cut off.

Nulty borrowed a generator and eventually managed to get his basic utilities back. His career had suffered, and he was now at an extremely low ebb. This made it even more difficult for him to financially get back on track. Eventually, amid confusion and acrimony in a court hearing, he was sent to Castlerea Prison in Co. Roscommon for contempt of court. 'I remember being taken down to the cells in handcuffs. I was then put into a van and taken to Castlerea,' he said. He spent a week in prison before being transferred to Dublin for a new court appearance. He was released immediately. Irish Nationwide had faxed a letter saying it would not contest his being released.

But when he got back to Barna he discovered that the society had repossessed his house. Nulty claimed that the society had pursued him unfairly for years. It went as far as Fingleton himself showing up on his lane in a big car, he said. 'I knew something was happening when Skittles, my little three-legged dog, became agitated as a huge Beemer [BMW] came to half way up the driveway with the engine still running. I recognised Fingleton, with another person in the car. As soon as I approached my uninvited guests they left the property.'

As Nulty told his story the meeting was in disarray, with members shouting and interrupting each other. Michael Walsh struggled to regain control as members shouted both for and against Fingleton.

'You were told off by a High Court judge,' Nulty roared at Fingleton. Walsh said it was 'not appropriate' to discuss Nulty's case, as it was still before the courts.

Then Brian Thompson, another borrower, stood up to add another voice to the cacophony. He was the owner of Cloghan Castle, near Banagher, Co. Offaly. A seventy-year-old former American paratrooper, Thompson had worked in insurance in New York before returning to Ireland to restore the castle. Over thirty years he had spent €2 million in today's money. He borrowed about £30,000 from Irish Nationwide, he said, and was in a dispute with the society over alleged arrears, paying interest, he claimed, of 30 per cent. 'I have had over a hundred mortgages in four countries,' he said. 'Never in my wildest dreams could I have envisaged anything as appalling—nothing even close. It's the most troublesome I have ever known.'

Furious about his spiralling interest bill, Thompson said he had stopped paying the society in 1997. 'This is the time to show that we, the members, are the ultimate bosses,' he said.

Another member shouted at Thompson that if he wasn't happy why didn't he just move his loans?

'I spent five months trying to pay them off and they wouldn't let me,' he replied. Another roar from Nulty, 'I know that feckin' feeling,' led to laughter.

Shane Hogan stood up to press the society to appoint a members' director. He pointed out that nobody knew how many members the society had, or their addresses. He asked for members to leave their addresses with him at the end of the meeting so that he could write to them. 'If someone wants to go on the board,' Walsh said, 'it is the board's obligation to ensure all members are circulated.'

More unrest. A member said the society needed to be demutualised, as it was not being run for its members any more. 'We get the feeling on this side of the table that the society is being run for the benefit of those on that side of the table,' he said.

Amid chaotic scenes, another member called for the society to hold a day out on the *Christina O*, the yacht that was bought two years before by a syndicate using money from Irish Nationwide. The yacht was formerly owned by the Greek shipping magnate Aristotle Onassis, who had lovingly restored it. Guests of Onassis had included his lover Maria Callas, the opera singer, and his wife, Jacqueline Onassis, widow of President John F. Kennedy. Its Irish owners, assembled by the lawyer Ivor FitzPatrick by way of the Cook Islands, included the trucking magnate Pino Harris. The partnership had spent €50 million renovating the yacht as well as restoring its many features, including bar stools upholstered with leather from the foreskin of Minke whales.

Walsh told the society's members that he had never been on the yacht, and neither had the society's managing director, as far as he knew. Fingleton took the microphone again to correct him. Yes, he had been on the yacht, he said, but by then there were no loans outstanding on it.

The society's chieftain then addressed more important matters: the issues of demutualisation and even going public by listing on the stock exchange. 'People can't have it every way,' hc said. 'Mutual means giving everything away to everybody. If we went public, without five years of strong profitability we would be wasting our time.'

Irish Nationwide, he said, was storming ahead and in the last year alone had added €50 million to its reserves. 'That's our money,' he said. It was a telling comment that showed how closely Fingleton aligned his own worth mentally with that of the society.

Fingleton was at once bemused and dismissive of his critics. The managing director of First Active, Cormac McCarthy, he said, had got a standing ovation only the day before, for less good results. 'I don't want a standing ovation, but I would like to thank any of you who support me and have supported me over the years.' Fingleton felt he'd put his critics in their place.

Peter Tuite, a quiet-spoken financial adviser, then stood up and launched a devastating critique of the society. 'Irish Nationwide is like a prehistoric monster eating its young. There is a lack of transparency and we all know that means there is something to hide. It's like trying to draw the tusks of a boar trying to get any information out of this society.'

Tuite said that Walsh was wrong to claim that super-high interest rates had rarely if ever been applied since 1997. 'I am looking at a statement that shows 12 per cent was charged in March,' he said. Tuite knew what he was talking about. He was a career banker who helped set up Cork branches for Guinness Mahon and Citibank. Now retired, he had decided to use his financial nous to help distressed borrowers from the society. At the time of the AGM he had already tried to make the Central Bank take on the society by giving it a detailed dossier of complaints, including handwritten notes from customers setting out the pressures they were under. One of these complaints, later published in the *Irish Independent* by Bill Tyson on 12 September 2002, said: 'We have done everything in our power to get this situation sorted but we find that due to the high interest, which they promised they would look at, we are unable to cope with this. We have sold machinery, land, anything we could to keep up with repayments but again we are falling in arrears . . .'

Over the years Tyson amassed a stack of similar complaints as the public wrote in to him, which he followed up on in the *Irish Independent*, despite pressure not to do so.

The Central Bank did respond to Tuite's and others' complaints, but it did so in an ineffectual manner.

Tuite told the Central Bank that he could prove that borrowers were being charged up to 42 per cent on their arrears, but he got nowhere. 'They may have had a problem with it but they didn't appear to do anything about it. They accepted the Nationwide's account at face value. They kicked to touch.'

Instead of stepping in, the Central Bank told Tuite to tell his clients to 'contact the society again to see if a mutually satisfactory agreement can be reached regarding arrears.' Three years later Tuite said no deal had been done. 'I spoke to the wife [of the borrower] recently, who told me she had been attending the doctor for high blood pressure treatment and that their ordeal was still ongoing,' he told Tyson.

Tuite sent Walsh into a huddle with his board members. Eventually Walsh emerged and invited Tuite to discuss the matter with Purcell privately afterwards.

To the board's relief, the meeting finally ended, after two hours. Burgess sprang out of his chair and approached the board. He had a copy of Nulty's committal order in his hand and tried to give it to Walsh. Walsh brushed him off, saying he did not wish to discuss individual members.

Burgess then went to Cooney and asked him if he would come outside and meet the society's distressed borrowers who hadn't been allowed into the AGM. 'He just looked down at his shoes and didn't answer my question,' Burgess said. 'It was the usual thing: we can't discuss individual circumstances.'

Finally Burgess turned to Power. 'I said, "Mr Power, will you come out and talk to a borrower outside?" I had never met the man before. Power said, "Certainly I will, of course I will."'

As Burgess walked towards the door with Power they were approached by an Irish Nationwide official. 'Mr Power, can I speak with you a moment?' the man said. A hushed conversation ensued. Then Power raised his voice and said: 'Nobody tells me who I can and cannot meet.'

Power grabbed Burgess by the arm and they marched out to meet Gerry Mullin and the other borrowers. Mullin, a Monaghan garage owner and car dealer, had a powerful story to tell. Describing his ordeal anonymously in the *Irish Independent* three days after the AGM, he said:

It was sheer hell. Unbelievable. One day I had to give them £10,000 to get them off my back. In one year I paid back £20,000, and £15,833 of it was interest and penalty interest. You can't think straight; you can't sleep. The missus got diabetes out of it. Many a man would have cracked for less . . . Luckily I am the operator I am.

Mullin was unable to escape the society by refinancing his loan, because of his arrears record. He said he took out a loan of £75,000 in the 1990s and ended up paying back £221,699 in total. 'I don't know why—I can't get answers.'

Power listened to his tale of woe and the others and promised to raise it with the board. Finally, it seemed, the borrowers were getting somewhere. Walsh had made some big concessions, and now they even had someone on the society's board prepared to listen to them.

Burgess was happy as he went for a drink with his fellow-rebels in the bar of the Conrad. 'We felt we had really got our message across. They were expecting a great gig and they had a rough time. They were just expecting everybody to be happy and we weren't happy.' The rebels were more determined than ever to force changes.

The final sentence of an article in the *Sunday Business Post* on 14 April 2002 did not seem so far-fetched. 'However, recent controversies, competition from cross-channel banks, the loss of his unique grip on the media and what would appear to be the laying of foundations to appoint a successor all suggest that Fingleton may be contemplating life after Irish Nationwide.' Nothing, as it turned out, could be further from the mind of the society's feudal-style chieftain.

———

On 8 November 2002, Fingleton, Power and Purcell met Philip Williamson, chief executive of Nationwide, Britain's biggest building society, and his finance director, Stuart Bernard.

Williamson ran Nationwide conservatively, and the society's strong cash reserves led it to seek to break into the Irish market. He mentioned that he had already met Michael Walsh at an earlier meeting. They weren't interested in buying Irish Nationwide outright but instead they wanted a merger. Power told Williamson: 'That's a good idea. Let's keep up a dialogue and explore it.'

Fingleton took a different point of view. 'The members expect cash from a trade sale,' he said, 'and that's what I am going to give them.' The talks ended. An opportunity to prevent catastrophe was missed.

Ten days later Irish Nationwide held its next board meeting. Maurice Harte was absent. That summer he had confided in Power that he felt 'trivialised' by Fingleton. 'Relations between Michael Fingleton and Maurice Harte at board meetings were putrid!' Con Power recalled. Fingleton and Harte would snipe at each other across the head of Stan Purcell. Power told Harte he would back him at board level if he was prepared to really take Fingleton on. 'I can't carry you like a eunuch! Don't take it. Stand up to your man!' Power told Harte. 'I will do a tizzy fit at the board to support you but you need to give me an opening.' Harte replied quietly, 'Con, I don't think I can do that.'

Just like that, Harte—the best-qualified person to run Irish Nationwide—was gone.

On 20 November 2002 Power met Walsh in the head office of International Investment and Underwriting to discuss what to do next. 'We must find a replacement,' Walsh said. Power suggested a recently retired senior manager at TSB, Dermot Tippins. Tippins was interested. After months of Walsh pressing Fingleton to meet Tippins, he eventually did. Not long after the meeting Tippins withdrew. Asked by Power why he had withdrawn, he replied simply: 'I couldn't work with Michael Fingleton.'

———

Having made some progress taking on Irish Nationwide, Brendan Burgess and Shane Hogan decided in December 2002 to submit four motions to the society before its AGM the next year. When they looked at the society's archaic rules, which Fingleton showed little interest in updating, they realised they were already too late.

Members wishing to submit any motion for discussion at an AGM had to do so six months in advance, in this case by the end of November. 'We had missed the deadline,' Burgess admitted. 'But we decided to submit our motions anyway.'

Their motions were mainly designed to help borrowers, but they also included a proposal to put forward a vote of no confidence in Fingleton as chief executive.

Purcell refused to allow any of the motions to go to members, by arguing that they were submitted too late. Burgess and Hogan, however, went through the fine print of the legislation to try to find a loophole. 'Within the Building Societies Act you have the right of appeal to the Central Bank,' Burgess said, 'So, we appealed to the Central Bank.'

The Central Bank decided to make a concession to the rebels and their campaign by instructing the society to allow the motions go forward. However, it wanted to rephrase the vote of no confidence in Fingleton to the less provocative phrasing of a vote of confidence.

Burgess recalls his meeting with the Central Bank at the time. 'Mary O'Dea was the consumer director-designate at the time. She felt the motions were valid. The prudential side said that a motion of no confidence could undermine the society and even lead to a run on the Irish Nationwide.' In the end the rebels had more or less what they wanted, once the phrasing of this motion was changed.

———

Friction at AGMs did not prevent Walsh and Fingleton socialising together with the elite of Irish business. Both men were among a social set of businessmen who revolved around Michael Smurfit, one of the first Irish businessmen to become a player on the global stage. In February 2003 they both attended Smurfit's dinner which was themed the 'Brave New World'. Other guests included the Tánaiste, Mary Harney, Elan's former chairman Donal Geaney, ex-Senator Edward Haughey, and Denis O'Brien. Ben Dunne, Michael Lowry and Albert Reynolds were also in attendance.

The American private equity group Madison Dearborn had just bought out the Jefferson Smurfit Group, so the event was a raucous and good-humoured affair. Pat Leahy wrote in the *Sunday Business Post*:

> One of the most eagerly anticipated features of the evening was the announcement of the coveted Employee of the Year award.
>
> Two years ago, beating off stiff competition, the winner was Tony Smurfit. This year, after a similarly intense race, the winner was Michael Smurfit himself.
>
> This year an extra special gong was handed out. Drawing gasps of admiration, a special Employee of the Century award was announced. The winner? Michael Smurfit. What a night.

It was great fun—a million miles from the lives of Joseph Nulty and Irish Nationwide's tiny borrowers who were being pursued so ruthlessly.

The following month Walsh was back to the business of Irish Nationwide. Seeing the rebels gaining momentum, he decided to meet Hogan and Burgess to try to broker peace in the offices of Dermot Desmond's investment group. Power, the only board member prepared to listen to the dissenters, was also invited. Burgess was glad to see Power there, as he considered him independent and supportive of his concerns.

The meeting at Walsh's office in IIU took place at 8 a.m. 'It was down in the IFSC in very luxurious offices,' Burgess recalled. Stacks of paintings were piled against the wall of the meeting-room, waiting to be hung.

Walsh quickly got down to setting out his views as chairman of the society and what its future should hold. 'Michael Walsh told me that he would get very fat if he went out for lunch with all the people who had offered to take him out to lunch to discuss the demutualisation,' Burgess said. 'All the banks and guys over in England, all the stockbrokers of Ireland, all wanted to handle the demutualisation.' Burgess and Hogan pressed Walsh to put down a more specific motion that would set a time limit for demutualisation.

Walsh listened amiably. As he often did, he engaged intelligently and constructively but held back from being tied down to any specific deadlines. 'He was absolutely keen on the demutualisation,' Burgess said. 'He thought Fingleton was essential to the demutualisation . . . We would have been of the view that Fingleton should go.'

Walsh ably defended Fingleton, pointing to his years of record profits. Despite their fundamental disagreement over Fingleton, Burgess and Hogan came away impressed by Walsh. 'Michael Walsh recognised that there were problems with the society,' Burgess said. 'He wanted to fix the society and get it ready for demutualisation.' Equally, he did not dispute that some borrowers were being treated badly by the society. 'He recognised that Michael Fingleton kept costs to a tiny level. He had instructed him, as far as I remember, that it wasn't enough to just have low costs, it had to be the lowest appropriate costs.'

The meeting, while cordial, was not enough to convince the rebels to back down. 'We didn't really believe we would win the vote,' Burgess now recalls. 'But by putting down the motion we had an opportunity to write to all of the members, ahead of the AGM, outlining our case. We felt this was a good benefit from the whole exercise in raising awareness.'

They circulated a statement to members, which hit the society's failings hard. It was inflammatory stuff, which infuriated Fingleton.

Burgess and Hogan called on members to vote against the motion expressing confidence in Fingleton. They said Fingleton had taken the credit for Irish Nationwide's strong financial performance and low cost base. Therefore, he must also accept responsibility for the issues that had brought the society into disrepute.

Their statement noted a comment by the Director of Consumer Affairs, Carmel Foley, who said she was 'disgusted' with the society over 'swingeing' penalty interest rates and 'lack of information to borrowers.' The society was 'very aggressive' with borrowers in arrears.

The case of a nine-year legal battle between Eileen Malone and the society was cited as an example of Fingleton's bullying.

Malone's 47-year old husband, Seán, had died on 29 July 1989, leaving her with four children and a newly purchased grocery, house and pub in Rathmolyon, Co. Meath. The property had a £100,000 mortgage from Irish Nationwide. Before his death Seán Malone had agreed with the society that he would buy insurance cover from Caledonian Life, which would pay off his mortgage in the event of his death. He had to buy the insurance cover from Caledonian as part of the terms of his Irish Nationwide mortgage. He had even paid the society an extra £1,200, including £1,000 in administration costs, for it to handle the paperwork for his mortgage and insurance cover.

The society, however, had failed to effect the insurance cover on behalf of the Malones, despite their solicitor's promptings. Seán Malone had filled in a direct debit form to cover his mortgage repayment and mortgage protection insurance; but the society had failed to lodge it. Irish Nationwide had admitted its oversight but refused to take responsibility for it. It spent the next ten years chasing the Malones for £100,000 on their property, which multiplied in value as the boom took off.

Eventually the case went to the Supreme Court, which found in favour of Eileen Malone. It ruled that the society had been 'manifestly negligent' in its treatment of her. At least €500,000 had been spent by the society in pursuing its fruitless action against the widow as she struggled to bring up her family.

Burgess and Hogan then reminded members of the jailing of Joseph Nulty as further evidence that Fingleton was unsuitable. It also raised the question of the society's appearance at the Flood Tribunal and the claim by Patrick Hanratty sc, for the Tribunal, that Fingleton was 'cavalier in the extreme,' in his attitude to it. Their statement said that Fingleton was due to retire in January 2004 and, having by now driven out Maurice Harte, had no potential successor.

The two men dragged up other dirt from the society's murky depths. In August 1999 Judge Peter Kelly had threatened to jail Fingleton and sequester the society's assets for contempt of court in a case involving the alleged wrongful dismissal of the manager of the society's Cavan branch, Seán Martin. Martin had obtained an order preventing his dismissal from Judge Fidelma Macken on 8 March until his case could be heard. The society sacked him anyway on 18 June, claiming he had carried out alternative employment as an auctioneer and in any event, it claimed, was under-achieving as a manager.

Martin had appealed against his dismissal before even being given a chance to argue his case in court before Judge Kelly, who said he was prepared to jail Fingleton for doing so. A stay had been put on his order when counsel for the society gave an unequivocal undertaking that Martin could continue in his job. The society claimed that the judge had only made an order for them not to sack Martin; this, it believed, did not prevent them carrying out further internal disciplinary procedures. When Martin failed to co-operate with these inquiries, it said, it felt entitled to dismiss him.

Judge Peter Kelly dismissed this explanation. 'If the Irish Nationwide Building Society had felt Mr Martin was abusing the order of making life impossible for them, then their course was clear. They could have come back to court at any time and sought to have the order dissolved or varied.' The society, he concluded, had taken the law into its own hands by dismissing Martin and humiliating him by taking his office keys, credit card and society car from him without trial.

The case had been highly embarrassing for Fingleton and had been quietly and expensively settled over the summer months, while the courts were closed.

Hogan and Burgess also made reference, though not explicitly, to an even worse episode in Fingleton's career. 'The society has also made substantial settlements under confidentiality agreements with ex-employees. These awards reduce the profits of the society and ultimately reduce the value of the windfall.'

This was a reference to an article published in the *Sunday Tribune* on 3 November 2002. It stated that the society had paid €200,000 in a confidential settlement with an employee called Fiona Couse. She had worked her way up from being a mortgage administration manager in the 1990s to becoming head of compliance. She had worked closely with Fingleton for twenty years before suddenly leaving at the beginning of 2002. She had taken her case to the Office of the Director of Equality Investigations. A public hearing was due on 16 October, but Fingleton decided to settle the case, which the *Sunday Tribune* said at the time could have been 'highly embarrassing for the society. It is understood that Couse brought her case against Irish Nationwide after her close working relationship with the chief executive deteriorated and negotiations failed to reach a conclusion satisfactory to both parties.'

In truth, Fingleton was more than close to Couse. They had enjoyed a love affair. It was only on 1 March 2011 that this became public in the *Irish Mail on Sunday* under the headline 'Fingleton's mistress got £200,000 payout.'

Couse, a one-time captain of the Irish women's hockey team, was confronted at her home by the paper. She said the pay-out happened only a 'significant period of time' after the affair ended. 'It wasn't linked to it at all. It has absolutely nothing to do with it. It was a sexual . . . it was a harassment and bullying action that was taken under the guise of the Director of Equality Investigations. And that's what that settlement was in relation to. It was in relation to nothing else.'

Fingleton neither confirmed nor denied the affair but insisted that Irish Nationwide had acted properly in response to what was an internal employment claim. 'The matter was settled at the time for good and proper reasons,' he said, 'and in the best interests of the Irish Nationwide Building Society, and all matters in relation to this case were dealt with by the chairman of the society at that time.'

He categorically denied any suggestion that the complaint had been hushed up to save his embarrassment. He refused to say whether board members who approved the payment to Fiona Couse knew of his previous relationship with her.

Couse claimed the settlement had been dealt with by Harte and Purcell, but not Fingleton. 'He wasn't even involved in it . . . Maurice Harte was the person involved with it, and the company secretary. And it was unlikely that he [Fingleton] could have been involved in so far as he was a named individual. So he would have been there from the point of view if it was necessary to have a witness or something like that.'

Harte declined to comment on the issue, and declined to say whether

Fingleton had played a role in the settlement, saying, 'I'd prefer not to answer that.'

The paper then approached Con Power, a board member present at the time of the payment. He told it he was unaware of the nature of the settlement and that his understanding at the time was that it had been an unfair dismissal claim, which had eventually been settled amicably. 'The details had never been discussed by the board,' he said. Neither Power nor Harte recalled a letter that Couse was reported to have written to the Central Bank in which she outlined a number of compliance concerns.

Fingleton's salary also came under fire. The letter noted that his package was 'similar' to the scale of the chief executives of AIB and Northern Rock, 'which are far larger and more complex companies. His package is approximately three times the size of the package paid to the chief executive of the EBS, the only comparable institution in Ireland. His undoubted experience in cost-cutting and litigation might well be counter-productive to the more marketing orientated skillset required to sell the company.'

A new managing director was required to lead the society during the demutualisation and sell-off phase, it said. 'Vote AGAINST any motion of confidence in Michael Fingleton.'

Burgess and Hogan also took on the wording of the board's motion on demutualisation and the future direction of the society. They argued that its motion on demutualisation was 'essentially meaningless,' as it set no deadlines. They suggested it should demutualise within eighteen months and be sold immediately afterwards.

They put on the agenda three items of concern to borrowers. The first was the sore point of standard variable rates, which the society was finally proposing to introduce years after their rivals. They called for this not only to be offered to anyone taking out a new mortgage from January 2002 but to be extended to all.

The second item was the 'treatment of borrowers,' who were banned from attending AGMs or voting on the society's direction. The rebels argued that the society should give borrowers these rights so as to ensure that the society was run in a fairer way. 'Much of the financial strength of the society has been developed at the expense of borrowing members,' they claimed.

The third item was the society's decision to finally 'abolish penalty interest on home loans.' The rebels urged members to vote for this motion but also to become more lenient with any borrower in trouble. They called on the society to adopt a 'less aggressive approach and to use the courts only as a last resort.'

Walsh was having none of it. Despite his amiable private meeting with the rebels, when it came down to it he backed the status quo. In a separate note to members he attacked the rebels' concerns, and their motivation. 'The board emphatically rejects the innuendo contained in the statement that the managing director is in some way unsuitable to continue to lead the society.' Irish Nationwide's profits spoke for themselves, he said. 'The reserves of the society, which are the property of the members, increased by a multiple of more than two thousand times during the period, and pre-tax profits in the year 2002 were also more than two thousand times the level of thirty years ago.' The society's mortgage book was up 'seven hundred times,' and €3 billion in new business had been lent. 'Far from adopting a very aggressive approach to borrowers in arrears, the society only goes to the courts as a last resort,' he said. Irish Nationwide had not repossessed any residential property in the current year (2003) and had made only one repossession in 2002 and two in 2001. 'The number of cases of difficulty is indeed tiny relative to the mortgage book of the society, and it seems to the board that the high profile and imbalanced presentation of some of those cases is now being used in an emotive and selective manner as the context for totally subjective and personalised criticism of the managing director.'

The 128th AGM of the society took place in the Burlington Hotel on Thursday 24 April 2003. Walsh began the proceedings by addressing the members present. 'The results announced by the society today reflect once again the exceptional financial strength of the Irish Nationwide, particularly in a market that is increasingly competitive and over-supplied and where margins continue to be squeezed on both sides of the balance sheet.'

Despite private reservations, Walsh boasted to the society's members that its ratio of cost to income of 22 per cent was 'the lowest of any financial institution in Ireland.' The society, he said, had a 'high level of lending,' pumping out €1 billion in each of the previous two years. 'We could not lend this level of funds unless we were clearly competitive, which we are.'

Pre-tax profits were up 26 per cent, to €97 million, and the financial achievements of the previous ten years were 'outstanding.'

To give a picture of growth over the past thirty years, the net book representing shareholders' interest has increased from €210,000 in 1972 to €438m in 2002. Assets have increased from €5.6m in 1972 to €5548m at the end of 2002.

The foregoing statistics once again clearly demonstrates that your society continues to be a very strong, well-managed and an independently viable financial institution. We have continually outperformed other financial institutions, some of them many times our size.

Fingleton was the key to the society's success, was Walsh's clear message. Walsh then turned to the society's view of Ireland's property market, which was already showing signs of overheating. He said that the Planning and Development (Amendment) Act (2002) brought in by the Minister for the Environment, Martin Cullen, provided a 'welcome boost' for the housing market. It was a good thing that the amendment had 'abolished the two year planning rule which threatened to freeze the supply of housing going forward.'

This change had effectually taken the brake off the already super-charged housing market. In addition, it amended part 5 of the planning Act (2000) to remove the requirement on builders that one in five houses in their developments should be social housing, or failing this to pay a fee to the city or county council. This move too was designed to help developers, who were concerned that it would dampen the crazy prices they were able to charge for small houses and apartments if they had to make some of them available to less fortunate people.

Walsh told members that he was not sure if the affordable-housing changes would 'help or hinder the supply of houses in the future.' He was aware, however, of the views of the big developers who had become so important to the society. 'Some developers believe that the amended provision will be negative for the industry. Only time will tell.'

Walsh then made a telling statement about the society's views of the property market. 'The society does not subscribe to the school of falling property values and expects prices to increase in the coming year by 8 to 10 per cent, particularly in the urban and greater Dublin area.' Outside those areas, price increases will be 'more moderate.'

It would be some time in the first half of 2004, he said, before supply would equate to demand. Demographic changes, low interest rates and modest unemployment were the fundamentals underpinning this prediction, he said. Competition, Walsh said, was strong among banks for new business. 'There is now no prospective borrower who complies with the normal lending criteria who cannot get a loan to buy a house.'

Updating members on his view of the society's future, Walsh said the Department of the Environment had established a review group and that he was confident that section 102 of the act would be amended and the five-year rule would go, allowing the society to be sold. In the meantime Fingleton would remain in the saddle, charged with continuing to 'build up shareholder value.'

> In conclusion, I would like to state that the Irish Nationwide is an exceptionally well managed modern progressive building society with a record of achievement second to none. We would be very concerned if after many years of successful growth that the society would be damaged in any way. The controversy currently prevailing is not helpful to the overall interests of members. Members who deliberately misrepresent the society and damage it have no place in the organisation.

The rebels' direct threat and detailed criticism ignited fury at the top of the society. A decision was made somewhere near the top that their motions must not only be beaten—which was almost certain—but trounced. The hope was that this would intimidate them into never trying again to oust Fingleton and win a fair deal for borrowers. To achieve this object, the rules would have to be broken.

In the weeks before the AGM the rebels became aware that the society appeared not only to be canvassing for votes but to have failed to pass their criticisms on to members. Both actions were illegal under the Building Societies Act.

Burgess received a phone call from one borrower, Brendan Gavin, who told him he had gone for a meeting with his local building society manager. While there he had been given a sheet of paper and asked to tick all the boxes in favour of Fingleton and the society. The manager told him his vote was needed to see off some troublemakers who were damaging the value of the society.

A pile of printed papers seeking proxy votes was stacked on the manager's desk. They were not attached to the notice of the AGM, which contained the rebels' criticisms. Crucially, Gavin could prove this, as he kept his sheet, which did not have the serrated edge it should have had as part of the notice of the AGM. 'It was very, very clear what they were doing was wrong,' Burgess said. 'People were just coming up and they said, Oh, Tom, look, there's this fellow causing trouble and they've put down a motion of no confidence in Michael Fingleton. Would you mind giving the chairman your proxy? They'd say, Oh, not at all, and they just signed it. They wouldn't have seen the arguments for or against.'

Burgess began to make phone calls to his contacts working in the society and quickly found out that the canvassing was not confined to one branch but was part of a concerted attempt to trounce any attempt at reform. Each branch was given a target of between 200 and 300 votes in favour of Fingleton. 'I was told this by people working in the Irish Nationwide . . . There were some seven whose job was to ring all the branches and check how many they had got and prove that they had met their target.'

One of those charged with gathering proxies was the manager of the Monaghan branch, Brendan Beggan. He had joined Irish Nationwide as branch manager in 1996. He recalls responding to an advertisement for the job and going to Dublin for the interview in the old Irish Nationwide head office in Camden Street. His first impression of the building was that it was 'pretty grotty'. Nevertheless he expected to be grilled by a team of three or four executives; but it didn't go that way at all. 'In walks Michael Fingleton himself. He was the only one. The interview wasn't about lending or anything like that. He spent the whole time asking about the GAA and my own connections with it.' Beggan had been an inter-county footballer with Monaghan and played with the prominent county team Scotstown. He recounts how Fingleton loved the GAA. 'A lot of his managers were in the GAA. The higher up you were in the GAA, the better chance you had of getting a job.'

Beggan recalls that the vote-gathering exercise was quite sophisticated in some ways. 'I would be given a list of people to approach. Depositors' names would come up in the overnight bags. I would tell them, If Michael Fingleton doesn't get back in you won't get your premium rates.'

He says that as a branch manager he was given targets for proxies for the Fingleton vote. He called to houses and secured votes in various ways. 'I used to get a phone call asking me how many I had got and how it was going,' he said. He claims that Fingleton was aware of the proxy-gathering operation by the society and that he discussed it with him by phone.

Unaware that all this was going on, Burgess was determined to follow up on the piece of evidence he had received. The document he had been given clearly showed that people were being presented with a paper to sign without knowing of the serious concerns about Fingleton.

In an angry e-mail message Burgess complained to Con Power, the only director who had shown any interest in his criticisms. Power was furious. He had not been told about the canvassing. He attended a special board meeting to find out what was going on, and he insisted on being told the truth. Barely containing his anger, he began with the chairman. 'Did you know about this, Michael Walsh?'

'No,' the answer came back.

Staring hard at his unruffled chief executive, he asked, 'Did you know, Michael Fingleton?'

Fingleton gave a curious answer that was not an explicit No. 'There is nothing happening that was initiated by the board.' Turning then to Purcell, Power asked the same question. Purcell hesitated, then gave a staggered 'No.'

Power's fury was unquelled, and he told his board they must co-operate with any investigation by the Central Bank. He was assured that this would of course be done.

Burgess and Hogan meanwhile lodged a formal complaint with the Central Bank, and asked it to attend the AGM and block the vote until an investigation was concluded into what looked like illegal canvassing and the deliberate suppression of the dissidents' arguments. 'They said No, they wouldn't,' Burgess said. 'They didn't attend the AGM but they said they would investigate the matter.'

The campaigners' complaint was made to the Central Bank's head of supervision, Con Horan. He was a career civil servant who had joined the Central Bank in 1979 and was firmly embedded in its 'light touch' culture. He would later emerge as the person who would oversee the regulator's handling of Anglo Irish Bank in 2008 when it was embroiled in a scandal ranging from funding its own clients to buy its shares, to pumping up its balance sheet with billions from another financial institution.

The campaigners thought they had a clear-cut case that canvassing was taking place, a clear breach of the Building Societies Act. Burgess meanwhile wrote a letter to the Central Bank outlining his concerns.

'One supporter was sent an additional proxy form to his home address, complete with a stamped addressed envelope. We have reports of staff being asked to work late in recent weeks to phone members and canvass their votes. We have one particularly disturbing report of a non-member being offered his expenses and a "feed of drink" by a branch manager to go to the a.g.m. as a proxy because they need "arses on seats".'

Despite the mounting evidence that the rules were being flouted, the Central Bank dragged its feet and said it would not halt the meeting to run the vote again. 'We think it is important that it goes ahead and that the issues we worked hard to get on the agenda are discussed,' a spokesperson said. He assured the media that the matter would eventually be looked at. 'When we come across any breach of the law, we would take follow-up action.'

The vote went ahead. Fingleton easily vanquished the rebels, with 11,823 votes in his favour and 2,254 against. The dissenters got a hard time at the AGM, Burgess said:

> We were in a total minority. There was only a few of us there speaking. When I stood up I got barracked and people spoke about how fantastic Michael Fingleton was and how much money they'd raised and how the profits had gone . . . We were troublemakers and could we not finish the meeting quicker and go over and have our tea and coffee.
>
> They were not interested in borrowers and generally speaking borrowers should just go and repay their money. Michael Fingleton was a nice guy and a good guy.

Afterwards comments by two journalists reflected the widely held view that Fingleton, while perhaps a rogue, also had many admirable qualities. One quality outweighed all others: the ability to make a profit. Writing in the *Irish Times*, Colm Keena, the leading journalist on the corruption tribunals, concluded on Friday 25 April 2003: 'Mr Fingleton is seen as unique not just in the level of involvement and control he has over every aspect of the financial institution he runs, but also in terms of the dynamic, entrepreneurial attitude he takes. He is seen as someone who is prepared to take risks, to get out and make business . . .'

Keena, like many other journalists, appeared to have a grudging respect for Fingleton.

Mr Fingleton is 65 years old. If legislation to allow Nationwide be sold had been enacted in 1997 or 1998, the society could have been sold in the middle of the boom and Mr Fingleton could have realised a better price. Now he is working against the clock, and market conditions are much less favourable. On the other hand, Mr Fingleton is an able and determined man. The game is not over yet.

Senator Shane Ross, writing in his influential column in the *Sunday Independent*, was much more admiring. Ross was friendly with Fingleton, who gave him the occasional juicy tip-off. 'Fingleton, for all his faults, has delivered the only thing that matters in business: profit.' Ross, a regular campaigner for corporate reform in companies like First Active and Eircom, nonetheless dismissed Burgess and his band of rebels. 'It was a classic example of how not to challenge a board of directors. Real reforms had already been conceded. The wrong target was now being picked at the wrong time. As the meeting progressed, the punters turned against the rebels. They had blown it.'

With mixed media support (with the noted exception of Bill Tyson in the *Irish Independent*), and even less political will, the rebels may have had the high moral ground, but nobody was listening.

Behind the scenes, however, matters were coming to a head between Power and Fingleton. The society boss was convinced that Power was feeding the rebels information, and encouraging Burgess to run for the board. The society asked Brendan Watchorn, a barrister, to write a letter on 19 August 2003 to its board, headed 'Re: Brendan Burgess & Complaints against the society.' Watchorn said that he had reviewed documents on behalf of the society in relation to Burgess and his 'campaign against the society.'

'At this stage I am of the opinion that the society should disengage from any direct contact with Mr Burgess,' Watchorn wrote. 'In particular the practice whereby he has direct access to individual members of the board should cease.' Watchorn advised that borrowers who made allegations of overcharging or failure to pass on cuts in interest rates were free to make a complaint to the Financial Regulator. 'If Mr Burgess wishes to make a complaint he is free to do so.'

Watchorn said he believed Burgess was approaching board members directly in an attempt to flush out who was sympathetic to his views. 'This is not a proper role for such board members. They have no right or authority to act individually in relation to issues concerning the society. It is certainly improper to discuss individual cases other than collectively as a board.'

Con Power knew that the letter was aimed directly at him. He was an expert in corporate governance and knew exactly how constrained he was as a non-executive director. But he also knew that Irish Nationwide was a mutual building society, so he had both a right and a duty to listen to any member who wanted their concerns brought to the board for discussion.

Power gave out to Purcell for allowing the letter to be written at all. He reminded him that he had asked him at one point to meet Burgess to try to improve relations. 'You can't censor me or who I meet or don't meet,' Power told him at a board meeting. 'It's not your business.'

'Ah, Connie, will you cool it!' Fingleton interjected.

'You keep out of this!' Power responded.

Three board meetings later the letter was rescinded. Power continued his contacts with Burgess, who was tipping him off about the complaints of small borrowers. Power's records show that he stuck up for small borrowers in sixty different cases during his time as a non-executive director.

Six months after the rebels had made a formal complaint about vote-canvassing, nothing had happened. Burgess wrote to the Central Bank asking it what was going on. He received an angry phone call from Con Horan. 'He was extremely annoyed. He said, I told you it is still under investigation.' Horan was not pleased at Burgess's persistence, which was in marked contrast to the regulator's own shillyshallying.

On 22 December 2004, with the Dáil closed for the Christmas break, the Financial Regulator finally concluded his investigation, a full twenty months after it began and on a date certain to bury any reaction to the story.

> The investigation found, and Irish Nationwide has accepted, that preparations for the 2003 annual general meeting did not comply fully with the legislation. In contravention of the legislation, the Society issued separate proxy forms to some members, which were not appended to a notice of the AGM and were issued in the absence of any written request for these forms. This breach did not invalidate the exercise of proxies in any way. No such issue arose in relation to the 2004 AGM.

The chief executive of the Financial Regulator's office, Dr Liam O'Reilly, wanted to assure the public that 'strict compliance is necessary to ensure that mutual societies retain the confidence of their members.' In a shameful cop-out, he applied no sanction on the society—not even requiring it to pay the cost of his eighteen-month investigation. Instead he sought to play down the seriousness of the society's breach of the law in unfairly rigging its own vote.

> Regardless of the technical nature of this issue, it is clear that the actions of Irish Nationwide in this case were in contravention of the legislation governing building societies. It is a cause for some concern that this breach was permitted to occur.
>
> It is important to stress that the new sanctions powers of the Financial Regulator will be available where contraventions of requirements occur in the future. We will continue to monitor compliance with the requirements of the legislation.

At first one of Fingleton's managers was blamed for the affair. Farcically, it was maintained that he had gone on a solo run in Ireland's most tightly controlled financial institution. 'He was left to carry the can,' Power reflected.

When Burgess heard the result he thought to himself, 'That's it for Michael Fingleton. He'll have to go.'

'We gave them a slam dunk,' Burgess recalled bitterly. 'We gave them a full file. The evidence was crystal-clear. But it took Con Horan a year to do the investigation! They rang me that morning to say they were doing a statement that afternoon. It was a gross breach of the Building Societies Act.'

Even had it wanted to, the Financial Regulator's office had few powers to take on Fingleton. Under the Building Societies Act (1989) it could only fine the society up to €1,270 if it was found guilty in court of wrongdoing. This was a paltry sum, and would cost tens of thousands in legal fees to collect. Taking and winning the case might have been enough to dislodge Fingleton; but the regulator's decision to dismiss the breach as merely of a 'technical nature' clearly showed it had little interest in doing so.

Fingleton had yet again failed to bear the brunt of a regulator's sanction. His chairman, the eminent professor of banking, Dr Walsh, despite finding this out, did not see it either as a resigning matter or one that raised questions about the leadership of the society. Instead he remained firmly in place as the society entered an ever more rapid phase of reckless expansion. Nobody was prepared to hit the brakes, and the incident faded into the past.

Chapter 5

THEY HAVEN'T GONE AWAY: FINGLETON, BURGESS AND THE REGULATOR

Michael Fingleton was furious. An article by Jane Suiter had appeared in the Irish edition of the *Sunday Times* on 18 January 2004 under the headline 'Watchdog examines Irish Nationwide.'

'Irish Nationwide building society is being examined by the financial watchdog over issues ranging from lending practices to corporate governance,' the article confidently began. 'Sources said the examination, which was described as "wide-ranging," is expected to take a number of months to complete.'

The article said the Central Bank was questioning both the board's independence and their expertise. It said the regulator's office had considered appointing its own directors to the society but had held back for fear of 'moral hazard.' This was a concern that the independence of the Irish Financial Services Regulatory Authority as a regulator would be compromised if it did so.

As he read the article, Fingleton felt his blood boil. He pondered about who could be the source of the article, which had been written despite the society's denials, on the record, that there was any inquiry.

The article contained quotations from the chief executive of the new Financial Regulator's office, Liam O'Reilly, who had launched its three-year strategic plan earlier in the week. It quoted O'Reilly as saying there was a need for 'ethical standards' and for people with 'probity' at the top of Irish banking. He said that boards must commit themselves to a 'culture of integrity, competence and best practice.'

Suiter's carefully worded article quoted unnamed sources to the effect that 'some of the practices at Irish Nationwide were not covered by industry standards or regulations and would have to be approached by reference to first principles such as openness and transparency.' It also stated that 'practices that members have objected to in the past include the absence of a published standard variable rate and penalty interest payments.' Irish Nationwide, the article said, had eventually agreed to stop charging penalty interest, but refused to repay the interest it had already received.

Fingleton was convinced that the Financial Regulator must have leaked the information in the article. He angrily rang his lieutenant, Stan Purcell, and demanded that something be done urgently. He felt that the article—regardless of the fact that it was substantially true—was an affront to his credibility. If it was allowed to gather steam, and be repeated in the media, it could be very damaging.

A legal letter was despatched to shut the journalist up, and a meeting was arranged to take care of the regulator.

At 4:30 p.m. on Friday 23 January 2004 Michael Walsh and Con Power were shown into the Financial Regulator's office. It was not the first time they had visited it. Power remembers that Walsh was very friendly with Liam O'Reilly, Patrick Neary and other officials there. Indeed Walsh had brought Power with him to meet O'Reilly to discuss what needed to be done with the society even before he became chairman in February 2001.

Fingleton himself rarely met the regulators personally, preferring to keep them at arm's length and leave the official meetings to Purcell as well as the society's internal auditor, its compliance manager and his other subordinates. As he occasionally mentioned at board meetings or to employees, he preferred to spend time with their bosses in the Dáil.

Con Power's detailed notes of this meeting, revealed here, give an account of how directors of a large lender dealt with and were treated by the senior officials of the Financial Regulator's office. They provide an extraordinary insight into the misguided nature of the regulatory regime, its misdirected sense of priorities and its blatant lack of guile when tackling regulatory deficiencies and breaches of rules.

O'Reilly greeted both Walsh and Power warmly. 'Pat will be along in a minute,' he said. The three men chatted amiably as they awaited the arrival of O'Reilly's number 2, Patrick Neary. Tea and coffee were served.

After fifteen minutes Neary, prudential director of the regulator's office responsible for keeping manners on the banks, arrived. A diffident man, he was prone to the occasional ill-judged outburst. There was to be none of that on this occasion. Neary was a confirmed 'don't rock the boat' official who had risen steadily through the ranks after joining the Central Bank in 1971, armed with a degree in Latin and Greek.

There were many things this 75-minute high-level meeting could have discussed regarding the society's regulatory failings, but instead it had at the top of its agenda the *Sunday Times* article. O'Reilly was anxious to assure Walsh and Power that the Financial Regulator was not the source of the story. According to an e-mail message circulated to Irish Nationwide's board by Power after the meeting, he said: 'Liam O'Reilly assured us that there are no issues between IFSRA [the Financial Regulator] and the society other than the type of issues that arise in the normal course of the activities of a regulatory authority between the regulator and the institutions that are regulated. There is certainly nothing that would merit the thrust of the article in the *Sunday Times*.'

The message went to all the directors' personal e-mail addresses, with the exception of Terry Cooney, who received it at his general company address, and Fingleton, who got it from his secretary, Melody van der Berg. Fingleton, like his counterpart Seán FitzPatrick, chief executive of Anglo Irish Bank, even in 2004 never used e-mail.

Power said that O'Reilly and Neary were 'seriously concerned' at the suggestion that somebody inside the regulator's office with access to the Irish Nationwide file had briefed Suiter. O'Reilly promised to conduct a 'thorough' investigation. Neary was indignant at the suggestion that his office was the source. Under the legislation, he said, any staff members who did such a thing can 'go to jail.'

The regulator assured the society's directors that it was working hard on facilitating the enactment of new legislation to facilitate a trade sale of the society. 'Anything that would damage the standing of the society in the context of a trade sale would concern IFSRA,' Power noted.

The Irish Nationwide directors and the regulator then discussed what they could do to 'assist' the society in playing down the article. O'Reilly promised to 'include in a public speech at an early date a strong statement and the integrity and confidentiality of [the regulator]' and would also state that the regulator never commented on individual institutions. 'If adverse media comments relative to the society gain momentum,' he added, according to Power's note, '[the regulator] will reconsider its position and may deem it necessary to issue a statement in refutation of suggestions being made.'

The substantive issue of the article having been dealt with, the meeting turned to what were seen as lesser matters. There was a 'brief' mention of the fact that the society had breached regulations in large exposures or lending to big developers.

There was a 'brief reference' to the vote-rigging affair. A single line said the directors told the regulator that they had engaged the solicitors McCann Fitzgerald to advise on corporate governance issues.

> We acknowledged that the issues outstanding between [the regulator] and the society must be resolved and that some of those issues are immediate whereas others can only [be] resolved over a period of up to 18 months or so.
>
> It was acknowledged by all four present at the meeting [Michael Walsh, Con Power, Liam O'Reilly and Patrick Neary] that the society must engage with [the regulator] as a matter of urgency in the resolution of immediate issues, and must agree what are the longer-term issues, with dates and context for their resolution.

The issue of co-opting Brendan Burgess to the board of Irish Nationwide was also discussed. O'Reilly told Power he was supportive of the idea and wanted the society's board to be strengthened. Power agreed to meet Fingleton in his office to discuss the possibility. He recalls that Fingleton said, 'That's fine with me, Connie, if that's what the three of you [non-executive directors] want.' As this meeting ended, Power asked Fingleton a pointed question. 'Michael, what is your self-perception?' Fingleton did not reply, and he appeared not to understand the question. 'I'll tell you what it is, Michael. Your self-perception is that you are sole proprietor.'

Fingleton rocked back in his chair with his arms fully outspread. 'Connie, you've got it in one!' he laughed.

On Tuesday 27 January, Power had breakfast at the home of Michael Walsh to discuss how to make Burgess a non-executive director of the society. Walsh said he was prepared to support him. Burgess was a terrier for the rules; he could be expected to challenge Fingleton at every turn.

Two of the society's five directors were now in agreement; all they needed was one more. Walsh and Power then asked Cooney for his support, which was not forthcoming. 'But Terry,' Walsh said, 'We need to have all three of us in agreement,' Power recalled. To which, he said, Cooney coolly replied: 'Well, Michael, now you know who the three are.'

———

Brushing off the Financial Regulator was not the only preoccupation of Fingleton that year. Brendan Burgess and his rebel band were as determined as ever to oust him.

The 2004 AGM would become known as the battle for the Burlington—even though there was always only one winner: Michael Fingleton.

A frustrated Burgess had decided to up the ante and run for election to the board of directors. For an institution growing so rapidly, its board remained small, with only five members. 'I wanted to continue to highlight the issues,' Burgess said. 'By standing for election you are not expecting to get elected but you do get to write to the members, and you get to speak at the AGM.'

Burgess knew that the society was moving ever closer to being sold, and he was determined to stop Fingleton from cashing in. It was speculated that the society was worth about €1 billion; it was widely rumoured at the time that Fingleton would bag €15 million of the proceeds.

Two sources with direct knowledge of the sale of the society said that Fingleton was careful never to put in writing how much he hoped to make. 'Chatting informally, we believed the number Fingleton hoped to pocket was much bigger than this,' a source said. 'He may well have been looking for €50 million when you include earn-outs and so on.' Burgess was determined, however, that he should get no more than any other member.

The society's employees were fully behind Fingleton getting a big pay-day, as they were being promised 15 per cent of the eventual sale price. 'I wasn't happy about that, as it reduced our money,' Burgess said. 'The employees were firmly on Fingleton's side. They spoke at the meetings about how wonderful Fingleton was. They were annoyed at me because if they were getting €150 million between them—how many was there? It could be €300,000 each. The big incentive was "When we demutualise you are going to get a lot of money".' With the average salary of the society at €30,000, this was a huge carrot for its employees—and a massive incentive not to challenge Fingleton, despite his demands and bullying. Members too did not care for Burgess, who was so against the man who promised a windfall, so he was easily defeated.

———

In January 2005 KPMG was again asked by the society, on the instructions of the Central Bank, to carry out a review of internal audit or what controls the society had on its lending. The regulator was concerned at the rapid growth of the society's commercial loan book at a time when the position of internal auditor, an essential brake on bad lending, was vacant.

The report began by describing some of the half-measures the society had taken over the previous five years to improve things, before again listing a long series of failings.

Internal audit, the report concluded, 'could be improved.' It 'lacks the experience and business knowledge to provide a real and robust challenge to some of the more complex areas including commercial lending, treasury and IT.' It noted that the society did not use computers to help it analyse risks, while the 'test samples' it used to gauge how well the society was lending were 'not representative.' Internal audit was 'weak' at following up when it found something wrong. It also commented that 'certain members of the internal audit team lack credibility with management.' This was perhaps not surprising, given that 'only one member of the internal audit team has a recognised internal audit qualification . . . Most of the credibility issues arise because the internal audit section is perceived to be very young with limited business experience.' The section, the report found, did not co-ordinate its work with any of the areas that it would normally be expected to, such as compliance or mortgage audits. Incredibly, the acting internal auditor, Killian McMahon, did not attend crucial committee meetings, including the credit, provisioning and asset liability committees. Nor was he even included in the circulation of the agenda or minutes of those meetings, effectually leaving him in the dark. This was not McMahon's fault and he was praised in the report as having a 'good grasp of the business' and being a 'breath of fresh air,' with a 'commercial focus'. Otherwise the report was damning.

Despite its many deficiencies, the society was not doing enough to change things. The KPMG report noted that training was not directed towards the development of individuals' competence. Even more remarkably—as the society would discover to its cost when it turned out to have lent tens of millions to the rogue solicitor Michael Lynn, among others—'internal audit have not developed a fraud awareness policy.'

As the society careered its way through the boom, KPMG noted that the management had held a workshop to 'identify and assess the key risks being faced by the society.' But the remedies being proposed were clearly cosmetic, to do enough to get the regulator off the society's back.

The accountants looked at sample file reviews of commercial loans and found that 'recommendations by internal audit do not state the risk to the business or assess the potential impact of the risks.' In a clear reference to Fingleton's unchallenged dominance, it concluded that the 'testing of authority levels were not clearly evidenced or prioritised.'

Reports on commercial loans tended to be 'very long' and rambling, in a manner that meant that 'key messages were not clearly evident or prioritised.' There was 'no evidence' of any follow-up of recommendations KPMG had made many times to try to curb risky lending.

Worse still, internal audit only assessed the risks of giving new loans: it never looked at what happened to old ones when Fingleton changed, for example, the interest rates being charged or allowed additional draw-downs. The sample files KPMG was given access to were only for the Republic. This was a massive flaw in its methods of work, as the lax practices in the society's Belfast branch were let slip under the radar. How the society was lending billions to low-profile London developers from there simply wasn't looked at.

KPMG also reviewed Irish Nationwide's treasury function. This is the engine room of any bank: it ensures that the bank remains liquid and has enough money to trade. Its most important function is ensuring that it is never at risk of going bust by the amount of money going out exceeding its capacity to meet that demand.

In an eerie premonition of what was to come, KPMG produced a damning assessment of the society's treasury arm. 'There was no evidence of specific tests in respect of funding requirements and counterparty concentrations,' it found. The society tested its liquidity ratio at the end of every month but never looked at its day-to-day level.

KPMG made a number of other technical points, all showing a catastrophic weakness in the society's engine room. These cracks, identified clearly in 2005, would doom the society three years later, when the credit crunch came.

In total, KPMG interviewed twenty senior people in Irish Nationwide when preparing its report, including all the members of the audit section. Afterwards it published quotations (unattributed) from senior figures, including Fingleton, on their views of internal audit, the most vital brake for slowing the society down and making it lend better.

IA [internal audit] need more oomph or gravitas.

Overall I have been disappointed with the quality of IA staff.

I would like IA to be more street-wise.

Training has been piecemeal with no overall strategy.

IA are lacking in confidence and hide behind the detail in their reports.

IA need to improve knowledge of processes in order to be more challenging.

I do not place any value on the work performed by some of the audit team and they need more mainstream business experience.

There is a skills deficit in the areas of treasury, commercial lending and IT.

There is a question mark over IA's understanding of key risks and processes.

The accumulation of all these factors left the society vulnerable as it expanded rapidly. There were simply no systems for stopping Fingleton running riot.

Yet again Walsh and his board digested the report, as did the Financial Regulator, but only superficial changes were made. Instead of taking up KPMG's legitimate criticisms, Michael Walsh—a former professor of banking—wrote an extraordinary letter on 1 February 2005, dismissing the regulator's fears. In his twenty-page letter he defended the society against the array of concerns put forward by the Financial Regulator, Liam O'Reilly, about the conduct of the society. The regulator, Walsh said, was 'not justified' in trying to curb its rampant lending. The society, he claimed, had an 'exceptionally strong balance sheet,' which could weather any storm.

He admitted that it had 'found it difficult' to hire good people. He blamed this on the 'perception in the recruitment market' that the society would soon come under new ownership. (He made no reference to the domineering character of Fingleton, who had driven away potential challengers, such as Maurice Harte.) Walsh denied that the society had no succession plan. He claimed that Stan Purcell, its finance director, and Gary McCollum, manager of the society's British operations, were both 'potential in-house candidates' for taking over.

He then dismissed the regulator's concerns about the society's rapid expansion into commercial lending. 'We operate in a niche market with high net worth customers who have a proven track record of success,' he insisted. (Concentration of risk from lending too much to too few people was an idea that was well established in banking long before 2005 but was clearly not on the radar of the former banking professor. This was later one of the factors behind the society's collapse.)

Walsh insisted that there were adequate controls to monitor this lending to its high-rolling clients. All loans over €635,000 were approved by the credit committee and 'recommended to the board for final approval.'

From October 2004 Walsh claimed the society had a specialist commercial lending administration section 'to enhance the formal control of lending by regular compiling of information and reporting on large exposures including fee sharing arrangements.' He assured the regulator that even more steps were in train to safeguard against bad lending. These included 'up to date reporting on the entire loan book on [a] formalised and regular basis,' and 'regular visits to large projects.'

In addition there was the function of 'supplying the board with quarterly reports that will monitor and assess the risks on large exposures,' and a complete review of its information technology to ensure that information on lending was only a push of a button away. All this, he said, would be completed by 31 March 2005.

(The reality, however, was that none of this was done adequately. Instead the society was allowed to career out of control for another three years.)

Walsh dismissed concerns put forward by the regulator and KPMG that the society was ill prepared to handle the fall-out if one of its larger clients went bust. In his letter he insisted that it had 'sufficient expertise to deal with loans in difficulty.' In the previous thirty years, he said, 'we have been through three recessions and we have not suffered any material loss in this area of activity.'

He dismissed KPMG's concerns that the society would struggle badly if the credit markets dried up. Only that January he said it had raised €750 million from European banks, money that had to be repaid in three years. (Again Walsh failed to see the danger of borrowing short from the money markets to lend long to developers, who could take far more than three years to get projects to the point of sale.) Instead he boasted how the society was the darling of German and French banks. 'We were offered funding of €1 billion in one day,' he said. 'This is clearly an endorsement by the financial markets of the society's performance and business strategy.'

Walsh also dismissed concerns that the society was getting in over its head in various mega-deals. The regulator was wrong to be worried, he insisted. A €109 million deal with the London property investors Giris Rabinovitch and Sheikh Sagir Bin Sagir Al Quassime, a member of the United Arab Emirates royal family, was not too risky for a small Irish building society. The society, Walsh said, would earn fees of €20 million from backing the two men on property deals in London. (In the two pages he dedicates to these borrowers he repeatedly mentions the society's projected profits while making no mention of what security or recourse the society had if anything went wrong.)

The society 'disagreed' with concerns that being in joint ventures with developers could lead to 'conflicts of interest'. The society, Walsh said, was making big profits from its joint ventures with developers like Gerry Gannon and Seán Mulryan, and the regulator was wrong to be concerned about its growing exposure to just two men. For example, he said, the society 'feels strongly that it is not correct' that the regulator wanted it to add up its total exposure to Seán Mulryan's Ballymore Properties by adding in both normal lending and joint-venture lending. Loans to joint-venture partners were given in a 'proper manner' and were 'vetted at the highest level of the society with the principals of our joint venture partners.' He also defended the society's habit of rolling up interest rates for its developer pals. 'The society is not taking a "punt",' Walsh insisted.

He admitted that the society had lost €1 million of its members' money when it went out on its own and built a housing estate in Dungarvan, Co. Waterford. The site, he said, was not only 'too remote' but had also been devastated by a 'freak tide'.

He also objected to attempts by the regulator to curb the society's lending by insisting that it keep more capital on its balance sheet. 'The society is concerned with this increase,' Walsh said. 'The increase does not reflect the performance of the society, is not commercially justified and will undoubtedly affect our credit rating.'

He concluded: 'The board is satisfied that the society is run in a professional manner as evidenced by the consistent and strong performance with an unbroken record of increased profitability over 30 years.'

This rejection by Irish Nationwide's most qualified board member of every concern put forward by the Financial Regulator would cost the taxpayer dearly. The society was ill prepared for curbing its recklessness as the final years of the boom approached.

Chapter 6

FOUR YEARS THAT PRIMED THE BOMB (2003–7)

There was a certain self-satisfaction among politicians, bankers and property developers as 2002 came to a close. They believed they were invincible: the 'Celtic Tiger' was immortal and the prosperity they now enjoyed was really all due to their own great efforts.

When we look back across the wreckage of the most expensive banking collapse in a developed economy and try to establish when it went wrong, all roads lead to 2003. If we analyse the banking, economic and exchequer figures, the entirely sustainable growth and prosperity of the late 1990s stalled in 2001 and 2002 and morphed into debt-fuelled fantasy from 2003 onwards.

Writing in 2003 in the annual report of Irish Nationwide for 2002, Michael Fingleton summed up what he wanted everyone to believe about the years ahead. 'In the present weakening economic climate the society is fully conscious of the dangers of sacrificing credit quality in pursuit of greater market share and greater profits. Our policy continues to be cautious and prudent and we fully support and acknowledge the frequently repeated warnings of the Central Bank against aggressive lending and inappropriate credit expansion.'

It didn't work out that way. Compound average loan growth from 2003 to 2006 was 40 per cent per year—second only in the Irish banking system to Anglo Irish Bank, which came in at 43 per cent. When the governor of the Central Bank, Patrick Honohan, wrote his assessment of the banking crisis and of what went wrong it covered the period from 2003 to 2008. Many Irish banks had taken a somewhat cavalier attitude towards lending for property, but it was only after 2003 that it became downright dangerous. Mike Soden, the former chief executive of Bank of Ireland who resigned in 2003, tells how it took Bank of Ireland two hundred years to build its assets to €100 billion by 2003, but it only took until 2007 for it to reach €200 billion.

The deregulation of euro-zone money markets meant that Irish banks could obtain access to enormous amounts of money to lend on to house-buyers, credit-card owners, businesses, property developers and just about everyone else. Given the tiny size of the Irish economy relative to the euro zone, in a sense an infinite supply of European money was available to Irish banks—and they used it!

Traditionally, Irish banks lent to borrowers the money they held on deposit from their savings customers. In 1997 only 5 per cent of the money lent had not come from deposits. The banks began moving away from this approach and relying more and more on wholesale funding—borrowing from other banks—to finance the loans they made. In 2003 the figure breached 30 per cent for the first time, and the loan-to-deposit ratio hit 142 per cent. It kept on climbing as bankers, high on the drug of bonuses, encouraged by government policy and let loose by the regulator, became addicted to wholesale money. By 2007 nearly half their funding was coming from the wholesale market, up from 5 per cent a decade earlier.

Also in 2003, lending by Irish banks to the property market broke through the 30 per cent mark for the first time. This was to climb steadily until 2007. Figures compiled by Klaus Regling and Max Watson for their investigation into the causes of the banking collapse show that in 2006, 77 per cent of Anglo Irish Bank's loan book was on commercial property. The figure for Irish Nationwide was 75 per cent. By 2006 Irish Nationwide had lent nearly 7½ times its own capital or funds to property developers.

Also in the mix were loans to ordinary house buyers. As bank lending was taking off, the 100 per cent mortgage arrived in Ireland. Rising prices left many young couples priced out of the housing market.

Middle-class children could depend on their parents stepping in with deposit money. In September 2004, in what now seems unthinkable, the National Economic and Social Council put into a draft report a plan to help less well-off first-time buyers get on the ladder. For someone on the average industrial wage a typical deposit then equalled a year's earnings, compared with one-third in 1989. The NESC proposed that the government should step in and introduce measures that would help younger lower-income people who are 'not in a position to acquire housing deposits from parental gifts or other sources of wealth' to bridge the affordability gap. It suggested that the state could intervene by either introducing tax relief on savings for a deposit or lending buyers a 10 per cent deposit in exchange for a 10 per cent stake in the property, to be repaid later. 'This would provide the effective opportunity to secure a 100 per cent mortgage on a property, something financial institutions seem reluctant to do,' the draft report said.

Such was the madness forming around property that taking measures to cool the market seemed unthinkable. Instead government think-tanks were coming up with ways to increase the borrowings, risk and state exposure to ever-rising prices.

In 2004 only 3 per cent of residential mortgages were 100 per cent loan-to-value, in other words the loan for the house was 100 per cent of its value. In 2005 First Active became the first bank to really push 100 per cent mortgages. The former building society was then owned by Ulster Bank. Within weeks the others all piled in. One of the first banks to announce 100 per cent mortgages held a press conference in Dublin in 2005. Executives fielded questions from journalists about the wisdom or otherwise of lending all the money to buy a house.

One of those present was Brendan Keenan, group business editor of the *Irish Independent* at the time. Executives batted back the questions by saying these 100 per cent mortgages would only be available to, and marketed towards, high-earners. They would be controlled and marketed in a targeted way for those most capable of paying the money back.

On his way back to the office Keenan was handed a leaflet on O'Connell Bridge advertising the new 100 per cent mortgages from the lender. He phoned the regulator and the bank and was told the leaflet was a mistake, caused by an over-enthusiastic branch manager.

Within a few months nobody even cared. Banks were handing out 100 per cent mortgages all over the place, and it was no longer even questioned. By 2007 they accounted for nearly one in eight mortgages. But first-time buyers were the ones really queuing up to get these loans. In 2004 only 3 per cent of first-time mortgages were 100 per cent; by 2007 the figure had reached 25 per cent.

The apparently booming economy, with full employment, was going so strongly that several hundred thousand eastern Europeans arrived in Ireland and found work. The Ahern government felt it could do whatever it wanted in regard to exchequer spending, because the tax revenue, although it was from boom-time sources, kept flowing in. With Charlie McCreevy as Minister for Finance, the government really let things rip.

By the end of 2003 Ireland was already some way down the road to failure. On Wednesday 3 December, McCreevy stood up in the Dáil to present his budget. 'It is easy to forget the progress we have achieved—the defeat of unemployment as an economic scourge, the doubling of real income in the economy, the massive investment in infrastructure, and the substantial enhancement of social benefits for the welfare of all our people.' He went on to list the plaudits Ireland had received from outside agencies, such as the International Monetary Fund. 'The IMF also praised not only our prudent fiscal management and our tax reforms but it also commended our sensible incomes policies and our investment in education. All of these policies have laid the foundation for a virtuous circle, reinforcing growth and strengthening the resilience of our economy.'

He then announced one of the greatest wastes of public money in recent decades: decentralisation. Without any real logic, cost-benefit analysis or assessment of social benefit, McCreevy announced that more than ten thousand civil servants would move to fifty-three centres in twenty-five counties. The whole debacle cost hundreds of millions.

The government went on to announce the benchmarking of public-sector pay, which resulted in average increases of approximately 9 per cent. On the back of all this self-congratulatory recklessness it began to increase current spending by more than the increase in GDP. During the boom years of the late 1990s, increases in day-to-day government spending were always lower than the increases in GDP. That changed in 2001, and the pattern continued until the collapse in 2008.

But perhaps the most damaging thing the government did to encourage property speculation was tax relief. Banks were never going to rein in their property lending when government policy was to promote it and subsidise it. At the height of the boom, in 2004–6, we had tax relief schemes for urban renewal, multi-storey car parks, students' accommodation, buildings used for third-level education, hotels and holiday camps, holiday cottages, rural and urban renewal, park-and-ride facilities, living over the shop, nursing homes, private hospitals and convalescent facilities, sports injury clinics and child-care facilities. Many of them were due to expire in 2003; McCreevy extended them to 2006. Brian Cowen then announced that he was closing them but allowed for a transition period, which in fact extended many of them until 2008.

The total gross tax cost to the exchequer of these reliefs from inception to mid-2007 was €3.2 billion. The net cost was about €2.2 billion. Without them, some projects would not have been built and those loans would not have defaulted, because they never would have been taken out. In his budget speech on 7 December 2005 the Minister for Finance, Brian Cowen, said: 'We are living in the midst of the longest and strongest era of sustainable prosperity in all of Irish history. This didn't happen by chance. This involved careful planning. As a nation we now enjoy a much enhanced quality of life. We are a prosperous country.'

Two-and-a-half years later his government announced its first round of spending cuts. The budget had to be brought forward to October 2008 as an emergency measure.

But back in 2004, 2005 and 2006, against a backdrop of wads of cheap money, of government policy subsidising property and construction, a voracious property boom and heaps of praise from reputable international think-tanks, the banks just went crazy.

Michael Fingleton could see that, while house prices continued to go through the roof, there was a lot more profit in lending to developers than in lending to people buying houses. This was because the mortgage market was highly competitive, whereas loans to property developers were all about relationships and not tying them up too much in paperwork. The virtuous circle seemed to apply to Fingleton's property-developer clients, who could borrow more than 100 per cent of the cost of a site, then borrow all the money for developing it. Once they agreed to a profit share with Irish Nationwide they could then have non-recourse loans, enabling them to walk away if things went wrong.

But as the boom went on, Fingleton seemed to get everything right. His commercial property loans were often repaid when developments were successfully completed, encouraging both the lender and the borrower to go again but for even more money.

Developers lived like kings. One owner of a wine shop in the south Dublin suburbs recounted how it was not unusual for a developer to ring up at five o'clock on a Tuesday or Wednesday evening to say he was having a few people around for dinner and then order €5,000 worth of wine to be delivered to his house.

The Ahern government loved the developers, and the feeling was mutual. Bankers just sat back, handed out loans, did their lobbying in private, stood up to a weak regulator, and collected their ballooning salaries and bonuses.

The property developer Seán Dunne invited both Charlie McCreevy and Bertie Ahern to his five-day fiftieth birthday party and wedding reception. Charity events became major social events, as these lines from Paul O'Kane in a *Sunday Tribune* article in April 2004 show:

> The scene is the Four Seasons Hotel in Dublin on a balmy, early summer's night. The event is a black tie ball for a third world charity that is run by a tireless Irish priest, who everyone agrees is a saint. The tables have been purchased at several hundred euro a plate and when the auction starts, the bidding is less than furious. A fifth century doubloon struggles to edge over its reserve, so too an original William Butler Yeats letter. Things really hot up, however, when a week-long stay at a glorious villa in Antibes and a similar package at the seven star hotel in Dubai come under the hammer. Bids move up in €5,000 notches and the whiff of cigar smoke fills the chandelier laden ballroom. This is Dublin's new wealth at play. Gotta go there. Gotta have it.

The deception of wealth over borrowing, of asset prices over cash and of vanity over reality resulted in a remarkable speech by the German ambassador to Ireland, Christian Pauls, in September 2007, just on the eve of it all falling apart. He caused consternation when he told a gathering of mainly German business people in Dublin that in Ireland everyone drives 2006 or 2007 cars, hospital consultants describe €200,000 per year as 'Mickey Mouse money,' junior ministers earn more than the German chancellor, and a house in Clontarf sold for €20 million—the price of a skyscraper in Frankfurt. He had captured the madness of it all, and inadvertently reminded Irish people of several very uncomfortable home truths.

Fingleton didn't keep the promise he made in Irish Nationwide's annual report in 2003. He increased lending massively. Commercial property loans shot up to a peak of about €9 billion. But during the period from the late 1990s onwards lots of loans were successfully repaid. In total the society lent out more than €17 billion in new loans. Its profit growth reflected this. But people outside probably didn't fully appreciate how much of it was coming from developers and arrangement fees. In 2003 the society made a profit of €117 million. By 2005 this had grown to €176 million, and in 2007 it shot up to €390 million.

Fingleton's pay, like that of other bank chief executives, went up too.

In March 2006 things finally came to a head between Con Power and Irish Nationwide's board. Power had many other interests besides his non-executive directorship of Irish Nationwide. In 2004 he had been made inaugural chairperson of the statutory Financial Services Ombudsman Council. This had been set up to deal with the complaints of customers of financial services companies. Power had become something of an expert in the area, thanks to Irish Nationwide.

Late on the evening of Wednesday 22 February 2006 he got a phone call from Brendan Burgess, telling him he had got a tip-off that Irish Nationwide had lodged papers in the High Court seeking a judicial review of a decision by the Financial Services Ombudsman. The society wanted to quash a €30,000 refund the Ombudsman had ordered it to repay to a mortgage customer.

Nobody in Irish Nationwide had bothered to tell Power that the society planned to take such an action. The following day he phoned Stan Purcell and told him he planned to resign from the board to avoid any perception that he might have a conflict of interest. He then discussed the matter with Michael Walsh, who urged him to stay on with Irish Nationwide and instead resign as chairperson of the Ombudsman Council. Power said no.

Late in the afternoon Michael Fingleton rang Power from London, where he was on a business trip. 'I declined a request from Michael Fingleton to reflect on the matter and to discuss it with him at the weekend,' Power said, 'on the grounds that nothing he would say to me could alter what had been done by Irish Nationwide.' Later that night he resigned from the society.

The following day Patrick Neary, who had been promoted to become Financial Regulator after Liam O'Reilly retired, rang him. Power's contemporary note of what Neary said reads: 'Great regret to see you go; it was a hard one to call; I appreciate why you did it, but we here are terribly sorry to see you go. You devil—you have put the cat among the pigeons, but you had no option.'

Just as Power moved on from the society, what he had originally joined the board to achieve was finally about to happen. Demutualisation always hung in the air but finally it was becoming real. In the summer of 2006 the bill introduced by Brian Cowen as Minister for Finance allowing for Irish Nationwide to be sold became law.

Power had earlier come close to achieving the same thing with the Housing (Miscellaneous Provisions) Act (2002). At the time the change was seen as a certainty, as in opposition in the 1990s Charlie McCreevy had been in favour of demutualisation. Power knew that the matter had been considered by the government in 2002 but had been shot down. It is not clear for whose benefit it was deferred, but not selling the society back then would prove a costly mistake in time.

The summer of 2006 saw the peak of the residential property market, but it was nearly twelve months before prices began to fall. In June that year MyHome.ie, owned by a group of estate agents including Sherry Fitzgerald, was put up for sale. The estate agents Hamilton Osborne King were sold. A percentage of Jackson Stops was sold. Gunne Residential was also sold.

Cowen had delivered Fingleton's long-term wish. But had it come too late? There was no evidence of those feelings on the night the legislation was passed. Finally it was happening. The promised land. Demutualisation.

Michael Fingleton sent Stan Purcell, Olivia Greene and Brendan Beggan down to watch the historic vote from the public gallery of the Dáil. He already knew the result; he wanted to see who would oppose him, Olivia Greene recalled, so he could 'deal with them.' As they sat in the public gallery, Greene noted that Éamon Gilmore and Noel Ahern were among those opposing the vote.

Afterwards Beggan and Greene said they went for a drink with Purcell and Francie O'Brien, a Fianna Fáil senator, in the Leinster House bar. O'Brien introduced them around, studiously avoiding any representatives of the Labour Party but greeting members of his own party warmly. Brian Lenihan was among the politicians who shook their hands briefly. As the night wore on, the drinking moved to Doheny and Nesbitt's, a popular pub in Baggot Street, famed for hosting a mix of politicians, businessmen, developers and civil servants, leading to the coining of the term 'Doheny and Nesbitt School of Economics.'

'Brian Cowen was there,' Greene recalled, 'and he had had a few drinks. He put his arm around us and said, "You're working for a great man," and so on.' Seeking a more private corner in which to talk, the society's group pushed their way towards the back of the bar.

Chapter 7 ∽

PORTRAIT OF A LENDER
DESTINED FOR DISASTER

By 2004 Michael Fingleton had chosen his own road for Irish Nationwide. That road led to Britain and high-risk property-lending. The old business of residential mortgages in Ireland was being left behind.

Irish Nationwide was still giving out more mortgages at home but was losing market share and was making less money out of them. And Fingleton appeared to be losing interest. By 2006 a third of all the mortgages issued by Irish Nationwide had come through head office, as more and more of them were residential mortgages linked to developer clients who wanted to buy more and more houses.

The more money the society lent out, especially to a handful of developers, the greater the risk it was taking but also the greater the profit it was making. By the fact that his defined-benefit pension would be two-thirds of his salary (including bonus), Fingleton was singularly motivated to drive up profits before his planned retirement or the sale of the society. The greater the bonuses he made on higher profits, the greater his final pay would be, which would fix the value of his pension for the rest of his life. This ridiculous situation, accepted by the board, motivated the chief executive in completely the wrong way.

Irish Nationwide was no longer functioning like a building society. It was a sub-prime lender, a property bank, an investment bank, an equity house and a property developer rolled into one. The Financial Regulator had ample evidence and reports to get rid of the board or the chief executive but failed to carry out any meaningful action.

Eventually, after years of lobbying, in the summer of 2006 Brian Cowen introduced the legislation that allowed for Irish Nationwide to be demutualised and sold in one fell swoop. Shortly afterwards the society was put up for sale. KPMG, the society's auditors, were hired in February 2007 to put together a highly confidential prospectus or sale document, known as a 'vendor due diligence report'. It was entitled 'Project Harmony'. It ran to several hundred pages and was presented to the society in June 2007. Its contents are revealed here for the first time.

The prospectus opens with a form of disclaimer. 'In preparing our report, our primary source has been internal management information, and representations made to us by management of the society. We do not accept responsibility for such information which remains the responsibility of the management.'

It was a fairly standard statement, but given that house prices had begun falling the very month it was submitted to the board, some lines in the disclaimer were extraordinary. 'We accept no responsibility for the realization of the prospective financial information. Actual results are likely to be different from those shown in the prospective financial information because events and circumstances frequently do not only occur as expected, and the differences may be material.' This was prophetic, and could have won first prize in the banking crisis Understatement of the Decade awards.

The report gave a snapshot of a business that was on the up, as long as the property market was on the up, but one that lacked the expertise, accountability, corporate governance, IT resources and restraint necessary to survive through a substantial change in the market.

According to the confidential KPMG report, the Financial Regulator's office had been concerned about corporate governance arrangements at the society for years. But it did very little about it. In 2004 it noted significant gaps in controls and 'a lack of knowledge in relation to obligations of the society under the Building Societies Act 1989.' It had already broken the law on issuing proxy voting forms to members.

In the face of all this, instead of booting out the chief executive or taking real action, it wrote a letter to the society.

The Financial Regulator outlined his concerns, including the need to increase the size of the management team, succession planning for when Fingleton retired, the expertise and experience of the internal audit team, and procedures and controls for commercial property lending. In 2004 Irish Nationwide had €3½ billion out in commercial loans and clearly insufficient resources, knowledge and expertise to back that up.

In 2006 the office of the Financial Regulator conducted another inspection. Once again it expressed its concerns but did little else. Commercial lending had by then rocketed to €8 billion.

The KPMG report reveals that by 2007 the society had breached rules on concentration of risk in too few clients and too few sectors for three years in a row. It had made fundamental mistakes in its reports to the Central Bank. It had been shown to have poor record-keeping and files on lenders.

The report also sums up findings made by the society's own internal audit committee. It had found that in 2006 there was no formal credit risk policy governing special arrangement fees that the society organised with developers as a way of splitting future profits from various ventures. These fees were not recorded on the society's loan administration system but were recorded and identified in accordance with entries made directly to the general ledger. This meant essentially that they were handwritten in a book.

Incredibly, the internal audit report also said: 'In 2006 it was identified that commercial files were situated in both the commercial administration and lending departments and the location of some commercial files were unknown.'

'Light-touch' regulation clearly failed throughout the banking system; but at Irish Nationwide there were multiple examples of things being done badly, or not being done at all. There were examples of failings in corporate governance and of breaches of Central Bank rules and guidelines. Yet they were not forcefully acted upon.

Ironically, the regulators had more power to remove a director of a building society than it had over executives in banks. Under the Building Societies Act (1989) the Financial Regulator had the power to remove a director for not being a fit and proper person if it considered that action to be appropriate. There was no similar explicit power in relation to other banks. This set things up for the regulator to insist that everything it felt needed to be done was done. If it wasn't, it could have moved towards deeming any director to be unfit.

A former board member of the Central Bank, however, says he could never recall any major push to tackle Fingleton during his years attending its meetings.

The Central Bank's view was the opposite of gung ho. We knew there were problems in Irish Nationwide but the Central Bank always felt we didn't have the powers to take him on. I don't believe this was true. We did have enough power to make life very difficult for Michael

Fingleton . . . The attitude was very much . . . sure this will go away when the society is sold, and good riddance! It was going to be sold and that was that.

Part of the background of Ireland's regulatory failure was certainly the fact that Irish Nationwide was going to be sold. Rather than take the proper steps to force change, the regulator—like the thousands of carpetbaggers who opened up accounts—was depending on Brian Cowen to change the legislation so that it could be sold off. This would make everything go away. It would be an easier solution than getting into the difficult work of actually regulating.

Brian Cowen, as Minister for Finance, was under pressure to change the law and allow the society to be sold off. Once Fingleton got the nod that this was happening he launched a new savings product to grab more badly needed deposits. The 'Advantage 30' scheme gave a good savings rate but also entitled the saver to a share of the cash pay-out from the sale of the society. Carpetbaggers flocked to it in their thousands.

By law, Irish Nationwide had to have a minimum of 30 per cent of its funds coming from members' savings accounts. The confidential report discloses that Advantage 30 took in more than €1.2 billion between May and December 2006. This was a quarter of all members' savings accounts.

Fingleton knew he needed these deposits. He was lending out so much money to property developers that he was almost in breach of the Building Societies Act on the 30 per cent rule. Even when he took in €1.2 billion on his new product, by the end of 2006 the crucial ratio was down to a wafer-thin 30.3 per cent. However, he had already approved and committed himself to a further €1.1 billion in loans that had not yet been drawn down. If Cowen had not changed the legislation, the society was heading for a clear breach of the law. It was on a collision course.

There were only two ways of dealing with this crisis: get the Central Bank to reduce the limit to 25 per cent, or make sure the society was sold off. By early 2007 Irish Nationwide had asked the Financial Regulator to cut the 30 per cent rule to 25 per cent, but it had not happened.

It was becoming more and more obvious to the government and the regulator that this thing had to be sold, and soon.

Courting the property developers and throwing ever larger amounts of money at them was paying dividends for Irish Nationwide and Fingleton's wallet as his bonuses went higher and higher. The problem with excessive lending for British projects was that there weren't that many customers. The society had built up a core group of large clients with a big appetite for borrowing. Thanks to Fingleton it was largely a one-way bet.

All British borrowers and all loans for developments in continental Europe were handled by the Belfast office. A mysterious low-key place, this oversaw €6 billion of British and European lending but only did one small property loan in Northern Ireland. The office was run by Gary McCollum, who had previously worked with a small building society before joining Irish Nationwide. Together with Michael Fingleton's son, Michael junior, and a small staff of five they doled out the cash, rarely with personal guarantees, through joint ventures and on a non-recourse basis, so that if things didn't work out, the client could just walk away from the project.

In 2004 Irish Nationwide had €1.9 billion of commercial loans in Britain; within two years this had exploded to €4.8 billion. It was almost double the amount of commercial property loans it had given out in Ireland.

The KPMG report discloses that when it came to lending to property developers the society's rules were incredibly loose. It found that up-to-date valuations were not sought as each property development continued over the life of the loan. About 30 per cent of the commercial loans, or €2.4 billion, had a loan-to-value ratio of more than 100 per cent. Once the property market turned sour this meant there was no financial cushion to soften the blow.

When it came to handing out loans of tens and hundreds of millions for property speculation to a handful of clients, Irish Nationwide had its own unique approach. The KPMG report boasts that the society based the success of its commercial lending on its business relationships, its ability to make decisions quickly and its low salaries for employees. 'Management believe that they operate in a niche market and the key differentiator is their ability to provide quick and efficient lending decisions while maintaining high security and low risk.'

The average salary for mortgage administrators was €25,000 per year, at a time when the average industrial wage was about €34,000. The report makes it clear that Fingleton knew he was paying below-average wages, but it emphasises that in the management's opinion the senior staff were paid appropriately.

The report reveals the society's formal loan approval process for commercial customers. It clearly states that loans must go to the credit committee, and in the absence of a formal credit committee meeting, where a loan was greater than €1 million it must be approved by Michael Fingleton and two members of the committee. Yet elsewhere in the report it talks about commercial loans being approved by Michael Fingleton or the credit committee (or both). The extraordinary powers and influence of Fingleton come across strongly.

KPMG found that when it came to property developers the special arrangement fees charged by the society on foot of profits made by clients' projects were not recorded on the society's loan administration computer system; instead they were just recorded by hand in a general ledger. It also found that the terms and conditions of loan facilities on developer loans were often changed later. As far back as 2004 it had emerged that for some of these amendments to the original loan no new signed facility letter had been issued or approved within the normal procedures, and approvals had not been updated. So nobody, other than a couple of senior executives, knew what the new terms of some developer loans were, or why they had been changed.

KPMG concluded that the compliance structure was adequate, given the size of the institution, but that it could be improved. It also recommended that the Belfast office be included in any new supervisory arrangement.

KPMG found that Irish Nationwide expected to rake in about €750 million over the following five years from developer fees. But perhaps the most shocking revelation of all is how it treated its high-flying developer clients when it came to finding out how much profit the property ventures had actually made.

Irish Nationwide would agree arrangement fees when the loan was given. These were based on how much profit the borrower estimated the venture would make. According to the report, the society

depends primarily on the borrower for information in respect of the development project. A percentage of profit and an estimated profit figure are set out prior to the loan being advanced in respect of supplemental arrangement fees. The group places trust in the customer in respect of the information being provided. Once the profit handed to the society in respect of such fees is similar to the original amount stated at the outset, management do not dispute actual profit generated on the development. This is to ensure that the group does not breach its relationship of trust with the customer and increase the likelihood of repeat business going forward.

This extraordinary and highly irregular arrangement defies belief. The picture that emerges of how the society lent to developers where extra fees based on profits were paid is truly shocking. Irish Nationwide did not even check what the profits of the venture were. It didn't take personal guarantees. The agreed fees were not recorded on the computer system but by hand in a ledger. Developers frequently obtained loans above 100 per cent of the value of the property. The terms of the loan were often changed without proper recording and back-up information. Files were often incomplete and sometimes just missing.

This level of complacency, blind trust and largesse in lending to a golden circle of borrowers is in stark contrast to how Fingleton pursued some residential borrowers who fell behind and tried desperately to hold on to their homes.

THE GREY GOOSE: SEÁN MULRYAN

It is hard to say exactly when Michael Fingleton and Seán Mulryan first met. Their business relationship goes back quite a long way. But it seemed quite fitting that the son of the garda from Tobercurry would end up getting on extremely well with the property developer who grew up in a thatched cottage in Co. Roscommon.

Friends say that after meeting Mulryan and identifying him as a potentially significant client, Fingleton worked hard at developing that relationship. They also say that Mulryan cultivated the relationship too, and both saw a mutual benefit.

Part of the toxic lending mix at Irish Nationwide was Fingleton's love of doing commercial property development joint ventures. It was great when the market was going up but disastrous when things collapsed. The first joint venture on a development was done with Mulryan's company Ballymore Properties in Lucan, Co. Dublin, in the early 1990s. Together they built more than five hundred houses and a shopping centre.

The Fingleton-Mulryan business relationship took off from there. Both men saw themselves as self-made country lads who had conquered Dublin and made a lot of money. They loved big corporate days out at

Croke Park, where they were regular visitors at each other's corporate boxes.

The inextricable links that were to grow between Fingleton's Irish Nationwide and Mulryan's Ballymore Properties developed over several years. It ended up with Mulryan's companies collectively having the biggest loans from Irish Nationwide and one of his senior executives, David Brophy, sitting around the board table of Irish Nationwide as a non-executive director.

'From the age of 18 I always wanted to start my own business,' Mulryan told the *Sunday Telegraph* in 2006. He started Ballymore Properties when he was twenty-six. It wasn't easy, and he worked extremely hard to make it happen. It was the early 1980s and not a particularly good time to go into any kind of business.

It is said that Mulryan sold his house to help finance his first development. He moved into rented accommodation and traded in his car for a cheaper model. He became a developer and plugged away throughout the 1980s and early 90s. Like so many others who hit the big time with the property boom of the late 1990s, he didn't really make headlines in the business pages until the end of the 1990s. More newspaper articles were appearing on specific deals Mulryan was doing. But it was only when he began doing big deals in London and buying up development land in places like Bratislava and Budapest that he really came to national attention.

He had developed political friendships, such as with Charlie McCreevy of Fianna Fáil. His companies made improper payments to Liam Lawlor TD totalling £50,000 over a period of four years in the mid-1990s.

One of his most prominent deals in Ireland was the development of the Whitewater Shopping Centre in Newbridge, Co. Kildare. He developed this in partnership with the developer Seán Dunne. The idea was conceived around 2000 as a mass-market fashion retail centre with 32,000 square metres of retail space, though it didn't open until 2006.

Other big deals Mulryan did in Ireland included the purchase of a large site at the former Baldoyle racecourse in Co. Dublin. He bought an option to acquire the lands from a company called Pennine Holdings, in which Frank Dunlop had an interest. Mulryan bought the land for £30 million in the mid-1990s, got it rezoned for housing, and sold half of it to Séamus Ross's Menolly Homes for €95 million.

Mulryan was very similar to other developers in that a stint in England in his youth had stuck with him, and he saw the London property market as the ultimate big prize. In 2004 he developed the 29-storey Ontario Tower at New Providence Wharf in the London docklands. It was the city's tallest residential building. Then came the Pan Peninsula, two towers with more than seven hundred apartments in total. He was selling apartments in the Pan Peninsula in November 2005 for up to £1.6 million each.

Mulryan became personally involved in the campaign to bring the Olympic Games to London for 2012. He donated nearly £1 million to the organisers and another £250,000 towards the celebrations in Trafalgar Square when London was chosen as the venue. He was described as the second-largest landowner in the London docklands. All this placed him in very powerful circles in the City of London. He was invited to 10 Downing Street, where he met the Prime Minister, Gordon Brown.

At his peak it is difficult to say just how wealthy Seán Mulryan was. Some estimates suggest that he had a net worth of €350 million; others have said it was much higher.

As we now know, when it comes to property developers it doesn't really matter what the number was: it depends on the extent of their borrowings and the optimism that can be shown in placing a value on their assets at a particular moment. Mulryan was certainly a very wealthy man. He had two helicopters, which he used almost like a bus service. He would regularly use them to fly from his 250-acre Ardenode Stud in Ballymore Eustace, Co. Wicklow, which was packed with works of art and thoroughbred horses, to his offices in the eighteenth-century Fonthill House in Lucan. He also had a €20 million jet, which he took delivery of in 2008, known as the *Grey Goose*. He reportedly leased it to Hollywood actors, including Johnny Depp, and a number of wealthy Middle East business families. Mulryan told the *Daily Telegraph* in 2006 that he owned between fifty and a hundred racehorses. But as the credit crunch began to bite and the property crash deepened, Mulryan was forced to sell his horses, his jet, and his helicopters.

Again like many property developers, Mulryan decided to place the parent company at the top of his property empire in unlimited-liability status. He did this in 2005. Other developers did the same thing around that time. It was a mechanism that meant they did not have to submit full group accounts to the Companies Registration Office and that only snatches of the success of his business empire could be gleaned from subsidiary accounts, never a full financial picture.

Mulryan's group of companies is listed as the biggest exposure of Irish Nationwide Building Society. An analysis in 2007 showed that the society had a net exposure to Ballymore Properties of €265 million. However, the Irish Nationwide approach of doing joint ventures through special-purpose vehicles, sometimes with different shareholders, meant that the actual indirect exposure may have been higher.

One joint venture in particular illustrates the relationship between Irish Nationwide and Mulryan. The company was called Clearstorm and it was a fifty-fifty joint venture between Ballymore and Irish Nationwide. As was normal with these deals, the society took an equity stake but also lent the money for the project, though on a non-recourse basis; this meant that if anything went wrong the assets of the project were the only real security.

Clearstorm was a joint venture to develop sites in London in the Tower Hamlets district. The entire project was lent around €163 million by Irish Nationwide. In 2007 the society sold its stake in the venture to Ballymore, making it a full subsidiary of the Ballymore group. Media reports at the time suggested that Irish Nationwide made a profit of about €40 million on the sale of the stake. However, by 2010 it had made a provision against the €163 million in loans of €108 million.

The total group debt of the Ballymore companies cannot be obtained, because it did not have to submit group accounts since 2004. But it was estimated at its peak to be approximately €2 billion, spread over forty projects. This was owed to a large number of banks, including Irish Nationwide.

Ballymore's British operations do submit accounts. The latest figures show that in the year to March 2011 it made a pre-tax loss of £93 million, having lost £225 million the previous year. It had total assets of £619 million but owed its creditors £839 million, which had to be paid within one year. It had a net shareholder deficit on its balance sheet of nearly a quarter of a billion pounds.

Its continental European business, with developments in Slovakia, Hungary and the Czech Republic, had assets of €990 million at the end of 2010, with bank borrowings and loan notes outstanding of €984 million. Irish Nationwide was not among its lender banks, while NAMA has taken up loans previously owed to Anglo Irish Bank and Bank of Ireland.

As the largest borrower from the society, Mulryan was close to Fingleton. This relationship would have been further deepened as the society continued to make good money from Mulryan projects in Ireland and Britain that went spectacularly well in the late 1990s and early 2000s. In the end, however, when the music stopped and the property crash hit, the Ballymore group had substantial outstanding loans with the society. Those loans are now being handled by NAMA, which is working with Mulryan. The agency has not disclosed the level of discount applied to these loans, which would reflect the extent of the society's losses on them.

MAKING A BALLS OF IT IN BALLSBRIDGE: SEÁN DUNNE

As 2004 drew to a close, the Irish commercial property boom was in full swing. Things were going very well for Irish Nationwide. Things were also going extremely well for a core group of twenty-five to thirty big developers. Michael Fingleton had built relationships with several of them early on in the boom and in some cases before it even happened. So they were loyal to him, as long as the easy, non-recourse loans kept coming.

But Seán Dunne was a little different. The former builder from Tullow, Co. Carlow, was getting bigger and bigger in the property game. He had been close to Fingleton, and the society had backed him with loans on residential developments from the early 1990s. Their business relationship had been mutually profitable. However, in the early 2000s tensions had emerged. Minor disagreements that sources say they cannot even remember meant that by the end of 2004 Dunne had paid back almost every loan he had borrowed from Fingleton. The society's net exposure to Dunne, later dubbed the Baron of Ballsbridge, was a modest €13 million. This was nothing for a man who spent €1½ million on his wedding bash the same year.

Dunne was very wealthy at the end of 2004, but what he had would never be enough. He wanted to think big, earn big and spend big. But that meant borrowing big. At a time when Fingleton's list of clients in Britain was growing rapidly, he was still keen to do big commercial property deals in Ireland.

So, in one way, the two men needed each other; that common profit motive drew them back together again. They had become friendly again some time in 2004. By that summer they were close enough for Dunne to invite Fingleton to his wedding party on the *Christina O* in July 2004. At the bash, which went on for fourteen days, Fingleton mixed with such celebrities as Ronan O'Gara, Mick Galwey, the fashion designer

Karen Millen, P. J. Mara's son John, and the Gate Theatre director Michael Colgan.

The wedding invitation must have worked. 'It was extraordinary in one way,' said a former senior executive at Irish Nationwide.

> Dunne had been a good client years earlier, but he and Michael had some kind of falling out. Dunne had paid up practically all of his loans and was basically gone from the place. Then suddenly he is back, and Michael is shovelling out money to him again in 2005. It would have saved the society a lot of money if Dunne had not come back at all.

As Dunne decided to go on a borrowing and buying splurge in 2005, he turned to Fingleton to finance some of it. By the end of 2005 the society's net exposure to Dunne had shot up to €58.7 million. A year later it had ballooned to €131.5 million, placing the man behind Mountbrook Homes and DCD Builders in twenty-first place in the list of the society's biggest exposures. Those years when the two men did not do business together must have saved Irish Nationwide quite a lot of money in the end.

Dunne's exposure to the society was nothing compared with what he owed other banks, including Bank of Ireland and Ulster Bank. All of them would rue the day they lent big to Seán Dunne.

Dunne's father was a local fire officer and town clerk. Dunne studied surveying at Dublin Institute of Technology, and when he graduated he emigrated to Canada. He spent three years in Alberta, working in tough conditions on tar sands, extracting oil for the American market. He came back to Ireland in 1979 and in 1983 set up his own company, DCD Builders. His first project was the construction of twenty houses in Sallynoggin, Co. Dublin. He then went on to build more houses in Co. Kildare, Bray, and west Dublin.

But within two years the market was in the doldrums. Dunne emigrated to England, returning four years later. He got a taste of a big development when he teamed up with a group of blue-chip Davy Stockbrokers executives and clients to form Berland. This company bought and developed the seventy-acre St Helen's Wood site at Booterstown, Co. Dublin. It was bought for £17 million. The investors included Kyran McLaughlin and David Shubotham of Davy's and Martin Naughton and Lochlann Quinn of Glen Dimplex.

The project was launched into a tough market, but Dunne made good money out of it. He bought up lots of land around Dublin with the proceeds, including 50 acres between Swords and Malahide and 166 acres in Rathfarnham. He went on to develop the Whitewater Shopping Centre in Newbridge, together with Seán Mulryan. He eventually received more than €100 million for his shareholding following a court settlement. He told people he made €80 million from the development of houses and commercial units in Greystones, Co. Wicklow.

Dunne was the typical party animal. He gave lavish parties at his house in the K Club in Straffan, Co. Kildare. He was known to fly friends by private jet, costing about €4,000 per hour, to rugby matches. He bought a corporate box at Lansdowne Road stadium for approximately €470,000. Dunne jointly financed a €1 million all-weather rugby pitch at Clongowes Wood College at Clane, Co. Kildare. For his wife's thirtieth birthday he hired the Park Hotel in Kenmare and held a fancy-dress party, on the theme of Pirates of the Caribbean. Gossip among local people at the time claimed that one guest asked if he could park his helicopter somewhere else, because he was embarrassed at how small it was compared with some of the others.

In 2009 he was the subject of an extraordinary article in the *New York Times*. The journalist spent a day with Dunne and described him downing champagne cocktails, copious amounts of wine and pints of Guinness to wash down a dinner of potatoes and turkey soaked in gravy. Dunne told friends that when he was bidding for Jury's Hotel in Dublin he asked his wife to think of a number between 253 and 275. Without knowing what he intended, she picked 275. This was the price in millions he then bid for the hotel.

Dunne was close to Bertie Ahern and Charlie McCreevy, and both were invited to his wedding reception on the *Christina O* and sent spoken messages of good wishes. He was a regular in the Fianna Fáil tent at the Galway Races, where he met his second wife. He attended Ahern's constituency fund-raisers and invited him to his son's twenty-first birthday party in 2008. Ahern had invited both Dunne and his wife to be present in the gallery when he made his historic address to the joint houses of the US Congress in April 2008.

The earliest record of Dunne borrowing from Irish Nationwide is in 1995, when he borrowed about £2 million, secured on lands in Rathmichael, Co. Wicklow. Other lands were also used as security on another £2 million that year. These loans were repaid in 2004. In 1996 he borrowed again, the security being land in Celbridge, Co. Kildare. 'Fingleton and Dunne were two of a kind, destined to get on and destined to fall out,' was how one source who knows both men put it. They were both headstrong, determined and ambitious.

The rapprochement in 2004 coincided with the eve of Dunne's biggest buying spree. In 2005 a mystery buyer acquired a house in Shrewsbury Road, Dublin, on 2½ acres. The price paid was €58 million. Dunne immediately denied that he was the one behind the purchase. He was so determined to dispel the rumour that he had a statement read out to a meeting of the Shrewsbury Road residents' group, telling them he had not bought the house.

Dunne already lived in Shrewsbury Road, and had a number of run-ins with neighbours over various residential issues. The new purchase stuck out because it was the most expensive house ever bought in Ireland. Years later it emerged that the beneficial owner of the house was not Dunne but his wife, the former *Sunday Independent* gossip columnist Gayle Killilea.

Another landmark deal in 2005 was the purchase of Jury's Hotel in Ballsbridge, Dublin, and later the Berkeley Court Hotel, along with the nearby office block Hume House. Dunne didn't stop there but went on to buy one of the blocks in the AIB Bankcentre just up the road. He spent €710 million buying up chunks of Ballsbridge, with a further €15 million in professional fees. He paid €260 million for Jury's, €119 million for the Berkeley Court, €130 million for Hume House and €200 million for his slice of AIB Bankcentre.

The biggest lender in all of this was Ulster Bank. Dunne has said that he sank about €135 million of his own money into the purchase of the two hotels, suggesting that he borrowed more than €250 million from Ulster Bank. The bank, which is owned by Royal Bank of Scotland, later syndicated some of this debt to a group of smaller banks.

There are mixed stories about why Fingleton did not participate in lending money for the Ballsbridge hotel deals. Former Irish Nationwide sources say Fingleton was bragging afterwards that he had not financed the purchase of the hotels at what was an outlandish price. Other sources have suggested that Fingleton wanted to get in on some of the action but Ulster Bank muscled him out with a better deal.

But Fingleton did lend Dunne €70 million to partly finance his purchase of four blocks of the AIB Bankcentre. Dunne used a company registered in the Isle of Man as the borrowing entity. This was a mechanism he used many times, as did other developers. By borrowing money through an Isle of Man company the business does not have to submit accounts. It also has tax benefits and greater privacy surrounding the transaction.

AIB had signed a twenty-year lease on the premises but had a break clause scheduled for 2011, which meant it could get out of the rental agreement if it wanted to at that stage. AIB informed Dunne that it wanted to exercise the break clause and vacate the premises. With the property market on its knees, Dunne would have found it very difficult to find suitable commercial tenants willing to pay the same boom-time rents as AIB.

This reality forced Irish Nationwide to write down the value of the €70 million loan to €18 million, a substantial loss for the society, a 74 per cent write-down on the Dunne AIB loan and a loss to the society of €52 million. The loan was secured on the value of the property, which had tumbled, and a personal guarantee.

Another boom-time Fingleton loan to Dunne came in 2006. This related to two adjacent sites in Kilcock, Co. Kildare. Dunne bought the site of a former sweet manufacturer called Zed Candy and a smaller nearby site. He acquired the Zed Candy site through an Isle of Man company, called Waterside Kilcock Property Company. A loan facility of €38 million was granted by Fingleton to cover the Zed Candy site and the smaller adjacent site. Dunne secured planning permission for 180 apartments and a 29-storey shopping centre, but An Bord Pleanála overturned the permission.

The deal was done at the peak of the property boom. Even if the planning had worked out, the value of this site would have fallen anyway; but once An Bord Pleanála shot it down, its value tumbled. Irish Nationwide wrote down the value of this loan from €38 million to €5 million, an 87 per cent loss. Dunne gave a personal guarantee of €35 million on the loan. This reflected the complacency and the casual approach taken by the society towards big clients who borrowed tens of millions, in sharp contrast to how it dealt with ordinary borrowers.

In 2008 Irish Nationwide had to petition the court in the Isle of Man for permission to formally register the charges or security on the loan. In its submission it said that 'by inadvertence, accident or otherwise the said two legal charges have not been registered within the time prescribed under Section 79 [of the] Companies Act 1931.' Fortunately for the society, the judge did extend the time limit, and the charges were allowed to be registered.

But both of these Dunne loans ran into trouble. Waterside Kilcock Property Company was placed in receivership after the loan was transferred to NAMA. It is likely that NAMA paid about €5 million for the €38 million loan. Dunne's personal guarantees have proved to be virtually worthless.

Dunne's property empire collapsed. He moved to the United States with his wife and family and is now the subject of litigation by NAMA, which is accusing him of transferring several millions in assets to his wife. Gayle sold an apartment in Geneva for several million and used much of the proceeds to acquire two multi-million luxury houses in Connecticut. The Dunnes deny any wrongdoing.

A syndicate of lenders behind the Jury's and Berkeley Court purchases secured judgements against Dunne for €165 million. NAMA has secured judgements totalling €185 million. Dunne gave personal guarantees to NAMA banks in the region of €135 million. His main holding company, DCD Builders, went into receivership. Its last accounts show that it had a loss of more than €250 million in 2008. In the same year that its turnover collapsed from €48.7 million to €10.7 million, payments to two of its directors, Seán Dunne and Ross Connolly, doubled to almost €1.9 million.

A SLIPPERY SLOPE: HUGH O'REGAN AND THE KILTERNAN HOTEL

The publican and hotelier Hugh O'Regan had the dubious distinction of being the first person to be taken down in the property collapse on foot of a sizeable personal guarantee granted to a lender. Irish Nationwide secured a judgement of €60 million against O'Regan, primarily related to loans it had granted him for the Kilternan Hotel. O'Regan was financially ruined, and he died in November 2012 at the age of forty-nine. He had made his money through the pub trade by buying, developing and later selling 'superpubs'. He sold his Thomas Read chain of bars at the top of the market in 2005 for €30 million.

Born in Dublin, O'Regan had done extremely well in business and found himself in the right place at the right time on many occasions. He used an inheritance of €19,000 from his mother to get himself onto the property ladder, buying a house in Sandymount, Dublin. In 1988 he remortgaged it to buy a pub in Temple Bar.

After that he never looked back. He opened up a string of upmarket and trendy bars around the city centre at just the right time, including Thomas Read's at the corner of Dame Street and Parliament Street. Other large drinking-houses followed, including Hogan's, Searson's, the Bailey, Pravda, and Life Bar. O'Regan also became a hotelier when he opened the Morrison Hotel on Ormond Quay, which was designed by John Rocha.

Somewhat annoyed at the prices publicans were paying for drink from the breweries, O'Regan set up a web site, bartrader.com, which was aimed at selling wholesale to publicans at better prices. He sank close to €2 million in the venture. But he had the business acumen to sell out his Thomas Read group at the best possible time. He held on to the Morrison Hotel, which was owned through a separate company. He bagged €30 million and became a very wealthy man.

O'Regan could have retired very young at that stage, but two things instead took his interest. His big vision was a hotel at Kilternan on the Dublin–Enniskerry road owned by the Irish-American businessman and philanthropist Chuck Feeney. The Kilternan Hotel, built decades before, was a fairly nondescript building, noted for having an artificial ski slope, where wealthy Dubliners went to improve their skill before taking to the piste in the Alps, where without practice they might look a bit foolish. But O'Regan had a much grander plan for the hotel.

Though it was miles from Dublin and had a poor record as a hotel, in 2001 O'Regan bought the Kilternan Hotel and Country Club from Feeney for €12.7 million. Irish Nationwide subsequently lent O'Regan close to €150 million to turn it into a massive new hotel, leisure centre and conference centre. The redevelopment was also supposed to include a theatre and a 'global innovation campus'. This was O'Regan's big idea.

He poured money into the venture, which was originally backed by First Active PLC, the former building society. Sources close to O'Regan said that Fingleton never came out to see the development for which he had approved tens of millions, though it was only a few miles from his home in Shankill or his office in Dublin.

As with many ambitious projects on this scale, as the building proceeded the costs mounted. Having guzzled about €150 million, it still wasn't finished.

O'Regan had other loans with Irish Nationwide. His immediate loan facility on the Kilternan Hotel was €135 million. A further €31 million was granted in relation to a development site at Cóbh, Co. Cork, part of the former IFI fertiliser plant, which was zoned for mixed-use development. O'Regan wanted to acquire 110 acres of freehold and leasehold property from the Department of the Marine and planned to build 1,200 residential units. He also had loans from Irish Nationwide in relation to his plan for a fashionable private members' club at 8 St Stephen's Green, the former Hibernian United Services Club, and a facility in relation to an investment property in central Dublin. The loans were granted on the basis of a capital and interest moratorium, which meant that he didn't have to pay back the principal or any interest for a few years.

In the spring of 2009, just as Irish Nationwide was in the process of being effectually nationalised, it approved a fresh loan facility, which would bring the total amount owed to €180 million.

O'Regan had his own financial difficulties from the crash in relation to other borrowings. The most tricky was the €80 million owed to Anglo Irish Bank. This had been built up as he spent money on such ventures as the purchase of the former Hibernian United Services Club. As part of the deal with Irish Nationwide for the €180 million facility, O'Regan agreed to release funds from Clubko, the company behind the St Stephen's Green project. He also agreed to provide fresh guarantees from his Thomas Read Holdings venture, which included assets like the Morrison Hotel. The deal didn't wash with Anglo Irish, and Irish Nationwide also decided not to proceed.

The Kilternan Hotel needed another €10 million or so to be completed. By the end of 2006 the company behind the development, Dashaven Ltd, had borrowings of €122 million but a turnover of only €15,236. It was also losing €2 million per year. In 2006 Dashaven's cash outflow was €85 million. That year about €85 million of new Irish Nationwide loans flowed in and was spent. At the end of 2006 the company had cash in hand of €2.

The jig was up for Dashaven and O'Regan, and for Irish Nationwide. An application to appoint an examiner to Dashaven was made in July 2009. The following month a receiver was appointed, and then a liquidator. The receiver began trying to find a buyer for the unfinished hotel. In 2010 there were reports that two American companies were interested, but no announcement of a sale was made.

A statement of affairs for the company showed that it was generating rental income of €30,000 per year from the outdoor centre but the building was costing €270,000 a year to insure and had €80,000 in ESB bills, €85,000 in gas bills, and €155,000 for security. These bills and others, including consultants, legal fees and receiver's fees, were being met by Irish Nationwide, which provided more than €1 million to the company between February 2010 and February 2011.

The extent of the loss to Irish Nationwide, NAMA and the taxpayer will be significant. The hotel has extensive land around it, but industry sources estimate that it will not make more than €25 million in a sale. This would be a loss of well over €100 million to the state.

ELYSIAN DREAMS: O'FLYNN CONSTRUCTION

O'Flynn Construction is owned by Michael and John O'Flynn. It has been involved in building and development projects in Ireland and Britain for decades. Highly regarded for the quality of its building, the company nevertheless went on a borrowing binge during the boom years of the property market. When the property crash came, it had debts of about €1 billion.

Michael O'Flynn began doing business with Irish Nationwide in 1998. The company was growing and profitable. In 2002 it was not quite big enough to make it into the *Sunday Tribune* 'Richlist' but was included as one of those companies 'bubbling under'. In 2000 it was a €50 million business and had made a profit of €10 million. Much of its work at that time was in Munster; but even at that stage it had a stake in Tiger Developments, which had a London investment portfolio of €200 million.

O'Flynn ended up with five major loan facilities from Irish Nationwide. These were a €75 million facility for the purchase and development of the former army barracks in Ballincollig, Co. Cork. Irish Nationwide expected to make substantial supplemental arrangement fees from this project; in total it expected to make €36 million in such fees from O'Flynn Construction projects.

Another loan of €71 million had been granted to develop a site in Edinburgh, to include three hotels and office space. Another loan facility amounted to €65 million for a 65-acre development site in Celbridge, Co. Kildare. This was being developed in partnership with Seán Dunne. Irish Nationwide granted another loan of €17 million for a business park in Leeds and €2 million for a development in Rochestown, Co.

Cork. Irish Nationwide had already received €10 million in arrangement fees when it approved the final €2 million loan.

O'Flynn is best known for the development of the Elysian Tower in Cork. Named with aesthetics in mind (Elysian means delightful, glorious or blissful), at 81 metres (266 feet) it is Ireland's tallest building. It consists of a number of connected six to eight-storey buildings, with a seventeen-storey tower on one corner of the site. Its 211 apartments came on the market at exactly the wrong time, in 2008. Prices tumbled, and a year later four-fifths of the apartments and half the commercial units were empty.

O'Flynn Construction owed Irish Nationwide €88 million in 2005, but this rocketed to €230 million at the end of 2006. O'Flynn is now a major client of NAMA and is working with the agency.

FROM WILD NORTH TO WILD WEST: LARRY O'MAHONY AND TOM McFEELY

'You couldn't build a snowman!' shouted one of the angry residents of Priory Hall at the property developer Tom McFeely. The developer had been summoned to the High Court to answer questions about how the 187-apartment development his company had built in Donaghmede, Dublin, was a completely unsafe fire hazard that had to be abandoned. About 250 residents were forced to leave the complex just before Christmas, 2009.

McFeely was a typical boom-time builder turned developer, except in one major respect: he was a convicted IRA man who had been sentenced to twenty six years in prison in the 1970s and had gone for fifty-three days without food on hunger strike.

A native of Co. Derry, McFeely emigrated to England for a while to do labouring jobs, then returned to his native county at the height of the Northern conflict. After carrying out an armed robbery on a post office, he and another IRA man took over a small country house, which was put under siege by the police and army. 'It was a bit Wild West, to be honest,' he later told the *Guardian*. 'The idea was to go out and take as many of them out as possible.' He shot a policeman, who survived.

After coming off hunger strike McFeely was later released and left the IRA to join the so-called 'League of Communist Republicans'. After a fairly lucrative period labouring on Dublin building sites he bought a pub in Dungiven, Co. Derry.

After that McFeely's business simply took off. His building company, Coalport, built houses around Ireland and in Britain. He tended to employ ex-prisoners and later said that during the boom 'everything was done in a rush. The attitude was, Get it up, get it off, get on to the next job. Come back and finish it later.'

Following an investigation by the Criminal Assets Bureau in 2006, McFeely had to pay more than €8 million in unpaid tax, dating back to his arrival in the Republic. The following year Coalport was the subject of eight High Court actions. McFeely took out a loan of €10 million from Irish Nationwide for his house, the former German embassy in Ailesbury Road, Dublin, but stopped paying the mortgage. In 2009 he was ordered to repay €6.2 million to a bank, as well as a further payment to the Revenue Commissioners of €580,000. McFeely was so annoyed at the CAB pay-out that he went out and bought a €50,000 Bentley, just to 'give them the two fingers,' he later said.

McFeely's partner on many of these projects was the Dubliner Larry O'Mahony. Eventually both men applied for bankruptcy in Britain. During the former IRA man's bankruptcy application he said, 'As a British citizen I have always objected to being forced into bankruptcy in a foreign jurisdiction. I maintain this is a breach of my human rights.' His British bankruptcy was overturned, and he was made bankrupt in Ireland.

Larry O'Mahony had an address in Manchester when he went into British bankruptcy in 2011 and then emerged from it a year later. He and related companies had debts totalling £197 million.

McFeely and O'Mahony were major borrowers from Irish Nationwide. Together they owed the society €186 million in 2006. The biggest portion of this related to an eighteen-acre site adjacent to the Square, the large shopping centre in Tallaght. Irish Nationwide also bankrolled their development at Priory Hall. Irish Nationwide agreed a 'supplemental arrangement fee' with the two developers whereby the society would be paid €2 million from the sale of the 194 apartments. It was indicative of its carelessness that it funded the construction of a fire-trap. Residents who spent hundreds of thousands buying property there had to leave. The High Court later found that McFeely had failed to comply with orders to deal with fire safety risks in the apartments. He was fined €1 million and given a three-month prison sentence. This sentence was later overturned on appeal.

The poor and hazardous state of the Priory Hall building meant that even NAMA refused to buy it from Irish Nationwide—at any price. McFeely was later evicted from his Ailesbury Road mansion by NAMA and complained bitterly that he and his wife had been 'thrown out on the side of the road.'

FROM PROPERTY TO PHILANTHROPY: NIALL MELLON

Niall Mellon was never the best-known property developer in Ireland. He quietly built up a successful financial consultancy and investment business; he then began to dabble in property development.

Mellon became something of a national figure by setting up a South African township trust to build houses for impoverished families. Over a period of ten years the foundation built twenty thousand houses, which provided a roof over the heads of 100,000 people. He got people from all over Ireland to go over and chip in with labour or other help. A close friend of the property developers Paddy Kelly and Seán Dunne, Mellon was also a big investor in South Africa.

Among the purchases made by his company, Knockrabo Developments, was the Bank of Ireland playing fields in Goatstown, Co. Dublin, in 2003 for €50 million. By the end of 2006 Mellon owed Irish Nationwide €145 million. His total borrowings from other lenders is not known, and he tended not to submit single group accounts for his business operations. His biggest Irish Nationwide loan was €52 million, relating to a development of 291 apartments at Swansea docks. He had other loans relating to a development site in Bristol, apartments in Nottingham, and a raft of other apartments in Glasgow and in Ireland.

Mellon was granted the loans on the basis of a moratorium on capital and interest for the full term of the loans. This meant he didn't have to pay back anything until the projects were completed and he had got his cash in. The properties were given as security, and he also gave a personal guarantee.

In 2001 Mellon hired Joseph Murphy, an eleven-year banking veteran with Irish Nationwide, to advise him as a financial accountant. Mellon considered his borrowings to be relatively low-geared before the bust.

In 2010 Mellon hit the headlines when, after having loans transferred to NAMA, he said he was moving out of his mansion, which sat on five acres in the exclusive Mount Merrion area. He said the move was part of an effort to cut costs. He also sold his 242-acre estate in Co. Kilkenny for €3¾ million, with the proceeds going towards his NAMA debt. Mellon told the *Irish Times* in November 2012 that he left his Dublin home with just €1 in his pocket.

THE MAN IN THE HAT: GERRY GANNON

A native of Co. Roscommon, Gerry Gannon began working in construction in London in the 1970s. Like so many other boom-time property developers, he built close relationships with two banks: Anglo Irish and Irish Nationwide. Michael Fingleton appears to have backed Gannon in various ventures as far back as the late 1980s.

As well as being a developer of housing projects Gannon also simply bought and sold sites, or entire buildings, as the property market was going up. Once he had access to finance he could turn a very rapid profit by 'flipping' land or office blocks, or anything else.

Gannon's closeness to Anglo Irish Bank is reflected in the fact that he was chosen as one of the 'Maple 10' borrowers who were financed by Anglo Irish to buy shares in the bank as part of a take-up of Seán Quinn's shareholding, which had been accumulated through 'contracts for difference'. These loans were not fully recourse-to-borrower and were largely secured on the Anglo Irish shares themselves.

Gannon's close relationship with Fingleton is reflected in the fact that the latter was a secret investor with him in the purchase of lands at Clongriffin, Co. Dublin, in the late 1990s. Details of Fingleton's personal investment in the project came to light only when he sued Gannon for a share of the profits. Gannon had originally bought an option to acquire the Clongriffin site in the late 1990s. Fingleton claims that he personally invested £75,000 of the £300,000 used to acquire the option, and that he is entitled to a quarter of the profit from the enormous Clongriffin development of houses, apartments and retail space.

Gannon was part not only of Anglo Irish's golden circle but also of Fingleton's elite core of favoured borrowers. He was introduced to the Co. Kildare estate agent turned developer Arthur French by Noel Smyth, the solicitor who had also become a property developer. French in turn was friendly with Fingleton and with Michael Smurfit. When Smurfit was trying to buy the K Club from the owners of the former Jefferson Smurfit Group in 2005 he knew he needed a developer as a joint-venture partner. The development potential of the site was seen as one of its main attractions. French knew both Gannon and Smurfit. Fingleton was in the mix and agreed to bankroll the purchase.

By the end of 2006 Gannon had done quite a lot of business with Irish Nationwide. He had set up a joint venture with the society whereby a subsidiary, Vernia Ltd, bought land from Gannon, and he in turn helped put together a sizeable site at Drinan, near Swords, Co. Dublin.

At the end of 2006, the peak of the property boom, Gannon was listed as the eighteenth-largest exposure to Irish Nationwide, with loans totalling €137 million. The society had provided a €55 million facility for a 115-apartment development in Malahide. His loans also included a €27 million facility for the joint purchase of the K Club with Michael Smurfit and a €22 million facility for a residential and commercial development in Dundrum, Co. Dublin, comprising 400 apartments and 130,000 square feet of commercial, office and retail space. The society also provided him with a €22 million facility to purchase and develop retail units, a pub and offices at the Plaza shopping centre in Swords. There were other loans for land purchases and a €5 million loan for Gannon to buy a luxury villa in Portugal.

The KPMG report compiled in 2007 as a prospectus for the sale of Irish Nationwide makes no reference to personal guarantees as security on these loans. It refers only to mortgage debentures and charges over land and property. Yet Gannon was in the habit of giving substantial personal guarantees on his borrowings, especially those with Anglo Irish. He even gave personal guarantees on separate loans in his wife's name.

As the property market began to collapse, Gannon was in trouble. His main trading company, Gannon Homes, lost €50 million in 2008. He had to sell his private jet and helicopter. He had transferred eighteen properties to his wife over a two-year period, and by the time his loans were bought by NAMA he had approximately 700 acres of land and borrowings of about €1 billion. He has agreed a business plan with NAMA that includes a personal salary of more than €150,000 a year.

Gannon and his wife were filmed in 2010 by RTE's 'Prime Time' loading bags of Brown Thomas shopping into their €110,000 Mercedes, as part of a programme on how heavily indebted developers were coping with the crash. The car belonged to his wife, and she sold it shortly afterwards, with a price tag of €69,000.

But Gannon was ultimately a beneficiary of the lax controls and personal style of lending dished out by his friend Michael Fingleton.

Forensic accountants hired by the board in 2009 had a lot to say about the poor controls the society operated on some of Gannon's loans.

FINGERS'S FRIEND: LOUIS SCULLY

Louis Scully was an estate agent with an office in Merrion Square, Dublin. He was a long-time personal friend of Fingleton, and the two holidayed abroad together with their wives. Scully had done quite a lot of valuation work over the years with house-builders such as the Abbey Group. Fingleton hired him to assess property deals that he was going to invest in himself. He clearly trusted his judgement.

Scully was also an old friend of the Dublin businessman Louis Maguire. When Maguire's son, also Louis, identified a potential multi-million property investment in the former Yugoslav state of Montenegro, Scully was able to introduce the young Maguire to Michael Fingleton.

But Scully became something of a property developer himself. He borrowed heavily from Irish Nationwide during the boom years, mainly for the purchase of land in Co. Meath. By 2009 loans connected to this little-known estate agent totalled €130 million.

NORTHERN LIGHTS GO OUT: ALASTAIR JACKSON

One of the borrowers who illustrates some of the madness of Fingleton's boom-time lending is Alastair Jackson. A native of Co. Antrim living at Templepatrick, Co. Down, Jackson had set up a successful property business even before the big boom. His Eassda group was profitable and diversifying into more types of property investment. His investment foray south of the border proved to be disastrous and ultimately very costly for the Irish taxpayer.

Jackson had been a borrower from Irish Nationwide since the late 1990s. He appeared in the KPMG list of exposures at number 23, owing €130 million. This included a €49 million loan facility for a 58-acre development site outside Wicklow, which Jackson had bought in December 2005. It had planning permission for 650 residential units.

He had an outstanding loan of €32 million in December 2006 for the purchase of a nineteenth-century house and golf course on 512 acres in Moyvalley, Co. Kildare. The Moyvalley Hotel and Golf Resort opened its doors in April 2007. The €60 million development included a 54-bedroom boutique hotel, a country residence with ten rooms, and fifteen original luxury courtyard cottages. It was built on the Balyna estate, ancient home of the O'Mores and later the O'Farrells, going back over four hundred years. In 1961 it was bought by the Bewley family, and in the early 2000s it was purchased by Alastair Jackson. The estate house was converted into meeting-rooms and an exclusive corporate centre. Jackson then set about building a hotel and a golf course, with the intention of building and selling houses around the course.

Irish Nationwide seized possession of the resort in July 2010, three years after it opened. The idea behind the golf club was that it would be exclusively for members, and no societies or day-trippers would be allowed use it.

The resort opened at exactly the wrong time in relation to the downturn; when it began selling membership it sold precisely two at the full price. It was in the wrong place—too far from Dublin, not particularly scenic—and opened too late. Everything went wrong. The whole financial proposition behind the golf course was the construction and sale of houses. The resort opened in April 2007, and house prices began to fall about two months later; but prices had already been static for about six months before opening. The sale of only two golf-club memberships at full price prompted a sharp reduction in membership fees and a rethink.

The resort really began to get into trouble when its parent group, Eassda, owned by Alastair Jackson and his family, was caught out in the property crash. It ended up in receivership in the North.

It was a massive fall from grace for the developers, who had begun building houses in the North many years ago. Irish Nationwide also bankrolled the Jacksons on a number of other building projects. The society had even provided a loan facility of €12 million for the New Forest Golf Club development on 300 acres at Tyrrellspass, Co. Westmeath, half an hour's drive away. But the Moyvalley resort was its biggest mistake. Irish Nationwide ended up foreclosing on the Moyvalley project and New Forest, and a receiver was appointed.

The extent of the collapse in fortunes for the Jacksons, who had their own helicopter and jet, was apparent from the statement of affairs for the Eassda receiver. An update from the receiver submitted to the Companies Registration Office describes how Jackson insisted that the directors put down a deposit of €2,000 if they wanted to continue using the company's mobile phones.

PRIZE FIGHTER: PADDY MCKILLEN

Clarendon Properties, backed by the low-profile property developers Paddy McKillen and Tony Leonard, became a major borrower from Irish Nationwide. Only two photographs of Paddy McKillen were ever published in a newspaper before his battle with Barclay Brothers in the English High Court for control of some of London's most prestigious hotels. McKillen also fought not to have his loans transferred to NAMA, but didn't win.

McKillen has fought two High Court battles during the crash: one against NAMA, challenging its right to buy his loans, and the other the London hotels showdown with the Barclay Brothers.

For McKillen, the relationship with Irish Nationwide also goes back a long way. Clarendon was listed as owing the society €129 million at the end of 2006. Its biggest loan facility, amounting to €32 million, was for the Powerscourt Centre in Dublin and the Savoy Shopping Centre in Cork. The two men bought Powerscourt House in the mid-1990s at a cheap price in the wake of the collapse of Power Corporation, the salutary tale of the Cork dentist Robin Power, who fell in love with property development in the 1980s. Power Corporation had been floated on the stock exchange in 1987, and by 1990 it was valued at £250 million. Less than four years later it was worth only £2 million.

Power had created the Powerscourt Centre and was behind the development of St Stephen's Green Shopping Centre, together with British Land. Over-extending the company's balance sheet on property development in London was its undoing.

Leonard and McKillen were both wily and astute operators who rode the property rollercoaster very well. McKillen also went to Irish Nationwide for Château La Coste, his French castle and vineyard (€14 million), and the purchase of office space in the Place Vendôme in Paris (€24 million). Other Fingleton loans included €12 million for retail space in Limerick and a further €8 million for investment property in London.

McKillen's personal and family assets include an art collection worth €20 million, mansions in California and a plush pad in the centre of London. He has owned four properties in the billionaires' playground of Cap Ferrat, where neighbours include the owner of Chelsea FC, Roman Abramovich, and a vineyard and other assets in Argentina. He is also known to have invested in Hong Kong and Vietnam. Closer to home, he owns a significant amount of property around South Anne Street in Dublin and has held a stake in Captain America, Wagamama, Muji and Champion Sports. He likes to keep a low profile when at his home in Foxrock, Co. Dublin, but drives classic Porsches abroad and uses a private jet. Clarendon has suffered its own setbacks with the property crash but retains many good property assets.

MUIRISÍN DURKIN: BRIAN AND TONY DURKAN

Durkan has been a big name in house-building and property development for decades. Two Durkan brothers, Brian and Tony, began to become more heavily involved in property development during the boom, but perhaps not in the biggest of housing schemes. They tended to do smaller, specialist developments, such as one in Foxrock involving twenty apartments and two town-houses on a quarter of an acre. Elsewhere in the Dublin region they received planning permission for twelve to fifteen-house developments.

When it came to borrowing from Michael Fingleton their ambitions just seemed to get bigger. By the end of 2006 their company, Devondale Ltd, owed Irish Nationwide €147 million in connection with a number of developments. One was a loan of €25 million in relation to an 8½-acre site in Saggart, Co. Dublin. The site was purchased in December 2006 with a view to selling it on if a suitable purchaser came along.

While the first half of 2006 had seen house prices continue to skyrocket, in October that year they began to stall. There were fewer transactions, and prices froze as people held off buying to see what might be in the budget that year regarding stamp duty. So when Brian and Tony bought this site in December the first real cracks were beginning to appear in the invincibility of the market. They had another €22 million facility to develop 152 residential units and a creche in Saggart, which was due to be completed in late 2007.

Devondale's biggest loan facility was €94 million in relation to a development site purchased in July 2005 at Celbridge. The site consisted of a period house on 66 acres, 49 of which were zoned for development. The master plan was not accepted by Kildare County Council until January 2007. Given that asking prices began to fall in early 2007, and house prices began to fall around June that year, this was a very late development indeed. The Durkans were about to pay the price, as ultimately was the taxpayer.

House prices collapsed in 2008 and 2009 and really only stopped falling (sort of) in 2012. Irish Nationwide had granted a capital and interest moratorium for the full term of the loan. This meant that neither the principal nor the interest had to be paid until the loan matured. The total security on the loan was essentially the property itself.

For the year ending December 2011 accounts for Devondale showed that it had assets valued at €20½ million but had borrowings due within one year of a staggering €175 million. The company was showing a deficit of €154 million and had generated trading losses of €144 million.

BLIGHTED BY OLD BLIGHTY: THE LONDON GOLDEN CIRCLE

Michael Fingleton's passion for property investment and lending inevitably took him to England. Many of his clients were from rural Ireland who had gone to London to work on building sites and wanted to go back there and buy up the place.

Michael Fingleton was more than ready to write the cheques to fulfil their personal and financial ambitions. At first he followed Irish developers who wanted to do deals in London in particular. Seán Mulryan was a typical builder from the west of Ireland who had lived in England and now wanted to make it big in property in London. Johnny Ronan of Treasury Holdings was the same, as were the O'Flynns, Gerry Gannon and Noel Smyth.

One Irish property developer tells the story of how in the late 1990s he was in London to complete the purchase of a building as an investment. He had borrowed the money, about £25 million, from Anglo Irish Bank. While there he happened to bump into Michael Fingleton in a posh hotel. They knew each other slightly, and began to chat. The developer told Fingleton what he was doing in London. Fingleton was a little annoyed that he hadn't gone to him for the money. 'The next time you want to buy something over here, why don't you come to me first?' The developer had another building in mind, which he immediately told Fingleton about. 'Within thirty minutes of meeting him he had agreed to lend me £15 million.'

But the really big opportunity (or risk) came from lending to British clients for property development and joint ventures in Britain. To pull this off, Fingleton needed to have an office there.

The first thing he did was to open an office in Belfast, even though it only made one loan in Northern Ireland. He then hired his own son, Michael Fingleton junior, to run a London branch, which would report to Gary McCollum in Belfast. Fingleton developed a pattern of lending in Ireland that thrived on the close social and business circles here. Developers knew each other and met each other socially, and therefore one referred the other for business. Fingleton was at the centre of that high-flying circle.

In Britain it was a little different. There were fewer clients, and they tended to have higher borrowings, with greater profit shares for the society. But, unlike Ireland, the same small group of big borrowers kept forming consortiums, alliances, joint ventures and partnerships with each other, and financing them through Irish Nationwide.

LONDON CALLING: GALLIARD, THE LANDESBERGS, THE ROSENBERGS, AND DAVID BURKE

After Ballymore Properties the three biggest borrowers from Irish Nationwide were in Britain. They owed a total of €720 million by the end of 2006 and were interlinked in several ventures.

The first of these was Galliard Homes. This was, and is, a house-building company that has diversified into all kinds of other property development and investment. It is run by Stephen Conway and owned by him and a group of other investors. A big part of the way it does business is through joint ventures. These tend to be separate business vehicles put together for specific projects, such as buying hotels, pubs or development sites.

At the end of 2006 Irish Nationwide had a net exposure to Galliard of €252 million. Based on group accounts for the period, this suggests that Irish Nationwide was a substantial banker to the group and probably its biggest lender. Examples of loans to Galliard were €25 million for a former hospital being developed into 245 residential units, a €100 million facility for a joint venture with Frogmore Property Company (Irish Nationwide's 28th-biggest borrower) for an apartment development, and other joint-venture loans with Frogmore for hotels in London and elsewhere in England.

Galliard shows up as an investor in several projects with two wealthy British families, the Landesbergs and the Rosenbergs. These two families were partners in a raft of ventures backed by Irish Nationwide and in which Galliard was a shareholder and sometimes did the renovating or building work. The main movers here were Alan Landesberg and his son Gary Landesberg on the one hand and the brothers Elliot and David Rosenberg on the other.

Their biggest venture backed by Irish Nationwide was Admiral Taverns. Irish Nationwide provided approximately €240 million on different pub and hotel-buying sprees. Admiral Taverns, financed by Bank of Scotland and Irish Nationwide, began buying pub chains around Britain. At one point it owned 2,500 pubs and was talking about floating on the stock exchange. Pubs were bought and certain properties were sold, which brought in a good profit on the better establishments. Its two lenders had done a major refinancing of the debt in 2007, which allowed Admiral Taverns to boast that it had a £1 billion 'war chest' to keep buying more pubs.

By the time the economy began to turn downwards Admiral Taverns had borrowings of £1 billion, and it had to start selling off pubs to stay afloat. The group owed Bank of Scotland £855 million and Irish Nationwide about £105 million when it was forced into administration in 2010. Bank of Scotland was forced to write off about £600 million and do a debt-for-equity swap under which it took a half share in the business. It has now emerged that because Irish Nationwide's security was secondary or subordinated to other lenders, the state-owned building society got nothing back on the Admiral Taverns loans.

Somewhat more upmarket, the Landesbergs, Rosenbergs and Galliard teamed up to buy St James's Club in London in 2005. This was one of the most exclusive members' clubs in the city, frequented by well-known actors and other celebrities, including Michael Caine, Liza Minnelli, Richard Attenborough and Dudley Moore. The Landesbergs and Rosenbergs closed the club in 2006 for a multi-million-pound renovation, and it reopened in 2008. All the rooms had handmade silk wallpaper, black lacquered furniture, Murano glass chandeliers and handmade mattresses. But in 2010 it was put up for sale. The asking price was in the region of £60 million; the sale price was never disclosed, but it is likely to have fetched a high enough price to clear its £45 million in bank borrowings.

Another major borrower was a company called Roadnumber Ltd. At the end of 2006 it owed approximately €230 million. The company was originally part of the Oracle Group, set up by the publican turned property developer David Burke. At one point the company had the

Galliard boss Stephen Conway on its board and became a joint venture partner with Galliard. It then teamed up also with Seán Mulryan's Ballymore Properties as part of a proposed £1 billion London Docklands Tower development. This meant that Irish Nationwide's first, second and sixth-biggest exposures were jointly doing a development.

It wasn't their first joint venture. Oracle Group, Ballymore and Galliard announced plans to redevelop a seven-acre site next to Pan Peninsula in east London as a 2 million square foot mixed-use scheme. The developers sought to buy the Audi garage site at Marsh Wall, London, which they plan to redevelop as five hundred flats, two hotels and 100,000 square feet of shops. Burke wanted to be the third-biggest developer in the London Docklands, after the Canary Wharf group and Ballymore.

Roadnumber borrowed heavily for the development in London's docklands. The company was Irish Nationwide's sixth-biggest exposure in 2006, according to the KPMG report of 2007. It later became a joint venture with Galliard, changed its name to Millharbour Developments and in 2010 became fully owned by Galliard. Burke's Oracle Group ended up liquidating four of its major ventures. Accounts for Millharbour show that at the end of March 2012 it had assets of £22 million and borrowings of £60 million. It had retained losses and a shareholders' deficit of £36 million.

One of Oracle's big coups came in May 2008 when it sold a pub site in the Isle of Dogs, London, to Ray Grehan's Glenkerrin Group for £32 million. Oracle had bought it only twelve months earlier for £6¾ million. At the time Oracle was reported in the press to have built up a 'war chest' of £80 million. Two years later four of its companies were in liquidation.

One of the biggest challenges for Fingleton and his Belfast lieutenant, Gary McCollum, was to get introductions and referrals of business in London. After all, Fingleton knew the Irish scene very well but he was drifting into a whole other market. Central to forming these relationships was a firm of London solicitors called Howard Kennedy. This firm acted for the society on several big property deals, and on a number of occasions acted for both sides of the transaction, representing the borrower also. KPMG noted in its sale prospectus in 2007 that growth in commercial lending in Britain was through their existing customers 'and those potential customers that are being introduced to them by existing customers, through their UK law firm, Howard Kennedy, and direct approaches to the society.'

Links with the Howard Kennedy firm were strong. Fingleton's daughter Eileen, a solicitor, worked there, though she is not known to have worked on any Irish Nationwide contracts. But the strength of the links is illustrated by a hotel investment. Galliard teamed up with the Landesbergs and Rosenbergs to buy a number of hotels in Britain that were leased to the Radisson and Folio Hotel chains. Another investor in this deal, which was also backed by Irish Nationwide, was a company called Deedchoice Ltd. This was a British investment company owned by Elizabeth Philips. She is the wife of Maurice Philips, a consultant to Howard Kennedy and a former partner in the firm. Irish Nationwide's net exposure to Deedchoice was listed as €204 million at the end of 2006.

Deedchoice operated three joint ventures in hotel investments. Each one had a loan with Irish Nationwide. Total loans from these joint ventures amounted to €278 million at the end of 2009. The loans defaulted in the summer of 2009. One of them related to an investment with Stephen Conway of Galliard and the Landesbergs, which was subsequently restructured to include cross-collateralisation with two other hotels, Jefferson Hotels and Jefferson Hotel (Cardiff) Ltd, which had a Landesberg connection.

Business breeds relationships, whether one is an investor or a lender. In the case of Irish Nationwide in Britain the tightness of the relationships left large amounts of Irish Nationwide loans with a relatively small number of people. It was a very significant concentration of risk. The second, third and fourth-biggest borrowers had formed multiple joint ventures together. Irish Nationwide's solicitors in London often acted for the borrower and the bank. A consultant and former partner with the firm, whose wife was the seventh-largest borrower from the society, was also a major investor in shared projects with the second, third and fourth-biggest borrowers.

In total, six of the thirteen biggest borrowers from the society had connections through participation in various joint ventures funded by the society. Irish Nationwide had a net exposure to those six borrowers of approximately €1.3 billion in 2006.

One British borrower who seems to have no connection with the other group was an elusive multi-millionaire property developer called Cyril Dennis.

WHERE DO YOU GO TO, MY LOVELY?—CYRIL DENNIS

Cyril Dennis was made for Irish Nationwide Building Society. Shy of publicity but with a good record in property development, the wealthy British developer thinks big and enjoys the good life. He was awarded membership of the Order of the British Empire for services to the Jewish community. He began his development work as half-owner of an Essex house-building firm, which he sold in 1987. After a period advising the Berisford Group he built up his own property business with a portfolio spread around different cities. In 1994 he sold three-quarters of the portfolio to Legal and General for £116 million, reputedly netting him a profit of £50 million.

Dennis spends a lot of time at his luxury villa in Monaco, the purchase of which was financed by Irish Nationwide. In 2009 his net worth was estimated by the British property journal *Estates Gazette* to be £130 million. When many property developers were on their knees in 2009, Dennis spent £23 million buying the 403-bedroom Le Méridien Beach Plaza Hotel in Monte Carlo. He had a good pedigree in property, having sold a 3.3-acre site in the Isle of Dogs, London, for £47 million in September 2006 that he had bough nine years earlier for £2 million.

Dennis has also secured approval for a development at Peruvian Wharf in the London docklands, at the fourth attempt. Irish Nationwide provided some of the finance for the original purchase of the site. He has owned the land, which at one point was touted as a site for Britain's first giant casino, since 1999. A £67 million development in Liverpool was also completed by Dennis in 2006.

But his most spectacular luxury purchase, which also went wrong, was financed by Irish Nationwide. In 2006 Dennis bought the abandoned Le Provençal hotel in Juan-les-Pins on the Côte d'Azur. Built in 1925 by the American millionaire Frank Jay Gould, it was a landmark on the French Riviera, nestled between Juan-les-Pins and Cap d'Antibes. It had been host to an array of celebrities, including Charlie Chaplin, Winston Churchill, Coco Chanel, Édith Piaf and Ernest Hemingway. Juan-les-Pins was at the time a luxury getaway for the rich, made famous from 1969 by the lyrics of the song 'Where do you go to, my lovely?' by Peter Sarstedt.

But in recent decades the town had gone somewhat downhill while the neighbouring Cap d'Antibes was booming. Since the glory days of wealth and excess, when F. Scott Fitzgerald took the Le Provençal orchestra hostage and Charlie Chaplin entertained his lover May Reeves on the beach, the town had really lost a lot of its five-star appeal. Cap d'Antibes has sprawling villas, electric gates, and high hedges, but the forests of Juan-les-Pins have been replaced with ugly 1970s apartment blocks, and whatever rich or famous do still visit have to sunbathe on concrete pontoons in front of the decaying hotel. 'Nothing has changed in forty years, yet people still come here and sit on the concrete like sardines,' Dennis told one journalist.

Le Provençal was part of that story. In the 1970s the hotel staff pushed for a pay increase. In response its eccentric owner, the Parisian jeweller Alexandre Reza, closed the place, never returned and refused to sell. Along came Cyril Dennis and Michael Fingleton, who planned to change all that. In 2006 Dennis bought the building through a company registered in Luxembourg called Provençal Investments SA. The purchase price was never disclosed but was reported to be in the region of €50 million. Two years later Fingleton attended the lavish launch party for Dennis's plan to redevelop the old hotel as fifty luxury apartments that would sell for between €2 and €40 million each. Fingleton was on the beach mingling with the local worthies and enjoying what the *Irish Times* called a 'break from the dire economy at home.'

Dennis described the potential for the building at the time.

It may be in disrepair, but you still feel the sense of its elegant past when you enter the huge reception. There is a spirit and soul in the walls. We are bringing back the historic splendour to Antibe and the old spirit of Juan-les-Pins, to recreate the days when Le Provençal was frequented by people who made a difference in our world— Churchill, the Kennedys, Marlene Dietrich.

He said it was a sleeping beauty, waiting for someone to breathe life into it again. Under the original plan a site beside the old hotel would be developed, with 'cheap' apartments priced between €2 and €6 million. It was extraordinary old guff. Buyers from such places as Russia, India and the Far East were expected as the company began selling off the plans. But nothing really happened. Four years after buying Le Provençal the company tried to stamp out speculation that it would never happen. The developer said he would open up parts of the development and wanted to adjust his plan for new market requirements and realities. Instead of the fifty gigantic apartments at €2 million plus there would be seventy smaller units. Accounts submitted in Luxembourg for Le Provençal SA show that at the end of 2010 the company had total assets of €127 million and total liabilities of €155 million, including bank borrowings of €147 million.

Irish Nationwide had a charge over the shares but once again no sign of a personal guarantee sought from a man who remains quite wealthy. The loan was based on repayment of the capital at the end of the loan, and quarterly interest payments were due.

Confidential documents show that Cyril Dennis had total borrowings from the society at the end of 2009 of €486 million, and the society had at that point made a provision of €137 million, suggesting the amount it believed at the time it might not get back.

A SHARD OF GLASS: SIMON HALABI

Simon Halabi was regarded as one of the richest men in Britain. A native of Syria, he had made a number of successful property deals in London. In 2007 his wealth was estimated at £3 billion. Big deals included the Aviva Tower and the European head office of J. P. Morgan at London Wall.

Halabi put these up for sale in 2006 with a price tag of £1.8 billion. But as the credit crunch came and his highly leveraged position was exposed, his wealth crumbled. His advisory business Buckingham Securities was placed in liquidation. Halabi himself disappeared after being made bankrupt.

His business deals tended to be accompanied by a degree of complication and sometimes strife. He was a major backer of the Shard Tower in London. Its construction began in March 2009 and was completed in March 2012. Standing 310 metres (1,017 feet) high, it is the second-tallest completed building in Europe. Halabi's 50 per cent stake was half-funded by Irish Nationwide. His partners, Irvine Sellar and the Swedish group CLS, thought he had only a 25 per cent stake. There was a huge legal battle, ending with each taking a third after it emerged that Irish Nationwide had sold its 25 per cent to Halabi.

After Halabi's collapse Irish Nationwide ended up taking a legal action in Jersey to secure the repayment of £7 million (€8.4 million) from companies linked with Halabi. The action opened the way for Irish Nationwide to consider moving on Halabi's luxury holiday home development in the south of France, which was used to secure a

£2½ million (€3 million) loan. The society had advanced the money to a Jersey company called Stormex Holdings in 1997, court documents showed. As part of that deal Halabi and one of his Luxembourg companies provided guarantees.

The Luxembourg company, Immofra, owns the Château des Bois Murés development in Grasse, north of Cannes. Accounts for Immofra show that Irish Nationwide has a charge over it. At the end of 2009 it was listed as being worth almost 9 million Swiss francs (€7.4 million). Stormex Holdings is also linked to the French property.

UPSIDE-DOWN LENDING: UPDOWN COURT

When it comes to getting it spectacularly wrong, Updown Court is perhaps one of the most insane banking propositions for an Irish building society ever to have financed. Bought out of receivership in 2002, the unfinished mansion in Surrey cost its new owner, Leslie Allen-Vercoe, also known as Les Allen, approximately £20 million (€22.6 million). Allen met the head of British lending at Irish Nationwide, Gary McCollum, to tie up the deal. With the backing of Fingleton, who had to ratify major loans, the society bankrolled the project to the tune of about £40 million. Further loans and accrued interest meant that by the end of 2009 the society was owed about £61 million.

The project was simple and ridiculous at the same time. Allen planned to spend £20 million buying the place and another £30 million doing it up. He would then sell it to a billionaire buyer for £70 million. Irish Nationwide even had a profit-share deal with Allen on the proceeds. There was only one snag: there was no billionaire buyer.

The house went on the market in 2005. To avoid time-wasters, Allen had a leather-bound brochure printed that cost £500 to buy. Savills were hired to find a buyer. A tour of the house took two-and-a-half hours, and Savills were happy to arrange for prospective buyers to be driven to Updown Court in a Rolls-Royce or flown in by helicopter.

The house has 103 rooms, 22 bedrooms, 27 bathrooms, five swimming-pools, a heated marble driveway, a fifty-seat cinema, eleven acres of landscaped gardens, fifty acres of parkland, a double staircase modelled on Gianni Versace's mansion in Miami, and enough marble to satisfy Emperor Augustus, as one newspaper put it. The marble alone cost £6 million. 'If Elton John were a house, he would be Updown Court,' Allen told the *Evening Standard* in March 2005.

Allen is a larger-than-life character. He enjoyed the trappings of wealth and, not unlike Fingleton, was known for his love of expensive watches. He told the newspaper that he had forty-two British companies, flew in jet helicopters and used to have his own plane. He said his assets included forests in Russia, coal mines in Ukraine and land in Latvia. At the time he said he was a preferred bidder to buy Antwerp Airport.

The British press were curious to know how this relatively unknown businessman had ended up selling the country's most expensive house. The son of a bricklayer, Allen originally became an estate agent. He had been involved in a court case in 2002 because he wanted to build luxury houses on land in Chelsea that had been bequeathed to the local borough by the aristocratic Cadogan family solely for the purpose of providing housing for the working class. Lord Cadogan objected to Allen's plans. Allen argued that there was no definition of working class. 'Is it because you wear a flat cap? Is it because you earn less than so much a week? Is it because you speak with a funny accent?'

He was quite calm about the prospect of finding a buyer for Updown Court when the *Evening Standard* interviewed him, just as the £70 million folly went on the market. He arrived in a £100,000 Mercedes coupé (one of his six luxury cars) and wore 'a £12,000 Cartier gold watch.'

'My estate agents tell me it will be gone in six months,' he told the paper. 'We've already had interest from buyers from Russia and the Middle East. And three Chinese called to enquire this morning.'

But there were no takers. Accounts for the company behind the project, Updown Court Ltd, paint an interesting picture of how things went wrong. It was owned by Allen and his former associate John Anton, who died in 2004. The company had no real income and has never had any turnover. Its only real source outside funding came from Irish Nationwide loans. The company accounts disclose that the loans were secured on the property but were non-recourse to Les Allen. He was able to walk away from any losses.

Between 2003 and 2009 the property increased in value on foot of the directors' own valuation at cost, from £28 million to £60 million. Naturally the more money they pumped into it the more valuable they said it was. Auditors began qualifying the accounts in 2008, querying the lack of an independent valuation on the property. They noted that the directors said the cost of an independent valuation would outweigh the benefit.

At the end of 2005, the year it came on the market at £70 million, the company had £5 in the bank and the property on its books was valued at £45 million. As the value of the property kept going up on the balance sheet, so too did the amount of money owed to Irish Nationwide, which reached a peak of £61 million in 2009. Meanwhile Allen and his partners must have been working very hard to finish the project before 2005 and then find a buyer. Between 2003 and 2006 directors' remuneration totalled £1.2 million. Not all of it was received.

Another company owned by Allen, Rhymer Investments, borrowed a total of £1.4 million from Updown Court, of which nearly £800,000 was written off as unrecoverable in 2008. Rhymer also received management fees totalling £382,000. Anton, Allen and Allen's wife also received consultancy fees from Updown totalling £294,000, while two other Allen companies owed Updown £61,000, which was written off. Rhymer went into administration in 2009.

NAMA took over the Updown Court loans of approximately €70 million. The agency appointed a receiver, who eventually found a Middle Eastern buyer in 2011 for €40 million. The loss to the Irish taxpayer was approximately €30 million.

Chapter 8

TOO LATE FOR HALLELUYAH: FROM FAILED SALE TO STATE BAIL-OUT (JANUARY–NOVEMBER 2008)

Michael Fingleton mingled merrily with 150 members of Ireland's business and social elite. It was November 2007 and he was at a $2,300-a-plate fund-raising dinner for Hillary Clinton, who was then an American presidential hopeful.

The party was in the Ballsbridge mansion of the American lawyer Brian Farren and his wife, Linda O'Shea-Farren. Among the guests who paid for the pleasure of the company of Hillary Clinton and her husband, Bill, the former two-term President of the United States, were many of Fingleton's old pals and clients. They included Niall Mellon, builder turned philanthropist, one of his biggest clients; Arthur French, auctioneer and borrower; and Terence O'Rourke, managing partner of Irish Nationwide's auditors KPMG. Also there were the Glen Dimplex boss Martin Naughton, the broadcaster Gerry Ryan, the actor Vivienne Connolly and her then husband Mark Dunne (son of the tycoon Ben Dunne), and the glamorous Lisa Fitzpatrick and her hotelier husband, Paul.

Fingleton happily pressed the flesh with the Clintons, with whom he was acquainted from their visits to Ireland. In June 2005 records show that Fingleton handed over a cheque for €20,000 to the Clinton Foundation. The multi-millionaire boss then charged this to the building society as an expense.

Fingleton's attendance at the dinner demonstrates how he filled his days with distractions in 2007, one of the most important years in the history of the society. Only the previous month he had finally appointed Goldman Sachs, the giant global investment bank, to sell his beloved society. It should have been put on the market sooner, but the society was in such a mess that getting the necessary documents in order had taken longer than expected.

All that summer Irish Nationwide had entertained informal approaches from about a dozen potential bidders. These included Hypo Real Estate, an aggressive German lender; General Electric Money; the financier Derek Quinlan, in combination with Halifax Bank of Scotland; and Landsbanki, the Icelandic bank that was in the middle of a crazed buying spree. Bank of Ireland and Ulster Bank also took an initial look.

The problem was not that none of these bidders could be convinced to nibble: on the basis of the society's initial undetailed sales documents they were interested; but once it got to the stage of making a bid they had all pulled back. The global environment was rapidly changing, and the few potential bidders who began to look under the hood were scared off by what they saw.

Fingleton, Purcell and the board's years of ignoring the basics of banking were now acting against them. Nobody was prepared to buy the society for anything like the valuation of between €1½ and €2 billion that Fingleton placed on his toxic creation. He had fatally delayed in not putting the society up for sale sooner. By not doing this immediately the legislation was passed, in the summer of 2006, he had missed the boat.

'We might still have been able to sell Irish Nationwide for something,' a source close to the sale process said, 'but Fingleton wasn't prepared to even countenance a fire sale.' Despite no buyer emerging, he continued to act as if the society was on the brink of being sold.

————

During much of 2007 Fingleton spent his weekends relaxing at the K Club as well as enjoying trips abroad. His eyes were often off the ball. In November, Irish Nationwide spent €40,000 on sponsoring and launching the autobiography of the Kerry football legend Mick O'Dwyer, *Blessed and Obsessed*. O'Dwyer, then manager of the Wicklow team, told the *Sunday Independent* that Fingleton would be his choice as Minister for Finance, because he has 'done wonders for his members.' O'Dwyer launched his autobiography in the Burlington Hotel, where six hundred guests partied from 5 p.m. to midnight. The *Irish Independent* described the bash as being 'sponsored by Micko's VBF [very best friend], Michael Fingleton of Irish Nationwide.'

Fingleton's client and friend Arthur French, the estate agent, was in attendance, as was Seán FitzPatrick, then chairman of Anglo Irish Bank, and a former president of the GAA, Peter Quinn (brother of Seán Quinn, the billionaire tycoon). 'Michael Fingleton's speech was another *tour de force,*' the *Independent* reported, 'tracing the Waterville man's career, which everyone agrees makes him one of the greatest footballer managers the country has ever seen.'

In December, Fingleton again got out the society's chequebook, despite the worsening of the economic climate and there still being no sign of any potential buyer for the society. This time he decided to sponsor the production of an album in tribute to the Dubliners' singer Ronnie Drew, who was suffering from the throat cancer that would eventually kill him. This was another chance for Fingleton to associate himself with a good deed—using his members' money. The idea of making the record came from the editor of the *Sunday Independent,* Aengus Fanning, himself a talented musician. He had interviewed Drew about his illness and asked Fingleton to finance a new record to cheer him up. The society spent €25,000 on the record, called *The Last Session: A Fond Farewell,* which featured the jazz musician Hugh Buckley and Aengus Fanning on the clarinet together with Ronnie Drew. It was a kind deed, but even still Fingleton saw no need to pay for it himself but instead got his building society to do it.

As 2008 began, Goldman Sachs realised there was still no hope of selling the society as the world's economy teetered, and told Fingleton as much. Fingleton, however, remained hopeful that things would turn around once sense prevailed again in the international markets.

———

On 26 January 2008 Michael Fingleton stepped down from the board of his beloved building society. It was his seventieth birthday, and the society's rules decreed that nobody could stay on the board beyond that age.

Fingleton made no objection. He was staying on as chief executive, so the change was largely cosmetic. James Morrissey, Irish Nationwide's spokesperson, was quick to assure the *Sunday Tribune* that week that Fingleton would remain 'very involved,' despite his advancing age.

The society's board had now shrunk to a mere four people. Nothing was done to seek a new member to replace Fingleton, even though the society badly needed more banking expertise and someone capable of challenging the ageing boss. The chairman, Michael Walsh, let the opportunity slide. This meant that, as the society faced into the toughest year in its history, there was nobody on the board who had not been compromised by all the bad decisions made over many years.

Terry Cooney and Stan Purcell, who had acted as faithful yes-men to Fingleton for more than a decade, lacked either the financial skill or the strength of character that was needed in the months ahead.

David Brophy, who had joined the board in March 2006, was better qualified. At the time of his appointment he was an executive with Smurfit Kappa, the packaging company founded by Michael Smurfit. At the end of 2007 he went to work for Seán Mulryan's Ballymore Properties, one of the society's biggest clients and a partner of the society in a British property development joint venture. He continued to be a non-executive director of Irish Nationwide despite this conflict of interest. 'All financial institutions face situations where directors find themselves in potential conflicts of interest because of their personal business interests,' Irish Nationwide said. The Central Bank must have agreed, as it allowed Brophy to remain.

Brophy had financial ability, but, like Con Power, who he replaced after the latter's departure in February 2006, he was only a part-time non-executive director.

There were no new faces around the boardroom table who might have asked awkward questions as Irish Nationwide faced into the toughest year in its 135-year history. This would have consequences for the state. An uncompromised outsider might have taken a harsher view of the challenges facing the society and blown the whistle on some of the extraordinary things that happened that year.

2008 began quietly after a bad 2007 for Irish Nationwide, when it got caught up in the scandal of lending to the rogue solicitors Michael Lynn and Thomas Byrne, the embarrassment of former staff members suing the society, and the continuing war of attrition with Brendan Burgess. What was ahead could not be batted off by the right phone call, a word in an ear, delay or subterfuge.

A cataclysmic fall in confidence in world banking had been sparked by the American sub-prime mortgage crisis. Fingleton and other senior Irish bankers had insisted all through 2007 that Ireland was insulated from this crisis. 2008 would prove them wrong.

Irish bankers' claims that losses incurred from the reckless packaging of bad home loans to the poor in America by investment banks had nothing to do with them would be shown to be nonsense. In 2008 it became clear that sub-prime loans were going to blow massive holes in the balance sheets of America's biggest banks that would prove big enough to sink them.

In a world where banks were all interconnected through the international money markets, this had to have a knock-on effect on Ireland. Banks around the globe began to fail like dominoes, and Irish banking shares all began to fall. Global investors fretted about their exposure and sought safe havens for their deposits. The global money markets, which had sloshed with cash from France and Germany, dried up.

These were the steroids that had driven Irish property values ever higher. Suddenly, the Irish banks were racked with pain as their overseas drug-pushers ceased supplying them. Month by month, Irish property prices fell into a dizzying decline as the banks, cut off from their foreign suppliers, simply stopped lending.

On 17 March things came to a head when the shares of Bear Stearns, the American investment bank, collapsed. This caused what became known as the St Patrick's Day massacre in Ireland. The value of the Irish stock market fell by €3½ billion in a single day, and the shares of Anglo Irish Bank fell by 15 per cent. Anglo Irish's woes were worsened by the secret punting on its shares by the country's richest man, Seán Quinn. This made it especially vulnerable to being shorted by hedge funds in London and New York. From March onwards the Financial Regulator became preoccupied with trying to sort out the terminal connection between Anglo Irish and Quinn. It took its eye off Irish Nationwide as a result.

Irish Nationwide wasn't listed on the stock exchange, so it escaped the drama of a plunging share price. But away from the limelight, every day it had to battle to assure depositors that their money was safe. The society pointed to its big deposit book and its decent credit rating from international agencies as proof that it was in a strong position. But clever investors weren't convinced. They could see that the society had a big exposure to the Irish and British property markets, and as the year went on they became less enthusiastic about the society's fortunes.

At the same time the society's big developer clients, who had huge lumps of cash on deposit with the society, either on or offshore, came under strain. As they watched the share price of Anglo Irish, AIB, Bank of Ireland and Irish Life and Permanent shudder downwards, suddenly the society's top hundred developer clients became afraid. They began to think about how much they had borrowed just as their banks began to urgently ring them and ask them when they would be paying it back. Developers who had cash in Irish Nationwide, whether in Ireland, Britain or its overseas branch in the Isle of Man, began pulling their money out to pay their bills to other banks. Irish Nationwide's lax lending practices made it harder for the society to grab the developers' cash before their rivals. Money was leaking away, causing fissures in the society's balance sheet.

Irish Nationwide offered high interest rates on deposits to try to counteract this. It also had a much smaller balance sheet than its peers, so it was in less danger early in 2008. In addition the society had a residential mortgage book, which it could use to obtain liquidity from the European Central Bank. This was an option not open to its rival Anglo Irish, which was involved only in commercial lending, further ensuring that it was the most vulnerable card in the house of cards that was Irish banking.

But the fissures remained, and grew larger every week. Fingleton could see daily his life's work straining under the pressure of the international crisis. His underpaid managers struggled to stop the widening of the fault lines that Fingleton had created over many decades of greed and neglect by failing to invest in his staff. The society's boasts about its spending on staff versus income being at a record low ratio of 10 per cent acted against it when really skilled people were needed to hold things together. The decision to ignore warnings from KPMG in 2000 and again in 2005 that it needed to employ more experts in such areas as risk and treasury left it vulnerable when it needed all hands on deck.

Fingleton, who had begun his career when the society kept its documents in tin biscuit boxes and who still didn't use e-mail, did not fully recognise the danger. He insisted to all-comers that his society would survive the crisis.

His chairman, Michael Walsh, did not agree. Walsh was a banking expert who worked for the financier Dermot Desmond in his investment vehicle

International Investment and Underwriting. He had a much better grasp of the scale of what was going on and what it would mean for the society. He privately warned Fingleton that the society could be in real trouble. He began turning up in the society more often, and there was some friction between him and Fingleton, according to building society sources.

Stan Purcell remained steadfastly loyal to Fingleton but at the same time tried to help Walsh. The society was sinking.

Fingleton, however, still had confidence in his Frankenstein monster. He knew there was a lot of work ahead. Lending had stopped and he remained focused on trying to get more deposits by raising interest rates. The society spent heavily on advertising, plugging its latest offers.

Fingleton's concern about trying to keep money inside the society, however, did not extend to his own salary. Every week he was personally making very big money—a consolation prize for missing out on his ultimate pay-day from selling the society. Just how well he was doing was revealed in April 2008 when the society published its annual report. While ordinary staff members plodded away on pay below industry norms, among the small number at the top things were different. The report showed that Fingleton was paid €2.3 million in 2007—an increase of €477,000, or 26 per cent, as the society turned in pre-tax profits of €391 million. His basic salary was €812,000, but his board had approved a bonus of €1.4 million—a third higher than in 2006. This was a year in which Fingleton had failed to sell the society because nobody wanted it. But in the topsy-turvy world of Irish Nationwide this meant he was paid more, not less. A bonus of €1 million was approved by the society's remuneration committee for what it described as 'the excellent performance of the society in very difficult market circumstances.' An additional payment of €400,000 was also paid, which was not specifically explained although it was classified as a bonus. In total, Fingleton was paid €2.3 million for steering the society onto the rocks.

In the space of two years Fingleton's salary had doubled, under the approving eyes of his board. What the annual report didn't say was that Fingleton had quietly struck a deal with his board whereby, in order to stay on as chief executive in 2008, he would be paid at least as much as he was in 2007. This meant he believed that not only his salary but also his bonus of more than €1 million would be matched, come what may for Irish Nationwide. This decision by the board would prove a very controversial one in 2009.

There is no known evidence of any complaints at the top of the society about Fingleton's salary, or his lucrative new deal for staying on. But then, why would there be? In 2007 Stan Purcell was paid €486,000 (€80,000 more than the previous year), while the society stuffed €492,000 into his pension scheme. Meanwhile its wealthy chairman, Michael Walsh, who approved executive salaries on the remuneration committee, took home €100,430.

To put this in context: Fingleton was now being paid more than AIB's chief executive, Eugene Sheehy, who took home €2.1 million while running a much bigger bank, which made €2½ billion in 2007. It was still less, though, than David Drumm in Anglo Irish Bank, who, at €3.2 million, was paid most of all.

A statement by Irish Nationwide in its annual report for 2007, which was signed off on 10 March 2008 by Walsh, Cooney, Purcell and Fingleton, showed that the society was as delusional about its prospects and performance as it was about the value of its chief executive. 'We have built up a very strong balance sheet with the net book worth of the society now standing in excess of €1.5 billion. Because of the present uncertainty in the financial markets and the weakening economy it is as stated earlier the society's policy in 2008 to manage its affairs in a prudent and conservative risk adverse manner.'

This assertion that the society was acting in a 'prudent and conservative' way would come back to haunt all four signatories when it emerged that a series of extraordinary decisions was taken that year by the society.

Later that month there was more keeping up of appearances and claims that the society was fundamentally in good shape. Nonetheless, its AGM in April in the RDS was a boisterous affair. Among Fingleton's once well-wishers there was now considerable ingratitude. Twenty months had passed since the government had removed the last remaining legal obstacle to the 133-year-old society being sold, and members wanted to know when they would finally get their windfall. Elderly member after elderly member took the floor to ask Fingleton, who sat up at a high table flanked by his board, when they were going to get their windfall from the sale of the society.

Fingleton told the meeting that two potential buyers had jilted the society at the altar. He said the European arm of one potential buyer had been 'all for it.' A deal had been agreed in principle, only for its international board to shoot it down because a change in corporate strategy meant that 'everything was put on hold.' Another institution was 'very anxious to buy us' but 'they were obliged to merge with another major institution for other reasons, and that put an end to that.'

'We weren't slow off the blocks,' Fingleton insisted. 'We weren't wasting our time.' He said the society had got firm offers but they would not represent 'fair value' for its shareholders. 'We are not going to give the institution away.'

Casually, Fingleton reinforced his old mantra that only he could run the society, as both potential buyers, he told members, had insisted that he stay on for two years.

Although Fingleton and his members did not know it then, the society's boss and his deferential board, in an act of greed or stupidity, had let slide the last chance they would have to sell the toxic society. This would later prove to be the most expensive single missed opportunity in the history of the country.

Far from realising that the society might collapse, its members retained their bubble mentality of easy money. They complained to Fingleton that a delayed sale would allow yet more carpetbaggers to clamber on board. They called for Fingleton to make it harder for new depositors to become full members of the society, at a time when what the society needed was to get hold of every euro it could.

Fingleton tried to reassure them. He told reporters that his wife qualified for a windfall the previous year and hinted that she would be among the last. 'I don't want any more carpetbaggers coming in,' he said. At the same time he was wary of frightening new members away, so he made things ambiguous. 'What we're after is deposits. We will not turn down a deposit. We're open for business,' he said.

Walsh, however, presented a downbeat assessment of the outlook for the society, in contrast to his rosy statements over the previous seven years. He said it could be two years before the markets returned to normal and the society could be sold. 'We are continuing to work with our advisers to see if there is a way to realise value. We have to unfortunately balance that ambition with where the financial markets are at the current time.'

Fingleton remained more confident. He was not prepared to admit to being fallible. 'Markets will have to normalise, and two years might be a very long time. But one thing is sure: we are determined to effect a trade sale of Irish Nationwide at the earliest opportunity. We ain't hanging around.'

Pressed about whether he intended to remain in charge, for the first time Fingleton gave a hint that he was thinking of life beyond the society. 'I don't intend to stay there for ever. I have a finite life, and I intend to enjoy some of it.' He dismissed a suggestion from one member that he should stay on for another seventy years. 'The genes aren't that good,' he replied.

Walsh said he planned to appoint more members to the board now that a sale was off the table. He added that the society planned (too late in the day) to become conservative and that it did not plan to grow its loan book that year. 'We are not out there looking for market share,' he said. He told the members that the society's liquidity had remained unchanged since the end of the previous year. Deposits accounted for 63 per cent of loans at 31 March 2008, compared with 59 per cent at the end of the previous year.

Only the pugnacious Brendan Burgess caused Fingleton to lose his cool as he provoked him from the floor. He harangued Fingleton for his treatment of borrowers. He said the society had levied interest of up to 20 per cent and tried to repossess people's homes in the past, and the board of the society must 'take him [Fingleton] off the backs of borrowers.' He did acknowledge, however, in his mini-speech that Fingleton seemed to have a 'great nose' for mega-property deals, while he was 'not good at looking after people in trouble.' The plucky borrowers' champion simply didn't see that the real problem facing the society was not Fingleton's bullying of the little guy but the big guys who owed it vast sums.

'Did you or did you not serve as chairman of the consumer advisory group?' Fingleton barked in response to Burgess.

After Fingleton repeated the question a second time, Burgess quipped, 'Do you play golf?'

When Burgess finally admitted that for two years he had chaired the consumer advisory panel set up by the Central Bank, Fingleton rounded on him. 'I didn't hear you on other institutions who came in offering sub-prime loans.' Fingleton's sense of being persecuted unfairly yet again revealed itself.

Walsh, as usual, could be relied on to defend Fingleton publicly, even if behind the scenes he may have had his doubts. He said that Irish Nationwide had changed its rules and no longer imposed penalty rates on borrowers who got stuck in arrears.

Burgess said this was only for those with home loans and did not apply to 'other loans.' Eventually the drama fizzled out.

Fingleton glided from the hall. It was his last AGM.

Just as Fingleton's reign was coming to an end, so too was Bertie Ahern's as Taoiseach. Ahern's reputation was in the process of being destroyed by tribunal investigations into his financial affairs. More importantly, however, it was also becoming clearer that he had blown the profits of the boom by allowing public expenditure to run out of control. Ireland didn't have much in the tank, despite collecting huge sums in taxes over the previous decade.

Wednesday 7 May 2008 was Ahern's last day as head of the government. He dashed from the Dáil to attend the INBS-*Sunday Independent* Irish International Cricketer of the Year awards. It was a measure of the *Sunday Independent*'s success and influence under its brilliant commercial editor, Aengus Fanning, that Ahern was prepared to travel to the awards in the National Yacht Club in Dún Laoghaire on his final day as the country's second-longest-serving Taoiseach and second-longest-serving leader of Fianna Fáil.

He was greeted warmly at the soirée, at which the attendance included Senator Eugene Regan, Ulick O'Connor and George Hook and which was paid for by Irish Nationwide. The *Sunday Independent* reported that weekend: 'Michael Fingleton, chief executive of the awards' sponsors the Irish Nationwide Building Society, was in good voice and said Bertie Ahern was the best Taoiseach the country has had and predicted that he would continue to hit his critics for six.'

By the summer of 2008 Fingleton hoped to have pocketed millions from flogging his society and to be spending more time making himself even richer by working on his plan to build a holiday resort in Montenegro. He had also hoped to spend more time on holidays. 'Barbados, Marbella, Portugal were among his favourite spots,' an old friend said. 'He was very sociable, and liked the sunshine.'

Fingleton usually holidayed with his wife, but he also liked spending time with a select group of his business buddies. The tensions between Fingleton and his wife over his relationship with Fiona Couse seemed to have melted away. 'He told me at the time it was very rough for her,' an old friend recalled, 'but "She'll get over it" was his attitude.'

Now Fingleton realised that his dreams of an easier life seemed unlikely. It was going to be some time yet before he was able to retire.

At the same time he was worried about his personal fortune. He had investments in land banks with Gerry Gannon, the developer, and

Francie O'Brien, the former Fianna Fáil senator. These were now looking rocky. He had other investments too in various corners that he was worried about. Worst of all, though, was his €27 million pension from the society. He had ploughed most of into Irish and British banking shares. These too were tumbling, but Fingleton felt sure they would recover in time once the market saw sense. As far as he was concerned, Fingleton was still rich.

———

As the summer ended Fingleton was back firmly in his creased green leather chair on the top floor of the society's head office. At all times he could see through his window the Central Bank as he schemed and plotted how the society and his favourite customers might escape.

The situation was dire, and while Fingleton didn't fully recognise it, Walsh did. Late in the day he finally began to use his expertise as best he could. The society faced a series of big cash calls that needed to be repaid, and Walsh feared it might not be able to meet every one of them with the credit market in complete lock-down as investors worried that one of Wall Street's big investment banks might fail. The writing was on the wall for the society, and each week made things harder, but Fingleton remained in denial. Then things really got bad.

On 4 September, Moody's credit rating agency sharply downgraded Irish Nationwide's long-term bank deposit grading, from AAA to BAAA1. Essentially this meant that one of the world's top three rating agencies no longer considered the society a safe haven with a high investment grade.

The main reason given by Moody's for saying the society was now riskier was that 80 per cent of its loan book was in commercial property and development in Ireland and Britain, where there was a 'rapid deterioration' in land and property values. The society, Moody's concluded, was 'weakly placed' and 'on review for further downgrades.' In fact it hinted that it might have downgraded the society more only it believed that the 'probability of systemic support for INBS in the event of a financial crisis is moderate.'

The downgrade caused a minor shock wave for the government, already hugely concerned as Ireland's listed banks daily hit new lows. Michael Manley, a senior official of the Department of Finance, prepared a memo on the situation for his minister, Brian Lenihan, which was stamped 'top secret.' He said that the downgrade would make it more expensive for the society to fund itself and would cause corporate deposits to be withdrawn from it, especially in its Isle of Man subsidiary. Irish Nationwide, Manley said, expected that €200 million at least would be taken out. (This would turn out to a very optimistic expectation.)

In a handwritten note on the secret memo, William Beausang, an assistant secretary of the department who worked tirelessly during the crisis, addressed Lenihan directly. 'Minister this is not good news for INBS and while INBS is currently financially stable with high levels of liquid assets, there is clear potential for future difficulties if further downgrades materialise.'

In the fevered climate of the time, Irish Nationwide was facing a run against its deposits. That Friday, 5 September, at 6:15 p.m. things got dramatically worse. Reuters, one of the world's most credible news agencies, reported that Irish Nationwide was in serious trouble. The society, it said, was 'in talks with its lenders to avoid insolvency.' The story was published without a comment from the society, which first heard about it when an eagle-eyed journalist from the Irish edition of the *Sunday Times* rang its spokesperson, James Morrissey.

The Financial Regulator was also caught on the hop; but within an hour its press office was ringing around to tell journalists that the story was without foundation.

At 8:31 p.m. the story reappeared updated on the wires. This time it included a strong denial from Irish Nationwide. At 10:45 p.m. the story was removed from the Reuters system and replaced with a retraction, and an admission that there would be no substitute story.

Irish Nationwide had forced Reuters into an embarrassing climb-down. Michael Fingleton had managed to gag the biggest news organisation in the world

The same night Ronald Quinlan, a reporter with the *Sunday Independent*, confronted the Taoiseach, Brian Cowen, immediately after his broadcast on the Late Late Show, which was taking place in the new Wexford Opera House. Cowen had just told the presenter, Pat Kenny, his reasoning for hastily bringing forward the government's budget to 14 October. The budget, he said, would be 'about sending a signal to the country that we are in a new set of circumstances. There is no doubt about that. The deceleration is happening much faster than anyone ever expected. We must take whatever steps are necessary now so that we can get back to the good times as soon as possible.'

Cowen also resisted pressure from developers, the banks and some quarters of the media to cut stamp duty on house sales in the mad expectation that this would get the property market moving again. 'We are not going to tinker around with the market. There is a correction taking place in the residential housing market. The problem is that with houses becoming more affordable people can't get access to credit. That is the issue. It is really a question of trying to tackle that issue.'

It was too little too late for Cowen. Despite the Irish Nationwide story sending business news desks into a tizzy, Cowen wasn't questioned by Kenny on the matter. Ronald Quinlan was determined to as he approached the Taoiseach.

Cowen reacted angrily to his line of questioning. To even ask whether an Irish bank could be in trouble seemed an affront. He said he was unaware of the story that was causing so much trouble for the society.

As I said to you now, I don't know anything about it, so there's no point in pursuing it when I don't know anything about it, and I've said that the company says there is no basis to it, so I really don't think that it's helpful for me to talk off the top of my head when I don't know anything about it. That's only fair, isn't it?

Pressed further, he added:

Rumours and unfounded rumours are not good at all. They shouldn't happen. So, I think it's important for me not to speculate on the basis that what you say appears to be a rumour. I don't want to add to it whatever because I don't think it'd be very sensible.

The Irish banking system is well capitalised. There has been no indication whatever that there is any difficulty there. The financial soundness of the banks is not in question. There is always dialogue there to make sure that we know exactly what the position is.

I think the point has been made by the regulator and the Central Bank in their various reports, that the Irish banking system is well capitalised.

The following day Lenihan also defended the society. He told 'Saturday View' on RTE radio that he believed Irish Nationwide was fine. He dismissed the claim by David McWilliams that the banks had pursued 'explicit and delinquent policies' by lending money to 'people who couldn't afford the houses they bought.' Lenihan replied:

> I don't accept this, and I think this is very dangerous. The Central Bank chairman gave evidence to a parliamentary committee this summer and clearly indicated that stress-testing had been done on all the Irish banks and there was no danger at all.
>
> Irish banks are not exposed to the sub-prime problem which US banks are exposed to. There is exposure in the Irish banks, but they made it clear they can accommodate it. The analysts of the different firms that look at bank shares and bank performances have said the Irish banks can weather this crisis.

While Lenihan was on air, Quinlan wrote his story, kicking off with Cowen's angry reaction. He submitted the article to his editor, Aengus Fanning, who was in phone contact with Fingleton, who assured his friend that he had been the victim of unprofessional conduct by Reuters. Fingleton was incandescent.

Fanning burst out of his office after talking to Fingleton, convinced that the failure of Reuters was the real story and not Cowen's angry reaction. The following day the *Sunday Independent* led with Fingleton's reaction, complete with a smiling picture of him posing in a yellow jumper. Cowen's telling response was relegated to half way down the article.

'This was the most irresponsible piece of financial journalism that I have experienced in my 35 years at the Irish Nationwide,' Fingleton told the *Sunday Independent*. He lashed out at the 'perpetrators' of the 'totally malicious' Reuters story, describing their actions as an 'attempt to sabotage' the building society.

> The story was irresponsible, false and untrue, and Reuters have accepted that. They have admitted to their subscribers around the world that 'material elements are incorrect' in the story and that it 'contained false information.'
>
> In the present highly sensitive economic, financial and commercial climate, the putting out of such statements is tantamount to commercial sabotage by people who are trying to undermine Irish Nationwide Building Society.

> We emphasise that the Irish Nationwide was, is, and continues
> to be a strong, profitable financial institution with record levels
> of capital and liquidity, both of which are essential in the present
> climate. We are rock solid.

The deputy leader of Fine Gael, Richard Bruton, had a more insightful
response.

> Confidence is the core of banking, and that has to be protected. We
> have to make sure that the confidence that is expressed in our banking
> system by the Central Bank is firmly based.
>
> I think it would behove the minister to look hard at these stress-
> testing models to see if they are robust enough to pick up any
> difficulties in a timely way so that we can anticipate them.

The Reuters story, while inaccurate, was not entirely untrue. At the highest
levels of the state there were real fears about Irish Nationwide's future if
it continued to be downgraded by the rating agencies. The question of
how to respond if it failed was being looked at. While Cowen, Lenihan
and Fingleton reassured the nation, behind the scenes the Financial
Regulator's office was looking at its options. That weekend the heads
of the country's main banks were contacted about Irish Nationwide.
The regulator feared a big run on Irish Nationwide's deposits when
it opened that Monday morning, which might spread to other banks,
already under pressure. The remedies discussed included preparing a
contingency plan for AIB and Bank of Ireland to pump in several billion
in deposits to bolster the society. This was rejected by the two banks:
they had no appetite for being dragged into Irish Nationwide's morass.
The talks ended inconclusively, with no contingency plan adopted.

Events internationally, however, moved in the society's favour. That
same momentous weekend the US Treasury was forced to step in to
rescue the Federal National Mortgage Association (FNMA, or 'Fannie
Mae') and the Federal Home Loan Mortgage Corporation (FHLMC, or
'Freddie Mac').

While all this was going on that Sunday morning, an article by David
McWilliams in the *Sunday Business Post* raised the possibility of the state
guaranteeing Ireland's banks. Though McWilliams says the article was
entirely his own idea, it was not inconsistent with views expressed by a

Biafran soldiers with rifles aboard army tugs during the Nigerian civil war (1967–70). Michael Fingleton, while never based in Biafra during the war, managed to play a part in the relief effort as well as helping with existing good works in Nigeria through his involvement with first the Church and then the Irish charity Concern (© *Getty Images*)

Fingleton wanted to make a bold statement for his growing building society by buying this prominent building beside O'Connell Bridge, Dublin, as the society's head office. Fingleton's office was renowned for hosting Christmas parties for journalists. (© *Alamy*)

Michael Fingleton and Michael Walsh, pictured in 2002 not long after Walsh had become chairman of Irish Nationwide. Walsh was a staunch defender of the society's plunge into commercial property lending and denied any suggestions from the Central Bank that the society was 'taking a punt' with its loans. (© *Irish Times*)

The property developer Gerry Gannon, a close associate of Michael Fingleton for several years, went into business with the society through a joint venture. Fingleton later sued Gannon, claiming a share of profits from a separate development in Co. Dublin in which Fingleton claimed they were both investors. (© *Photocall Ireland*)

Seán Mulryan's Ballymore group of companies became the biggest borrower from Irish Nationwide. The society bankrolled numerous developments by Ballymore in London. In 2010 it made a provision of €103 million against loans of €163 million owed by a Ballymore company, Clearstorm Ltd. (© *Rex Features*)

Irish Nationwide lent the money for building the most expensive house in Britain.
By 2009 the society was owed €72 million on the lavish house, which included 103
rooms, 22 bedrooms, 27 bathrooms, five swimming pools, a heated marble driveway,
a fifty-seat cinema, eleven acres of landscaped gardens, fifty acres of parkland, a
double staircase modelled on Gianni Versace's mansion in Miami, and enough
marble to satisfy the Emperor Augustus, as one newspaper put it. The marble alone
cost £6 million. NAMA bought the loans and put the property into receivership. It was
sold in 2011 for €40 million, a loss to the Irish taxpayer of approximately €32 million.
(© *Rex Features*)

The €50 million luxury yacht *Christina O* was bought and renovated in 2000 by a partnership of investors registered in the Cook Islands. It included the Irish trucking magnate Pino Harris. Irish Nationwide provided some of the funding, and Fingleton enjoyed the good life on board on a number of occasions, including the wedding of the developer Seán Dunne. (© *Getty Images*)

At the races: The developer Seán Dunne and his wife, Gayle Killilea, chat with the Taoiseach, Bertie Ahern, in April 2008 while attending the Punchestown National Hunt Festival. Dunne was a major borrower from Irish Nationwide, which had to write down a €38 million loan facility to Dunne on a site in Co. Kildare to €5 million. (© *Photocall Ireland*)

Patrick Neary was appointed Financial Regulator in late 2005. Previously he was head of banking supervision. Neary had concerns about Irish Nationwide but did not take effective action to force the society to change direction. (© *Photocall Ireland*)

The Taoiseach, Bertie Ahern, and Minister for Finance, Charlie McCreevy, during the 2002 general election campaign. McCreevy was a supporter of legislating for the demutualisation of Irish Nationwide in the late 1990s but did not deliver on it while in office. The records show that McCreevy borrowed €1.6 million from Irish Nationwide to buy a house at the K Club in 2006, two years after ceasing to be Minister for Finance. (© *Photocall Ireland*)

The chairman and chief executive of Anglo-Irish Bank, Seán FitzPatrick (*right*), with its chief executive, David Drumm, pictured in February 2008 at their last AGM in charge of the bank. Later that year they were both forced to resign when details of the extent of their personal loans with the bank emerged. FitzPatrick had 'warehoused' loans totalling €87 million with Irish Nationwide over several years. (© *Photocall Ireland*)

Michael Fingleton with the veteran chairman of Irish Nationwide, Peter D. O'Connor. O'Connor retired as chairman in 2001. He had taken over the role from his father, Peter O'Connor. (© *Irish Times*)

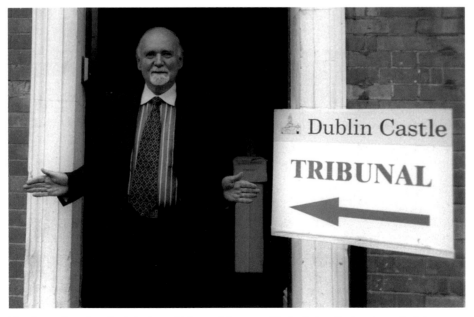

Fingleton leaving the Moriarty Tribunal in 2001. He had the distinction of giving evidence at both the Mahon and the Moriarty Tribunal. He told the tribunal he could not direct employees of the society's bank in the Isle of Man to come to Dublin and give evidence. Judge Moriarty expressed his disappointment that the subsidiary would not co-operate fully with the tribunal. (© *Photocall Ireland*)

Fingleton stands proudly over the financial results for 2003, which showed that lending had gone through the roof. He was by then rapidly increasing the society's exposure to property developers. (© *Photocall Ireland*)

Irish Nationwide financed the purchase of the K Club by Michael Smurfit and Gerry Gannon in 2005 for €115 million. When Gannon ran into financial difficulties, NAMA sold the luxury venue to Michael Smurfit. (© *Collins Agency*)

Hotel Fjord at Kotor, Montenegro: Fingleton invested more than €5 million of his own money into buying the derelict hotel on the Montenegrin coast. He and his business partner Louis Maguire planned to build a luxury hotel and resort on the site. After they had sunk millions into the project, the Montenegrin property bubble burst and the development never happened.

The small borrowers' advocate Brendan Burgess addresses the 2006 annual general meeting, at which he sharply criticised the board of the society. At the top table the secretary and chief financial officer, Stan Purcell, Michael Fingleton and the chairman, Michael Walsh, show little sign of engagement with the issues being raised. (© *Photocall Ireland*)

Con Power joined the board of Irish Nationwide in 2001. He clashed with Michael Fingleton on a number of issues, including the treatment of small borrowers who got into arrears. He also worked to get the legislation permitting demutualisation introduced, which eventually came in 2006. (© *Photocall Ireland*)

David Brophy (*left*) was a senior executive in the Smurfit Kappa Group. After being appointed a non-executive director of Irish Nationwide he joined Seán Mulryan's (*right*) Ballymore Group. He ended up on the board of Irish Nationwide while also a senior executive in a group owned by the society's biggest borrower. (© *Irish Times*)

Irish Nationwide lent more than €150 million for the redevelopment of the Kilternan Hotel in Co. Dublin. A brainchild of the publican Hugh O'Regan, the project ran out of money before it was completed. A receiver was appointed, and the unfinished building was placed on the market. (© *Collins Agency*)

The chief executive of the Irish Bank Reconciliation Corporation, Mike Aynsley, took control of the remnants of Irish Nationwide when the former building society was merged with the new agency. Aynsley immediately became active in seeking the return of Michael Fingleton's €1 million bonus and a retirement gold watch. He also initiated legal proceedings against Fingleton and several other former members of Irish Nationwide's board. (© *Photocall Ireland*)

Fingleton believed he had been offered a deal by the former Taoiseach Brian Cowen regarding the voluntary return of his controversial €1 million bonus to the society in 2009. (© *Photocall Ireland*)

Brian Lenihan pushed the former chairman of Irish Nationwide, Danny Kitchen, to seek the return of a controversial €1 million bonus received by Fingleton. Lenihan later asked one senior executive of the society, shortly before he left office because of his terminal illness, 'Do you think we will ever get Michael Fingleton?' (© *Photocall Ireland*)

Gerry McGinn took over as chief executive of Irish Nationwide a few months after Fingleton's departure. A career banker and Northern Ireland public servant, McGinn and the new board hired Ernst and Young and the legal firm McCann Fitzgerald to conduct a review of corporate governance at the society over several years to get to the bottom of how the society was run. The reports have never been published. (© *Photocall Ireland*)

John McGloughlin became chief financial officer of Irish Nationwide after it was nationalised. He remained with the society through the transfer to the IBRC and remains its most senior executive. (© *Photocall Ireland*)

number of banking and wealthy business insiders about how to get the country to rescue the bust banks. Whether there was an orchestrated campaign from bankers and business people remains unclear; what is certain is that a number of prominent business people, who were also supporters or clients of either Anglo Irish or Irish Nationwide, reached the same conclusion at the same time: the state would have to put its weight behind all Ireland's banks. McWilliams's article would act as a rallying-cry in the days ahead as Ireland's banking system approached the brink of collapse.

America's show of strength in bailing out its two biggest sub-prime mortgage lenders ensured that, when Monday morning came, stock markets rallied. A big run on Irish Nationwide failed to materialise, and the society limped on.

The Financial Regulator, however, was still very concerned about the society. Anglo Irish Bank was under even more pressure and was its great priority, as it had a balance sheet of €101 billion, as against Irish Nationwide's €16 billion. Unknown to Fingleton, the Financial Regulator, Patrick Neary, rang David Drumm, chief executive of Anglo Irish, asking to meet him to discuss the building society. 'What Neary said was, Would we look at Irish Nationwide,' Seán FitzPatrick, chairman of Anglo Irish, said in interviews for a book about his life and Anglo Irish, *The FitzPatrick Tapes*, by Tom Lyons and Brian Carey, published in 2011.

He said, We asked AIB and Bank of Ireland to do something but [they] wouldn't. David said, Yeah, maybe, and he came back and he talked to me about it. I sort of said maybe what we should do here is, this could be a great chance for us here of actually getting the government to back us.

So what we should say is, Lookit, we will do it. We will take over the loan management of the loans. We are in a much better position.

And Michael Walsh wanted us to do it as well. Michael Walsh saw us as the obvious people to do it because we had a better knowledge of their loan book than anybody else and we wouldn't be as scared of it and therefore wouldn't write off as much and more importantly we would be able to handle it.

On the other hand the negative about that was that you were going to actually get a concentration of loan borrowers—not all borrowers but for instance Seán Mulryan, a big one of ours, was a big one of his.

Michael Walsh was quite keen. He spoke to David on a few occasions.

Michael Fingleton wasn't part of the discussions. There was tension between Michael and Michael Walsh. Michael controlled the whole thing and Michael Walsh was trying to [come up with a solution].

This was done behind Fingleton's back.

As these talks went back and forth, the credit market continued its vice-like tightening. Drumm told FitzPatrick to meet Lenihan to discuss the possibility of Irish Nationwide merging with Anglo Irish. They met in Lenihan's private office in Merrion Street. It was the first time the two men had met. Kevin Cardiff, the civil servant in charge of banking, was also in attendance.

'Basically what they were talking about was Anglo,' FitzPatrick said. 'It was a lead on the whole issue of Irish Nationwide. I spoke to him about that but I didn't really speak to him.'

Lenihan was preoccupied and kept getting up to take phone calls. FitzPatrick thought he would have encouraged a merger, as it was Neary's idea, but no dice. 'He wasn't really interested,' FitzPatrick said.

Lenihan seemed to know that bolting two wrecks together wouldn't solve anything. He had more to think about than the views of Seán FitzPatrick. Irish banking was falling apart, and he knew that it was almost inevitable that Irish Nationwide would continue to be downgraded. He became anxious to get his own eyes and ears at the society's boardroom table, someone he could trust to tell him what was going on.

On 10 September the society announced that it had beefed up its flimsy board with the appointment of Seán Carey, a former assistant city manager of Dublin, as a non-executive director. Carey was hardly a banking heavy-hitter but he knew something about finance from his days with Dublin City Council, and was uncompromised, unlike others who had been on the board for too long. This happened the same day that Fitch, another rating agency, followed Moody's and downgraded Irish Nationwide, moving it from A– to BBB+ or seven levels below its former AAA rating, the highest level. Fitch welcomed the appointment of Carey as a step towards strengthening the society's corporate governance but also fretted about its huge exposure to commercial and residential property.

Irish Nationwide knew better, of course, than either Fitch or Moody's. Responding to its downgrading, it said it 'fundamentally disagrees' with both and that their views did 'not reflect the underlying financial strength of the society. It is important to emphasise that the society is and continues to be a strong, profitable financial institution and that profit budgeting projections are on target for the first half of 2008.'

The society said it had made a profit of €391 million in 2007 and expected to have earnings in 2008 that would again be greater than the EBS, First Active, ACC and National Irish Bank combined.

Fitch wasn't as convinced of the society's brilliance. It noted that it had billions to refinance over the coming fifteen months. 'The increasing cost of funding, together with reduced revenue from lower volumes of business, has begun to impact profitability,' it said, 'although, currently, performance ratios remain strong.'

Within days, Irish Nationwide's views of its own prospects would be shown to be woefully out of touch with the emerging harsh reality for banks around the world.

On 15 September the crisis reached a new apex: Lehman Brothers fell. It was the biggest bankruptcy in American history, as the investment bank had assets of $600 billion. Suddenly it was clear that nobody was too big to fail—not least a small building society on an island on the edge of Europe. Anglo Irish was in even worse straits as depositors withdrew billions from their accounts. While other banks were not that far behind, Anglo Irish knew it could topple in days. Its treasury department was besieged with phone calls as investors tried to get their money out.

Anglo Irish now urgently needed to take over Irish Nationwide, but with some form of state support, which would show the market that not only was Anglo Irish able to do deals but that Ireland was in some way behind it. It wanted the state to give them a guarantee that it would pick up future losses related to the building society. It also knew that getting access to the society's billions in deposits and residential mortgages (which could be used to obtain liquidity from the European Central Bank) would put it in a position to survive longer. As FitzPatrick explained,

> the advantage was that here was a company or a bank that was falling, and who did the Irish government give it to? Not another bank that was going to fall but a bank who they think a lot of.

That was what was in it for us, that it would state that we were beyond it. We were saying that if Irish Nationwide fell someone has got to pick it up because if it falls someone else will fail.

We didn't see it as an opportunity to create more profitability but we did see it as an opportunity to eventually paint a picture of ourselves in the eyes of the new world of aiding and abetting the state with a weak institution.

On 16 September the US government seized control of American International Group in an $85 billion deal that showed how fearful the world's biggest economy was that its financial system could be about to collapse.

That night David McWilliams appeared on 'Prime Time' and warned that Ireland's banks were going to go bust. In response, the Irish Banking Federation accused him of 'loose talk.' Driving home that night, McWilliams rang Lenihan to tell him of his fears.

The following morning, 17 September, the *Irish Times* had an article by Noel Smyth, a major client of both Anglo Irish and Irish Nationwide, apparently off his own bat.

If the Government was to persuade the Central Bank to guarantee all deposits in Irish banks operating under a banking licence from the Central Bank in the State, the effect would ensure that depositors considering investing in Ireland would know they had a State guarantee and that the banks would always ensure their money was repaid.

A guarantee must always be unequivocal.

None of our banks in Ireland are in the remotest area of trouble or of any concern. So surely now is the time to step in and confirm that all deposits made in our banks are fully guaranteed.

Smyth did not disclose in his article that he owed hundreds of millions to Anglo Irish and Irish Nationwide.

Under Irish law, deposit-holders were ranked equally with senior bond-holders. If the state fully backed deposit-holders it would have to do the same for senior bond-holders, the highest class of bond-holders, at the very least.

McWilliams too had an article that morning, this time in the *Irish Independent*. 'Put simply, we are looking into the precipice. However, there is a solution. The first should be a shotgun marriage between two of our banks.' This might see either AIB or Bank of Ireland 'take over one of the smaller banks,' a reference to either Anglo Irish or Irish Nationwide, or both.

This marriage should be forced by the Central Bank to save the system.

The Central Bank should also look at selling one of the country's bigger banks too if necessary.

At the moment, the banks are playing chicken with the market, pretending that they don't need to go to the Central Bank for money.

If we don't see these moves quickly, there will be serious trouble. It is highly likely that a bank will go bust and the entire financial system could come crashing down. Let's not wait for this. Let's not repeat the mistakes of our Irish American cousins. We can act now and do it decisively.

After they had read these articles over their morning coffee, it was further hammered home to bankers and the state that the crisis was much closer to home than America.

Late that Wednesday it was announced that Lloyds Bank was dramatically taking over Halifax Bank of Scotland—the parent company of Bank of Scotland (Ireland)—in a £12 billion merger. Bank of Scotland (Ireland) had been among Irish Nationwide's fiercest competitors in paying ridiculous prices for land banks around the country.

In that momentous week, titans of international banking fell. Would an Irish bank or building society be next? Lenihan was on a knife edge. He was being besieged with different messages from bankers, regulators, civil servants and business people and didn't know who to trust. That night at 10:20 p.m. he turned up at McWilliams's door to seek his advice. In his book *Follow the Money*, McWilliams said he 'looked exhausted. He had been working day and night and he was trying to understand everything.'

The Department of Finance, McWilliams wrote, was then looking at getting AIB and Bank of Ireland to take over both Irish Nationwide and Anglo Irish. AIB, however, the country's biggest bank, was Lenihan's biggest fear, as it was then facing huge funding difficulties. McWilliams told Lenihan that things were now so bad that he needed to guarantee not only deposit-holders but also the banks' main source of funding: the bond-holders.

He was worried that this guarantee idea was too radical. And I could understand this because he was the man who had to make the decision, not me.

I told him he simply had to guarantee everything for a limited period to make sure that an illiquid dilemma didn't lead to an insolvency catastrophe.

But, he argued, warming to the idea, what if we got the insolvencies? We could never afford to cover all the liabilities.

This was the risk, a huge risk, but one that could be reduced if the guarantee was not extended beyond a fixed period.

I argued that over the two years of the guarantee, the true extent of the bad debts would become apparent as would the depth of the recession and, armed with this knowledge, he could then choose which banks to save, or not, in an orderly fashion.

The key to McWilliams's idea, however, which had been used in other countries, was that any guarantee should be temporary. Sadly, this is not what later occurred.

Events continued to accelerate. On 18 September, Fingleton met the secretary-general of the Department of Finance, David Doyle. The meeting was acrimonious, as Fingleton despised Doyle. He insisted that the society was in good shape, but Doyle was sceptical.

Later that day the office of the Financial Regulator announced that it was banning the short-selling of banks from midnight. The move was of great advantage to Anglo Irish and the other listed banks.

That night Tony Garry, head of Davy Stockbrokers, the largest firm in the business and stockbroker for Anglo Irish at the time, met David Doyle. 'It was a private conversation between myself, David and one of my colleagues,' Garry told Tom Lyons in the *Sunday Independent* in 2012. However, sources told Lyons that the economic crisis was the subject of the conversation and that the prospect of a guarantee was mentioned, among a range of solutions. No notes appear to have been kept of this meeting.

The following day Fingleton wrote to Doyle to repeat what he had told him the day before. A 'realistic provision' for Irish Nationwide's future losses, he said, would be only between '€60m and €100m.' The society, he claimed, was 'a very profitable and viable institution.' Nothing had fundamentally changed, he insisted, and the society 'can deliver above-average profits on an ongoing basis subject to us resolving the short-term liquidity problem.' Irish Nationwide would make a pre-tax profit of between €150 and €175 million in 2008. Not a penny would be lost on its €1 billion European commercial loan book, while its €3½ billion British loan book was a 'very robust and good quality book where the borrowers are extremely successful and professional.' Only 'a small number' of transactions in its €2.9 billion Irish commercial loan book would lose any money, as 'the body of the book is sound.' This letter, Fingleton said, was written to ensure that 'you did not leave yesterday with the impression that we envisaged any serious problems with our book on an ongoing basis.' The letter was also circulated to the Financial Regulator, Patrick Neary.

Everything in the letter would be shown to be entirely wrong, the only real question being whether Fingleton knowingly lied or was merely blind to the fallibility of his creation.

On the same day the *Irish Times* got wind of the moves by Anglo Irish to take on Irish Nationwide. In a front-page story, which Fingleton was convinced had been placed by Anglo Irish, it said there had been talks over the previous ten days about a merger. Combined with the ban on short-selling, the news caused Anglo Irish's share price to rally strongly. Fingleton, however, was furious, as he believed the bank was using his society for its own ends.

He was right. Ireland's banks were battling for survival. They were prepared to play dirty against each other in order to survive.

At about the same time that the *Irish Times* story was published, Anglo Irish became aware that the government had asked Goldman Sachs, the world's biggest investment bank, to give it its views on Irish Nationwide. Goldman Sachs had advised the society when Fingleton was trying to flog it. It was familiar with its balance sheet and its problems, so in some ways the government asking it for help made sense. In other ways it didn't. Goldman Sachs had been prepared to value the society at over €1½ billion less than twelve months previously, so it was not ideally placed to give an independent assessment.

Anglo Irish, however, didn't know what Goldman Sachs was going to report. It was anxious that if the investment bank was too negative this would read badly for Anglo Irish, as it had a similar loan book, only ten times the size. Drumm told FitzPatrick to ring Peter Sutherland, his pal from UCD, a former member of the European Commission and now chairman of Goldman Sachs International. FitzPatrick describes the call as a 'soft chat.'

'I sort of said, Where are the guys in Goldman Sachs going with this [review of Irish Nationwide]? We were trying to ensure that we were going to get a fair crack of the whip from them.' Whether Sutherland expressed FitzPatrick's views to the Goldman Sachs management is not known. Events, however, were now moving downwards for Irish Nationwide.

On Friday 19 September, after the *Irish Times* article appeared, Tom Lyons of the *Sunday Times* submitted a series of questions to the society, asking how it could possibly pay its bond-holders as the year went on. His questions were based on a presentation the society had given to bond-holders. According to this presentation, the society needed to go to the capital markets to fund €1.5 billion of the €2.3 billion in scheduled loan repayments due the following year. The largest tranche of these, €1 billion, was due in May 2009.

The bank told investors in June that €800 million would be funded from its existing deposits. That December it was required to pay back another €634 million to bond-holders. 'This would not be a problem for Irish Nationwide in normal circumstances,' a capital-markets source told Lyons, 'but with global capital markets in lock-down this is a tremendous challenge.'

Lyons's questions essentially related to what the society would do if the markets did not unlock. The questions did not say the society was going to go bust immediately, but they did suggest it would really struggle to survive in the long run.

Lyons also rang the society directly and left his mobile phone number with Fingleton's secretary. Irish Nationwide's spokesperson, James Morrissey, rang back and said he would endeavour to get a response from Fingleton. He came back later that day to say that Fingleton was unable to comment to anyone.

The following morning, a Saturday, Lyons and his colleague Brian Carey wrote their story. It drew attention to the capital-raising issues, and it said there were now talks behind the scenes to try to rescue the society, which was under mounting pressure. As he was in the middle of writing, Lyons's phone rang. It was Michael Fingleton.

'Is that you, Aengus?'

'No, Michael, it's Tom Lyons from the *Sunday Times*. Can I ask you a question?'

The phone went dead.

About 4:30 p.m. that Saturday, James Morrissey rang Lyons on his mobile phone. He said the *Sunday Times* story was totally wrong, but he couldn't explain why. 'Irish Nationwide is not the problem here,' he barked. 'Somebody is spinning here, and you need to think who—the society is in good shape. You have to listen to me, you are wrong,' he said. Morrissey threatened to go above Lyons's head to ensure that the society's side of the story was heard.

'Why don't you tell Fingleton to ring me, and not Aengus [Fanning], then, if everything is okay?' Lyons asked. 'Look, go ahead. Complain if you want. You won't get anywhere.' The conversation ended.

Minutes later Seán Dunne rang up, unprompted. He wanted to discuss the crisis and the wild rumours circling Irish Nationwide. 'I'm telling you, Irish Nationwide is not the problem,' he said. 'I hear Anglo is in real trouble.'

Dunne seemed to have an inside track of sorts on what was going on. He made reference to contacting senior Fianna Fáil sources, who were keeping him briefed. He also said he was in touch with Fingleton, who had assured him about the strength of the society.

'We'll see,' Lyons replied. 'I've just heard the same thing from James Morrissey. He is telling me this far too late in the day—I sent him questions yesterday. The story is written. If we're being spun he should tell me why. Now all he can say is I am wrong but can't explain why.'

Morrissey, however, was only partly wrong. He was right that Anglo Irish was under greater pressure and was desperately trying to turn the spotlight onto Irish Nationwide instead. But he was wrong that Irish Nationwide was much better off. At the highest levels of the state it was known that the entire banking system was under severe strain and heading towards a possible breaking-point.

That Saturday, in the hope of calming the markets before the banks opened again on Monday, the government announced that it was increasing its deposit guarantee limit for individuals from €20,000 to €100,000. Lenihan stated:

I want it to be known that the Government is confident about the strength and resilience of the Irish financial system. The Government is committed to the stability of our financial system, so that money placed with an Irish credit institution would not be at risk.

As I said yesterday, the Irish Government wants to protect the whole financial system, secure its stability and ensure that all deposits in Irish financial institutions are safe.

The Central Bank and Financial Regulator have stressed the soundness and stability of the Irish financial system. This measure provides additional reassurance to depositors in Ireland that their savings are safe. The new guarantee level is now among the highest in the EU.

This was good news for all the banks, but especially for Irish Nationwide. The negative publicity had been scaring its older members, who were anxious to protect their nest eggs. They were constantly ringing its branches to ask if their money was safe. Irish Nationwide assured them that things were okay. But the reality was that they were right to be afraid.

The following day, Sunday, a secret briefing by Goldman Sachs revealed that Irish Nationwide was within days of going over the edge. (This briefing document was released to the Committee of Public Accounts of the Oireachtas in 2010.) A managing director of Goldman Sachs, Basil Geoghegan, gave the presentation about the society to the Domestic Standing Group. Geoghegan had earned Goldman a hefty fee the previous year for advising the society on its aborted sale process; now he was in front of some of the most senior civil servants charged with protecting the state during this crisis.

The high-level Domestic Standing Group was set up to ensure that all branches of the state worked together by allowing senior officials from the Central Bank, the Financial Regulator's office and the Department of Finance to meet regularly to exchange information. Among those at the meeting that Sunday were Kevin Cardiff and Con Horan, prudential director in the office of the Financial Regulator, who was in charge of supervising the banks. Patrick Neary is also recorded as being there for part of the meeting.

Notes kept by the group record the principal points made by Geoghegan. He said that Goldman Sachs had reviewed the society's top thirty borrowers. 'Lot of reassurance in those that there is real value there,' he said. His next point, however, was the qualification that this was only 'based on management discussions.' Even at this late stage there was an information gap that saw the state still relying on Fingleton and his cronies. 'Very few loans above €250m. Irish bank well diversified,'

Goldman Sachs said. Despite this, 'KPMG are looking through a worst case scenario.'

> So far, could see hits eat through capital but nothing to suggest it would go further than that.
>
> Auditors do not see performance here being worse than anywhere else.
>
> Management's central case assumption is a loss of a few hundred million.
>
> Liquidity a big issue—at current rates reaches limits in 11 days but real danger of acceleration.
>
> Convinced help from authorities will be required—soon.
>
> Suggested range of options for discussion with pros and cons (1) nationalisation (2) stand alone with liquidity support (3) break up.
>
> Mark to market value right now maybe 50/60% but a lot of value in loans if worked through.

The group listened to Goldman's assessment. It knew that the government was planning to send the global accountancy firm Price-Waterhouse Coopers into all the banks, including Irish Nationwide, to get an independent view in the coming days.

The following day, 22 September, Michael Walsh—without Fingleton's knowledge—met the secretary-general of the Department of Finance, David Doyle, to 'press his case.' In a six-page paper he outlined four possible scenarios for the society. It provided, for the first time, an honest assessment of the perilous situation facing it.

The first scenario, Walsh said, was 'Do nothing.' Capital markets were now entirely closed to the society and it was impossible to refinance its loans with other institutions.

> Assuming current market conditions prevail the do nothing option will inevitably result in the collapse of Irish Nationwide. A collapse of Irish Nationwide would have implications for the circa 180,000 depositors and result in a distressed sale of the loan books. Given the high level of property related lending in all financial institutions this could have serious consequences as valuations in all institutions might then have to be set to reflect distressed levels.

The rating agencies, Walsh said, would then downgrade Ireland's other banks, causing a massive run.

Irish Nationwide, he said, was facing a run on three fronts. He predicted that the society would lose €2.3 billion held by overseas depositors; in addition it had debt securities in issue of €5.9 billion, which were all obtained overseas and would have to be repaid; finally, its Irish depositors were also taking money out and putting it into Northern Rock Bank, which had been guaranteed by the British government. 'Inaction leading to collapse will be seen as a lack of leadership,' Walsh concluded, 'and confirm the international perception that Ireland does not know how to deal with its problems.'

The second option was an 'orderly run off.' In the previous year, Walsh said, the society had 'reduced the size of its loan book by €600 million, but it was unable to do anything more. 'In the absence of support, in the current market conditions, it is unlikely that INBS will have sufficient funding to get the time to have an orderly run-off.' The state had to help the society, Walsh said, either by providing it with liquidity, overtly or covertly, nationalising it, merging it with another institution, or guaranteeing deposits.

Providing covert funding, Walsh said, would allow the society to keep going by secretly tapping into cash from the state. But, he said, this would not prevent the rating agencies continually downgrading the society, creating an ever greater need for more covert funding. 'Utilising covert funding is likely to require much more money from the state than would be required if public confidence was restored.' Overt funding, he said, while good for Irish Nationwide would have implications for everybody else, as depositors would choose to put their money with the society over other banks if it was backed by the state. 'At its simplest if one knows one institution is safe but one is uncertain about the others then inevitably one will put one's money with the safe institution.'

Walsh also argued against simply nationalising Irish Nationwide, because once the state did this 'the market would begin to speculate about who would be next. 'The threat of nationalisation of institutions is effectively a threat to wipe out the equity in those institutions. In such a position no rational investor is going to provide equity or near equity to an institution which might be nationalised.' The nationalising of Irish Nationwide might hasten the nationalising of other banks, such as Anglo Irish, which Doyle knew was vainly hoping to go to the markets to raise more funds with which to dig itself out of the hole it had created.

'Nationalising a single institution, in the absence of guaranteeing the deposits with the others will inevitably exacerbate the problems with the others,' he said.

Walsh was pushing for the state to introduce a deposit or equivalent guarantee to Irish Nationwide. He described this as the 'least disruptive option from a national perspective. It gives a clear signal from the state that it is not prepared to countenance failure and that no creditor of an Irish financial institution is at risk.' He warned that any ambiguity about this would create problems. 'With the state giving public comfort on the security of funds with INBS (as the smallest institution) this will inevitably imply that the state will provide similar comfort to larger institutions.'

Most analysts already assumed, Walsh said, that the state would be prepared to do this for its biggest banks. If it did this for the building society it would also have to do it for Anglo Irish or risk accelerating a run on the bank.

Walsh then looked at what he saw as the third option for the society: break-up. This would involve breaking Irish Nationwide into parts and selling them off rapidly. He argued against this, because 'it would lead to greater value destruction and almost certainly cause wider market problems' than running it down over a longer period. Any break-up would have to be done overnight, and nobody would be prepared to pay much for the various bits of the society in such circumstances. Worse, he added, 'such a forced sale valuation would provide a very negative cross read to other Irish banks with property exposures.'

Walsh made his strongest argument in favour of merger with Anglo Irish. This was the plan he had already privately discussed with its chief executive, Seán FitzPatrick, a close friend for twenty years.

Anglo Irish, Walsh said, already knew many of Irish Nationwide's clients and had the expertise to manage them. However, the bank would need a state guarantee to protect it from any negative consequences. 'In effect the state will have to guarantee Anglo at the same time.' He warned, however, that the other banks would kick up about such a 'sweetheart deal', and the state might be seen to be taking on a much bigger problem than it needed to. 'There is a real danger that the market will not accept this as a solution unless there is an unequivocal statement from the State that it will provide whatever support is necessary to Anglo.' Anything less might lead to 'cynicism' by the international markets, which instead would focus on how bad both their loan books were.

In short, Walsh was arguing that in order to save Irish Nationwide the state should take on the much heavier burden of rescuing Anglo Irish.

Having completely failed to prevent the society going mad during the boom, Walsh was now proposing that the state should be prepared to accept every risk taken not only by Irish Nationwide but also by Anglo Irish Bank. It was catastrophic advice, capable of bankrupting the entire country.

As things worsened daily, Lenihan had secretly brought in Price-Waterhouse Coopers to trawl through the balance sheets of Ireland's banks. He wanted to know what was facing him. Unfortunately for the country, he was badly let down. From inside the bubble, nobody could see the real danger.

The government was now days away from making the disastrous decision to unconditionally guarantee the banks.

The lobbying for a bank guarantee continued unabated. On 25 September the former head of treasury at Anglo Irish Bank, Tiernan O'Mahony, met the civil servant in charge of banking, Kevin Cardiff. O'Mahony, whose debt investment vehicle ISTC had collapsed with debts of €850 million in November 2007 at the beginning of the credit crunch, said the state needed to consider some form of guarantee in order to restore confidence to the market and halt the flow of deposits. 'Tiernan requested the meeting,' the department said in 2012 when this meeting finally became public. 'Kevin listened to what he had to say but that was it. He gave no indication as to government policy.'

Other meetings took place between Lenihan and senior figures in Irish business during the hectic final weeks of September 2008. These meetings were not entered in official diaries, and no notes are known to have been taken, adding yet another layer of complexity to the final days before Ireland guaranteed its banks.

Whether or not Fingleton lobbied members of the government during this time is also not known. While he was not close to Lenihan, Fingleton was both friendly with and in possession of the mobile numbers of many members of Fianna Fáil, at all levels, as well as knowing senior civil servants and other influencers.

Did Fingleton pick up the phone in the final days of September? It would be easy enough to check his phone or mobile records, but this has not been done. Like Ireland's other bankers, Fingleton has never been asked to publicly explain what happened, and there has been no official inquiry into the events leading up to the decision to guarantee the banks.

In any event, as September ended, what Lenihan badly wanted to know was whether the suspicions he expressed to McWilliams about Ireland's banks were correct. Were the banks totally broke, or just temporarily running out of cash?

Price-Waterhouse Coopers were already inside the country's biggest banks, instructed to find out the answer to his question. Irish Nationwide, because it was smaller, was less of a priority.

On 27 September the accountants visited the head office of Irish Nationwide for the first time. It was a Saturday, to ensure that the arrival of a group of suited strangers with their check-lists of questions went unnoticed by nosy staff members. Fingleton was there to greet them, and calmly he assured them that his society was in good shape. It was other banks they needed to worry about, he said, in particular Anglo Irish.

It was now three days before the bank guarantee, and the accountants simply hadn't time to grasp the threat Irish Nationwide posed to the taxpayer. Instead, in preparing their advice for the government they partly relied on the assurances of the society's compromised insiders, notably Michael Fingleton and his lieutenant, Stan Purcell. They also reviewed information supplied to them by professionals.

But this information was flawed. Many of the documents were prepared by KPMG and Goldman Sachs during 2007, when the world was a different place and the society was trying to look its best for a potential buyer. The information was not useless, but it didn't drill down deep enough. It would have been impossible to really get to grips with the society in such a short time. It had a poor IT system and stored its files badly, making it hard to see what it was really like. The failure by the Financial Regulator to make the society address these issues over the decades allowed this situation to continue. At the moment when Ireland was most vulnerable, it was making crucial decisions in the dark.

Late on the night of 29 September 2008 the government took the decision to give a blanket guarantee to the entire banking system, at a cost of some €440 billion.

Earlier the heads of the country's two biggest banks, AIB and Bank of Ireland, had pressed for the state to guarantee their liabilities and also to nationalise Anglo Irish and possibly Irish Nationwide. According to a detailed account of the night's events by the *Sunday Business Post*, Cowen's response was, 'We're not fucking nationalising Anglo.'

Once the decision not to take out Anglo Irish was made, Irish Nationwide too, by the logic of the time, was in the clear. The two banks were so similar that to say that Irish Nationwide alone was doomed would have caused the market to desert Anglo Irish, as the obvious one next in line to fall.

A guarantee had been only one of the options given to the government by its advisers Merrill Lynch, who warned that such a decision threatened the ability of the sovereign to pay for itself. However, that was the course the government chose that fateful night.

In a press statement the Department of Finance said:

> The decision has been taken by [the] Government to remove any uncertainty on the part of counterparties and customers of the six credit institutions. The Government's objective in taking this decisive action is to maintain financial stability for the benefit of depositors and businesses and is in the best interests of the Irish economy.
>
> This very important initiative by the Government is designed to safeguard the Irish financial system and to remedy a serious disturbance in the economy caused by the recent turmoil in the international financial markets.

The decision not to look harder at Irish Nationwide would prove to be a very expensive decision made by Cowen's inept and shell-shocked government. Within a year the guarantee, designed to safeguard the banking system, would bankrupt the country. Immediately after the announcement, however, Irish bankers were euphoric. They had been saved.

Fingleton's son Michael junior was among the first to jump up and down, in the process creating a diplomatic incident. On 2 October an e-mail message from Fingleton junior emerged on the internet, which was picked up soon afterwards by the *Financial Times*. It had been sent from the society's London office to a friend in an unnamed large investment bank, touting for deposits.

> As Irish Nationwide qualifies under this scheme we now represent the safest place to deposit money in Europe with a AAA guarantee from a country with the lowest national debt to GDP ratio of any AAA country.
>
> Please, be so kind, as to pass on to friends, colleagues and clients as you see fit. Should you have any queries, please do not hesitate to contact me directly.

A furious British Prime Minister, Gordon Brown, contacted Cowen to voice his concern. 'Downing Street wants to avoid a public row,' the *Financial Times* reported, 'but officials say Mr Brown is determined "to restrict the inflows into these Irish institutions".'

Lenihan tried to defuse the situation by issuing a strongly worded statement. 'The Minister has said that he will have no tolerance for any financial institution which seeks to exploit competitive advantage from this guarantee. The Minster had not yet entered into a contract with the institution in question.'

The implication was clear: Lenihan was threatening Irish Nationwide that he would leave it out of the bank guarantee if it did not apologise. An apology was quickly forthcoming.

On 7 October the Financial Regulator fined Irish Nationwide €50,000 for sending out the message. 'Irish Nationwide failed to act professionally and with due regard to the integrity of the market,' the regulator said. It was the first time the regulator had fined a bank since the agency was set up in 2003. It was both a seismic and an absurd moment: an action by a Fingleton had been punished—but only for sending an indiscreet e-mail message.

———

On 13 October 2008 Price-Waterhouse Coopers were back inside the society, this time for a deeper dig. They took three weeks to review the society, which by now had been guaranteed by the state. They visited both its head office in Grand Parade, Dublin, and its Northern Ireland office on the Ormeau Road, Belfast. The code-name for the project was 'Canal.'

Meetings were held with Michael Fingleton, Stan Purcell, Darragh Daly (credit risk manager), Tom McMenamin (commercial lending manager for Ireland) and Gary McCollum (head of UK credit risk), as well as other members of the society's senior management, such as it was. Notably absent was the society's chairman, Michael Walsh.

The meetings were positive: the 'Canal' was bearing up well in the global economic storm, the accountants were assured. They told the government, however, that it was Fingleton and his men who were guiding them around in the the darkness of the society's lending engine-room. In its 'strictly private and confidential report' it stated:

> Our information was obtained primarily from the management completed templates [explaining how the society was doing], 30 September 2008 management accounts and discussions with management / loan officers.
>
> In addition we reviewed a sample of loan files.
>
> We checked a sample . . . No major issues arose from our review of the sample.

This wasn't surprising. The society had provided the sample, so naturally the worst of its excess and madness lay hidden away.

Then came yet another pile of qualifications, designed to protect Price-Waterhouse Coopers from their failure to spot how toxic the society was. 'The building society is a complex business which produces a substantial amount of financial information for internal and entity reporting requirements. As a result of the time taken to undertake our review we have not been able to review all the relevant financial management available at 30 September 2008.' In other words, they were admitting that Irish Nationwide couldn't get it together to provide them with up-to-date information. 'We note that we have undertaken only a high level review of the September 2008 balance sheet. We have not been able in the time available to us to check all the underlying documentation, the adequacy of security, valuation reporting etc.'

In short, the accountants hadn't really looked at what would have been a major problem for the society, even if the property market had never crashed. Its lax and negligent approach to lending made it a disaster waiting to happen, no matter what occurred overseas.

For good measure, Price-Waterhouse Coopers added that they hadn't looked at some of the other issues that would later dog the society, including, most notably, 'regulatory matters.' The whole thing was too rushed. There wasn't time to delve deeper into potential problems in any of the banks. The review should have taken place a year earlier, when the credit crunch began internationally. This would have been long before the guarantee was introduced.

'We have shown a draft of this report to Michael Fingleton (Chief executive) and Stan Purcell (finance director),' they reported, 'who have confirmed to the best of their knowledge and belief [that] it does not contain any material error of fact, there has been no material omission and it fairly sets out the results, state of affairs and prospects of the society.' Based on the information from Fingleton and his pals, they argued that the society might have had problems but its balance sheet was strong enough to make it bomb-proof.

Under 'all capital scenarios,' Irish Nationwide's tier 1 capital—the core ratio for measuring its financial strength—'remains in excess of 9% in all years with the exception of 2008.' For 2008 they said that tier 1 capital would slip back slightly to 8.3 per cent, reflecting the tough market, but this would still give the society one of the strongest balance sheets in the country.

Buried in the report, however, were some startling admissions that should have set alarm bells ringing. As so often before, they didn't.

The society faced a huge concentration risk, as it had allowed a small number of people to run out of control with their borrowings. In September 2008 the society's commercial loan book was €9½ billion, the report said, with about €3 billion of this managed by Fingleton from Dublin and €6½ billion handled by McCollum and his five-person team in Belfast. The numbers were scary and staggering when stripped of Price-Waterhouse Coopers' cold prose. For example, €5.6 billion of the society's lending was for land or development—and of this, €2.3 billion related to sites that had not even obtained planning permission.

Irish Nationwide wasn't even very Irish any more: it had pumped €5.4 billion into Britain, or 46 per cent of its total loan book. (It was a good thing in a way that it wasn't entirely bogged down in Ireland's shockingly overheated property market; but in other ways it could be seen that much of Irish Nationwide's bad lending was in Britain. If this had been allowed to collapse it would have been Britain's problem, not that of Irish citizens.)

The top seven customers alone owed the society €2.1 billion, or 22 per cent of its commercial loan book, Price-Waterhouse Coopers said. These seven—Seán Mulryan, Michael O'Flynn, Gary and Alan Landesberg, David and Eliot Rosenberg, Stephen Conway's Galliard Homes, David Conway, and David Burke's Roadnumber—owed the society more than €250 million each. With the exceptions of Mulryan and O'Flynn, none of these big exposures had any profile in Ireland.

Looking slightly deeper, Price-Waterhouse Coopers found that the society's top twenty-five customers owed it €5.1 billion on 30 September 2008, or 54 per cent of its commercial loan book. These twenty-five people would later cost the state more than €2 billion of the total €5.4 billion spent to prop up Irish Nationwide.

The accountants said that a number of Irish Nationwide's large customers were running out of cash and were either sacking staff or selling non-core assets to keep themselves going. They didn't spell out the fact that sacking a few employees and selling a few shares or other liquid assets was hardly going to make a dent in their borrowings.

Niall Mellon, the house-builder and philanthropist, Larry O'Mahony, who jointly built with the former IRA man Tom McFeely, and Alastair Jackson, the Northern developer, were all under pressure, the report said. (Oddly, even though McFeely was the driving force in the O'Mahony-McFeely partnership, his name is left out of the Price-Waterhouse Coopers report.) 'In the event that these customers default, the quality of the society's security and the value it will realise will dictate the level of impairment, if any, the society will incur,' they said, rather obviously. Loan-to-values were already reaching dangerous levels for all three, with Mellon at 89 per cent, Jackson at 85 per cent and O'Mahony at 82 per cent. In other words, the society had very little wriggle room for recovering its money if any of the three toppled. They were borrowed up to their necks.

Incredibly, despite it being clear that the property market had begun to crash, Price-Waterhouse Coopers said Irish Nationwide rated only 6.6 per cent of its €9.5 billion commercial loan book as grade 5, 'unacceptable risk,' or 6, standing for 'provision required.'

Despite huge sums ploughed into development land that was yielding no income, and huge bills for interest roll-up, the society (unchallenged by Price-Waterhouse Coopers) was insisting that 93 per cent of its loan book was in good shape. 'There are a number of high risk customers,' the accountants reported. 'The society deems Alastair Jackson, Seán Dunne, Larry O'Mahony, Hugh O'Regan, Niall Mellon, Northern Way Properties and Devondale to be the most likely to raise potential concerns should the current market environment persist over the next 18–24 months.'

All these clients were on the society's 'watch list,' those who might default or go bust. However, they were not written off—despite being heavily underwater and with little prospect of recovery. Price-Waterhouse Coopers noted that the society was giving some of them 'equity release facilities': in other words, it was lending more to them even as they fell off the cliff. The society's business model 'has been successful over the past number of years, however changing economic circumstances highlight a number of underlying risks.' The society, they said, had very late in the day slowed its lending in late 2007, when it decided to concentrate on new lending to its old developer clients rather than chasing new ones.

It was only in August and September 2007, as the property bubble reached its limit, that Irish Nationwide finally stopped allowing its developers to buy sites without planning permission. By then, of course, the damage had long been done.

Irish Nationwide's business model was to 'lend against property assets with collateral.' However, Price-Waterhouse Coopers noted that 'in some instances' the society asked only for 'limited equity' from borrowers when they were guiding sites through the initial stages of getting planning permission for development land, and after this it might finance construction too.

They did not spell out the fact that 'some instances' did not mean rarely or on occasion but commonly. Irish Nationwide was habitually giving 100 per cent loans to developers to finance the most risky type of project in the event of a property crash: fields and sites that produced no income and that nobody would want in a downturn, let alone a global crash. They also said the society's model was that 'loans are normally given for periods of two to three years, which allows INBS to renegotiate more favourable terms as the project collapses.'

Even worse, huge sums were being lent to the society's biggest clients on an interest roll-up basis—where the society, rather than the developers, was paying the interest cost of loans until the projects were completed. At the end of 2007 the society had rolled up interest of €514 million, with €309 million of this owed by its top twenty-five clients.

The accountants did not spell out what this type of lending meant in the event of an extended downturn: the devastation of Irish Nationwide's balance sheet. Instead they spent ages poring over Fingleton's fantasy numbers, which assumed that the property market would pick up again.

Fingleton told Price-Waterhouse Coopers that he believed the society's various joint ventures with developers would make €903 million in profit for the society in the best case, or €616 million if things worsened. 'Market conditions will determine the ultimate outcome,' the accountants concluded.

In total, Irish Nationwide expected to make a 'core business profit of €248.5m before loan provisions in 2008.' The society said it expected to make the same amount in the future, even though it accepted that it would take some losses on its loans. In 2008 it predicted that loan impairments would cost it a mere €142 million. Fingleton's delusions were being presented in all seriousness to the government.

The truth, however—that the building society was a toxic time-bomb—was there in the report. Price-Waterhouse Coopers noted that the society's jumbo borrowers also had 'significant exposures' to other domestic and overseas banks. At this stage of the crisis Irish Nationwide and the government simply had no idea how developers had stacked one loan on top of another until the top ten developers in the country each owed between €1 and €3 billion personally, through their companies and in joint ventures with others. They said there was a 'risk' that if other banks called in their loans Irish Nationwide's customers wouldn't have the money to repay the society, and that those banks that could be relied on in the past to sell on overvalued property among each other might simply refuse to do so.

Not to worry, however, Irish Nationwide assured the accountants: 'INBS has identified these exposures and is satisfied with its overall security package.' When the society's loans entered NAMA two years later these claims would be shown to be very far off the mark and bordering on the fantastical, as Irish Nationwide's sloppiness and recklessness saw it top the league of rubbish lending. This was quite an achievement, given the fierce competition.

A cliff could be seen looming for the society's developers if the market did not unlock itself. 'Given the current economic environment,' the accountants said in their understated style, 'borrowers may find it difficult to refinance these loans.' This was 'exacerbated', they said, by how many of the society's sites needed more money pumped into them to ensure that something was built that might eventually be capable of generating income, or of being sold.

In total the society said it needed to lend €502 million more in the next twelve months just to dig out its existing clients. Once it had done this it would slam on the brakes and reduce commercial lending to €10 million a month.

To finance itself, the society had a number of short-term obstacles to surmount. These included raising €500 million by securitising its mortgage book by February 2009 and raising €1 billion by securitising its commercial book. On top of this it needed to tap the European markets for £500 million that December and in 2009 to roll another £689 million of European money that was due to be repaid in May 2009. It was a colossal amount to raise just to keep going; but there was optimism at the top.

In a speech on 23 October, Brian Lenihan said the guarantee was 'a necessary first step' and the cheapest bail-out in the world so far compared with other countries, where 'billions and billions of taxpayers' money are being poured into financial institutions.' Ireland was being run by geniuses, was the message. He said that after the guarantee the government would 'move on and examine other questions which may have to be addressed to ensure that the banks are put on a sound footing.'

In the weeks after the guarantee, Lenihan briefly looked right. The Financial Regulator, Patrick Neary, told politicians in confidential meetings on 11 November 2008 that €65 billion had flowed into Irish banks in the six weeks following the guarantee. The most any bank would lose, he assured them, was €3 billion. Everything was coming back great from Price-Waterhouse Coopers. 'All institutions appear at this stage to be resilient under this "aggressive" stress test,' Neary said. There were 'no plans for recapitalisation' of any Irish bank, although this could change if the economy worsened.

Michael Walsh was not convinced that Irish Nationwide would pull through. In the final weeks of October he engaged in secret talks with the chief executive of Irish Life and Permanent, Denis Casey, about a possible tie-up. While it had a profitable life business, Irish Life was greatly exposed to the international money markets through its Permanent TSB mortgage business. It was interested in getting access to Irish Nationwide's large deposit book and residential mortgage book, which could be used to get money from the European Central Bank.

The minutes of a meeting on 30 October show that Casey met the top brass at the Central Bank and the Financial Regulator to discuss taking over Irish Nationwide, or merging with the French bank BNP Paribas. Casey circulated his notes of this meeting to the board of Irish Life and Permanent. 'I said we were working with MW [Michael Walsh] and things were progressing in a workmanlike way,' he recorded.

Not everybody was as realistic about the society's lack of a future as Walsh. Fingleton still had the attitude of hope-for-the-best, and he tapped into his contacts within the government and politics to assure them that the society's future was sound. He cleverly positioned himself as the only person capable of pulling the society through these difficult times, even though his own chairman was by now convinced that Irish Nationwide was finished.

For Fingleton, only he and his close-knit band of cronies knew how to pull the levers in the society's lending files to keep it going. In his own head—and for the moment in some parts of the state—he was still in charge, and he continued to spend the society's money lavishly.

At Christmas 2008 Irish Nationwide spent €11,000 on gifts from 4giftsdirect.com, including ten Supreme Christmas Feast Hampers at €840 each, which it sent to its developer clients. It also donated €25,000 to All Hallows' College, Dublin, where Fingleton had trained as a priest, to sponsor a gala Christmas concert in the Vicar Street theatre featuring the singer Rebecca Storm and the Derry musician and composer Phil Coulter. It was incredible that even after the bank guarantee the society kept spending in this way.

A later analysis of Irish Nationwide's spending on presents to developers and others would show that at Christmas 2005 it spent €14,700 on twenty-four bottles of wine (or €612.50 per bottle) from the Dublin branch of Berry Brothers and Rudd. The same year it spent €25,000 in Terry's, a high-end wine retailer, to cover the cost of seventy-two bottles of Cristal champagne and other drinks. The society also gave a cheque for €5,000 to the Fianna Fáil senator Des Hanafin (whose daughter Mary was a government minister) to support a national antidrug campaign. Hanafin was a social buddy of Fingleton, and the two were often seen chatting in the Shelbourne Hotel.

Fingleton used such gifts to charity—paid for with the building society's funds—to develop a reputation for generosity. In 2006 the society spent €5,000 on a table at a charity auction for the Jack and Jill Children's Foundation, set up to help seriously ill children and their families. Over dinner Fingleton gleefully bid €6,000 for a Gucci watch, which he then magnanimously returned to be auctioned again. Afterwards the bill for the watch was paid by Irish Nationwide.

At Christmas 2006 nine Supreme Christmas Feast Hampers were bought for €840 each, €8,300 altogether, also using the on-line retailer 4giftsdirect.com. A further €20,000 was spent with Watercourse Gift Deliveries on the most exclusive bottles of Irish whiskey in the world: six bottles of Midleton 20th Anniversary and six bottles of Midleton 1973, at more than €1,400 a bottle.

Christmas 2007 saw the society spend €12,000 with 4giftsdirect.com for eleven hampers priced €840 each as well as €5,500 on forty-eight bottles of wine (or €114.58 each) from Berry Brothers and Rudd.

It was all very different from the harsh treatment doled out by Fingleton to his smaller borrowers when they fell into arrears. Sure didn't the developers deserve to be indulged . . .

| FINGERS WAVES GOODBYE

T he year 2009 would prove to be an extraordinary one in the implosion of Irish Nationwide Building Society. After benefiting from Brian Lenihan's bank guarantee in September 2008, the society simply accelerated towards the cliff.

It became obvious within a relatively short time after the guarantee that the banks had much deeper problems than simply getting liquidity or access to cash because of a perceived lack of confidence in the banking industry. It was becoming apparent that banks, including Irish Nationwide, had huge losses pending on their commercial property loan books.

International banks hadn't just stopped lending money to Irish banks because of rumours or unfair perceptions: it was because they were right and the reality behind the banks' balance sheets was even worse than the perception. Irish banks in general, but Anglo Irish Bank and Irish Nationwide in particular, had lent too much money to property developers. The façade that the banks simply had a liquidity problem crumbled very quickly; so too did any lingering naïveté about the behaviour of those running them.

Even hours after the bank guarantee was announced there were those who said that, whatever about the main retail banks (such as AIB and Bank of Ireland), Anglo Irish and Irish Nationwide should not have been saved. The premise of the guarantee was that it would save the banks without actually costing anything. If they merely had a liquidity problem, the guarantee would never be called upon. But if the government got it wrong and property developers could not repay their loans, the result would be a multi-billion calamity.

By December 2008 the sceptics who questioned whether a neat little arrangement had been reached with Lenihan and Cowen for Anglo Irish and Irish Nationwide began to feel vindicated.

Behind the scenes, Fingleton took the curious decision to write to the Irish Rugby Football Union. Back in July 2005 Irish Nationwide had bought six ten-year tickets for the West Stand in Lansdowne Road at €6,600 each per year. This allowed Fingleton to entertain both his inner circle of cronies in the society and his developer pals. On 2 December 2008 he quietly asked the IRFU to send the tickets from then on to his home address in Shankill, and not to the society. This would allow him to continue to enjoy their use in the future, come what may. Perhaps he sensed that a storm was brewing.

On 18 December, fifteen days after announcing its full-year results, and a provision of a paltry €500 million for bad debts, it emerged that the chairman of Anglo Irish Bank, Seán FitzPatrick, had moved his own personal borrowings out of Anglo Irish, just before the end-of-year accounts, by refinancing his loans with Irish Nationwide. It emerged that the amount involved was an enormous €87 million, and that FitzPatrick had done this every year since 2000. At its peak his loans from Anglo Irish had reached €129 million.

It was inconceivable that Irish Nationwide would refinance or temporarily 'warehouse' FitzPatrick's loans without Fingleton sanctioning it. The public outcry was enormous, and Fingleton would inevitably face scrutiny. The idea that the most influential figure at Anglo Irish Bank had warehoused his personal borrowings with Irish Nationwide for seven years, without the investment community being told, dealt a severe blow to the sinking credibility of Irish banking. Investigations began into the Anglo Irish situation that would have included any role Irish Nationwide had in warehousing loans. But there was no clear evidence that Irish Nationwide or Fingleton had broken any rules by facilitating this eight-year process.

FitzPatrick said in *The FitzPatrick Tapes* that he never discussed this transfer with Fingleton. He acknowledged, however, that it was impossible that Fingleton did not know about his loans. Documents relating to the transfer are signed by more junior officials in the society and not by Fingleton.

FitzPatrick resigned after his loans emerged, and the day afterwards his chief executive, David Drumm, followed him.

On 15 January 2009 Anglo Irish Bank was nationalised. At first the reasons put forward were failings of corporate governance. The reality, however, was that the bank would have collapsed if the government had not intervened.

It was chaos. A guessing-game began about which of the banks would be next as share prices continued to tank. A stunned public was infuriated as scandal after scandal emerged from the Anglo Irish woodwork.

On 4 February the Taoiseach, Brian Cowen, announced in the Dáil that he planned to take a tougher stance on bankers' pay. The taxpayer was being asked to pump €8 billion into the country's two biggest banks, AIB and Bank of Ireland, and Cowen, not surprisingly, wanted cuts in return.

> If there were to be recapitalisation, I would expect the directors' fees to be cut by 25 per cent, and I would expect that when they appoint their top executives, there would be an upper limit on remuneration. I would expect that whatever it is at the moment would be cut by at least another 25 per cent as well.

Lenihan was in agreement. He believed the banks needed to be pushed harder to accept pay cuts. Eugene Sheehy, chief executive of AIB, had given up his bonus, so he was down €1 million, but he was still on €1.1 million for 2008. Dermot Gleeson, AIB's chairman, had taken a 10 per cent pay cut, but he was still making €427,000 a year. This was hardly hairshirt pay, and Lenihan wanted something done.

On Monday 16 February, Moody's downgraded Irish Nationwide again, on concerns that it had too big an exposure to commercial property while also referring to its 'poor quality' residential mortgage book. The society was now one notch above 'junk' status, and the rating agency suggested that things were likely to get even worse.

There was now no way that any financial institution would lend to the society, making it dependent on the state for its survival. The game was well and truly up.

———

On Thursday 17 February RTE announced that Irish Nationwide's chairman, Michael Walsh, had resigned. No reason was immediately available, as RTE had been unable to reach its spokesperson for comment. Clearly, however, someone reliable had been able to confirm his departure.

That night the society held an emergency board meeting to decide what to do next. Terry Cooney, who had been ineffectual for so many years, was appointed interim chairman.

The timing of Walsh's exit was terrible. Despite his failings as a chairman, he had some credibility in the money markets, partially through his association with Dermot Desmond.

Things were very bleak for the society. The *Irish Times* reported the following day that the government had still not been given any reason for Walsh's resignation, causing yet more confusion. Finally, later in the morning, the society issued a statement.

The board of Irish Nationwide Building Society accepts with great regret the resignation of Dr Michael Walsh as chairman of the board and a director of the society and thanks him for his enormous contribution as a director from April 1995 and chairman since May 2001.

Dr Walsh has informed the board that there are no commercial issues which would have impacted on his decision.

The board understands and fully accepts that he can no longer devote the increasing amount of time required to provide the necessary oversight and leadership in the current challenging times for all financial institutions.

After so many years of allowing Fingleton to reign supreme, Walsh had finally jumped ship, supposedly because of time commitments. The explanation simply wasn't credible. The following day the *Irish Times* published two leaked letters from Walsh regarding his resignation, only a day after they had been written to the society's secretary, Stan Purcell. The real reason for his departure emerged. 'In the light of unfolding events at Irish Nationwide and my responsibility as chairman of the society, I believe that the board and ultimately the Minister should have an opportunity to provide new oversight and leadership,' the first letter said.

His second letter gave greater insight. 'It is clear to me that Irish Nationwide Building Society cannot survive without reorganisation and significant Government support.' Having helped create an epic mess, Walsh had lost any interest he had in going down with the ship.

Lenihan moved fast to kill off such a dangerously frank letter, which admitted that the society was finished. Hurriedly he rang Walsh. A watered-down explanation was agreed. 'Dr Walsh has informed the minister that his reference to Government support was in fact a reference to the importance of the Government guarantee. The minister wishes to state in the strongest possible terms that Irish Nationwide Building Society has all the necessary Government support it needs to conduct its business.'

Commenting in the *Sunday Times* that weekend, its Irish business editor, Brian Carey, made a prescient criticism of Lenihan and his decision to guarantee Irish Nationwide.

> Of all the financial institutions covered by the guarantee, including those now being pilloried from pillar to post, INBS is easily the least deserving.
>
> Before we vouch our support—in the 'strongest possible terms'— it would be nice to know exactly what is going on.

Working ever harder to control the crisis, Lenihan was now frustrated with Fingleton. He wanted rid of him, but the society was in such a mess it would be difficult to replace him. Winging its way to the minister, however, was a more than adequate reason: Fingleton's final-year bonus.

After Cowen's comments earlier that month about reducing bankers' pay, Lenihan had commissioned an expert review. This reported on 27 February 2009. The report, by the Covered Institution Remuneration Oversight Committee, recommended that the most any banker should be paid was €500,000. In the case of Irish Nationwide, it said, the chief executive's pay should be €360,000—a small fraction of what Fingleton had been used to. During this review process his final-year salary came into sharp focus. Things went nuclear for Fingleton, and the board of the society, as a result. Lenihan was furious at what he discovered and demanded that something be done.

On 14 March a story was leaked to the *Irish Times* that Fingleton had received a bonus €1 million in November 2008. This was only weeks after the government had been forced to guarantee its debts, at a massive financial risk.

The story provoked an outcry. Lenihan wrote to the society, saying he believed the payment of the bonus was in breach of the terms of the bank guarantee. The society called an emergency board meeting before counter-claiming that the deal was above board, as it had been agreed before the guarantee.

Pressed on the issue, a furious Lenihan told reporters: 'That is being investigated and the department are discussing the matter.'

The bonus became a major source of friction between Fianna Fáil and the Green Party, their minority partner in government, at a time when unity was needed. 'He should have retired before now, and the extension of his employment has never been explained,' Senator Dan Boyle of the Green Party said on 20 March.

In the media, Fingleton's bonus became a totem for bankers' greed. It was a dangerous distraction for a society that was fighting for its survival, but Fingleton showed no interest in budging.

Irish Nationwide had to repay a €1 billion bond in May and it was scrambling to come up with the money, but management time was being wasted on defending its chieftain's bonus. It was all a long way now from Walsh's boast in 2005 to the Financial Regulator about the society being offered €1 billion in one day from the money markets.

That Sunday, 22 March, the *Sunday Tribune* picked up a minor comment buried in a 73-page document prepared for investors in Irish Nationwide. This comment acknowledged that the society realised there was now a risk that it could be nationalised, despite its public protestations to the contrary. The same day, Fingleton's reputation was further damaged in the *Sunday Business Post*, which reported the enormous size of his pension. Fingleton had transferred his pension out of a special Irish Nationwide scheme to a personal scheme in 2007. The amount in his defined-benefit pension pot was €27 million.

This figure had been declared in the society's annual report that year, but it was heavily disguised. It was referred to as 'one of the groups defined benefit schemes' that had now been settled for the 'members of the scheme.' This gave the reader the false impression that the €27 million scheme was for more than one person, when in fact it was for just one: Michael Fingleton.

Fingleton's pension was an enormous sum that had been compiled in the context of a society scheme that provided him with two-thirds of his salary on retirement.

That Sunday night the leader of the Green Party, John Gormley, claimed that the position of the bank boss was now 'untenable.' His colleague Dan Boyle said Fingleton's conduct was a disgrace; 'that he has remained so long in position while others have fallen on their swords is a complete mystery.'

As the news broke that the banker had been paid so much money, and that the bonus was paid after the guarantee, Lenihan demanded a meeting with the two public-interest directors he had appointed to the board in the wake of the guarantee, Adrian Kearns and Rory O'Ferrall. On Monday 23 March they were summoned to the Department of Finance. They were told to conduct an internal inquiry into the precise circumstances of the bonus payment and how such a large pot of money could have been built up in Fingleton's pension scheme. Lenihan wanted the report as soon as possible, but this was later extended to giving them a month to compile it. He also told them he wanted the board and the management reviewed.

In the meantime, political capital was being made from the bonus. On 24 March the leader of Fine Gael, Enda Kenny, said in the Dáil that Fingleton had 'given fingers' to the taxpayer by accepting the payment.

The leader of the Labour Party, Éamon Gilmore, said the matter should not be put on the 'méar fhada' or long finger, given that the taxpayer was going to be asked to take more cuts in an emergency budget that had been called on 7 April. 'The public, who are being asked to shoulder the burden of the difficult economic circumstances, need to have this dealt with before budget day,' he said, 'not leave it until afterwards.'

The Green Party just wouldn't shut up either. That night Senator Dan Boyle attended the launch of Deirdre de Búrca's ill-fated campaign for the European Parliament in the Science Gallery of Trinity College. In the middle of the proceedings, he recalls in his political memoir, *Without Power or Glory*, he received a voice-mail message from the Department of Finance, asking him to contact its minister urgently. 'I stole away from the function and rang the Department,' Boyle recalls. 'Brian Lenihan told me that he had met with the board of Irish Nationwide that day. The board was agitated, he claimed, at my criticism of its long-time chief executive Michael Fingleton.'

Even at this stage Fingleton's board remained loyal to him. His house was now under a media siege, as journalists from radio, television and newspapers wanted to know how he got this bonus at a time when the society was clearly in dire financial straits. Fingleton explained very little publicly but said he wanted the board to spell it out that the bonus payment had been made on foot of an agreement reached with the board in March 2008, whereby Fingleton would stay on as chief executive for another year.

The chairman of Irish Nationwide, Danny Kitchen, contacted the Department of Finance and said it was a bonus for agreeing to stay on and not linked to the financial performance of the society, which was clearly on the brink.

Kitchen, it also emerged, turned down the opportunity to take on Fingleton's job, because he believed the cap of €360,000 on pay for the post was too low. Asked by the *Irish Times* whether he would accept the job if the salary was increased to the government's higher cap for senior bankers of €500,000, he replied, 'It is what it is.' This made it hard for Lenihan to simply sack Fingleton, as he needed somebody to replace him.

On 26 March, Lenihan finally acknowledged in the Dáil that he couldn't just take the bonus back without having more information.

I don't have the power to do that, because the payment itself was sanctioned before the guarantee was given. In fact the particular issue is, there was a prior decision to make this bonus. Now, clearly it's for the board themselves in the first instance to establish the facts on that, see what remedies are open to them, then at the conclusion of that, if they cannot progress this matter further, it goes to my desk. There is a process to be followed here.

The following day Lenihan attempted to dampen down the controversy by telling the Dáil he believed Fingleton's €27 million pension fund had been badly hit by the stock-market crash. 'The value of the amount transferred into the pension fund in the first instance is substantially less than the figures quoted,' he told the Dáil. 'The current value of the pension fund has substantially diminished with changes in stock values.'

Finally, after the controversy had raged for two weeks, badly distracting the society from its efforts to survive, Fingleton caved in. On 27 March he issued a statement saying he would repay his €1 million bonus, despite insisting that he remained legally entitled to it. He said he had decided to give back the bonus 'because of the effect on his family with a continuing 24-hour media siege on his home and also because of his concern for the effect it may have on the society.' He claimed, however, that the bonus was 'a contractual and binding agreement with the society which he was legally entitled to receive and was entered into long before the implementation of the guarantee scheme.'

Fingleton described his bonus as a 'pre-contracted incentive bonus,' which had been agreed in April 2008 even though it was only paid that November, after the bank guarantee. He said he was 'pleased' that Lenihan had admitted earlier that week that 'he could not be compelled to return this payment.' The statement added that legal opinion obtained by the building society concluded that Fingleton had 'full legal entitlement to this payment and that it has nothing to do with the Government guarantee scheme.' The statement said it was 'very clear that Mr Fingleton's payment was paid under a valid binding contract entered into between himself and the society and that he has no obligation to be beholden to any other third parties in this regard.'

The decision to repay the bonus eased the public pressure on Fingleton. But Lenihan still wanted him out. Government sources immediately began to brief the media that Fingleton would step down 'within days.'

On 30 March came much more worrying news. Standard and Poor's removed Ireland's AAA rating, its top grade. The country had held the coveted rating since October 2001; in less than six months it had lost it by tying its citizens to the reckless decisions of Fingleton and his like. The Department of Finance tried to play down the news by saying that Ireland remained 'committed to restoring order.' But Standard and Poor's did not believe it, with Brian Cowen's emergency budget only days away, on 7 April.

'S&P has no confidence that the budgetary measures will be enough,' the head of fixed-income strategy at Société Générale SA in Paris, Ciarán O'Hagan, wrote in a note. The downgrade 'is worse than expected and will weigh on Irish gilts and AA sovereigns generally.'

There were already omens that Irish Nationwide and Ireland's other banks would, over time, take the country with them over the edge. It was against this background that Fingleton's selfish and arrogant decision to not immediately return his €1 million bonus must be seen.

On 2 April 2009 Lenihan finally got his wish. Irish Nationwide issued a statement that Fingleton planned to step down on 30 April. 'The board wishes to thank Mr Fingleton for the enormous and unique contribution he has made to the society over the past 37 years and wish both Michael and his wife Eileen many happy years of retirement.' It also revealed that the board of the society would be restructured, with Daniel Kitchen becoming its non-executive chairman following Michael Walsh's departure two months earlier.

The long-serving director Terry Cooney had been filling in until then. He quietly retired not long afterwards. Lenihan had expressed frustration at the veteran director's explanations for Fingleton's €1 million bonus, but Cooney appears to have left of his own volition. Perhaps it was before he was pushed.

The decision by Fingleton to go, after thirty-seven years at the helm, was seen as bowing to government pressure. In fact it was widely believed that he had simply been fired. The real story is that he had served out the full extension to his employment agreed in March 2008. But this did not fully emerge for some time.

———

The society was now keen to focus on the scramble to keep going. On 8 April it settled a claim of constructive dismissal taken by its former home loans supervisor, Olivia Greene. She left the society in 2008, claiming she was picked on after she had testified in 2007 in favour of Brian Fitzgibbon, one of the society's former home loan managers. Fingleton had tried to blame Fitzgibbon for bad lending to the rogue solicitor Michael Lynn, but Greene claimed that Fingleton himself had been involved in approving this lending, and it was unfair to blame Fitzgibbon. The fact that the society had continued to employ considerable efforts to pursue a few former managers even during such a crisis reveals the petty and nasty side to Fingleton's nature.

It was best to settle the case, as the society could ill afford to risk taking on Greene, who was armed with dangerous information about its careless approach to lending. This tidying up, however, did not kill off bad news for long.

On 16 April, Irish Nationwide revealed its first loss in its history under Fingleton. It made a net loss of €243 million after it wrote off €464 million in bad loans to developers. It was a dramatic u-turn for a society that had made a profit of €309 million in 2007.

Everything was going south. The loan book shrank by 15 per cent, to €10.47 billion, driven by a €1.3 billion hit from the decline in value of sterling. Operating profits halved, to €260 million, as the society's business model of generating profits through doing deals with developers fell apart. Worse, the results stated that Irish Nationwide had to repay its bond-holders €2.3 billion that year, with €1 billion of that due the following month. It had €1.2 billion in reserves; but how long would that last?

Knocking on the door now was the state's new property bank, the National Asset Management Agency. Once that began to pull the society's toxic loans out, a huge hole of still unknown size would open up.

Not that Irish Nationwide was prepared to admit as much. Instead it insisted it was 'confident that with the continuing support of the Government,' and its reserves, it would continue as a 'viable and stable systematically important credit institution.' Incredibly, it still dangled before its carpet-bagging members the prospect of some day seeing a return. Once things had settled down, it said, it would go on again to 'realise maximum value for members.' The society was finished, but it was still in denial.

As Fingleton's final days in Irish Nationwide approached, John McGloughlin, an experienced banker, quietly joined the society as chief financial officer. He had worked as an executive with Citibank and as an accountant with Arthur Anderson. Stan Purcell stayed on as finance director and secretary but was now reporting to McGloughlin.

McGloughlin joined the society without fully realising the challenge ahead of him. He would later say to friends, 'I was really shocked, really taken aback by what I saw.' He knew Michael Walsh, who was widely regarded in banking circles as a brilliant banker, making all the more surprising what had been allowed to go on unchecked for so many years. As McGloughlin entered the society, Fingleton exited.

The night before he retired, Wednesday 29 April 2009, Fingleton enjoyed a dinner that turned back the clock to when he was in his prime, a powerful man to be feted. In the stately National Yacht Club in Dún Laoghaire a group gathered to celebrate the annual dinner for the *Sunday Independent* International Cricketer of the Year awards. Fingleton had been an avid supporter of the *Sunday Independent* Cricket Society, formed by the editor, Aengus Fanning. Over the decades Fanning had grown fond of Fingleton, who inevitably got the inside track on any big story. 'Most of what Fingleton said was unprintable but highly entertaining,' a source who knew both men well said, 'so it wasn't surprising that Aengus got on with him. He knew every secret, from the state of somebody's marriage to what was really happening inside a big business deal.'

Bertie Ahern, less than a year after he resigned as Taoiseach, was one of the guests, along with the Irish cricket star Andre Botha and the former English cricket star Graham Thorpe. Fanning had tried to get

Lenihan to go to the dinner too. Lenihan liked Fanning but he cried off, as he was snowed under, trying to deal with the fall-out from the decisions of his predecessors.

Fingleton was in fine fettle amid the celebrations. Despite the scandals of the previous six months, it all appeared to be behind him. He quaffed wine like the old days. Ahern saw no reason not to be drinking with the building society boss.

It was a sociable crowd of about 150 people, which also included the former Minister for Defence Willie O'Dea, the law-and-order Fianna Fáil TD from Limerick; the Fine Gael senator Eugene Regan; and the former Minister for Justice Michael McDowell. Also there were Jack Kyle, the rugby player; Ulick O'Connor, the writer; Michael Mortell, the designer; Anne Harris, deputy editor of the *Sunday Independent*; Nigel Blow, then managing director of Brown Thomas; and Trevor White, former publisher of the *Dubliner*. Nobody objected to the presence of Fingleton, who had so recently agreed to return his €1 million bonus to the state.

In his speech the president of the cricket society, Charles Lysaght, praised Ireland's sporting greats. But he also complimented the goateed building society chieftain, despite having had a spiky enough relationship with him in the past. 'He was a wonderful young fellow, and his work in Nigeria is of particular note. He built up a building society from nothing to the major force it is today. Turbulent times have come, but we shouldn't forget his benevolence. He will be remembered when others' benevolence is forgotten.'

Fingleton lapped up the praise. Most of those attending assumed he had something to do with paying the bill for the evening, and he was described afterwards as having jointly hosted it. It appears, however, that the taxpayer was asked to pay part of it.

Earlier that month Fingleton ensured that two cheques totalling €4,000 were handed over to the *Sunday Independent* Cricket Club. This was in the same month that the society announced a colossal loss. No invoice was supplied to say what the society's money was used for, but it seems almost certain that some or all of it was to pay for that wonderful night. Irish Nationwide stopped sponsoring the cricket society in February 2010, quite a while after Fingleton stepped down, when it made a final donation of €5,000. After it ceased sponsoring the dinner Fanning convinced Richie Boucher, chief executive of Bank of Ireland, to pick up the bill.

The next day was Fingleton's last at Irish Nationwide. He had already painstakingly cleared out his seventh-floor office. His filing-cabinet, which ran along an entire wall, was now empty. His meeting-room table, where, over maps and drawings, he would plot with his favourite clients the society's next move, was clear. He left nothing behind him.

As his last day ended, Fingleton's trusty sidekick Stan Purcell, who had been rewarded so richly down the years, said a few words to a small group who gathered to say goodbye in the society's boardroom. He recalled how Fingleton as a dynamic young man had taken the society by the scruff of the neck and shaped it into a much bigger institution. He wished his old boss all the best in the future.

Then, like the parties of old, the beer, brandy and whiskey flowed. Fingleton finally relaxed. He reminisced about the deals he had done and the celebrities he had met.

Then it was over. He put on his trilby and walked out the door of the society for the last time.

Chapter 10

I'M KEEPING THE €1 MILLION (APRIL–DECEMBER 2009)

M ichael Fingleton was now gone from Nationwide House. With the chieftain finally down, it fell to Danny Kitchen to rally the shell-shocked staff. Their morale was low, as they had endured lower-than-average pay for years while they awaited a pay-off from the society's sale. Now many of them feared they might lose their jobs if the society disappeared.

Kitchen told them the society had a five-year plan for moving out of commercial lending and more into residential lending. He said its emphasis from then on would be on bringing in more deposits, and that a number of new senior appointments were in the offing. He dismissed the belief that the society had no independent future and insisted that Irish Nationwide would live on and that its staff could rest assured that they had a future there.

This, however, was looking increasingly unlikely. By that summer NAMA was beginning to step up its preparations to take over the society's commercial loan book, worth some €8 billion, or 80 per cent of its entire book. The society's days had to be numbered.

'If they set up NAMA in the way that they say they are doing, it will leave Irish Nationwide with a very small loan book,' Oliver Gilvarry, head of research at the stockbrokers Dolmen Securities, told the *Irish Times* on 1 May 2009. 'The vast majority of the €8 billion will be moved into NAMA. Irish Nationwide as an independent entity will not be sustainable.' This would leave a rump residential loan book of €2.3 billion and substantial customer deposits, which might be better run by another institution.

Gilvarry raised the prospect that Irish Nationwide might be rolled into a so-called 'super-mutual' or 'third force' in banking to counter AIB and Bank of Ireland. This might see it merged with its once-loathed rival, the EBS, or even stuck together with Permanent TSB, the troubled banking division of Irish Life and Permanent. Everything was certainly being looked at by the government. The only thing certain was that Fingleton's dream was going to be killed off.

Like Kitchen, however, the Department of Finance was not prepared to admit this publicly. In the first week of May the Labour Party's spokesperson, Joan Burton, who had been questioning why the state had guaranteed the society at all, got her answer. William Beausang at the Department of Finance wrote to Burton to tell her that the state had to guarantee Irish Nationwide because 'the society is an important actor on the Irish banking system and has many dealings with other covered institutions and customers of other covered institutions.' He claimed the society was of systemic importance because it had forty-nine branches and €6.7 billion in customers' deposits, which had to be protected.

In an argument very similar to Michael Walsh's in the period before the bank guarantee, Beausang said that any perception that the government 'would adopt a selective approach' to supporting individual guaranteed institutions 'is likely to be interpreted negatively by international markets, including in relation to the credibility of the guarantee overall.' The counter-argument to this—that it was madness for citizens to be asked to pick up the bill for every reckless decision made by a society that lent primarily to thirty-odd property developers—was not made or considered. The government still did not understand the scale of the losses facing it by guaranteeing banks like Irish Nationwide, and so it ploughed blindly ahead.

The immediate priority for Irish Nationwide now was for something to be done to replace Fingleton as chief executive. The previous month Danny Kitchen, its non-executive chairman, had tentatively agreed to become Fingleton's successor.

Kitchen was already familiar with the society's loan book in Britain, having been deputy chief executive of Gerald Ronson's Heron Group from 2003 to 2008. Ronson was a larger-than-life character who had survived the Guinness share-trading scandal in 1990 to become one of Britain's most successful developers and philanthropists. He was one of Irish Nationwide's top ten borrowers, but this was not seen as a conflict of interest or as an impediment to the experienced Kitchen being a potential successor to Fingleton.

Kitchen knew the London market and was a credible figure to the society's bigger clients, such as the Landesbergs and Rosenbergs. Kitchen might indeed have been capable of running the society had he been bothered to.

It was now more than a week since Fingleton's departure. He had not, however, got around yet to repaying his €1 million bonus. On 8 May 2009 Kitchen wrote to Fingleton at his home address in Shankill.

Dear Michael,

On Behalf of the board I would be obliged if you could let me know when you intend to repay your 2008 bonus to the society, as per your press statement.

Yours sincerely,

Daniel J. Kitchen, chairman.

It was a tame enough letter, more a gentle reminder than a demand.

Fingleton fired back a response on 11 May. He had changed his mind. He was keeping his €1 million.

He was annoyed by Lenihan's insistence on digging further into his financial affairs. He felt his decision to return the money was enough. His sources inside the society told him that the investigation was much more than a cursory review of his pay and pension. He was very displeased.

'Because of the Minister's decision to continue to pursue this matter by seeking a full investigation by the government appointed directors,' he wrote, 'I have decided to defer this repayment until this matter is concluded to my satisfaction.'

He recalled a meeting on 23 January 2009 at which the society had told the government's review group on executive pay that his bonus

had nothing to do with the government guarantee scheme or indeed constituted in anyway a performance bonus.

In response to the Minister's letter of the 12th March the board responded in clear detailed unambiguous manner again stating that this payment had nothing to do with the government scheme and was simply a contractual agreement with me to continue as CE [chief executive] for a further year.

I had an undertaking at a senior government level that on my promise to repay the bonus there would be no further government interest in this or any other matter and that the timing of my departure from the society would be my own decision.

This final comment by Fingleton is intriguing. He states that he believes an unnamed senior person in the government had offered him a deal whereby if he returned the bonus the state would agree not to pursue him on anything else. The person who Fingleton believed offered this deal was the Taoiseach, Brian Cowen, according to a source who has spoken to Fingleton. Brian Lenihan, a source said, told them before he died that he had never made an offer to Fingleton, but admitted that others had. There was certainly no formal deal sanctioned by the government. Fingleton was furious that the government, as he saw it, had backed out of its deal. However, even if Cowen did make such an offer, either directly or through an intermediary, it is unlikely that he made it as open-ended as Fingleton believed it to be.

As the cracks in the society worsened, such an offer was simply impossible to fulfil. It would have been political suicide to let Fingleton off the hook. The secretary-general of the Department of Finance, David Doyle, also distrusted Fingleton and was opposed to any action that might favour him.

Three days after writing this extraordinary letter Fingleton flew to London and booked into the five-star Dorchester Hotel on 14 May with his wife. He met his old developer clients in London to assure them that the society would still respect all their old agreements.

A bill for £2,300 was submitted to the society for his stay. It was duly paid, even though Fingleton was no longer working for the society. Somebody within the society's walls believed he was still worth picking up the lavish bill for.

The same week Brian Lenihan was ploughing through his paperwork, trying to cope with the crash. An inexperienced Minister for Finance, he was under enormous pressure, staying up late at night attempting to read himself into his brief. He had a lot more serious things to worry about than Fingleton's bonus; but the building society's impunity and arrogance meant he had to make it a priority.

On 12 May, Lenihan received the Kearns and O'Ferrall report on Fingleton's pay and pension, which had been completed with the help of KPMG. It showed that under the society's rules Fingleton had to step down from the board of Irish Nationwide once he turned seventy. This happened in January 2008. He remained as chief executive but he was not happy with the situation and wanted the board to change the rules at an AGM to allow him to remain as a director. The board did not accede to this request and instead the then chairman, Michael Walsh, opened up negotiations with Fingleton about staying on. The board wanted him to remain as chief executive, saying that his knowledge of the clients and his experience were important in steering the society through difficult times as the property market began to soften and the credit crisis first reared its head.

Fingleton negotiated an incredible deal. He agreed to stay on if he got a 10 per cent increase on his 2007 salary, bringing it up to €893,000; a bonus equal to his 2007 performance bonus of €1 million but irrespective of the performance of the society; and the additional €400,000, in monthly instalments, that had been agreed in 2007. It was as if he knew things were going to get rough and he was going to stick around to take the flak but wanted to be paid a total of €2.4 million to do so.

The Kearns-O'Ferrall report failed to adequately explain the additional payment of €400,000. Despite producing a 54-page report with the assistance of KPMG, the solicitors Arthur Cox and others, they fudge what these payments were about and why they were given.

The 2007 accounts say that Fingleton's bonus for that year was €1.4 million. In March 2008, in agreement with Walsh, he was to receive a bonus of no less than his 2007 bonus in return for staying on. He was awarded €1 million. There is what is described as an additional payment of €400,000, awarded in 2007, but it is not clear if this was paid. It was paid in 2008. No clear explanation was provided for how this came about.

The report explained Fingleton's pension situation in great detail. He had joined a private defined-benefit scheme for executives in 1981, which provided him with two-thirds of his final salary after his retirement. In 1991 Fingleton took over the investment strategy of this pension fund, so he decided where the money should be invested. Then in 1995 a separate pension fund was set up for him, and two years later the board agreed that the definition of terminal salary in any year should include the basic annual salary plus the bonus payments averaged over the three previous years.

The incredibly generous board decision in 1997 meant that Fingleton was in an extraordinarily fortunate financial position. The more profit he earned for the society, the bigger his bonus. The bigger his bonus, the greater the amount he would receive after he retired. Pushing profits up for the three years before he retired would multiply the value of the pension he would receive for the rest of his life.

Fingleton had been given a massive incentive to blow the lights out when it came to short-term profit, especially in the three years leading up to his retirement. This required a massive financial gamble; but the property market was on fire, so it looked like paying off.

The decision in 1997 to include bonuses in the calculation of final salary meant adding €12 million to the pension fund needed to fulfil the obligation to Fingleton. A further decision to upgrade his wife's pension entitlement, should he die, from two-thirds of his pension to 100 per cent of it added another €2 million to the cost.

Yet, despite building up a €27.6 million fund, the society had to put in only €4.3 million of its own money; the rest had come from investment gains that the fund made under the direction of Fingleton himself. He primarily invested his fund in bank shares, and by 2007 it had €12 million worth of shares in AIB alone. He also had €6.8 million in Bank of Ireland and €1.3 million in Irish Life and Permanent. He didn't invest a cent in Anglo Irish Bank, the report found.

The report of the public-interest directors, which was presented to the Committee of Public Accounts, also found that by managing the pension investments himself Fingleton had saved the society €2 million in fees that would have been charged by a pension advisory or investment company. But, irrespective of how his investments performed, he was on track to receive a pension of €890,000 per year. It was one of the most gilt-edged pensions in Irish corporate history. As it happened, Fingleton invested wisely during those stock-market boom years. However, the Midas touch he showed in investments ran out, and his investment portfolio of bank shares collapsed after 2007.

It is not known, however, whether Fingleton switched the investments out of those shares and into something else. If he didn't, according to an analysis by KPMG, by 2009 his pension fund of €27.6 million would have had assets worth less than €4 million.

Fingleton has never disclosed the present value of his pension fund, but when pursued in the High Court by Ulster Bank for an unpaid loan of €13 million and pressed to provide a full list of his assets he did not include any value for his pension at that time, something the court described as 'remarkable.' Clearly Fingleton's personal wealth in 2007 was well above €30 million when his pension is included. He had also been earning more than €1 million per year since 2003. In fact in the six years 2003–8, inclusive, he was paid a total of €11 million. His pay was criticised, but not unduly so, as year after year the society turned in record profits. 'Shovelling out shed loads of money in this manner is considered to be the natural order in the corporate jungle,' Frank Fitzgibbon concluded in his *Sunday Times* column in April 2003.

At the board of directors his salary was never really challenged either. Con Power had made sure there was an independent review of Fingleton's salary after it was criticised by a member at the society's AGM in April 2003. Michael Walsh selected an experienced independent human resources consultant from the Hay Group to review Fingleton's pay; the consultant concluded that his pay at that time was reasonable relative to that of his peers. In any event, Fingleton was one of the best-paid executives in Irish business for many years.

His most lucrative year was 2008, when he earned €2.4 million. This was the year in which the society made a loss of €243 million. Again he got a bonus of €1 million, plus the additional payment of €400,000. The society went on to lose more that €5 billion over the next three years on the strength of loans sanctioned by Fingleton.

The value of Fingleton's pay each year, including salary and bonus, was determined by the remuneration sub-committee of the board. Extraordinarily, this included David Brophy, a non-executive director who was also an executive of Ballymore Properties, owned by Seán Mulryan, Irish Nationwide's biggest borrower. The remuneration committee was chaired by Michael Walsh; the third member was Terry Cooney.

Journalists could see a potential conflict of interest but could not easily have found out the extent of Mulryan's borrowings from Irish Nationwide. But the Financial Regulator would have known how much the society's exposure was. If he didn't, he probably could have found out with a single phone call. Yet he did absolutely nothing about this glaring conflict.

Now, with the bank guarantee, Irish Nationwide's warehousing of the FitzPatrick loans, the €1 million bonus paid after the guarantee and the €27.6 million pension pot all public knowledge, Fingleton's position was untenable anyway. Brian Lenihan's inability to forcibly reverse the €1 million payment had left him looking powerless and frustrated. The Financial Regulator too was beginning to look ridiculously naïve about what was going on in Anglo Irish and Irish Nationwide.

In June 2009 Gerry McGinn was finally appointed chief executive. A 52-year-old with a degree in French and philosophy from Queen's

University, he had spent eighteen years working for Bank of Ireland in Dublin, London and Belfast. In 2001 he changed direction to become permanent secretary at the Department of Education in Northern Ireland, under its then minister, Martin McGuinness. After that he worked in the Department of Regional Development, where he ran the North's transport network. For the two years before joining Irish Permanent he headed the Belfast office of Goodbody Stockbrokers.

At Irish Nationwide, McGinn found an organisation that had been dominated by one man for a generation. It was now in free fall. There had been no real management team: real power had rested with Fingleton. Administration was chaotic.

NAMA had been set up to buy bad loans, including billions in loans from Irish Nationwide. Yet another report by Price-Waterhouse Coopers for the Department of Finance was finally uncovering how bad the loan book really was. The society was now effectually in state hands, and the big question was, How much is it going to cost the taxpayer from loan losses?

Against this backdrop McGinn and the recently appointed chief financial officer, John McGloughlin, approached Danny Kitchen and said they needed a competent third party to assess what had gone on inside the society. 'They weren't sure if skulduggery had gone on' was how one former insider at Irish Nationwide put it, 'but from all they could see, the whole think stank.'

The society hired the accountants Ernst and Young and the solicitors McCann Fitzgerald to conduct a review of corporate governance at the society over the years. What they would find was mind-blowing, but finding it wasn't easy. Files and documents were spread out all over the society's head office and its various branches.

During the first months of 2009 there had been extensive shredding of files and documents, but it was hard to know what they contained. 'How could you prove that what was shredded was bank documents and not personal documents?' a society source said.

———

While the Ernst and Young review was taking place in painstaking secrecy, the saga of the €1 million bonus rumbled on. On 24 July, Kitchen picked up the baton again and replied to Fingleton's refusal on 11 May to return his bonus.

> In light of the fact that the report by the government appointed directors has been completed for several weeks I wondered what progress or otherwise you had made regarding the bonus.
>
> Clearly the likelihood of adverse press comment looks much less remote so whatever you choose to do should stay below the radar.
>
> On another matter could you let Meryl know some dates which would suit regarding the dinner we discussed.
>
> I hope you are keeping well, yours sincerely, Daniel Kitchen.

The letter received no immediate reply. On 1 September, after enquires from the *Irish Times*, Irish Nationwide stated: 'The society has written to Mr Fingleton on a number of occasions seeking the return of the money. As of now, the money has not been returned to the society.' By text message, an unnamed spokesperson for Fingleton said that 'the question of repayment does not arise at this time. There are several outstanding issues in relation to this matter and until such time as those issues are resolved Mr Fingleton has no comment to make on this subject.' The *Irish Times* admitted it was baffled by what these issues might be.

The Fine Gael spokesperson on finance, Richard Bruton, said:

> To be getting a payment after the taxpayer had extended a guarantee seems to fly in the face of everything that is fair and reasonable. He made a commitment which I think people accepted that he was going to honour. It's not acceptable at a time when ordinary people are facing very severe constraints and are having to dig deep into their pockets to protect the financial system.

The issue was hugely embarrassing for Brian Lenihan. Internationally, politicians were trying to end the global culture of short-term decision-making linked to bonuses that had so devastated the world's economy. Lenihan was eager to join in.

At a meeting of EU finance ministers on 2 September to discuss bankers' bonuses Lenihan mingled with Europe's heavy-hitters and nodded his approval when the Swedish Minister of Finance, Anders

Borg, whose country then held the EU presidency, said that bankers were still 'partying like it's 1999, and it's 2009.' Pressed afterwards by the media, Lenihan admitted that he couldn't just take the €1 million back from Fingleton. 'The government doesn't have a right to sue for this money—it is between the society and Mr Fingleton.'

The bonus controversy was again an unneeded headache for Lenihan. He was in the thick of working out a new strategy for Irish banking, but over and over again the media quizzed him on Fingleton's bonus. 'It's been a very busy year,' he admitted to the *Sunday Tribune* on 6 September.

Almost a year after the bank guarantee Lenihan continued to defend that night's fateful decision, saying that forcing investors to pay for banks' mistakes would hit the consumer, as bank bonds were held by pension funds, credit unions and insurance companies. Burning those institutions, he argued, would affect the consumer by wiping out their pensions or making their premiums go higher. 'Let's be clear: who are these investors? Who are they? I think the "Who are they?" is an important issue in this debate.'

Indeed it was. The fact that it was German and French institutions and individuals who would take the worst hits in such an eventuality was an important distinction that Lenihan did not make. Nor perhaps could he, as Irish banks were by now dependent on the European Central Bank for billions of euros in liquidity. Antagonising Europe was a strategy Lenihan could not risk.

He also told the *Sunday Tribune* that he was working hard on setting out a new direction for the banking industry, which he would reveal on 16 September.

On 7 September part of that strategy arrived. Mike Aynsley, an Australian banker, began work in Anglo Irish Bank. A thirty-year banking veteran, he faced the difficult task of trying to hold the bank together.

Aynsley had worked in Australia, New Zealand and south-east Asia. He had been attracted to Ireland after his old friend Mike Soden, former chief executive of Bank of Ireland who resigned after an internet pornography scandal, tipped him about the job. Aynsley had diverse banking experience, including risk management, liquidity management and governance risk assessment, which were all among the challenges facing Anglo Irish.

Two days later Irish Nationwide made its own important appointment towards fulfilling Lenihan's strategy. Valerie Mulhall, who had worked with Barclays Bank and State Street, was named head of the society's NAMA unit. The society was in the thick of picking through its messy commercial loan book, and Mulhall faced a heavy work load. After her years working to the high standards of State Street she was shocked by the poor quality of record-keeping at Irish Nationwide. Files for borrowers who owed the society a small fortune were poorly kept. Some documents appeared to have been lost, while others were only half filled in. Time and again Michael Fingleton's signature or initials popped up as the society made reckless decisions, lending billions with little regard to best banking practices.

NAMA was not impressed by the standard or the security of documents dug out of boxes and files by Mulhall and her team. From early on, Irish Nationwide was, in NAMA's eyes, easily the worst of all Ireland's banks. NAMA began to gear up to give the society's valuation of its loans a massive haircut. The black hole inside the society was going to be enormous.

While the society's staff and board worked hard, its old boss was holidaying abroad with his wife. Fingleton, always so eager to speak to journalists, suddenly stopped answering his mobile phone, which more often than not now had an overseas ringing tone.

———

It was now clear that Irish Nationwide was finished, even if Kitchen and his crew continued to maintain that this was not so. The idea of a so-called 'third force' bank began to emerge at government level, which would merge Irish Nationwide with the EBS and Permanent TSB. The fact that such a radical combination was being looked at showed both how bad things were and how poorly the government still grasped the problems facing it. While millions would be spent working on what this third force might look like, it would in fact never emerge.

On Monday 14 September, Irish Nationwide's despised rival, the EBS, reported interim results. It said it expected that it would transfer €1 billion worth of loans to NAMA. It would need, as a result, €300 million from the state once NAMA took over its commercial property loan book. Most of these losses had been accrued in a few years when, under pressure from its members and some elements of the media, the

EBS had abandoned its traditional conservative approach to chase Irish Nationwide. If €300 million was the hit for the relatively conservative EBS, then Irish Nationwide had to be many, many times that.

After the results the chief executive of the EBS, Fergus Murphy, spoke openly for the first time about the possibility of heading a new 'super-mutual', which would include EBS, Irish Nationwide and possibly Permanent TSB. 'This entity would act as the "ultimate good bank" and would be built on the tradition of mutuals—building up savings from members and providing home loans,' he said.

This was a million miles from the direction in which Fingleton had so disastrously taken Irish Nationwide. The idea that EBS would take over his beloved society must have galled him.

That Wednesday, in a dramatic speech to the Dáil, Lenihan revealed just how bad things were for Irish banks and, by extension, its blanket guarantors: the taxpayer. NAMA, he said, would pay €54 billion for loans with a face value of €77 billion from the banks, a discount of about 30 per cent. In total, this would cover 21,500 loans owed by 2,000 people. Half the €77 billion, it would later emerge, was borrowed by a mere 150 people. The cost of any losses associated with these loans, however, would be shouldered by the Republic's 4½ million citizens. 'The final figure will depend on the detailed evaluation of each individual loan,' Lenihan said. Irish Nationwide would pass over €8 billion of its loans to NAMA; this compared with €24 billion from AIB, €28 billion from Anglo Irish, €16 billion from Bank of Ireland and €1 billion from the EBS.

The extent of the haircut for each bank was still not known, but banking analysts estimated that Irish Nationwide, with its big land-bank loans, could expect its loans to be bought at a discount of 40 per cent. This estimate put the cost of the society to the taxpayer at €3.2 billion—a huge sum but one that would turn out to be a gross underestimate. After so many years of trying, Irish Nationwide was now punching very much above its weight, although in the most horrendous way.

The Labour Party's spokesperson on finance, Joan Burton, spoke out against NAMA, which she was worried was putting too heavy a burden on the taxpayer. Anglo Irish and Irish Nationwide, she pointed out, accounted for a big chunk of the huge cost of the state bailing out its bankers and developers.

That's Fingers [Fingleton] and that's Seánie [FitzPatrick]. That is half of what the Irish taxpayer is having to carry. Do we trust Fianna Fáil and the Minister for Finance to head up the largest property firm on the planet? Do we trust a Taoiseach who pleaded that Ireland's economic fundamentals were sound when it was plain to see we were teetering on the brink of disaster?

Shares in the banks surged at the news, as investors snapped up shares. It now seemed clear that the taxpayer was to be landed with the bill for the stupid decisions that only two years earlier had been cheered by shareholders and stockbrokers. AIB surged by 30 per cent, pushing its value to €3 billion, while Bank of Ireland rose by 18 per cent, putting its value at €3.4 billion. The increases, however, would only prove temporary as the months dragged on and the truth about Irish banking in all its ugliness seeped out.

Nobody minded the two banks' shares picking up. There was an unshakeable general acceptance among politicians that neither of the two big banks could be allowed to go bust. The same, however, was not then true about Anglo Irish and Irish Nationwide.

On 22 September the leader of Fine Gael, Enda Kenny, voiced his concerns at the scale of the combined €30 billion allocated for Anglo Irish and Irish Nationwide. 'This will not result in one single person being taken off the dole queue,' he said, while clearly implying that if he was in charge things would be different.

As the month ended, the news from Irish Nationwide just kept getting worse. On 22 September the Department of Finance released new figures on the society, showing that in the first six months of the year €899 million had been pulled out of the society by worried depositors. It now had deposits of €5.8 billion; this was a full €1.7 billion lower than where it had been in June 2008, before the worst of the crisis hit. A run was under way.

Irish Nationwide's carpetbagging depositors, who had so happily piled in, giving Fingleton some of the money and the regulatory freedom to keep lending to developers, were now voting with their feet. The society's lending, meanwhile, had ground to a halt as it fought to survive. After years of Fingleton firing out cash every which way, now, in the first six months of 2009, it had approved only nine mortgages, worth a grand total of €340,000. Irish Nationwide was going bust, and the cost to the state already looked huge.

It is against this background that an extraordinarily arrogant letter from Fingleton must be read.

The five-page letter was written to Kitchen on 25 September 2009. The editor of the *Sunday Independent*, Aengus Fanning, knew about the letter. Over many months he tried to convince his old friend to leak his side of the story to him. Fingleton would take his battered version of the letter out of his jacket pocket when they met and dangle it; but he steadfastly refused to let Fanning publish it.

Finally, in a coffee shop in Blackrock, Fingleton handed a copy of the letter over to Fanning, who published it in April 2010. The leaked version of the letter, however, was only a draft. The sentences in bold type below are the parts Fingleton left out when he leaked the letter. They paint a terrible picture of a man delusional in his self-importance.

Fingleton began his letter by responding to a report in the *Irish Times* on 1 September in which a spokesperson for Irish Nationwide was quoted as saying, 'Michael Fingleton had been contacted several times but had not responded.' Piqued by this comment, Fingleton said he been contacted only twice by the society, on 8 May and 12 July. He had responded to the society's letter of 8 May, he said, and now he wanted to give his reply in detail.

On reaching retirement age at the end of January 2008, the Board of the Society requested that I be retained for a further year-long contract which was to expire on 28th February 2009. It was agreed that in exchange for agreeing to this extension that my total remuneration for 2008 be not less than my total remuneration for 2007.

The constituent parts of my 2007 remuneration package included a one million euro 'bonus'. At no point did the Board of the Society discuss or agree a performance bonus in relation to my remuneration for 2008. However for some reason, the one million 'bonus' payment became part of the contract in the official records of the Remuneration Committee.

On 23rd January 2009 the Chairman, Vice-Chairman and the two Government-appointed directors met with the Covered Institutions Remuneration Oversight Committee (CIROC), a Government body established to examine the remuneration of executives in the six covered institutions under the Credit Institutions (Financial Support)

Scheme 2008. At this meeting, the payment of one million euro as part of my 2008 remuneration was discussed extensively and exhaustively.

The Directors of the Society made it absolutely and abundantly clear to the three-person board of CIROC that this payment was in no way linked to performance and clearly demonstrated that it was a contractual payment due to me on foot of my agreement to enter into a one year contract after my due retirement.

It therefore came as a great surprise to me and the Board of the Society that the draft report of CIROC furnished to the Minister for Finance referred to this payment as a 'Performance Bonus'. As a direct result of this misrepresentation, the Minister wrote to the Board of the Society on 12 March 2009 expressing his 'serious concerns' about the circumstances of this payment and seeking an immediate response. The Minister's letter was delivered to the Society after 7pm on the evening of 12th March 2009 and sought a reply by 11am the following morning 13th March 2009, before the launch of the CIROC Report that same day.

The Secretary of the Society, who was still working in the office that evening, brought the matter to the immediate attention of the acting Chairman who summoned an emergency board meeting. By 11pm on 12th March 2009, the Board delivered a clear and full response to the Minister stating, in unequivocal terms once more, that the payment in question was a contractual payment established and agreed long before the Credit Institutions (Financial Support) Scheme 2008 and did not fall under the powers of the Minister under this same scheme.

As a result of this letter, CIROC was forced to change the reference in the final published report from 'performance-related bonus' to 'pre-contractual bonus' which appeared in their official report. This was clear and conclusive evidence that both the Minister for Finance and his Department had fully accepted the Society's position as set out in the letter of 12th March 2009. I am not aware that the Minister ever responded to this letter or officially questioned the content on any subsequent occasion.

It was now clear that my 'bonus' was contractual and that the Society was fully and legally obliged to honour it, and furthermore that I was legally entitled to receive it. It was therefore fully established that the powers of the Minister under the Credit Institutions (Financial

Support) Scheme 2008 had no legal implications whatsoever in relation to this matter. For completeness, the Board of the Society, at a later date, sought and obtained legal opinion from Michael McDowell SC. The opinion fully and comprehensively agreed with the Board's position. Mr McDowell's opinion was openly circulated to the media, however only one newspaper made reference to it. **It clearly did not suit the agenda at the time**.

Two days later, in a high profile report, the *Irish Times* on 14th March 2009 stated 'it emerged last night that the Department of Finance intends to put pressure on Mr. Fingleton to repay the bonus'. It went on: 'the Department of Finance sources said Mr Lenihan was not impressed with the bonus payment to Mr Fingleton in November 2008 after the Bank Guarantee Scheme was introduced and that the matter would be pursued'.

It was clear to me that the spin, denial and politicisation of the issue had begun. The resources and apparatus of the State were organised to create the perception, contrary to the legal position already accepted by both the Minister and his Department, that the repayment to me was 'tainted' and in breach of the conditions of the 2008 Scheme. The Irish media rowed in with a vengeance along with the Government and opposition parties who bought into the false perception now being created that the payment to me was in breach of the Guarantee Scheme and should be repaid. The Society's rebuttals were ignored and got lost in the frenzy.

The collective bullying and harassment was in full swing and persisted for weeks.

It became clear to me that the matter would have to be brought to a conclusion either by legal means or some other way. I chose the latter in the interest of the Society since under the terms of the Guarantee Scheme the State had effective administrative control of the Society, and the Society would have to work with them on a regular basis. At this point contact was made on a confidential basis through an independent intermediary. The Government contact stated that the question of whether or not I was legally entitled to the payment did not arise; it was the fact that there was a public perception that I was not entitled to the payment. The Government was on a 'political hook' and the only way the matter could be resolved was by returning the one million euro payment.

After two days of contact and discussion it was agreed by the government contact that if I voluntarily agreed to pay the one million euro, and thus releasing them from the political hook (a creation of their own making), there would be full and complete closure to this matter. It was stated that there would be no further interest in this matter or in my pension entitlements by the State.

Indeed I was assured that there would be 'positive official comment' made on the matter. At all times the Minister for Finance was fully aware of these discussions and the subsequent agreement.

This agreement with the government, notwithstanding the reasons given in my public statement of 27th March, 2009, was the reason I offered to pay back the Society the one million euro (less tax already deducted). For the record there is a further independent witness to this agreement other than the intermediary, who confirmed to me recently that my understanding as detailed above is correct.

Despite this agreement the Minister for Finance continued his personal attack by pursuing an inquiry into the payment of my 'bonus' and my pension entitlements by publicly giving instructions to the two Government-appointed Directors to carry out a full and detailed investigation of both issues and setting a deadline for it to be completed.

Clearly, as far as the Minister was concerned there was no closure or anything else. It had been established beyond doubt that there was and is no legal obligation on my part to repay any of the remuneration I received in 2008 and both the Minister and his Department were fully aware of this fact. The only possible reason to initiate such an inquiry was to establish some justification for their campaign, **which was as dishonest as it was flawed**.

By this action, the Minister has repudiated the agreement I had with the government and my act of good faith.

I was **bullied and** harassed into volunteering to repay money which I was under no legal obligation to do and to which I was contractually entitled. As a direct result of the minister's actions, I have no obligation legal or otherwise to account to any party with regard to the funds in question.

The remaining issues now outstanding as far as I am concerned relate to the results of the investigation ordered by the Minister. I am aware that the enquiry is complete and the ensuing report has been forwarded to the Minister some considerable time ago. I was to be given a copy of this immediately after it had been submitted. I now wish for official closure on this subject.

In addition to a copy of the report, I request confirmation from the two Government-appointed Directors that they found nothing irregular nor improper in their investigations and that in both instances I was fully entitled, both legally and contractually, to the payments in question. I also would like to request a copy of the response, if any, from the Minister and/or his Department to the report.

I believe that it would be in the best interests of the Board to seek a full and complete acknowledgement from the Minister that the repayments made to Michael Fingleton were proper, legal and contractually binding on the Society and that it was fully obliged to discharge them. This is a necessity in order to bring complete closure to this matter as far as the Society is concerned.

As far as I am aware, the Minister or his Department have never responded to or acknowledged in any way the numerous occasions the Society, the Board and its Directors have informed the Minister and his officials of the legal status of these payments.

Danny, as Chairman, you clearly set out the position of the Society in relation to this payment and my pension arrangements in the Chairman's statement to the AGM in May this year. It is strange, though not surprising that this statement got little or no media coverage. I presume you were requested to submit this statement in advance for clearance from the Minister under the terms of the Guarantee Scheme. Again this gave the Department of Finance further confirmation of the Society's position and indeed an opportunity to challenge it. In not challenging or amending the contents it can therefore be deemed that they accepted the position as articulated by you as Chairman.

In relation to my pension entitlements, I feel this is as good an opportunity as any to clarify the history of the creation of the fund and its cost to the Society.

In the late Eighties and early Nineties, I became concerned about the performance of my pension fund under independent management. I agreed with the Society that I would manage the fund myself and invest all pension contributions as they arose. The fund in the intervening years performed exceptionally well and delivered a sum to cover the Society's obligations to me but also delivered a lump sum of €1.17 million euro to the Society. The cost to the Society in contributions was less than €3 million. This figure was confirmed by the auditors and appeared in the 2007 accounts of the Society by way of a note.

Furthermore, managing the fund in-house meant there was an estimated saving in fees of circa €2 million. Overall it was an exceptionally outstanding result for the Society.

To put the cost into perspective, if a secretary general of a major government department were to retire now, the cost of his pension would be in the region of €7m as compared to the cost of less than €3m for my pension from the society.

In your Chairman's statement to the AGM, you also set out clearly the Society's position in relation to Mr FitzPatrick's loans. There was nothing improper, illegal or irregular about those transactions. They were commercial loans on commercial terms. For the record I wish to state that I never spoke to Mr FitzPatrick about those loans or he to me. I never had, nor do not have now any interests or business connections with Mr FitzPatrick or any of his associates. I do not have or never had any business interest or connections with any director, executive or staff member of Anglo Irish Bank. I never had or do not have now any borrowings from or deposits with Anglo Irish Bank. Nor have I ever owned or do not own any shares in Anglo Irish Bank.

It must be remembered that Mr FitzPatrick and his fellow Directors made an outrageous hostile attempt in mid-September 2008 to destabilise the Society and to mislead the public and the markets when Anglo Irish Bank announced unilaterally that they were taking over the Irish Nationwide. The media were also duped and bought enthusiastically into this fiction, despite strong denials by the Society.

I wish to state for the record that I have no issues with the Society nor do I expect to have any in the future. Any issues I may have are firmly focused elsewhere. To clarify, this is the response to your letter dated 4th August 2009. Therefore, the Society has contacted me twice and I have responded twice (if somewhat belatedly this time).

I trust that this clarifies for you and the Society my position and I look forward to full closure of this matter.

Yours sincerely

Michael Fingleton

Given the cost to the taxpayer of Fingleton's decision-making, he might have expected a sternly worded response. Instead, on 6 October 2009 Kitchen replied to Fingleton as follows:

Dear Michael,

Thanks for your letter of 25 September. First let me say that in relation to the legal position regarding the bonus the society is clear that the offer you made to repay it was entirely at your own discretion. Equally as you have noted from address at the AGM the board's view on the pension arrangements and the FitzPatrick loans coincides with your own. Consequently on the above issues there is nothing contentious between yourself and the society.

I was asked by the Department to ask you again to repay the bonus and I have explained to them that whilst prepared to do so, the society has no leverage to ensure you do so. I also agree that the number of times referred to in the press was two, and that the lack of response referred to the last occasion I wrote to you.

Like you I want to put the issue behind the society and consequently I will assume that you do not intend to repay the bonus and accordingly I will stop seeking such repayment.

I believe you understand the circumstances prevailing and hopefully from both our perspectives this will put an end to the matter.

Yours sincerely,

Daniel J. Kitchen

Chairman

Kitchen admits in his letter that he has no intention of pursuing Fingleton. He wants to put the entire annoying affair behind him and gives Fingleton no reason to pull back on his position.

On the same day as Kitchen's letter, Irish Nationwide appointed as a non-executive director Roger McGreal, a hardened banker who had previously been an associate director of corporate lending at Investment Bank of Ireland and executive director of Woodchester Investments. McGreal's speciality was risk, and his expertise would prove invaluable in a society that for decades had ignored the area. He would later confide in friends how shocked he was at the society's reckless approach to lending, which would have eventually toppled it even if there had not been a global economic crisis. 'How on earth was this ever allowed go on? What does that say about Ireland?' he would later say privately.

After decades with a tiny board, for the first time the society was beginning to make proper use of its large boardroom table, though it was still in poor shape, given the scale of its problems. Around him Kitchen had the government-appointed directors, O'Ferrall and Kearns, as well as McGreal. Seán Carey, the former deputy city manager, was also still there. Representing the old regime was Stan Purcell.

'The new board meetings were very constructive,' a society insider recalled. 'The public-interest directors were very good. It was always a struggle but deposits were good as they were spread across the branch network. Collectively [the board] all worked well together.'

There were signs that the society was facing other troubles than NAMA. On 25 September, John Mara, son of the former government press secretary P. J. Mara, sold his house in Sandymount, Dublin, for more than €1.9 million. The sale was part of an attempt by Mara and his wife to clear their debt of €6 million to Irish Nationwide. In evidence submitted to Dublin Circuit Court that July it was revealed that this debt was 125 times their combined annual income.

Mara's gradual engulfment in debt to the society revealed how badly things were turning out for the rich and influential who had once been courted by Fingleton. Mara had begun building a property empire by borrowing €2 million to buy a house in Heytesbury Lane, Ballsbridge. In 2006 he and his wife borrowed €2.98 million to buy the Sandymount house, on an interest roll-up basis for two years while they spent €1 million renovating it. The same year they met Fingleton and borrowed another €1½ million to buy a property in Croatia. This property too was on the block.

Irish Nationwide's use of equity releases and its stacking of one loan on top of another was a repeated pattern in its residential loan book, which would later push small investors into depression, bankruptcy or emigration.

Even the best-connected were being pulled down by Irish Nationwide. For Fingleton, however, life continued as usual. On 10 October he was one of hundreds of mourners at the funeral of Father Aengus Finucane, former chief executive of Concern. Fingleton chatted to an *Irish Independent* reporter, Stephen O'Farrell, at the fringe of the ceremony at the Church of the Holy Spirit in Kimmage, Dublin. He praised his old friend, who, he said, he had stayed in touch with up until he died at the age of seventy-seven. 'He was a gentleman, a great humanitarian and a great priest,' he said. He also made a more unusual comment to the paper, that he could still 'drop a couple of bombshells.' He reversed tack immediately when pressed by the journalist: what he had said was 'nonsense' and 'only a joke,' he said.

Whatever it was, it was a strange comment to make to the media at this time. It was almost as if it was a shot across the bows to somebody.

Meanwhile Brian Lenihan was pressing ahead with a plan to gain control of Irish Nationwide. He proposed amendments to the NAMA legislation that would give him a 'special share' in the society. This would give the right to appoint directors to the board and propose or veto motions. The legislation, which was winding its way through the Oireachtas, would mean that the minister could wind up the society, or do anything else he wanted, at five days' notice to its members.

Lenihan was laying the groundwork for the state to take over the society outright. The society's members, so many of whom had backed Fingleton to the hilt down the years, were being removed from its future.

Joan Burton claimed at the time that the state would need to put at least €1 billion into the society. This was not confirmed by Lenihan, but she was ahead of her time with this prediction, which would later turn out to be a serious underestimate.

There were heated daily debates in the Dáil on NAMA and the bank bail-out. On 13 October a Fine Gael TD, Paul Kehoe, made a comment about Fingleton during discussion of the NAMA Bill. Kehoe, who had legal immunity because his comments were made in the Dáil, compared the treatment of one of his constituents in Co. Wexford who faced losing his home with that of senior bankers. His comments stung Fingleton, who was furious that such comments had been made, which must only have reaffirmed his resolve not to be, as he saw it, 'bullied by the state.' On 21 October 2009 he wrote again to Kitchen.

Dear Danny,
    I wish to acknowledge receipt of your letter of 6 October in reply to my letter of 25 September last.

Because the government reneged on their agreement with me through the actions of the Minister for Finance, the voluntary repayment of the €1m so called bonus is no longer discretionary. It is now a matter of principle for me.

It is not an issue for the society, it is now an issue for the Minister for Finance and his department and if they wish to deal with me on the matter I would be happy to respond.

However there are still a number of issues outstanding as far as I am concerned which have not been addressed. In my letter to you on 25 September last, I requested a copy of the report from the government directors of the investigation sought by the minister into the payment of my so called bonus and pension entitlements. I also sought confirmation from the same directors that they found nothing irregular nor improper in their investigations and that in both instances I was fully entitled both legally and contractually to the payments in question. Furthermore I also need confirmation that there was no inconsistency with the stated position of the board of the society and their findings.

As this was [an] independent investigation carried out by the government directors on the behalf of the Minister, the obligation is on them not the society to furnish me with this information.

I look forward to receiving this information to bring a conclusion to the issues outstanding as per my statement to the *Irish Times* as per their report of 1 September 2009.

Yours sincerely,

Michael Fingleton

Fingleton had reinvented himself as a man of principle rather than the widely held view of him as a greedy banker.

It was a busy letter-writing period for Fingleton. On 24 October he wrote to the Ceann Comhairle of the Dáil, Séamus Kirk, demanding that Kehoe apologise for his comments, which he described as 'outrageous, reckless, misinformed and extremely defamatory allegations.' Under the Constitution he was 'entitled to defend my good name,' and he called on Kirk to uphold his rights.

I now demand that Mr Kehoe be requested by the Chair to publicly withdraw these false allegations and to apologise to the House for his

actions. I also invite Deputy Kehoe to make these allegations outside
the House and if he does so my action will be swift and decisive
under the law.

I look forward to an immediate response to this letter as both
my wife and my family are devastated by these false, malicious and
unfounded allegations, and they cannot be allowed to stand on the
record.

Kirk referred the complaint to the Committee on Procedure and
Privileges, which twice discussed the complaint over the following
months. In 2010 he wrote to Kehoe to tell him:

I am to inform you that while the committee found that the remark
made by you was inappropriate, it was agreed, taking into account
the circumstances in which it was made, that prima facie a breach of
privilege did not occur.

The committee now regards the matter as being closed.

While Fingleton raged at his name being trampled on in the Dáil,
the government was working flat out to try to solve the mess he had
bequeathed it. On the night of 29 October the Dáil Finance Committee
met to discuss NAMA's controversial 'valuation methodology,' which saw
it pay approximately the market value of impaired loans, in the hope
that they would recover in the future. Lenihan defended the approach
by saying it had the backing of the European Commission.

So the Commission accepts that this is not just appropriate but
inevitable in the case of virtually every member-state that adopts
an asset relief scheme. However, one hears in the public debate that
there is something unusual, that the Government is uniquely thick-
headed about this. These sections have been drafted on the basis of
the Commission advice and this is their foundation.

Joan Burton was not convinced.

By having a separate notion of long-term economic value the minister
is seeking to inflate the value of the assets artificially, thereby putting
the economy of this country at a significant disadvantage by the

decision to overpay on such a grandiose scale for the distressed loans of the banks. The loans were given by the banks to the construction sector, but particularly to property developers, to pay for massive speculation in land which created a bubble and then collapsed.

At this point the government believed it would have to put €4 billion into Anglo Irish and €1 billion into Irish Nationwide. 'Most of this money will be gone with the wind,' Burton said presciently. 'The Minister has decided to throw economic logic to the wind and for the sake of floating the boat of the bankers to come up with an artificial structure which seeks to overpay for the assets at the cost of the taxpayer.'

Gerry McGinn was now snowed under trying to deal with problem developers. He appointed Declan Ballance, a former property investment manager with D2 Private, as senior commercial banking manager. The society, however, had still not found anyone prepared to take on the job of head of commercial lending.

At about the same time Irish Nationwide leaned on the state guarantee to raise €500 million to bolster its funding. It would otherwise have been shut out of the market entirely, but it was still very tight and it was a battle to keep the society afloat. A spokesperson for the society said it was 'totally untrue' that it was running out of cash. The reality, however, was that it was sinking slowly, and a takeover by the state was now only a matter of timing. Its deposits at this point may have sunk as low as €4 billion.

The state and its banks were now competing to raise money. As the months went on, gradually the banks would pull the state down to their own level in the mire, making it impossible for Ireland to raise finance.

On 18 November the *Irish Independent* reported that Fingleton had not paid back his bonus. The story was by now a regular one.

On 20 November, Irish Nationwide finally appointed Declan Buckley as head of commercial banking. Buckley was former head of business banking at Ulster Bank (Ireland), which was facing its own problems because of its exposure to the property market. He took the job from Tom McMenamin, who had retired after a disastrous spell in charge.

The Department of Finance was again pushing hard for Irish Nationwide to be absorbed into the EBS. The losses facing both institutions were still not fully understood, and the government was prepared to take only a 60 per cent stake in the combined building societies. Even though Lenihan by now realised that both institutions might have to be nationalised, he was anxious to ensure that at least part of the merged societies remained in private hands. At the annual conference of the Association of Compliance Officers in Ireland on 23 November, both Lenihan and the chief executive of EBS, Fergus Murphy, pushed the so-called positives of such a merger. 'You would like to think that we could move this on quite quickly,' Murphy said, adding that he believed a merger could be implemented by that Christmas or early in 2010. At the same conference Lenihan stated: 'It is clear from the quantity of assets which both Nationwide and EBS have to transfer to the National Asset Management Agency that the state may well end up being a substantial shareholder in any resulting building society.' He declined to comment on whether Permanent TSB might also be merged later into a 'third force'.

Murphy, however, said Permanent TSB 'could become part of it,' in a comment that was unlikely to have been made without Lenihan's approval. He said he believed between €50 and €100 million would be needed from the state to cover any losses associated with Irish Nationwide's residential loan book.

The news that the society was going to lose up to €100 million more on its home loans lending barely registered with the public, who were already shell-shocked by the billions in new losses now being announced every few months. Brian Carey correctly described talks about the so-called third force in his column in the *Sunday Times* about this time as 'a wonkily assembled flat-packed, three-legged stool. Every time it looks as if it stacks up, logic collapses it.' Banging three rubbish banks together, he argued, would not solve anything; but the state would have to spend millions more on consultants before it realised this.

While these talks were going on, Gerry McGinn was trying to get to grips with the society's British business, which for so many years had been run only by Gary McCollum in Belfast and Michael Fingleton junior in London. The £4.4 billion loan book was a mess, with excessive loan-to-value lending and profit-share deals that were now worth nothing, leaving the society in a difficult position in trying to recover value. McGinn appointed four new people to the society's Belfast office to try to unpick the problem. But this also was too little, too late.

Lenihan, worn out and facing fresh challenges every day, was by now furious whenever he thought of Fingleton's bonus. On 25 November 2009, responding to the *Irish Independent* article seven days earlier, he wrote another letter to Kitchen, marked 'personal and confidential,' urging action by the society.

Dear Mr Kitchen,

I have been informed (a) that the former chief executive of INBS, Mr Michael Fingleton has stated that he does not now propose to return the bonus of €1m as promised and (b) that you do not intend to make any more approaches to him on the matter. Neither of these are acceptable outcomes.

In the absence of the state guarantee and a commitment by the state to provide capital, INBS would not have survived. As you know, there are significant decisions to be made in respect of INBS and, in such a context, this matter cannot be allowed to stand as you propose. It is essential, therefore, that you and your board pursue Mr Fingleton's promise to return the bonus to the society with the utmost vigour and that all available options towards this end be actively considered.

I expect that you will keep me fully informed on all developments in this matter as a matter of urgency.

Yours sincerely,

Brian Lenihan TD,

Minister for Finance

On 30 November Kitchen replied. It was a letter designed to put Lenihan back in his box and encourage him to finally drop the matter.

Dear Minister,

Thank you for your letter of 25 November. Perhaps you do not recall at our meeting in September I explained to you that Mr Fingleton had no intention of repaying his bonus. Also from our discussion and the report commissioned by your department from the two public interest directors on our board you should know that the society had no legal basis whatsoever to bring pressure on Mr Fingleton.

You may recall I informed you that senior counsel (Mr M McDowell) had opined in this regard. I would therefore be grateful if you could let me know exactly what you expect from us other than ritual requests which I have already determined will be refused.

Not being party to any discussions on the subject I cannot vouch for the accuracy of Mr Fingleton's position. He however has informed me that he had reached an agreement with Government to repay the bonus but that this agreement had been reneged upon by Government after he had announced he was prepared to repay. Further your Department's veto of our Board's decision to send him a copy of the above mentioned report has further hardened his attitude to the matter.

In conclusion I have already informed you that this matter is now between Mr Fingleton and the Government and whilst I and the board will do anything required to facilitate an agreement we are not the parties in dispute and thus have no leverage over Mr Fingleton.

Please let me know if I can be of further assistance.

Yours sincerely,

Daniel J Kitchen

Chairman

Kitchen was beginning to show his irritation with Lenihan, who just wouldn't let the €1 million bonus drop. Irish Nationwide's wealthy chairman appeared not to understand how the bonus had become a stick with which Lenihan's opponents in politics and the media would beat him. Kitchen knew that the prospects for the society were bleak but somehow couldn't see how unfair it was that Fingleton had walked away with another €1 million on top of the many more he had taken over the years—or, if he could see it, he was clear that nothing could be done about it.

On 8 December, Irish Nationwide stated that it would need between €1.2 and €2 billion in taxpayers' funds to pay for Fingleton's and his cronies' follies. The discounts being applied by NAMA on its sloppy and reckless commercial loan book were proving worse than expected. The society told its 200,000 members that it planned to hold a special general meeting on 18 December. In return for any capital injection, the Minister for Finance was to be given his 'special shares,' passing control of the society wholly to the state. Members were told there were 'no further options' other than a government investment of between €1.2 and €2 billion to 'raise material levels of capital to meet the society's requirements.'

Lenihan, who was being briefed daily on NAMA's progress, knew that Irish Nationwide would need at least €2 billion. He knew the truth that the taxpayer was being asked to write a blank cheque to pay for Fingleton's foolishness, and he knew that politically he needed to be seen to get the €1 million back in order to hold on to public support.

On 15 December he again wrote to Kitchen, pressing him on the issue of the bonus.

Dear Mr Kitchen,

I refer to your letter dated 30 November 2009 concerning the bonus of €1m paid by INBS in November 2008 to the society's then chief executive officer, Mr Michael Fingleton.

I note your reference to our meeting in September 2009 during the course of which the bonus paid to Mr Fingleton was one of a number of topics discussed.

As you know, at that meeting I was given a specific assurance by you, as chairman that the board of INBS would continue to pursue the former CEO for the return by him to the society of the €1m in question, as promised in Mr Fingleton's press release of April 2009.

With regard to Mr Fingleton's comment to you to the effect that he had reached an agreement with the government to repay the bonus, and that this agreement had been reneged upon by the government after he had announced he was prepared to repay, I have to state that no such agreement ever existed.

I am of the view that every available mechanism should be considered to secure the return of the bonus to the society. While I note that legal opinions have been provided to INBS on this matter, these relate solely to the compatibility of the payment with the requirements of the guarantee scheme. They do not, for example, consider the standing of the commitment made by the former CEO to the society.

However, apart from the strict legal considerations involved, in view of the fact that the former CEO, as an expression of his concern for the society and 'his respect for its members,' made a voluntary and public commitment to return the bonus payment, I believe it is incumbent on the board of the society to continue to pursue the matter on behalf of the society with all necessary determination to ensure that such a commitment is fully honoured.

I would request that you keep me fully informed of your board's progress and of all relevant documents in this matter.

Yours sincerely,

Brian Lenihan TD,

Minister for Finance

———

On Thursday 17 December, shareholders in Irish Life and Permanent approved the creation of a holding company to help the group spin off its loss-making banking arm, Permanent TSB. This would free the company's profitable Irish Life business to go on without it. The move was seen as another step towards the 'third force' idea.

The following day Irish Nationwide and EBS held simultaneous special general meetings to approve the injection of state capital into their balance sheets. The two societies needed €2.4 billion, taking the total put into the banks by the taxpayer up to that point to €13.4 billion. Close to 97 per cent of Irish Nationwide's members voted in favour of a motion to issue special investment shares to the Minister for Finance. Members of the EBS also voted overwhelming for state support.

'The society will need a substantial capital injection. Realistically, the only source for that is the government,' Kitchen said. 'It gives the minister the power to do whatever he wants with the board,' he admitted, in recognition that the society was now under state control in all but name. In a telling comment he admitted that the estimated loss of up to €2 billion was only a 'guess'. Cash would be provided by the state 'on a drip-feed basis,' as it needed it. 'There's little by way of legal redress that can be brought to bear,' he said in response to questioning by a member about Fingleton's bonus.

Brendan Burgess criticised the decision by the society to enter discussions for merging with the EBS. He said the society had failed and should be wound up, with the surplus returned to the members. The fact that Burgess believed there would be a surplus showed how even the more critical members of the society had little idea of the catastrophe the society had become.

One member, Reggie Irwin, compared the society to Laurel and Hardy. It was a case of 'here's another nice mess you've got us into,' he said; but even Stan Laurel would not have been 'so inept as to get us into this position.' He said the society should stay independent as a tiny building society. 'We could ask Michael Fingleton to come back and rescue us.'

Mark Fitzpatrick, an accountant, had greater insight. He asked the board, 'How could one man completely bring down this great institution,' which was 'supposedly a working man's society? As a taxpayer I cannot see how we are ever going to get €1 billion or €2 billion out of the society.'

On 21 December, 'Prime Time Investigates' broadcast a programme called 'Meet the Bankers.' It drew heavily on the evidence of Olivia Greene, who had turned whistle-blower on the society she had previously worked for.

An irate Fingleton rang the station just before the broadcast. He launched a blistering attack against the makers of the programme and threatened to sue them if they went ahead. His protests were ignored, and the broadcast went out.

The programme revealed that a loan of €1.6 million had been fast-tracked by the society to Charlie McCreevy, Irish member of the EU Commission and a former Minister for Finance, to buy a home at the K Club. The records showed that McCreevy and his wife had bought a property on the Ladycastle Estate for €1.6 million on 13 September 2006. The property was valued in June 2006, and its mortgage amounted to a loan-to-value ratio of 107 per cent. Irish Nationwide's guidelines said it was not supposed to grant 100 per cent mortgages, but this had been breached in this case. McCreevy declined to comment.

Other loans to Fianna Fáil politicians included €7 million to Francis 'Francie' O'Brien, a former senator, €3 million for Don Lydon, another former senator, and €300,000 for Seán McCarthy, a Fianna Fáil councillor.

Joan Burton seized on the programme's findings. 'The question now arises as to whether or not other figures in Fianna Fáil, including figures at senior level, were customers of Irish Nationwide, and whether the institution operated a system of favoured relationships for particular clients.'

Fine Gael's spokesperson on enterprise, Leo Varadkar, said: 'The year on the calendar has changed but another generation of Fianna Fáil politicians and their friends in banking and building have succeeded in bankrupting the country. A 21st-century golden circle has corrupted our banking system and destroyed our economy. The drivers of this phase of economic destruction were, again, a cheerleading Fianna Fáil Government and greedy speculators and banks.'

The leader of the Green Party, John Gormley, called for a banking inquiry that would include an investigation into the links between bankers, developers and politicians. 'I think it would be helpful in the context of any sort of inquiry. [Fingleton] had a habit of giving loans and mortgages to a lot of people . . . Mr Fingleton seemed to foster good relationships with these people, for whatever reason, and it is important to establish why this was so.'

The idea of such an inquiry, like so much else that concerned Irish Nationwide, was somehow allowed to fade away.

Chapter 11

SIFTING THROUGH THE WRECKAGE (DECEMBER 2009 TO MAY 2010)

On Sunday 12 December 2009 Miriam O'Callaghan interviewed the former Minister for Finance Charlie McCreevy and his wife, Noeleen. It was a soft Sunday-morning style of interview, which delved into the ups and downs of their lives together, broken up with a choice of songs. But, as usually happened with O'Callaghan, some tough questions were added to the mix.

'Do you ever doubt yourself?' she asked McCreevy, then a member of the European Commission.

'I don't stand up every day and say, I shouldn't have done that,' McCreevy replied, 'We did what we did, and they were in the best interests of the people.'

Steadfastly, he defended all his actions, from introducing tax relief for property development to weakening the civil service by pursuing a mad plan called decentralisation to scatter its offices around the country. It was the sort of bull-headed refusal to accept any blame that must have been familiar to Fingleton, who also remained in denial about his failings.

A few months earlier, McCreevy recalled in his interview, he had launched *Bertie Ahern: The Autobiography* in the Shelbourne Hotel. Brian Cowen had also been at the launch, but, unlike Ahern and McCreevy, he said nothing as the two men delivered self-congratulatory speeches.

'It was a great night, it was like a mini-ard-fheis.' McCreevy laughed as he remembered a night of pints and back-slapping.

'People said it was like you were living in a parallel universe,' O'Callaghan replied. 'You were both singing the praises of the past, and people were going, Hello, have you been living in Ireland in the past few months?'

'Well, hold on,' McCreevy replied. 'My dad died in 1954. You weren't born then. Ireland in the 50s and 60s, compared to the Ireland of the 2000s—there's no comparison. Even if the economy retrenches in '08, '09, '10 it's a damn sight far better place than it was even fifteen or twenty years ago. People have to get things in perspective in this particular country. Things are tough at the moment, but it's up to ourselves to get out of it ... People should have been around when it was really tough ... Times are tough, people are finding it difficult, but we have to be somewhat positive.'

Noeleen McCreevy added: 'As I keep saying to James [the McCreevys' son], it's a great time to be a student. Stay there for another while.'

The McCreevys could afford this sanguine attitude towards the bust. Charlie McCreevy was well insulated from the consequences of his political mistakes, with a TD's and minister's pension of €125,000 a year, paid by the taxpayer, on top of his EU commissioner's salary of €238,000. Not everybody was so lucky.

Ireland had not gone back to 1954, but a decade of growth was in the process of being wiped out. Ordinary people were now really beginning to feel the price of bailing out Irish Nationwide and Ireland's other toxic banks. By December 2010 unemployment had reached 13 per cent, compared with less than 5 per cent during the boom. Figures from the Central Statistics Office showed that emigration was at its highest level since the late 1980s.

Even the rich and the formerly rich were beginning to feel the pain. Nowhere was this more evident than at the K Club, whose acquisition with borrowings from Irish Nationwide was a high-water mark for the property bubble. The resort was still luxurious, with paintings by Jack Yeats and John Lavery adorning its walls, as well as a display case containing a uniform worn at the Battle of the Bulge by General Patton. But it wasn't the same. There was no longer as much money around as there had been in the glory years, when Michael Smurfit had worn Patton's uniform during a birthday cruise around the Mediterranean, to the amusement of his guests, including Michael Fingleton. Smurfit was now at loggerheads with Gerry Gannon over ownership of the resort, where income was falling as its former members' cash dried up. Residents like Séamus Ross, Noel Smyth and Seán Dunne were now on their way into NAMA. The agency wanted them at their desks working and not socialising and wheeler-dealing on the golf course.

Like his fellow-developers, Gannon, a former bricklayer from Co.

Roscommon, was no longer a very rich man. He owed his Irish banks €1.7 billion and in return for NAMA support was preparing to accept a salary of a mere €150,000 to €200,000 a year. He had no interest in paying the bills at the K Club to keep it going and was instead anxious to sell his stake. Michael Smurfit was not amused. In a letter to members at the tail end of 2009 he wrote: 'I am the sole financial supporter at this time.' Members were pressing him to reduce their annual fee from €6,950 plus VAT, but the tycoon declined, citing the additional expenses he had to pick up.

It was a constant battle for the ill-equipped society to keep things going. At every level it had slipped up, and it was hard work trying to unravel the past. On 28 January, for example, Tadhg Feeney, a businessman from Thomastown, Co. Kilkenny, was given a two-year suspended prison sentence for non-payment of tax on almost €1 million lodged in bogus non-resident accounts. In April 2009, Fingleton's final month in the hot seat, Feeney had opened twenty-nine Irish Nationwide accounts with a bogus address in England. It was incredible that he could manage to open so many accounts without this being picked up. But then, this was Irish Nationwide.

The society was dead on its feet. Gerry McGinn and his stretched management were under enormous pressure. It was constant firefighting to keep clients afloat and to claw back whatever money it could. As he dug deeper into the society's Belfast office in particular he was agog at the reckless lending and the poor quality of records. At the same time he knew that in September, only nine months away, Irish Nationwide had to refinance €3.7 billion of its bonds, a third of its entire business. This was an impossible mountain to climb.

Making it worse, in total that month Irish banks had to refinance €24 billion worth of bonds. Irish Nationwide would face fierce competition as it tried to raise funds. The September deadline was dubbed by the Royal Bank of Canada the 'wall of worry' for Ireland.

The clock was ticking; if Irish Nationwide couldn't manage to come up with this money, the state would have to intervene—assuming it had the money to do so. It was essential, then, that the society should get its commercial loans off its books and get new money in by transferring them to NAMA before September.

The dire situation the society was in was underlined when, in January 2010, Moody's published its global league table for bank financial strength.

From being rated as having some of the best banks in the world three years earlier, Ireland was now in the bottom quarter, behind Bolivia, Uruguay, Tunisia and Pakistan. Bank of Ireland, AIB and Irish Life and Permanent were graded D, making them well below investment grade. Anglo Irish Bank was rated E, placing it firmly in the toxic high-risk zone.

As always, however, Irish Nationwide did worse again. It was crowned by Moody's as Ireland's worst bank, with a rating of E–. This put it on a par with banks in Kyrgyzstan, then under a particularly corrupt and murderous regime, where Moody's considered the worst banks in the world to be.

As February began, Charlie McCreevy, who had been Minister for Finance from 1997 to 2004, finished his stint as EU Commissioner for the Internal Market. He was given a golden handshake worth €378,288 to ease his transition back into everyday life. Asked if he believed his actions had helped create the economic crisis, he replied: 'I don't. I have always said I certainly don't.' Asked if he believed Michael Fingleton should repay his €1 million bonus, he was more circumspect. 'Nothing to do with me. I've no opinion on any of these matters. They are Irish matters.'

On 9 February, a few days after McCreevy's comments, the new governor of the Central Bank, Patrick Honohan, told an event in Trinity College, Dublin, where he had previously lectured, that the state would have to take bigger stakes in the banks. NAMA, he warned, was going to blow holes in their balance sheets when it acquired their toxic property loans. 'It's pretty clear the government will be acquiring additional equity stakes,' Honohan said. It was 'possible', he said, that the state would have to take a majority stake in Bank of Ireland and AIB, where it already had an indirect 25 per cent holding. Tough spending cuts would be needed, he warned, to pay for the banks. However, he said he was hopeful that the crisis in Ireland's economy was bottoming out, as its gross national product had now shrunk by 16 per cent and its gross domestic product by 11 per cent. Honohan would be proved wrong on this issue: bad decisions both behind and ahead of the state would ensure years of future austerity.

Later that day Bank of Scotland (Ireland) announced a plan to shut down the forty-four branches of Halifax and other retail businesses, leading to the loss of 750 jobs, almost half its total work force. The announcement was made at 3 p.m. that day in a conference call throughout the group, which sent shocked workers spilling out into the streets afterwards. The company said that part of the reason it had decided to shut up shop was that its attempts to be amalgamated as a 'third-force' bank with Irish Nationwide and others had come to nothing. Under its chief executive, Mark Duffy, it had competed hard with Irish Nationwide to give loans to rural developers and competed for deposits in towns around the country but was finally chucking in the towel.

Other banks were also downsizing rapidly, with National Irish Bank shutting 25 of its 58 branches and First Active putting 49 branches up for sale.

It now seemed inevitable that Irish Nationwide too would have to swing the axe, to fire employees and close some or all of its fifty branches.

Speaking to Brian Carey in the *Sunday Times*, the former chief executive of Irish Life and Permanent, David Went, said he wasn't very surprised at the vicious banking retrenchments. 'We put too much capital and too much competition against a small market the size of Manchester,' he said. 'With hindsight, it was like putting a flame-thrower to a can of petrol.'

On 17 February the *Irish Times* reported that Irish Nationwide had suspended Gary McCollum, the head of its British operations. The society refused to comment on the suspension, which came as Ernst and Young were working their way steadily through the society's commercial loan book. McCollum had set a rental record in Belfast in April 2008 when the society had leased space in the ten-storey Centrepoint building. He would never again get to enjoy its views.

On 21 February there was further evidence of Fingleton's extravagance. The *Sunday Independent* reported that he was among a group of Irish business people who stumped up millions to pay for the restoration of the historic Pauline Chapel in the Vatican Museum. Three of the society's clients who made large donations were Johnny Ronan of Treasury Holdings, Seán Mulryan of Ballymore Properties and Paddy McKillen. Others who donated were Seán FitzPatrick, the former chairman of Anglo Irish Bank, and Denis O'Brien, the telecoms magnate. Donors were given special medallions after a private mass in the chapel celebrated by Cardinal Giovanni Lajolo in July 2009. Michael Fingleton's name is engraved on a five-foot-tall marble plaque in the sacristy of the chapel. The Vatican gave him a special gold-plated medallion for his donation of more than $100,000. It was another reminder of Fingleton's hubris and self-regard that in his own eyes made him bigger than the man in the street who had been saddled with the bill for his appalling mistakes.

Far from the glories of Rome, Ireland's sprawling so-called solution to the property loans sinking its banks was coming together. On Friday 26 February the European Union gave NAMA the green light. 'This impaired asset measure, which is specifically targeted at real estate assets, is [the] key to cleaning up Irish banks' balance sheets,' said the EU Commissioner for Competition, Joaquín Almunia. The EU was firmly behind the socialising of bad property debts onto the backs of Irish citizens.

Irish Nationwide had already packaged close to €1 billion worth of property loans to be transferred to NAMA. The haircuts being applied had originally been estimated at about 30 per cent, but as February ended it was widely speculated that the cut for the society could top 50 per cent.

'I am advised by NAMA that issues have arisen during the due diligence process regarding the quality of legal title and related matters,' Brian Lenihan said. 'Clearly this justifies the thorough and detailed due diligence process undertaken by NAMA.'

The work load within the society was now intense. With NAMA beginning to come together, a clamber began to explain to the public just what happened. Patrick Honohan said he would prepare a report on the crisis at the same time that two outside experts, Klaus Regling and Max Watson, were selected to interview the bankers and their watchdogs to determine what had happened.

On 18 March, Seán FitzPatrick was detained in Bray Garda Station and questioned for twenty-four hours on goings-on inside Anglo Irish Bank. It was a very public fall from grace for one banker at least.

The following day it emerged that Michael Fingleton junior had been moved from Irish Nationwide's London office and was now installed in Belfast. It was extraordinary, given who his father was, that he was still working in Irish Nationwide, though the society had to be careful not to mistreat him because of this.

With Irish Nationwide crawling with outside consultants and its ordinary staff working late into the night, Danny Kitchen wrote again to Fingleton on 23 March to ask for his bonus back.

Dear Michael,

I am writing to enquire if your situation with regard to your undertaking to repay the bonus has changed. Clearly I am not aware of any contact you may or may not have had with the government in relation to this matter and would therefore be obliged for an update.

On a separate matter I enclose a letter received by us today requesting your attendance at the inquiry being carried out by Klaus Regling and Max Watson. Could you reply directly to them as per the contact details contained therein.

Yours sincerely,

Daniel J. Kitchen

On 27 March, James Morrissey parted ways with Irish Nationwide after representing the society for fifteen years. He had staunchly defended Fingleton against any and all attacks by journalists like Bill Tyson as the society lurched from controversy to scandal.

As March ended, the focus turned to Brian Lenihan and Matthew Elderfield, the Financial Regulator, who were due to reveal the new post-NAMA banking landscape. Both Bank of Ireland and the EBS delayed issuing their results in order to allow this announcement. There was a sense of dread in the twenty-four hours beforehand as the market steeled itself for what promised to be savage haircuts. 'This is the big one' was how Goodbody's banking analyst Éamonn Hughes described it, 'when we find out about National Asset Management Agency haircuts, target capital levels and levels of state ownership.' An analyst with NCB Stockbrokers, Ciarán Callaghan, said: 'Tomorrow is shaping up to be a defining day in the history of the Irish banking sector.'

The night before that seismic 'bail-out Tuesday,' AIB's share price fell by 19 per cent, while Bank of Ireland was down 10 per cent. Things were so fraught that Lenihan decided to make his speech after the markets closed that Tuesday, 30 March. To a tense and ill-tempered Dáil, he stood up and began to make his speech.

This country has come a long way since we introduced the state guarantee eighteen months ago. Back then, our banks were on the brink of financial collapse and our economy had gone into reverse. Revenue had fallen steeply, and unemployment had risen sharply. For the first time in a quarter of a century we were experiencing negative growth. Economic activity remains weak, and we face further difficult decisions. But the crucial difference is that we now have a credible fiscal position. As a result, we are now in a position to stabilise the deficit, and we are on a firm path to economic recovery.

This adjustment has imposed a heavy burden on our citizens. Taxes have increased, public-sector workers have suffered significant reductions in their pay, and social welfare payments have been reduced.

It is regularly suggested in this house and outside it that these painful measures have been necessitated by our banking crisis—that the cuts in pay are funding a bail-out of the banks. That is simply wrong. The reason we have had to make very substantial savings is because of the huge gap that opened up between the revenue we take in and the cost of running this state. We are borrowing for day-to-day expenses, and that is not sustainable.

Our determination to deal with this imbalance in our public finances through firm and decisive action has engendered real confidence in our economy on the international stage. The world out there believes in us and in our ability to work our way through our difficulties and return to growth.

Jean-Claude Trichet said, 'In the case of Ireland, very, very tough decisions have been taken by the government, and rightly so.' More recently Mr Trichet's colleague José Manuel González-Páramo on the ECB said, 'The Irish measures are very courageous. They are going in the right direction.' The French Finance Minister, Christine Lagarde, said, 'Ireland has set the high standard the rest of us must follow.' On a recent visit to Ireland the German Minister for European Affairs, Dr Werner Hoyer, said, 'I think there is a deeply rooted trust and confidence in this country's ability to sort out its problems . . . There is a fundamental belief that the Irish are going to solve it.'

It was a bravura performance. While accepting the praise of European leaders, Lenihan made no reference to their culpability for Ireland's economic woes. It was the French and German banks that had lent so recklessly to Ireland's rogue institutions, such as Irish Nationwide. But they were taking no pain for their mistakes as a small country on the edge of Europe suddenly became saddled with the debts of a few hundred crazed developers. Instead Lenihan praised the Europeans, before dropping a series of domestic bombshells.

The state, he said, would have to put another €8.3 billion into Anglo Irish Bank immediately and a possible €10 billion more in the future. AIB needed to find €7.4 billion, but some of this money might be raised by selling off its good businesses in Poland and North America. The state, he said, would have to take majority control of AIB from its existing position of 25 per cent. Bank of Ireland would need €2.66 billion, but he hoped the bank would be able to raise some of this money privately. The state, he said, would remain a minority shareholder in the bank.

Then came Irish Nationwide's turn.

Irish Nationwide, Lenihan said, was about to transfer €670 million of assets to NAMA, at an average discount of 58 per cent. This was the worst haircut in Irish banking by a considerable degree, reflecting decades of unchecked mismanagement and bad decision-making. Anglo Irish, by comparison, came in at 50 per cent, while Bank of Ireland stood at 35 per cent.

Taking account of this and his broader assessment of the building society, the regulator has determined that INBS will need an injection of €2.6 billion to remain compliant with its current regulatory capital requirements. This is a very large bill for the taxpayer, but, as in the case of Anglo, it is the least costly solution. It is important to highlight that this level of capital support is required to maintain the institution's financial position in light of the large losses incurred on its loan portfolio. Without this capital injection the taxpayer would have to shoulder the significant and immediate costs in meeting the deposits, bond-holders, and the liabilities due to the ECB.

The detailed information that had emerged from the banks in the course of the NAMA process, the minister said, was 'truly shocking. At every hand's turn our worst fears have been surpassed. Some institutions were worse than others. But the fact is that our banking system, to a greater or lesser extent, engaged in reckless property development lending. In too many cases there were also shoddy banking practices. The banks played fast and loose with the economic interests of this country.'

NAMA, in a briefing later that day, said it planned to take over €81 billion of toxic assets, made up of between 14,000 and 15,000 individual loans. The first tranche of these loans would relate to the country's biggest developers, who had loans of €16 billion. NAMA would buy these loans for €8½ billion, or a discount of 47 per cent.

The public were shocked. AIB announced in the middle of everything that it planned to increase its interest rates by 0.5 per cent, in a clear signal that it badly needed to get more cash in to stay afloat. For customers already under pressure this added €65 to the monthly payments on an average mortgage of €250,000.

In an editorial the following day the *Irish Independent* concluded: 'If there is one thing you can bank on, it is that 2010 will go down as the year of the great bank robbery.'

Fine Gael's spokesperson on finance, Richard Bruton, said:

> With the stroke of a pen today Brian Lenihan will double our national debt. That's quite an achievement. You see, they are going to pump over €70 billion into NAMA and our existing banks, including the zombie bank, Anglo Irish. This money is effectively going to pay off the bad debts run up by these banks and their speculator friends. We have crossed the Rubicon. There can be no turning back from this decision.

The state was now going to own Irish Nationwide outright by putting €100 million into it in 'special investment shares.' In such circumstances, Lenihan said, 'the institution does not have a future as an independent stand-alone entity. The government's priority will be to secure a swift sale of INBS or its integration with another entity.'

During a lengthy briefing for journalists, Lenihan said he planned to shake up the society's board, and once this was done the issue of Fingleton's €1 million bonus 'would be raised.'

Joan Burton wasn't convinced. 'How did their managing director walk away with a retirement bonus of €1 million, which, when the heat was on, there were promises it would be given back, but it has never been returned? That is what ordinary people cannot understand. Can someone please stand up and explain how this can be?'

In a short statement that night Gerry McGinn warned the public that worse was to come when the society revealed its annual results in May.

> We are grateful to the Government for its financial commitment to the Society. The Society will post significant losses for 2009 due to the high level of provisions required on our commercial loan book. This injection of capital will cover both the losses for 2009 and the uncertainty we will have over the extent of discount emanating from the transfer of impaired assets to NAMA.

The following day the *Star* published an inflammatory front-page article featuring photographs of Seán FitzPatrick and Michael Fingleton with the comment that they had cost the taxpayer €25 billion. The next day, 31 March, Anglo Irish Bank posted a loss of €12.7 billion, the biggest in Irish corporate history, for the fifteen months to the end of December 2009. The bank wrote off an incredible €15.1 billion on bad loans—with €10.1 billion of this relating to loans going into NAMA. In total, the bank had now sucked up €12.3 billion in taxpayers' money.

On 1 April the state paid €100 million to take over the toxic mess that was Irish Nationwide Building Society. The same day Stan Purcell, a director of Irish Nationwide since 1994, resigned. A society insider said: 'He was one of the very people who knew the place inside and out. He helped to the extent that he had to. He knew where the baggage was buried but he did not volunteer anything for us to look at for attention.' Purcell had attended board meetings after Fingleton's departure, but he didn't say much. Every day he had gone into his office on the fifth floor and worked away at what he was asked to.

As the society's new management, aided by Ernst and Young, dug deeper into its lending files, Purcell was regularly confronted by McGinn and McGloughlin, who were demanding explanations. 'They confronted him about it from the summer of 2009 on,' a society source said. 'He'd take it all in and not say very much. Eventually Danny Kitchen told him: This is simply unsustainable, you have got to go.'

Purcell was paid €385,000 in his final year, at a time when the average salary in the society was €33,000. After twenty-four years at Fingleton's side, he left quietly, a wealthy man with a multi-million pension fund earned while the society operated like a rogue hedge-fund, piling risk upon risk, which now had to be paid by the taxpayer.

That night Lenihan insisted that Ireland wouldn't buckle under the cost of bailing out its bust banks. He told the *Irish Times*:

We are in danger of viewing Ireland as having a problem we cannot surmount, but that is not the case. Those advocating default would put us in the position of Iceland or Argentina, and that would leave us with insurmountable problems. People are perfectly entitled to be angry at the reckless lending of the bankers. I understand that; but Ireland is not Argentina, and we can't go around repudiating our debts.

In Lenihan's mind, Ireland could still come through this, even though the evidence was mounting that his policies, under the direction of the European Union, would bankrupt the country. In all, it was a horrific week.

That weekend, in an editorial on 4 April, the *Sunday Independent* concluded: 'The taxpayer has been taken for a mug for long enough. It's high time that the Government spread some of the Anglo and Irish Nationwide pain to the bondholders. Unlike many of the depositors, these were savvy professional investors. Big boys' games, big boys' rules.'

In the same edition Lenihan tried to put a brighter gloss on the disastrous decision to bail out the banks and their bond-holders. 'One of the good things about the steep discount, averaging 47 per cent, is that the residential property market will now be stabilised at a realistic level. You can now buy in confidence that the price is realistic.' Yet again he was both hopelessly optimistic and plain wrong.

———

Ernst and Young continued to trawl through Irish Nationwide's lending sewer. They were finding incredible things hidden away in its files. While their findings remained secret, the business editor of the *Irish Times*, John McManus, wrote an insightful opinion column on 19 April, the morning the society was to reveal record losses.

> The truly baffling thing about what happened at Irish Nationwide was that it pretty much happened in plain sight.
>
> Fingleton blatantly paid little more than lip service to the rules governing mutual societies and nobody shouted stop.
>
> Instead of being held to account, he was lauded as some sort of mischievous, but brilliant, rogue basking in that most dangerous of Irish sentiments, sneaking regard.
>
> In truth he was someone who was allowed hijack a friendly society through adroit use of its rules and, in particular, the omnipotence of a board that does not answer to institutional shareholders but instead to a disparate collection of members (or in truth customers) who were made feel profoundly grateful to have got a mortgage.

That day Irish Nationwide announced that its losses for 2009 had gone up tenfold, to €2.49 billion. McGinn told a news conference on the first floor of the building society: 'When you arrive at the scene of a car crash, you try to keep the patient alive and deal with the issues. What has happened here is an outrage. Let's not beat about the bush about that. I was very surprised and taken aback by how I found things here. There's little point in trying to disguise it.'

He said the reason NAMA had given the society such a big haircut was its high-risk lending, poor paperwork and security, and use of profit shares, which meant the society sometimes acted more in the client's interests than its own. 'There were gaps of some pretty basic information in the paper trail. Up until 2007 the rate of increase and values in the property market—fuelled by the banks themselves—meant there was always an "out", and they booked a profit. Everyone seemed to be content with that, until the music stops.'

He found it particularly shocking, he said, that the society's board had received reports about its failings that had been forwarded in turn to the Financial Regulator, and yet nothing had been done.

Merger with the EBS was on hold while the society submitted plans for its future restructuring to the European Union by the end of June. 'We have conducted a detailed analysis of the assets of the society and have created a fundamental change in the way the Irish Nationwide Building Society is managed, ensuring that robust corporate governance is in place and is effective.'

Danny Kitchen added:

> The losses reflect unprecedented levels of impairment on our loan book, which gave rise to losses on a massive scale in the context of the society. The collapse of property markets both in Ireland and abroad gave rise to the impairments, but this was exacerbated by the nature of the operation of the business, which was clearly a flawed model. The scale of the losses reflects the failure of the society's commercial lending strategy, which was over-reliant on asset value.

Afterwards McGinn did some television interviews before sitting down in a corner with Tom Lyons. He said the society had completed a review of its so-called 'celebrity loans,' to politicians, sports stars, socialites and well-known business people. He admitted that it had given favourable loans to many of these people, but he insisted there was 'nothing untoward' in this, as 'the board gave Michael Fingleton extraordinary powers.'

> He was able to make decisions on all sorts of matters without referral. Invariably the loans were within the powers granted to him by the board. These loans had a variety of characteristics: they could be interest-only, or with capital repayment holidays. The celebrity category was various well-known people. Even if it was interest-only for a period, the loans would still have to be paid back in full.

McGinn declined to comment on individual politician borrowers but said: 'I have not come across a loan made to a public representative where there were special favours done [beyond Fingleton's remit]. There was nothing untoward in loans being given on slightly generous terms.'

Later that day it emerged that Michael Fingleton junior had resigned. A society source said: 'It's not easy to sack people these days. Michael Fingleton junior was not very bright—he was very average. Yet he was one of two guys managing €5 billion. There was a lot of friction with him. Eventually he agreed to go. We all agreed it was better that way.'

———

The clear-out of most of the people who had destroyed the society and saddled the taxpayer with an ever-growing bill was now complete.

In the Dáil the following day, during leaders' questions, Éamon Gilmore demanded to know whether Brian Cowen had ever been made aware during his time as Minister for Finance of the bad lending practices in Irish Nationwide. 'I don't think it was ever brought to my attention that that sort of practice existed,' Cowen insisted. 'Certainly not. The idea that such losses were imminent or people were suggesting that that was going to take place when I was Minister for Finance during that time was not the case.'

This was an extraordinary admission of how far out of the loop he was as Minister for Finance, given the constant discussions between the Financial Regulator and the society during those years.

That night Brian Lenihan brought in draft legislation to merge the Financial Regulator's office with the Central Bank. This was to prevent the buck-passing of the boom happening again, when each had left it up to the other to monitor the banks. During the debate Richard Bruton brought up Irish Nationwide.

It reminds us of everything that was rotten, the way institutions were run as personal fiefdoms, and even still those who ran them have not in any way suffered any consequence for what has happened. And the consequences for taxpayers, for mortgage-holders, for people looking for jobs are extraordinary. Ordinary people have been brought to their knees, and they want accountability.

In the letters page of the *Irish Times*, Shane Hogan, who had campaigned for years with Brendan Burgess against Fingleton, addressed John McManus's opinion column of a few days earlier. He recalled the society's 2003 AGM, where the rebels had tried to have Fingleton sacked.

Over 80 per cent of members voted confidence in Mr Fingleton. Most members were mesmerised by claims such as 'strong leadership of our managing director,' 'our business model has clearly proven itself' and 'we will continue to build on our success for the benefit of all our members and staff' (direct quotations from the Directors Report for 2002).

Most members failed to see beyond the dollar signs flashing in front of their eyes to recognise the fundamental flaws in the leadership provided by Mr Fingleton and Mr Walsh.

I shouted stop, but few members listened. Now the taxpayer is left to pay the bill.

Hogan was right. The society's members had allowed Fingleton's absolute rule.

That summer, Ernst and Young completed their analysis of Irish Nationwide's lending. Their findings were a devastating indictment of the society.

Chapter 12

THE FORENSIC ACCOUNTANTS MOVE IN: THE ERNST AND YOUNG REPORT

'**C**orporate governance' is a broad term that reflects the way an organisation conducts its business in relation to probity, honesty, checks and balances, transparency, accountability and legality. It can also be used as a formula for going on what might be called a 'fishing expedition', with broad terms of reference.

Fingleton was gone. Irish Nationwide was essentially collapsing, and the state had taken it over. Gerry McGinn's job was to manage the meltdown, tidy up the balance sheet as best he could and manage the society in line with government policy.

The rationale for the Ernst and Young investigation was obvious. The society had lost hundreds of millions and would go on to lose a total of more than €5.4 billion. This was on foot of loans sanctioned by Michael Fingleton.

Basic questions had to be answered. How did this happen? Was the board weak? Were there adequate structures for ensuring that Fingleton did not have undue influence and control? Where did all the money go?

The sub-text of the investigation was to try to find out if Fingleton, other executives or board members had broken the law, or any society rules, or had been in breach of their fiduciary duty as directors.

The report looked at several areas. It examined Fingleton's authority and power within the society and whether it was legitimately granted or not. It looked at the banking relationships with clients. It also looked at how the society conducted its affairs on such issues as the traceability of funds, payment of invoices, ensuring adequate security or charges on loans. It also probed some aspects of Fingleton's personal finances, including an investment he had made in a hotel project in Montenegro. Fingleton's partner in the venture, the Dublin businessman Louis

Maguire, had gone to the Financial Regulator the previous year and made several allegations about Fingleton's role in that venture, raising questions about the origin of the funds Fingleton had provided for it.

What the investigators uncovered was truly shocking.

The accountants found that Michael Fingleton had been granted special powers by the board of the society as far back as 1981. These powers were reinforced by the board in December 1994 and again in August 1997. The measures empowered him to set, vary or alter interest rates and fees, and to make arrangements with individual members. This meant he could charge different people different rates of interest. He could structure a commercial or residential loan with one customer on certain conditions, such as interest-only for a decade, and on completely different terms with others. He could change the rates or the conditions attached to the loan at will. So, having lent out €1 million at a certain rate and repayable at a certain time in the future, he could then alter those conditions at any stage as he saw fit. He did not need to consult the board, or anyone else, in order to do this.

The board must have felt at the time that Fingleton could do no wrong. In reality by granting these powers they were giving the chief executive personal autonomy to do special deals with friends, change any deal he wanted, and run the society as he saw fit, without necessarily breaking the society's rules.

The ordinary checks and balances of having a chairman, a board, an audit committee, a credit committee, could become de facto irrelevant. It was the most extraordinary handing over of power in Irish financial services. It undermined and even eliminated any accountability by Fingleton for his actions within the society.

Yet nobody seemed to know about it. Newspapers didn't report it at the time, and while people inside the organisation and in the wider business community knew that Fingleton ran things his way, they didn't necessarily realise that he had been formally given the powers to do practically whatever he wanted.

Con Power, a non-executive director of Irish Nationwide at the time, has said that he knew nothing about these powers. He sat at the boardroom table for six years and was never told that Fingleton had been granted these powers. He said it was never raised or discussed by the board or in any meeting with the Central Bank or the Financial Regulator.

Power says that the rules of the society empowered the board to delegate certain responsibilities to the chief executive, but in his view it would never have been intended to hand over that kind of discretionary power to one person.

The existence of the powers should have been a red flag to the Financial Regulator. The first big question is whether the Central Bank and later the Financial Regulator even knew about them. The society was originally regulated by the Registrar of Friendly Societies, but the duty fell on the Central Bank in 1989 and then the Financial Regulator in 2004.

The second big question is, If the regulatory authorities didn't know, then why not? Surely they should have access to this kind of information, either automatically or by requesting it. Could it have been the case that the Central Bank was informed of all this through regulatory submissions but they were simply not read, ignored, or viewed as quite acceptable?

The office of the Financial Regulator is not telling us. They are not answering these kinds of questions. They may form part of the subject of an investigation by an Oireachtas committee in the future; but in the meantime the Financial Regulator is leading the investigation into what went wrong at Irish Nationwide, in a unique piece of Irish irony.

Whether the regulator knew or not, too much power had been given to one man. After all, he didn't own the society, and a lack of accountability on that scale could cause a registered lender of money to end up in disaster. And so it did. This should also have been obvious to the board.

Ernst and Young looked right down inside the corporate structure of Irish Nationwide under Michael Fingleton. Through interviews and an analysis of thousands of documents and e-mail messages the accountants discovered an organisation that was a corporate governance disaster area.

It emerged that Fingleton had twelve different people reporting directly to him. This was a most unusual way of doing things. Typically, even in enormous multi-billion companies, the business is divided into units or divisions; the further up the chain of command, the fewer the numbers. Businesses are usually classic pyramid structures. It would not be unusual to have as few as three or four people reporting directly to the chief executive, even in a much bigger organisation.

The Irish Nationwide structure revealed two things: firstly, how unorthodox the society was and, secondly, how Fingleton was all-powerful. One of the net effects of this structure was that no proper senior management team, familiar with different parts of the business, emerged. Fingleton was the only one who knew everything. Others knew a lot about their own patch, but not much else.

This was another warning sign, that a business with a loan book of nearly €12 billion could rely so much on one person. Clearly, that was how Fingleton liked it. It was up to the board to exert pressure to change it.

The accountants also built up a picture of who Fingleton was friendly with and how those people were treated commercially. One such was Louis Scully. A relatively unknown estate agent turned property developer, Scully was a personal friend of Fingleton. After Fingleton left, it emerged that loans connected to Scully, primarily for development land, amounted to approximately €130 million. The new management at Irish Nationwide had queried the status of these loans and whether they were recourse to Scully or not. A senior executive who had been there in Fingleton's time said the loans were on a profit-share joint-venture basis and therefore non-recourse. The new management had queried this. Fingleton then wrote to the society in March 2010 saying the loans were non-recourse. In other words, Scully was not personally liable for the debts in the event that he couldn't pay up. Six plots of land bought in Co. Meath had cost more than €50 million; they are now worth about €5 million.

The report found that Fingleton's letter absolved his friend Scully of all personal liability on a collection of loans, with various partners, totalling €130 million. They found evidence of Irish Nationwide paying deposits for property purchases that Scully was doing before approval of the loans by the credit committee. For example, an offer letter relating to the purchase of 36 acres in Clonee, Co. Meath, was dated 29 November 2005, a day before the credit application was approved. Two draw-downs totalling €6.9 million took place before board approval, and mortgage documents were completed on 20 December 2005.

Initial loans for the purchase of lands at Ratoath (€3.2 million) and Windtown (€0.5 million) were made to 'Stan Purcell in trust.' Purcell was chief financial officer, and he told the accountants that this was done on the instruction of Michael Fingleton. Purcell also signed a release of Irish Nationwide's charge over 17 of the 54 acres in Ratoath without the loan being repaid or any clear document on file explaining why. The balance of the loan was €15.3 million in June 2009. Purcell said this was done on the instruction of Michael Fingleton.

Irish Nationwide had a joint venture with the house-builder and developer Gerry Gannon. Its 50 per cent stake in the venture was held through a subsidiary it set up, called Vernia Ltd. The aim was to assemble a number of sites at Drinan in north Co. Dublin. It would then develop services on the land and acquire planning permission. The sites have since been sold. Vernia's registered address on the company returns for 1998 to 2000 is the home address of Stan Purcell, Irish Nationwide's chief financial officer at the time.

There were a number of payments to various individuals in relation to this venture, including Gerry Gannon, Louis Scully and the estate agent Arthur French, all three of whom were borrowers from the society. Ernst and Young said there was limited evidence to support what services had been provided in return for the payments by Scully, who received €609,000, described as for 'legal fees', and French, who received €529,000, described as for 'auctioneer fees'.

Purcell stated that Scully and French were paid these fees for introducing the property developers Séamus Ross of Menolly Homes and David Daly to the project. The society also invoiced for fees from the project relating to services for the same land sale. The accountants concluded that it was not clear what these services were.

Gannon Homes was responsible for progressing the project, in servicing works and obtaining rezoning and planning permission. The transactions appear to Ernst and Young's team to have been with Gerry Gannon personally and various companies controlled by him. Purcell told Ernst and Young that Gannon personally and Gannon Homes Ltd took fees for services provided with regard to servicing the sites. 'These fees do not appear to have a contractual basis,' Ernst and Young said, 'and the former CFO [Purcell] stated that the former CEO [Fingleton] negotiated personally with Gerry Gannon.'

The accountants also found evidence of a €2 million increase, to €20 million, marked on the sales contract on the day the parcel of land was purchased from Gannon in 2000. Purcell signed the contract on behalf of Vernia Ltd. 'There is no indication as to what the increase related,' the report concluded. 'When asked the CFO indicated that he had no knowledge about the increase in the price.'

Separately they found evidence of an increase in price of €1 million to Gerry Gannon personally for the sale of land to Vernia Ltd. The letter, dated November 2002 and signed by Purcell, states that the increase related to a right of way. 'No documents can be provided to support this,' they said.

All this is highly unusual for a regulated financial entity engaged in multi-million deals. There may be explanations for all these payments that would reflect well on those individuals who were doing business with Vernia at that time; but the complete lack of supporting documents and the lack of clarity and accountability regarding the purpose of the payment of the society's funds is an appalling indictment of how Irish Nationwide and Michael Fingleton did business.

In a way it has little to do with individuals like Gerry Gannon or Arthur French. Surely, if things were being run properly, Michael Fingleton would have absented himself from all financial decisions or loans involving Louis Scully, because of the obvious conflict of interest arising from the fact that they were personal friends. Surely the fact that Michael Fingleton personally invested in a business venture with Gerry Gannon on the purchase of lands elsewhere, in Clongriffin, Co. Dublin, in the late 1990s, should have precluded him from making any lending or commercial decisions involving Gerry Gannon. Here was another direct conflict of interest reflecting badly on Fingleton and Irish Nationwide. It was not a conflict of interest for Scully or Gannon: they were just businessmen doing business deals. But the situation regarding a regulated financial institution is totally different.

But the Ernst and Young report went on to make other extraordinary discoveries about how Irish Nationwide was run. Take the simple con- clusion it came to that when the new management went into Fingleton's office, following his exit in 2009, they found that after thirty-seven years with the society, and having had no access to a computer, Fingleton left no paperwork in his office at the time of his resignation (with the exception of a number of files relating to a personnel matter).

Access to information in Irish Nationwide was a very sensitive issue. The British operation, which was increasing lending and risk at an alarming rate, was perhaps the most secretive place of all. Former executives say they were never told anything about what was going on in Belfast or London, where Gary McCollum and Michael Fingleton junior alone ran a €5+ billion loan book.

Fingleton junior may have been a chip off the old block in many ways, but he did use a computer. Ernst and Young found that he used his own personal computer for business purposes and refused to provide access to the IT staff. The report also found that he had made what it described as an 'inappropriate approach' to the Ernst and Young staff, seeking information in relation to investigations into the conduct of the former head of British commercial lending, his former boss, Gary McCollum.

This was the real reason why McCollum had been suspended by the new chief executive, Gerry McGinn. The Ernst and Young report had triggered a series of follow-up investigations. However, McCollum never came back to the job, so the outcome of any internal inquiries is not known.

Just before he resigned as chief executive Michael Fingleton wrote a letter, dated 3 April 2009. It sought to indemnify the then head of branches, Meryl Foster, against all possible actions or claims by any person connected with Irish Nationwide in relation to the various jobs she held within the society. Foster had been Fingleton's personal assistant but in later years had been promoted to cover various duties within the society, including the very important position of head of branches. The letter also stated that 'all costs incurred therein will be the sole responsibility of the society.' So, after Fingleton's departure, if the society or anyone connected with it decided to sue her, the society would have to bear the cost and any pay-out that might ensue.

Ernst and Young also found that Fingleton had acted in relation to an Irish Nationwide account in the Isle of Man while not formally mandated to do so. The accountants revealed what they called 'unusual activity' concerning this account and sought further details about it from the board of the society in the Isle of Man.

They also found that there were ten occasions when Gary McCollum, then head of lending for Britain and Europe, asked for a board resolution to be signed *post facto*.

Fingleton also ran a special account within the society called the No. 3 Account. This account, which consisted of Irish Nationwide money, was used when there was a need for immediate disbursement of funds. It was jointly controlled by Fingleton and Purcell between 2002 and 2008. It could make payments without limit and was used for such things as a loan to a politically sensitive figure or for the settlement of disputes. Fast-tracked mortgage loans, of the kind advanced to the former Minister for Finance, Charlie McCreevy, came out of this type of account. McCreevy borrowed €1.6 million from Irish Nationwide to buy a house that was valued at the time at €1.5 million.

When it came to lending practices, the Ernst and Young report goes through a litany of failures. The report shows that Fingleton was able to use the special powers granted to him by the board to circumvent the credit committee. 'There is evidence that the credit committee could be circumvented by obtaining the approval of the CEO, due to the delegation of extraordinary powers by the board,' it reported. 'Allowing such discretion to one individual is highly unusual and contrary to normal practice.' Among its discoveries were:

- Lending files were brief and gave little understanding of the background, rationale or performance of the facilities. There was no supporting information behind section tabs in most of the files.
- Loans were poorly structured. Many loan cases were approved on the basis of 100 per cent of security value and outlay costs (fees and stamp duty), with profit-share elements rather than cross-collateralisation or recourse to the borrower. The society's own policy typically guided 70 per cent loan-to-value for such loans.
- Facility letters were poorly drafted, as the 'purpose of loan' clauses were non-restrictive and gave the society limited opportunity to demand repayment. There wasn't even a standard template for the letters confirming and outlining a commercial loan facility. This meant that some were simply better than others.
- Minimal evidence was found of any challenge to the original credit application at meetings of the credit committee. This suggests that the credit committee was not active in questioning aspects of loan applications and seeking amendments to how the loan would be issued and repaid.
- There was evidence of loans granted before approval by the credit committee or for amounts different from those approved.
- Funds were frequently drawn in excess of the approved limit or without preconditions being satisfied. There was also evidence of funds being issued to related companies rather than to the entity for which limits were approved.

- A lack of supporting documents was noted for certain draw-downs identified.
- There was no formal process for extending loan terms.

Certain issues were identified in an internal audit report in 2007 but they still kept happening, according to the three subsequent reviews conducted by Deloitte during the ten months to February 2009. The Financial Regulator was trying to 'butch up' and make itself look tough eight days after Fingleton announced on 1 April 2009 that he was retiring at the end of the month. A letter from the regulator dated 9 April 2009 referred to the shortcoming identified by Deloitte.

Deloitte made a presentation to the audit committee a month earlier. It wasn't pretty.

- Not all commercial loans were subject to regular review by the credit risk department.
- Adherence to the credit committee's terms of reference was not fully met.
- The quarterly reporting pack on credit risk management was not produced since September 2007.
- External valuations were not always obtained for facilities above €1 million.
- The society operated without an arrears management system.
- Terms were extended on certain loans in December 2008 without the request of the borrower.

The final point suggests that, probably like other Irish lenders, Irish Nationwide was trying to dress up the books by December 2008. This was three months into the state guarantee, and banks wanted to ensure that loan books and the position of borrowers looked as attractive as possible. It was giving its customers more time to pay back loans, without even being asked, to take some of the dirty look off their balance sheets.

The losses for 2008 and 2009 were astronomical. The society lost an amount in those two years alone (€2.7 billion) that was nearly twice the total profit it had made in the previous ten years (€1.4 billion). By 2007 the commercial loan book accounted for 80 per cent of the total. By 2009 half of all outstanding loans were owed by the top thirty borrowers.

After the guarantee in late September 2008 and the resignation of Seán FitzPatrick in December because of his warehousing of personal loans with Irish Nationwide, the Financial Regulator began to act tough. The society's business plan, submitted to the regulator in December 2008, was rejected by the mandarins in Dame Street. It demonstrated a failure of Fingleton to understand and deal with the risks inherent in the strategies previously adopted. It must have seemed a bit rich, even to Michael Fingleton, to have his business plan rejected by the Financial Regulator's office in that way. After all, they were aware of pretty much every aspect of the growth of the society's loan book, concentration of risk and internal shortcomings since 2000. All it had done was write letters.

Ernst and Young also found that Irish Nationwide was frequently using the same solicitors in Britain as the borrower. This arose on sizeable commercial property loans in some cases. One of the preferred firms used for big British deals was Howard Kennedy in London. Using the same firm on both sides of a deal is not a breach of any rules and is perfectly legal, but it falls well short of best practice when it comes to lending tens of millions to property developers.

There was no formal process for extending loans. For big clients this was simply done by Fingleton, who made the decision himself.

The British lending operation was perhaps even more dysfunctional than the Irish one. Just two lenders, Gary McCollum and Michael Fingleton junior, lent more than €6 billion for commercial projects in Britain and continental Europe. In corporate governance terms, the operation was a shambles. But clearly all major decisions were sanctioned by Fingleton.

The investigating team found a payment to a firm called Value Designs with an address in Madison Avenue, New York. The payment was on foot of an invoice for €435,000. But the team found no evidence that the entity existed at that address. 'The beneficiary appears to be a Luxembourg bank account,' the report concluded. 'There is no evidence that these invoices were challenged prior to reimbursement.' There may ultimately be reasonable explanations for what this payment was about, but the society's records were so poor that answers to such basic questions could not be found.

Some of the society's biggest borrowers were British property developers, who borrowed heavily during the boom years. One of these,

Cyril Dennis, was in business with his son. Ernst and Young found payments to a company called Capital Provident and Management. This was owned by a Jersey trust controlled by Dennis's son. The payments were listed as covering 'consultancy services'. A total of €6.6 million was paid to Capital and Amble Ventures, another firm linked to Dennis, between January 2007 and September 2008.

When asked about it, Gary McCollum said that management fees of that magnitude were appropriate at the time. The payments would have been linked to joint-venture property development projects between the society and Dennis firms. Again there is no evidence that there was anything untoward about these payments, but with regard to a lender's corporate governance there appears to have been little professional assessment, paperwork or scrutiny of the background, value or breakdown of the payment of these fees. This is simply poor corporate governance by Irish Nationwide.

When it came to loans to Dennis, as with other Irish Nationwide clients, the society took all kinds of short-cuts. According to Ernst and Young, a lot of lending was done quite late in the property boom, and it continued despite the evident weakening in the financial position of the projects for which the client was borrowing. The review found issues with the draw-down of funds, including missing invoices, invoices presented more than once, invoices related to other developments, invoices from entities related to the borrower, and invoice amounts not related to the purpose as stated in the facility letter.

They found a payment of €10 million to the borrower to settle a dispute with a third party over ownership of land. There is no authorisation in the file for the facility to be used for this purpose; however, the British lending manager said he received verbal approval for this from Fingleton.

A payment of €1.4 million was also made from the Le Provençal facility for the deposit on land at St George's before approval by the credit committee for the loan. There were draw-downs of €4.1 million from the Le Provençal facility that appeared to Ernst and Young to relate to invoices for other Dennis development projects. The British lending manager said this mixing was because the society viewed each of these developments as one, and that this treatment was approved by Fingleton. 'We note however, that there is no formal cross collateralisation in place between the various entries,' the report concluded, 'and hence some funds advanced in this manner could be considered unsecured.' It also found evidence of invoices totalling €2 million paid twice, as a result of being repeated on separate draw-down requests, and there was no evidence that they were challenged by the Irish Nationwide management.

The report again shows it was a bizarre way to run a bank. For the borrower it simply meant getting access to funds quickly and with ease. In that sense, all the culpability here rests with the society and not with Cyril Dennis. It was not his job to regulate how Irish Nationwide did its business.

By the end of 2009 Dennis's loans to the society on a number of projects had totalled €486 million. Reports in late 2011 suggest that NAMA had sold approximately €600 million of his loans to the American investment group Orion Capital Partners for approximately €320 million. We don't know how much NAMA paid for the loans, and it may have made a profit. Either way, the taxpayer loses about €250 to €280 million.

The Ernst and Young team also found some unusual connections between the society, a major borrower and a business venture by one of Michael Fingleton's sons. They found some correspondence discussing activity with William Fingleton and a company called Beijing Gateway. William Fingleton was living in China, where he ran a pub called the Paddy Fields. Beijing Gateway is registered in the British Virgin Islands but with activities in China. An executive at Irish Nationwide said he believed the company was involved in selling apartments in China. William was the beneficiary of the company's Irish Nationwide bank account in the Isle of Man. Ernst and Young found that one of the deposits to the account was challenged by the internal audit section in August 2009. According to the Ernst and Young report, there is evidence that Michael Fingleton himself had some interest in or control of the company, as e-mail traffic makes references to certain issues needing his action or approval.

A review of the bank account showed there were only five deposits to the account and no withdrawals since it was opened in 2006. The deposits totalled €443,500 and were all received from Ballymore Properties. This company, owned by Seán Mulryan, was a significant borrower from Irish Nationwide, being its biggest single exposure, and in fact one of its senior executives, David Brophy, sat on the board of the society. It is far from clear what these deposits were all about. It may simply have been that a plan to promote the sale of apartments in Beijing by Michael Fingleton's son was financially supported by Seán Mulryan's company. The company may have thought it was a good business idea and wanted to back Fingleton's son. Irrespective of the explanation, it reveals a further connection between Fingleton and the society's biggest borrower, which should have precluded Fingleton from taking part in any commercial decisions about Ballymore Properties.

Another venture involving Michael Fingleton was New Fjord Developments. This was a company set up in Montenegro by Louis Maguire, an associate of Fingleton's.

In Michael Fingleton he found a backer for a new resort in Montenegro. Fingleton invested about €5 million in a stalled hotel development in the coastal city of Kotor in 2005. The investment was part of a joint venture to build a €200 million luxury hotel.

Fingleton's Montenegrin investment was investigated by Ernst and Young, because Maguire later raised questions about the role he played in the deal and the origin of the funds Fingleton put into the project. Maguire made the allegations directly to the society after Fingleton had resigned, and he also complained to the Central Bank.

In the meantime the Central Bank decided to conduct a number of follow-up reports, approximately five in total, delving more deeply into specific aspects of the original corporate governance report. It got Ernst and Young to continue the work it had done with more detailed follow-up reports. Once completed, these were all forwarded to the Central Bank by the board of Irish Nationwide. The board considered whether the information it had could form the basis of a possible legal action against Fingleton or other former directors or executives of the building society.

No final conclusions were made. The legal advice received seemed to question whether Fingleton had broken any of the society's rules, because what he did was based on the special powers given to him by the board, but it was possible that some action could be taken if he had overstepped them. 'It's like saying that, Yes, Fingleton had special powers officially given to him by the board,' one source close to the action said, 'but what he did with those powers was nevertheless reckless and irresponsible.'

The Ernst and Young report has never been published. Copies of it were given to the Department of Finance and the Central Bank in the summer of 2010. That October, Éamon Gilmore raised the issue of the report in the Dáil. He asked the Taoiseach, Brian Cowen, whether the report had been presented, and whether it would be laid before the Dáil, 'as in effect this is a publicly owned institution.'

There has always been a feeling of inertia about going after those responsible for the destruction of the building society that cost the citizens €5.4 billion. Sceptics have suggested that Fingleton was so plugged in to political and business life that there was a lack of will to go after him. His connections in the political sphere included the two main parties. Certainly the coalition government of Fianna Fáil and the Green Party did not seek to publish the report, even an edited version, so as to provide some understanding of just how badly Irish Nationwide had been run.

The present Minister for Finance, Michael Noonan, has had the report in his department since he took office in March 2011. In that month a spokesperson for Éamon Gilmore, now also in government, said that while he remained of the view that the report should be published it was a matter for the relevant minister, in this case the Minister for Finance. it was not something the government had got around to deciding.

It is difficult to say whether this is all part of a strategy aimed at taking the right action at the right time or not doing anything that might jeopardise the chance of successful litigation or sanction being taken against Fingleton and other former board members. There is strong evidence to suggest that the late Brian Lenihan had an appetite for pursuing to the full any possible wrongdoing at the society. Just before he left the department he phoned a number of people he had worked with in relation to the banking crisis. One of them, who did not want to be named, said the phone call was the last conversation he had with Lenihan. The outgoing minister thanked him for his assistance in tackling various issues at the society and for all his co-operation. His final comment at the end of the conversation was, 'Do you think we will ever get Michael Fingleton?'

|LIVING THE LIFE OF FINGERS

In September 2005 Michael Fingleton and his wife flew to Portugal to attend the wedding of Julie Gannon and Peter Reynolds in the baroque chapel of São Lourenço dos Matos in Almancil. The church's exquisite eighteenth-century blue-and-white tiles depict the life of a local saint, surrounded by angels bearing medallions and garlands of flowers and leaves.

The church was packed for the marriage of the daughter of one of Irish Nationwide's biggest borrowers, Gerry Gannon. Fingleton took his seat alongside two other close friends of Gannon, Tom Brown, Anglo Irish Bank's gregarious head of lending, and Bill Barrett, the veteran Anglo Irish lender who had helped keep Gannon afloat during the 1980s when he ran into difficulties caused by the recession.

Gannon was in a mood to celebrate. At that point he owed Irish Nationwide approximately €130 million, making him its tenth-biggest client. He owed Anglo Irish Bank well over half a billion more, as well as having borrowings from other banks. Included in his Irish Nationwide borrowings was his half of the acquisition of the K Club four months earlier for €115 million, along with Michael Smurfit.

Despite only recently borrowing another €100-odd million, Gannon considered himself a very rich man, based on the bubble valuations of property and land that existed at the time. Having mountainous debts, much of them locked up in development land, was in his mind no reason to spare any expense.

White roses and candles adorned the altar of the church, and the plaza outside was festooned with white rose topiaries. It was bling, Irish developer style. Back then, such spending by the massively indebted was not considered crass. The *Irish Independent*'s social diary described the scene in gushing terms.

When the radiant bride entered this Algarve landmark on the arm of her father Gerry, there was an audible gasp from the congregation. In a gorgeous Vera-Wang designed couture gown of white charmeuse silk, Julie looked every inch the princess bride. The diamanté detail on each side of the deep V-front was picked up by her glittering diamond jewellery: studs, a solitaire necklace and a diamond headband which held her short veil in place. She carried a bouquet of tied white roses.

As Gannon stepped up the aisle with his resplendent daughter, his guests remarked with amusement that for once he was not wearing his trade-mark fedora.

Afterwards the guests retired to a champagne reception on the terrace of the Algarve Sheraton, a five-star golf clubhouse, before sitting down to a sumptuous dinner. As usual at these events, Fingleton took several turns on the dance floor after the meal.

A black-tie ballroom shindig back in the K Club was scheduled later to complete the festivities for those unable to make it to Portugal. Arriving back in Dublin, Fingleton was keen to impress the developer by giving his daughter a present before the K Club party. On 28 September 2005 a Mr M. Fingleton bought an 'antique fruit basket' from J. W. Weldon, the fourth-generation family-owned diamond and antique-silver retailers in Clarendon Street, Dublin. The basket, marked 'London, c. 1758,' was the work of the renowned silversmith Samuel Herbert. The payment was made with a cheque for €6,000 signed with just one signature, Fingleton's. He described it as a 'gift for Julie Gannon' as he chucked the bill in with the other expenses that he charged monthly to Irish Nationwide Building Society.

In Fingleton's mind, the building society's money had blurred with his own. And it never seemed to cross the mind of anyone who dealt with this bill to question it, as Fingleton had for decades charged the society for anything that took his fancy.

But the way Fingleton had spent the society's money on himself was the next area that came into sharp focus after the completion of the Ernst and Young report. The head of Irish Nationwide's internal audit department, Killian McMahon, was ordered to prepare a report on the expenses claimed by Fingleton and a small bunch of his cronies between 2005 and 2010. He completed this report in September 2010.

The investigation was sparked after it was discovered that a going-away present of a watch costing €11,500 for Fingleton had been purchased with an expenses cheque that had been cashed in the staff cheques account. The watch was a lavish gift for a man who had run a financial institution so badly that the state had been forced to take it over.

It was also discovered at about the same time that two significant claims had been made to benefit Meryl Foster, a close confidante of Fingleton in the society, that had not been taxed appropriately as a benefit in kind. Foster (also known as Meryl Coade before her separation) had been plucked from the ranks by Fingleton and accelerated upwards to be head of branch operations.

As Fingleton moved from the joy of recklessly expanding the society in its final years to brooding in his final months about how it all went wrong, Foster remained loyal. Often, according to other former staff members, she would work late into the night with Fingleton on whatever scheme was occupying him. McMahon's task was to determine what benefits had been received and whether they had been appropriately approved and correctly taxed. As part of this task he looked at whether duplicate expenses had been claimed, what paperwork was supplied to support them, and whether they related at all to the society's business.

Four individuals in particular were looked at: Michael Fingleton, Meryl Foster (Coade), Michael Fingleton junior and Gary McCollum.

Firstly, the circumstances surrounding the gift of the watch were looked at. What McMahon found surprised him. The society regularly paid for small departure gifts for staff members; but this time a very different mechanism was used that was very hard to spot. On 30 April 2009 Stan Purcell wrote a cheque for €11,500, using the society's expenses account, which he lodged in the so-called staff cheques account. The purpose of this account was merely to facilitate temporary summer employees who had no bank account with the society in cashing their pay cheques.

Soon afterwards €11,500 was withdrawn from this account and used to pay for the going-away watch for Fingleton. Purcell, when questioned on this expense, said that Meryl Foster had been the person who withdrew the money to pay for Fingleton's watch. Neither the payroll section nor the society's human resources department was informed of the present, despite the society usually informing them of any gift above €32 in value.

Alarmed by this finding, the internal audit team dug deeper. They found that on 8 April 2009 Fingleton had approved a cheque for €2,000 to be paid to the Castleknock Hotel and Country Club. He said this was a 'sponsorship' donation for Meryl Coade. Apart from the money leaving, there was no other record on file to explain this charitable donation by Fingleton to a member of his staff a few weeks before he quit the society— and after it had clamped down on expenses for lower-ranked employees. Coade herself drafted the cheque, which she also made payable to herself. Stan Purcell then signed the cheque, which Coade endorsed. No tax was paid on this benefit in kind at the time. (In July or August 2010 the society ensured that Meryl Foster paid tax on this benefit.)

Questioned by internal audit on the mater, Foster said: 'Unfortunately, I am none the wiser. All I know is that Mr Fingleton would not have authorised any expense without supporting documentation.'

That same day Fingleton approved a cheque for €1,250, payable to Educogym, a fitness chain founded by the colourful 'guru' Tony Quinn. The payment was again described as 'sponsorship' of Coade. Again Coade drafted the cheque, which was also payable to herself, before two other senior officials in the society also signed it.

Coade gave the same dismissive response to internal audit when questioned on this second hefty payment. 'Unfortunately, I am none the wiser. All I know is that Mr Fingleton would not have authorised any expense without supporting documentation.' (Again Coade was retrospectively forced to pay benefit-in-kind tax on this payment.) Pressed to provide proof of her payment to Educogym, she eventually produced an invoice for €1,500, which said it was for a one-year personal training programme.

Digging deeper still, the internal audit section found a cheque for €2,000 made payable to O'D Steel Products Ltd. The managing director of O'D Steel turned out to be John O'Doherty, who happened to be the owner of an Educogym. Meryl Foster filled out the paperwork for the cheque. Originally it was to be drawn in favour of Meryl Coade, but somebody scribbled this name out; instead the cheque requisition was signed by Michael Fingleton, on 7 May 2009. Fingleton had left the society on 30 April 2009 and therefore could not have authorised this payment. Yet again the payment was described as a 'sponsorship' for Meryl Coade.

There were more unusual payments associated with Fingleton's right-hand woman. In December 2008 Irish Nationwide was due to have its Christmas party in the luxurious environs of the Radisson Hotel in Golden Lane, Dublin. After the bank guarantee, not surprisingly, this was no longer considered appropriate. Unfortunately the society had already paid the hotel a booking fee of €5,275, of which the Radisson agreed to refund €5,000 in the form of a credit note, valid for one year. On 28 December 2009 Irish Nationwide discovered that a big chunk of the credit note had been used.

One of the rooms in the Radisson Hotel was booked in the name of Meryl B. Foster, while two rooms were booked in the name of Marion McGuire, the married name of Marion Kiernan, supervisor of Irish Nationwide's legal department. It is not clear who stayed in the third room, except that it appears to have been a relative of Meryl Foster. A bill of €1,140 was run up, including dinner in the hotel's Sure restaurant, noted for its cocktails. This was paid with the society's credit note. Nobody in the society approved this bill.

In total, undeclared additional benefits of €5,800 could be traced to Foster. It was also found that she had booked several stays in February 2009 in the Radisson SAS Hotel in Galway under the name Judith Mulligan. The society was not sure who this person was, or what link she had to the society's business, but the documents vouching for the expense appeared to have been altered to include Meryl Coade's name and address.

Coade was also found to have run up large bills in various expensive restaurants, including Dobbins, Trentuno, Canal Bank Café, Da Vincenzo and Pasta Fresca (where the same claim was submitted twice). Many of these bills ran to over €2,000 each.

Other expenses submitted by Coade were paid without any receipt or invoice being kept on file, including €1,000 described as covering the cost of a Christmas staff night out. One meal in Trentuno in April 2009 is described as being for 'Jackson / O'Flynn.' The bill came to €1,100, including a payment of €110 by Visa credit card signed by the mysterious Judith Mulligan. This expense was also submitted twice.

The audit then focused on Fingleton. It found that expenses of €68,109 had not been declared and had benefit-in-kind tax owing on them.

The receipts revealed yet more of the incredible life-style enjoyed by Fingleton in his pomp. He took large sums in cash from the society for walking-around money while on trips away. In February 2005 he took $2,000 for a trip to America and was reimbursed with €1,000 in relation to a trip with Michael Smurfit, Seán Mulryan and Arthur French. About €48,000 related to expenses run up in the K Club, together with everything from membership fees to dining. Green fees at the Real Club de Golf in Las Brisas, Marbella, a six-night trip to Dubai costing €3,500, €500 in cash for a trip to Moscow, €800 on a trip with Private Chauffeurs Ireland, and a medical fee of €495 in the Well health centre in Dublin ten days before he left were all included in these untaxed benefits in kind.

In addition there were the expenses that were treated as benefits in kind by the society and on which tax was paid. These included a bill for €12,000 for dental work in the Blackrock Clinic in 2008, and membership in Woodbrook Golf Club and Luttrellstown Golf Club.

Incredibly, it was found that Fingleton had been able to charge expenses to the society even after he had left it. A bill for £2,300 had been submitted for a stay in the Dorchester Hotel in London on 14 and 15 May 2009 and had been paid, despite Fingleton having resigned from the society two weeks earlier. Meryl Coade had authorised a payment of £3,799 to cover the cost of Fingleton's stay, despite not having the authority to do so from the account the money was paid out of. After Fingleton and his wife stayed in the hotel there was a credit of £1,600 on Irish Nationwide's account. In June 2009 Coade told the hotel to leave the credit there until her next stay.

It was also discovered that there may have been a reason why Irish Nationwide favoured 4giftsdirect.com when lavishing gifts on developers. An e-mail message from the managing director of the company, Lulu O'Sullivan, to Meryl Foster on 8 December 2008 refers to her being given €600 worth of free gifts of wine and champagne. Foster told O'Sullivan after placing her mega-order with the society's money that she was 'just wondering is Santa calling to me, seeing the size of the order!!!!' O'Sullivan replied: 'We can discuss whether you would like champagne & chocolates for yourself on Monday or champagne bottles same as '07.' No record of these gifts being declared, as was the society's policy, was available in either its payroll or human resources department.

Not surprisingly, Irish Nationwide internal audit concluded that there were major gaps in the society's procedures and significant control weaknesses in how it handled expenses by senior executives. The society was determined to get answers.

Fingleton used gifts to charity to develop a reputation for philanthropy among the elite and chattering classes, even though it was usually the society's members who were paying for his largesse.

Fingleton's spending of Irish Nationwide's funds reveals how he saw his personal interests and the society's money as the same thing. The society paid him a massive salary, giving him more than enough money to pay for pet projects or to reward favourites. But why would he do that when he could dip into the society's funds virtually unchecked? Nobody on the society's old board ever seems to have reviewed his expenses, leaving him free to do what he wanted.

———

Irish Nationwide's new regime under Gerry McGinn and John McGloughlin was determined that Fingleton would be made to repay some of his expenses. Fingleton remained unrepentant, however, and instead retreated into a bizarre world where every action, every whim, every waste was justified. In his mind, Fingleton had become the victim.

Chapter 14

THINK OF A NUMBER: THE
LOSSES RACK UP

On Tuesday 17 August 2010 the governor of the Central Bank, Patrick Honohan, gave an address to Renmin University in Beijing. The speech contrasted starkly with a visit five years earlier by the Taoiseach, Bertie Ahern, to the same city, where he had been lauded in China's Great Hall of the People by the Premier, Wen Jiabao. Ahern basked in Ireland's economic success as he toured China's greatest cities, lecturing them on the parallels between the great Celtic Tiger and the Chinese Dragon's economic success. His visit peaked when he announced that the Irish developers Johnny Ronan and Richard Barrett planned to build a new €2 billion eco-city on an island off the north coast of Shanghai in the mouth of the Yangtze River. Ireland, Ahern and his developer associates believed, was now ready to teach the Chinese its secrets.

Honohan, however, cut a more subdued figure in front of the students and academics of Renmin University. He was eloquent but forensic in his analysis, in a manner Ahern was incapable of.

From 2003 to 2007 the Irish banking system imported funds equivalent to over 50 per cent of GDP to fund a runaway property and construction bubble. The tax revenue generated by the boom came in many forms . . . Immigrants from the rest of Europe, from Africa, from China, flooded in as the construction sector alone swelled up to account for about 13 per cent of the numbers at work.

For over a decade the budget was in surplus almost every year. No need, it seemed, for restraint in spending, and so, after years of relatively disciplined government budgeting, there was a relaxation of spending controls—one, I will say, which was broadly welcomed across most of the political spectrum.

Alas, that the apparent solidity of the public finances was all a mirage was brutally exposed when global financial confidence collapsed.

The boom ended, house prices fell, and trade decreased as Ireland's global partners slowed down or entered recession.

> The progressive tightening of short-term financial markets during the second half of 2007 and through 2008, peaking in those dramatic weeks after the bankruptcy of Lehman Brothers, eventually exposed the fact that not only had the banks fuelled an unsustainable property bubble but they had not safeguarded their own solvency through adequate collateral and guarantees.
>
> The Government had little alternative to announcing an extensive guarantee of bank liabilities.
>
> This has proved not to be costless and is imposing a net cost which will place a heavy burden on taxpayers and the users of public services in Ireland for several years—though it is manageable and much less than some alarmist commentary had suggested.

Buried half way down Honohan's speech was a bombshell: 'Anglo may impose a net cost to the Government of about €22 to 25 billion, to which can be added about €4 billion mainly to cover one small building society.'

Irish Nationwide, Honohan almost casually let slip, was going to cost the taxpayer €4 billion. This was a billion more than the last estimate and four times the estimate of only a year before. His description of the society was a telling one.

Back home, politicians claimed that Irish Nationwide had been guaranteed by the taxpayer because it was of so-called 'systemic' importance. But in Beijing the governor of the Central Bank described it as what it actually was: a rather small institution that somehow was costing the public a huge sum of money.

Joan Burton was quick to accuse the government of using Honohan to 'drip-feed bad news' and called on Lenihan to 'come clean' about the banks.

> At every stage of Ireland's banking crisis, the Government has insisted that they have the costs under control, only for this to be blown out of the water by the next multi-billion euro announcement.
>
> Between Anglo Irish Bank and Irish Nationwide alone we are already looking at a bill for nearly €30 billion. This figure may have

risen yet further by the time NAMA loan transfers are completed next year.

Does he have any realistic idea of what the final bill will come to? It's as if he has left the taxpayers' credit card behind the bar for a bankers' free-for-all.

Three days after Honohan's speech, Michael Fingleton landed at Dublin Airport after a relaxing holiday in Spain. He had been spotted getting on his flight, however, and someone had rung RTE to tip it off about his arrival. RTE's business editor, David Murphy, waited with a camera crew in the arrival hall for Fingleton to emerge. Wearing a green flat cap, white striped shirt and yellow sports jacket, Fingleton was far from pleased when he saw Murphy, who insisted on pursuing him as he tried to escape.

'Do you not have any sense of remorse about what has happened in Ireland as a result of what happened at banks like your own?'

'Of course I have, of course I have, like anybody else. I have indeed.'

'What do you think should be done?'

'Everything is being done that can possibly be done by everybody concerned.'

'Do you feel guilty about what happened?'

'Come on. Just . . . I have already made my comment and that's it. I can't say any more . . .'

'Mr Fingleton, will you repay your €1 million bonus?'

'I have already made a full statement on that.'

'But you have received a lot of letters from Irish Nationwide.'

'Sorry, I have already made a full public statement on that, which you are fully aware of. Okay?'

Murphy followed Fingleton out of the airport, where cars were pulling up to collect passengers.

'And what about the loans to directors at Anglo Irish Bank? Do you regret your involvement in that, in terms that those loans weren't made public to the shareholders of Anglo Irish bank?'

'That is a matter under investigation. It will be made very clear in due course that we had no responsibility whatsoever.'

'Will you be co-operating with future investigations?'

'I have already co-operated and I continue to co-operate in every way I can.'

Then, having collected his golf clubs, Fingleton stepped into the back of a car and was gone.

———

As August ended, Ireland's economic situation just kept getting worse. At the beginning of the month the country had managed to raise €1 billion in six-month and eight-month treasury bills, but the price it had to pay for the market to trust it was creeping up fast. The yield on Irish ten-year bonds hit 5.4 per cent on 12 August, 2.94 points higher than the German bund and up almost half a point from the previous week.

Philip Lane, a professor of international and macro-economics at Trinity College, Dublin, told the *Wall Street Journal* that the market was worried about the size of Ireland's banking black hole. 'Financial markets can go into panic mode, and it's hard to say that the Irish fundamentals are sufficiently bad to warrant these spreads.'

Irish Nationwide's new management was still scrambling to hold on to deposits and get cash back in from developers. Everywhere, however, there were signs of Fingleton's madness. A lot of corners had been cut in turning the building society from a relatively conservative lender to the little guy into a 'player' throwing money at the rich and powerful. The society, the new management learnt daily, had strayed a long way from its roots. Two examples from August that the new team had to deal with illustrate this.

At the beginning of August, Michael Smurfit rescued his palatial Spanish villa at Marbella just as it was about to go into NAMA by paying off the remainder of a €20 million loan. The society, of course, was pleased to get its money back, but it was amazing that it had ever lent to anybody to buy such a house. It sprawled over 40,000 square feet on the Golden Mile and came complete with a gym, a cinema and a heated outdoor pool. It was so luxurious that Smurfit had once rented it out to an Arab princess for €20,000 a day. 'How on earth did we end up lending for this type of thing?' an Irish Nationwide source said.

Not everything went so well. That summer Irish Nationwide appointed a receiver for the €60 million Moyvalley Hotel and golf resort in Co. Kildare and a related course in Co. Westmeath called the New Forest Golf Club, both of which had been developed by Alastair Jackson. Moyvalley, set on 550 acres with a stunning golf course designed by Darren Clarke, should never have been built. Even if the economy hadn't collapsed there wasn't much demand for another golf resort with holiday homes selling for up to €1 million each in the Kildare area, where there were already four or five resorts of similar quality. Fingleton never seemed to consider the bigger picture when he doled out the society's money. Neither did Jackson, who went bankrupt in May 2012, dragged down by this and other follies.

To manage its ever-expanding mess, Irish Nationwide had to hire a whole new team to try to prevent the society falling apart. 'The quality of people was really poor in commercial; in residential it was okay,' an insider said. 'But what would you expect for the low salaries they were paying? Michael Fingleton had ruled the place with an iron fist.'

The Ernst and Young trawl had uncovered many bizarre things, but it also found more systemic mistakes in the way the society lent commercially. Time and again the society found itself at the wrong side of the deal when it came to trying to recover cash from developers, as too often it had lent millions on bad terms.

'The way things were done was all wrong,' a society source said. Of one group of British property developers they said, 'These guys would buy and sell you. They were a very tight bunch who were all interlinked. Everything was done through SPVs [special-purpose vehicles], where the loans were non-recourse. They were much smarter than anyone in the society.' Non-recourse meant the society had lent developers money in a way that it could take back the asset only if lent for them to buy or develop. What this meant was that even though many of its London clients were incredibly rich, the society had no way of pursuing them.

Fingleton, his son and McCollum, in their eagerness to win new business, had left the society terribly exposed if anything went wrong. The board, chaired by Michael Walsh, also had a lot to answer for. 'The thing about the directors was, they were all profits, profits, profits,' an insider said. 'They didn't think about risk. How was the society protected if anything went wrong?'

It would have been bad enough untangling the society's atrocious lending if things were not made much worse by the global financial crisis. On 30 August a financial expert with Roubini Global Economics, Jennifer Kapila, concluded:

The Emerald Isle is sinking under the weight of consistently bad news as escalating costs of Anglo Irish's bad loans precipitated the European Commission's third emergency capital authorization.

The next hurdle is September's immense refinancing schedule of roughly €26 billion for the largest three banks and Irish Nationwide. Clearly, the Irish condition is no longer just a bad situation in stasis but is deteriorating and should call into question the current forecasts of capital requirements of other Eurozone banks.

Roubini Global Economics was a think-tank set up by the influential economist Nouriel Roubini, nicknamed Dr Doom. It was closely followed by international investors and fund managers, who would increasingly call the shots on Ireland in the coming months.

The scale of the economic cliff facing Irish banks was actually less than €26 billion. This was because all year Ireland's banks had carried out smaller fund-raisings in preparation for this September deadline. But whatever the real funding challenge was, it was certainly many billions, which was looking increasingly insurmountable, particularly for Ireland's worst institution, Irish Nationwide. The stakes were very high.

The past mistakes of Fingleton-type bankers and their cheerleaders, the international bond-holders, were now not only threatening Ireland but putting in danger the euro itself.

The situation for Irish Nationwide was becoming as ridiculous as it was dangerous. On 6 September it issued a statement saying it had 'listed €4 billion notes under its Global Medium Term Note Programme, which are available to the Issuer as eligible collateral for central bank "repo" funding purposes. The Notes have a six-month maturity. The Notes have the benefit of the Irish Government Guarantee under the Credit Institutions.'

The society was quick to tell the Bloomberg business news service that the so-called global medium-term note programme gave it the ability to repay €4 billion in debt that was maturing at the end of September. This 'boosts the liquidity of the society,' a spokesperson told Bloomberg, and it 'may use some of the €4 billion of notes to repay maturing bonds.'

Simon Carswell in the *Irish Times* soon afterwards saw through the society's ruse. 'Irish Nationwide has issued €4 billion of government bonds effectively to itself,' he concluded. It had issued a bond that had no collateral except for the government guarantee, an instrument so worthless that only the society itself would buy it. This it did on the advice of the National Treasury Management Agency, the state body responsible for Ireland's funding, and BNP Paribas, an international bank.

Irish Nationwide had issued its €4 billion in bonds to its property development subsidiary, Pangrove, and then bought them all back, except for €50,000. The society then headed to Frankfurt to collect its money, completing the merry-go-round. An unnamed bond analyst told the *Irish Times* he had never seen a funding transaction structured in such a way, as it was 'a type of micro-quantitative easing' or a means of allowing a central bank to print money to support an institution.

Writing in the *Sunday Times*, Brian Carey concluded: 'Michael Fingleton, the former Irish Nationwide Building Society chief executive, had the look of a fairground magician, but not even the great Mephisto himself could achieve what INBS did last week: magic up €4 billion from thin air.' It was a dexterous financial move as Ireland headed into the financial dead-zone of the final quarter of 2010.

Increasingly, the reasoning behind the state's rescuing of Irish Nationwide at all was being questioned as more and more people realised that by doing so it had put the future of the country at risk. 'Who really gained from not allowing it to collapse?' was the question that now came to the forefront.

On 7 September, Fintan O'Toole in the *Irish Times* gave his answer.

We have been given, in all, five different explanations by the Government of why we must continue to pour money into Anglo and, lest we forget, its mini-me Irish Nationwide.

The first was that these institutions were basically sound but needed temporary rescue from a liquidity crisis. No one needs to be told how stupid that was.

The second was that we needed to give them the money to get credit flowing into the economy again. This was always a cynical line spun for the supposedly gullible masses—Anglo and Nationwide never lent significantly into the real economy and will never do so in the future.

The third reason we've been given is that it was vital to avoid having zombie banks. This actually has been achieved—as the *Financial Times* pointed out last week, Anglo is nothing as lively as a zombie. It's a 'rotting corpse'.

The fourth proposition was that saving Anglo and Nationwide was necessary to maintain Ireland's 'credibility' with the international financial markets. In fact, watching a State borrow endless billions at high interest rates to shovel them into a grave has merely enhanced our incredibility.

Which leaves us with the fifth reason for the strategy, and the only one that makes any sense: that the European Union, and more specifically the European Central Bank, have decided that no European bank should be allowed to fail.

Strip away the drivel and the spinning and this is the one truth left standing.

On Sunday 12 September the *Sunday Business Post* broke the story that the European Commission planned to pull the plug on Irish Nationwide by vetoing its plan to reinvent itself as a mortgage and savings provider. The move came less than a week after the government announced that Anglo Irish would be banned from any new lending and instead would be split into a savings bank and an asset recovery unit.

The paper also reported that Anglo Irish would cost a maximum of €30 billion—considerably more than the €24 billion the state had last estimated but less than the €35 billion that Standard and Poor's rating agency had recently predicted.

Irish Nationwide was to be banned by the EU Commission from engaging in new lending (though it could lend to existing customers to help them finish projects) and instead would concentrate on collecting repayments on its €2 billion residential loan book while managing its €4 billion book in a separate vehicle. Putting the deposits into a new unit would allow the government to move them more easily to prop up one of its remaining banks when required.

The society was now officially dead. Any dream of it living on, either as part of a so-called third force or going back to its roots as a small lender, was now over.

Reacting to the news of Irish Nationwide's closure, Brian Cowen told RTE radio later that day that 'horrendous mistakes' had been made by Irish banking, and he was prepared to take his 'full measure' of responsibility for his role as former Minister for Finance. There were, he said, 'liquidity issues for the whole banking system right throughout 2008,' but 'there was no suggestion that what we ended up with was around the corner.' He said he had not knowingly misled the Dáil when he said the banks were well capitalised. 'The regulatory system in our country and in the IMF and elsewhere were not suggesting we had an under-capitalisation problem. And if there was such a proposal, that we did have a problem on the capitalisation side, obviously it would have been incumbent upon us to do something about it.'

Soon afterwards Irish Nationwide appointed a former Bank of Scotland (Ireland) executive, Antoinette Dunne, to review its fifty branches. While her decision was some time away, she could only conclude one thing: they would all have to close. The hundreds of employees in those branches were on their way to losing their jobs—another price paid by others for Fingleton's profligacy.

On 30 September, Brian Lenihan delivered a speech with the rather unexciting title of 'Minister's statement on banking.' Its contents, however, were devastating, revealing yet again that Ireland's banking black hole was much larger than expected. Within minutes, the news wires were abuzz about the day that would become known as Black Thursday. The news agency AFP gave the speech an initial headline of 'Ireland reveals full horror of banking crisis' before updating it to 'Shocked Irish see years of financial pain ahead' as the full extent of the losses being announced sunk in.

The total cost of the banking bail-out was put by Lenihan at €50 billion. This equated to €11,000 per person, or €100,000 per household. Ireland's budget deficit was lifted to a record 32 per cent of gross domestic product, or ten times EU guidelines for member-states. The projected cost for Anglo Irish alone came in at €29.3 billion.

The *Financial Times* concluded: 'The rescue costs for this one bank represent a staggering 21 per cent of Irish GDP, more than the entire bill for sorting the Japanese banking crisis of 1997 and almost twice the cost of the Finnish crisis in the early 1990s.'

AIB would now have a majority state ownership, Lenihan said, as it needed a total of €7.9 billion even after deducting what it had raised from selling off its Polish operation. AIB's managing director, Colm Doherty, and its chairman, Dan O'Connor, both announced their intention to resign.

Bank of Ireland, Lenihan said, would not need fresh capital, and this had been confirmed by the Central Bank.

Then it was Irish Nationwide's turn. The society, Lenihan said, was now under state control. The state had already pumped €2.7 billion into the society, and now it needed even more.

> The NTMA has recommended that I provide a further €2.7 billion representing a prudential estimate of the capital required to cover expected losses on INBS's residual loan book and bringing the total capital support to €5.4 billion. I have accepted the NTMA's recommendation in order to establish a ceiling on the level of support provided to the Society consistent with the objective of providing final clarity on the public support required by the Irish banking system.

He said that Irish Nationwide, like Anglo Irish, would enter talks with some of its subordinated bond-holders to try to force them to share some of the pain being saddled on the taxpayer. 'I expect the subordinated debt-holders to make a significant contribution towards meeting the costs of Anglo [and Irish Nationwide],' he said. Senior bond-holders, however, whose debts have equal ranking with depositors, remained safe, despite having provided the kerosene that the Irish banks poured on property. To suggest asking them to share in Ireland's pain, Lenihan said, was 'completely unreal.'

> We are not going to tell the bank manager we are going to default prior to asking for more money. Were we to impose haircuts on senior bond-holders, equivalent haircuts would require to be imposed on depositors. We have to bring closure to this matter, and that is what we have done today. Yes, of course these figures are horrendous, but they can be managed over a ten-year period, and they will be managed.

Patrick Honohan said that yet more billions going into Anglo Irish would require a 'reprogramming' of the country's budget plans. Although he did not use the term, it was clear that austerity was going to be needed to pay for bank gambling.

On RTE Radio 1 that lunchtime Honohan was asked by an incredulous Seán O'Rourke, 'The worst-case scenario involving Anglo and Irish Nationwide is €40 billion—gone?' 'Gone,' agreed Honohan.

The National Treasury Management Agency announced that it was suspending bond auctions planned for October and November and that it planned to return to the markets only in the first quarter of 2011. Ireland was fully funded until June 2011, but after that it was anybody's guess what would happen. Irish ten-year government bonds had hit a record of almost 7 per cent before Lenihan's announcement, or 4.7 per cent more than Germany. The annual cost of insuring Irish bonds against default had also jumped sharply.

Both yields fell back a little on the news that at least Lenihan appeared to have drawn a line in the sand under Ireland's losses. Brian Cowen said the state might have to introduce budget cuts that December 'significantly' more than €3 billion from public services, such as health, education and social welfare. 'Obviously there will have to be revenue-raising as a contribution to closing that gap—it cannot all be done on the expenditure side,' he said, in a warning that Ireland would have to sell off its crown jewels—such as its energy companies or infrastructure—to find money to put into its zombie banks. The very sovereignty of the country was now at stake.

'This is not going to be easy but it has to be done,' Cowen said. 'Why does it have to be done? Because we as a country want to control our own affairs.'

The president of the European Central Bank, Jean-Claude Trichet, welcomed the government's decision to take one for Europe by picking up the entire bill for a madness that was fuelled by German and French banks. 'What is absolutely key for us is credibility and the delivery of this unequivocal commitment to correct the excessive deficit by 2014 as had been previously agreed. It will be key for the credibility of Ireland.'

The EU Commissioner for Economic and Monetary Affairs, Olli Rehn, added: 'We strongly endorse Finance Minister Brian Lenihan's handling of this issue.'

It wasn't just Europe, which had wilfully thrown hundreds of billions at Ireland's failed banks, that was insisting that the nation now take full responsibility for its bank debts. The Russian oligarch Roman Abramovich was also anxious that a small country on the edge of Europe should take its punishment in full. He owned subordinated bonds in Irish Nationwide, and he threatened to sue the society if Lenihan's suggestion that these types of bonds should share the pain was carried through. The fact that subordinated bonds, by definition, were more risky than either senior bonds or actual deposits and as a result were paid higher interest no longer mattered.

'We are fully prepared to vigorously defend our position using all possible legal avenues,' Abramovich's investment vehicle, Millhouse, said. The Irish government had promised to guarantee the bonds and have a strategy for the bank. 'We now believe that we have been misled and deceived. We believe that any attempt to force losses on Irish Nationwide lower Tier 2 debt holders will result in a huge reputation loss and ultimately financial cost to the Irish and European sovereigns and financial institutions.'

The message was clear: investors would charge more if the Irish government took on even the lowest-ranking bond-holders in an insolvent and hopelessly bust building society. The owner of the world's biggest yacht was adamant that the people of Ireland should stump up in full for Irish Nationwide's mistakes. If social welfare or disability benefits had to be cut as a result—tough cheese.

Danny McCoy, director-general of the Irish Business and Employers' Confederation, which had silently watched Irish bankers lend recklessly during the boom, now came out in agreement. 'Ireland should honour its debts if it can . . . The country makes a living taking capital from people and looking after it, and you don't want to get a reputation for carrying out partial defaults.'

The independent TD Maureen O'Sullivan took a very different view. 'It appears there is a bottomless pit of money and guarantees when it comes to banks, but when it comes to the needs and lives of Irish people, they are told they must accept the cuts and make the sacrifices.'

Writing in the *Irish Independent*, the economist David McWilliams said:

The Irish elite is prepared to sell the sovereignty of this country to protect the likes of Roman Abramovich and other vulture investors who bought up third-rate Irish banking debt at a discount and are hoping to get paid in full.

People such as Abramovich, like the other creditors, can be told to line up in an orderly queue and wait for the liquidator to give them the morsels that might remain from the broken Irish banking system. The crud Abramovich owns—an IOU from Irish Nationwide Building Society—is not the same thing as Irish government debt.

The last time I checked, there was a harp on the front of my passport, not a picture of Michael Fingleton.

Michael Walsh, who had remained relatively unscathed by the epic failure of Irish Nationwide, was challenged by the *Irish Times* a few days after Lenihan's announcement. It was a relatively rare public confrontation of Walsh about the society's mistakes. He agreed he was unhappy about what had happened but insisted that it 'isn't true' that the society had an ineffective board, which had let Fingleton do what he want and allowed the society run out of control. He refused to comment further. He retreated into the safety of Dermot Desmond's investment vehicle, International Investment and Underwriting, where he remained a board director and adviser. Privately wealthy, he was not one of the ordinary people that O'Sullivan was worried about.

In the first weeks after Black Thursday the world's biggest rating agencies all caused more shivers for investors in Ireland and its evil-twin banks. Standard and Poor's and Fitch both downgraded Ireland another notch, while Moody's warned that it was likely to do so. Ireland was now several notches below the euro area, which retained its AAA status.

Equally worrying was the continued downgrading of Ireland's banks as rating agencies fretted that talk about burning even low-ranked bond-holders in Anglo Irish or Irish Nationwide might spread to AIB or elsewhere. On Sunday 10 October, Lenihan landed in New York after attending the annual meeting of the IMF and the World Bank in Washington. He was interviewed by Bloomberg Television on 11 October in a carefully staged media outing designed to calm investors' nerves. 'We have already reduced public-service pay by nearly 14 per cent on average . . . Likewise, we've looked at our welfare bill, at our pensions bill,' Lenihan said. 'All of these areas will have to be looked at. They're on the table.' Increasing taxes on the general population would also have to play some part.

Lenihan also publicly defended Ireland's low rate of corporation tax, at 12½ per cent, designed to lure foreign investment. 'We want to encourage investment, not discourage it.' And, he insisted, 'exports have retained a lot of their strength.'

The following day Patrick Honohan was also asked by reporters about Ireland's low corporate tax regime, after giving a speech at the Philadelphia Federal Reserve Bank. 'A lot of people have been talking about there being pressure,' he said. 'So far I don't actually see that pressure being made explicit.' As a member of the Governing Council of the European Central Bank, Honohan would have been expected to know if there was any. 'I think there is definitely a general view in Ireland, "Why change this system? It works reasonably well", he said.

The view outside Ireland wasn't as benign. Behind the scenes, Ireland's low tax rate—the basis for its success in attracting some of the world's biggest transnationals, including Facebook, Google, Intel and Microsoft—was now under threat. Elements in France and Germany were beginning to push for the tax to be raised in return for further support. The price that might have to be paid for leaving the likes of Fingleton unchecked for so many years was growing ever larger.

On 4 November the Department of Finance published a new document, called *Information Note on the Economic and Budgetary Outlook, 2011–2014*. In bleak terms, which did not break down spending cuts and tax increases, it said the government planned to cut its borrowing by €6 billion the following year. A total adjustment of €15 billion over four years—double the €7½ billion previously estimated by Lenihan—was required to put the economy back on a sustainable path, it said. It was a huge sum to take out of a small economy like Ireland's in a relatively short period.

On 8 November the business news service Dow Jones reported that two hedge funds, Satin Finance SARL and Trimast Holding SARL, had begun a legal action against Irish Nationwide to prevent any write-down of the value of the subordinated bonds they held. Instead they tried to force the society's liquidation. The two funds held more than a quarter of the €250 million of subordinated bonds issued by Irish Nationwide, so there was a good deal of money at stake. But it was hard to know why they would want to liquidate the society, unless, as Dow Jones speculated, they had hedged for such an eventuality by buying credit default swaps to make sure they would get paid if the society went bust.

Irish Nationwide said it planned to 'vigorously defend' the action. A few days later it applied in London to have the case struck out, arguing that it was a ploy by its bond-holders to force full payment.

Brian Lenihan, however, had more to worry about than this sideshow. Late on Tuesday 16 November he was anxious to reassure the media and investors after a meeting with EU finance ministers. 'Ireland is now engaging in an intensive, and disclosed, engagement in relation to the problems in the banking sector,' he said. 'We will take whatever decisive measures that are required to stabilise our banking system as part of the stability of the wider euro zone.'

The following week representatives of the European Union, the European Central Bank and the International Monetary Fund were to visit Ireland to advise it on what to do. Lenihan tried to play down the visit, but it was becoming clear that Ireland was going to struggle hard to keep going under the burden of its banks. He was adamant that it would not need a bail-out.

The EU Commissioner for Economic and Monetary Affairs, Olli Rehn, said of the talks: 'This can be regarded as an intensification of pre-parations of a potential programme, in case it is requested and deemed necessary.' The head of the Euro Group, the sixteen states that use the euro, Jean-Claude Juncker, said that Ireland is making 'significant efforts' to deal with its budget deficit. 'However, market conditions have not normalised yet, and pressure remains.' He added that 'we will take action as the Euro Group . . . to safeguard the stability of the euro if that is needed.'

Yields on ten-year Irish treasuries hit 8.24 per cent that Tuesday. This was too high a level even if Ireland still maintained that it did not need to go back to the market for additional funding until June 2011. Combined with rising bond yields in Greece, Portugal and Spain, Europe had a lot to worry about.

The next day Brian Cowen tried to play down the prospect of a bail-out by telling RTE television:

> We have still not applied for a facility. We haven't started any negotiations. There is no solution yet formulated for us. We have not decided we are putting forward a proposal, because we need to decide what the best option is, and that is what these discussions are about . . . It is urgent. We accept it is urgent and we need to deal with it, but we will deal with it in our own interests as well.

Just how urgent things were was revealed the following day. The Central Bank disclosed that it had provided nearly €35 billion in exceptional liquidity assistance to its banks up to the end of October. It had been forced to put €13.4 billion of this amount into the banks in the month of October alone.

That Thursday morning Honohan pulled the rug on Cowen and Lenihan, who were still resisting being pushed into a bail-out. On the 'Morning Ireland' programme he said that Ireland needed a 'very substantial loan, tens of billions,' to support its economy. 'It's not my call. It's the government at the end. It's my expectation that that is what is likely to happen.' While he expected the talks in Dublin to lead to a loan, he was not concerned that Ireland would lose its sovereignty if a full bail-out took place. 'I think this is the way forward. I don't see it as something that is really worrisome or should lead to a huge change in direction.'

In France the Minister of Finance, Christine Lagarde, seemed to be pushing also for Ireland to accept its fate. She told AFP: 'If it is decided that a mechanism has to be put in place I have no doubt that the Irish government will be responsible and make the appropriate decision independently.' Behind the scenes, Jean-Claude Trichet, President of the European Central Bank, sent a letter marked 'secret' to Lenihan. Accept a bailout or face dire consequences, was the message from the ECB.

The game was now up. Cowen's government had been dragging their feet to avoid a bail-out in order to try to get a better deal on the bank debt and copperfasten its low corporate tax rate. Now Cowen tried to put a brave face on the country's pending humiliation. 'What we're involved in here is working with colleagues in respect of currency problems and euro issue problems that are affecting Ireland,' he insisted.

Enda Kenny dismissed the claim, accusing Cowen of raising the 'white flag' and subjecting the country to the dictates of foreign masters.

A new term entered the popular lexicon: 'Troika'. Officials of the European Commission, European Central Bank and International Monetary Fund would be in Dublin the following week for what was euphemistically called a 'consultation'.

———

On 28 November, after tense negotiations and under fierce pressure from the European Union, the government agreed that Ireland would be provided with an €85 billion bail-out. The National Pension Reserve Fund and other cash resources would be drained in their entirety of €17½ billion as the state's contribution.

Ireland had lost its economic sovereignty. The rottenness epitomised by Irish Nationwide had felled the state.

Chapter 15 ∿

FROM THE MAFIA COAST
TO CO. CAVAN

T he coastline of Montenegro on the Adriatic Sea has been nicknamed the Mafia Coast. Stunningly beautiful, it was tipped to become a rising tourism star. The Montenegrin government was determined to attract international investors to develop coastal resorts that could compete with the best of Italy and Croatia.

Investment, however, was certainly not for the faint-hearted. The tiny south-east European state bordered such trouble spots as Albania and Kosovo. Crime syndicates used Montenegro as a route into continental Europe for cigarettes, narcotics, arms and human trafficking. It was still a risky place to put your money.

As Michael Fingleton counted his ever-growing pension pot and dreamt of a big pay-day from the sale of Irish Nationwide, he felt he was able to meet the challenge. He had mastered the 'stroke' school of Irish business and politics and was confident that he could take on all-comers even in a country like Montenegro.

It was a time when his peers, the Irish developer barons, were striding the world stage as debt-laden buccaneers. Johnny Ronan was building houses on the grounds of the Catherine Palace in St Petersburg, while his school friend and business partner Richard Barrett planned to transform China's exploding cities. Derek Quinlan had opened a Four Seasons Hotel in Prague, while down the Danube, Seán Mulryan was building a new city quarter in Bratislava.

The second tier of small developers tried to match them by pushing into even more far-flung places. Cape Verde, Panama, Antigua and the Stans of Central Asia became the new 'new frontier'. You name it, it was all go. Everywhere in the world, Irish developers were chasing the next wave of money.

Fingleton was determined not to miss out. He wanted to chase the higher returns offered in exotic locations. As in banking, he did not think enough of the associated risk.

His problem, however, was time. He had, after all, a building society to run. When his then friend Louis Maguire, a businessman steeped in the culture of land speculation, told him about an opportunity in Montenegro, he was interested. Maguire's father, Louis senior, was friendly with the estate agent and valuer Louis Scully, an associate of Fingleton.

Maguire junior had joined the ranks of the frontier speculators in Montenegro. He had set up a company there in the early 2000s with a view to buying up land and developing property for the expected influx of tourists from around the world. He had established the investment structures, had got to meet people there and had big plans.

The place they chose was Kotor. It is a small city of about 13,000 inhabitants surrounded by an ancient town wall that dates from when it was a trading outpost of Venice. Epic limestone cliffs overhang the city, creating panoramic views of its natural harbour. What Kotor lacked was enough hotels to tap into its tourist potential.

The city was an up-and-coming port for cruise ships and had the potential to attract the super-yachts of the world's wealthy. Fingleton was familiar with both forms of transport, having holidayed on the famous *Christina O* several times. During his holidays he was also known to be partial to luxury cruise-ships. 'I love an old cruise,' he would sometimes remark to friends. Now was a chance to combine his fondness for the sea with his great passion: making money from property. Maguire's record helped convince him to open his pockets.

Maguire was a modestly wealthy man from wheeler-dealing in Irish property over the years. He had a nose for an investment and an ability to take risks. But what he was best known for was his grandiose plan to build a €7 billion 2,500-acre Disney-type theme park in Co. Dublin, which never happened.

Maguire and Fingleton began to plot out their plans for Kotor. In 2005 they began by purchasing the old Hotel Fjord. It was to be the bedrock of what Maguire promised would be a €200 million resort. The hotel itself was a 200-bed drab ruin that had been built in 1979. It was in a good site, however, with fabulous views. The plan was to rip it all down and replace it with a five-star hotel. As the next two to three years passed, Fingleton personally sank €5½ million into getting the hotel going, even before real construction began. He eventually had a three-quarters share in the company behind it. He was also a director of Paradise Bay Resort, another company set up to redevelop the general area.

In total, Maguire's UEP spent €12.4 million buying three different buildings. Alongside its stake in the Fjord Hotel it snapped up the URC Slavija hotel and leisure centre and the administrative building of Jugo-Oceanija. The redevelopment of the New Fjord was to be a flagship project, Maguire told local reporters, requiring an investment of €70 million. 'It will operate according to highest world standards,' he said. He even announced a plan to set up his own airline, flying directly from Dublin to Montenegro.

The project stalled, however, with planning and fund-raising issues. Fingleton was happy to keep writing the cheques, up to a point; after that he decided to reduce his risk by convincing some of his old pals to invest. It's not clear if any did, but he certainly tried his best.

One of those he hit on was his old friend Jim Mansfield. Mansfield was a colourful Dublin developer who, from beginnings on a small farm in Brittas, Co. Dublin, had gradually become lord of all he surveyed. He delighted in getting his son P. J., then married to the model Andrea Roche, to take him up in his helicopter just so that they could marvel at the thousands of acres he owned.

Mansfield owned a sprawling conference centre with two thousand rooms known as Citywest on the Naas Road, which had been built with little regard for local planners. It had hosted everyone from the Fianna Fáil ard-fheis to American presidents.

Irish Nationwide was one of Mansfield's biggest bankers. It had helped him to buy Weston Aerodrome at Leixlip for €13 million, which Mansfield dreamt of turning into an airport for executive jets. This never happened, and in 2006 it became notorious when criminals were nabbed entering the aerodrome with heroin worth €10 million. They were flying in Mansfield's private jet (unknown to the owner), which he had rented out.

Mansfield listened in his office in Citywest to Fingleton going on about his Montenegrin dream, but he just wasn't interested. Even the fearless Citywest boss, who had made his fortune selling scrap from the Falklands war, baulked. He felt, he later told friends, 'it was too risky.' Unfortunately, Fingleton hadn't the same foresight. Montenegro would later cost him considerable sums, and he would fall out bitterly with Maguire.

On paper Michael Fingleton was a multimillionaire when he left Irish Nationwide in April 2009. In reality, his personal finances would quickly prove to be in grim shape. As time went on he would gradually realise he had squandered the millions he was paid by the society. Like his clients, he had been lured in too deep by get-rich-quick property schemes, just as credit dried up and property prices tumbled. Instead of a happy retirement he was now stuck trying to unravel the mess he had created.

It was all happening too fast. Fingleton had believed he was insulated against ever returning to his modest roots. Now he wasn't so sure. His investments were crumbling as he lost his Midas touch. Worse, he became aware that Irish Nationwide's new management were delving into how he had accumulated his fortune over the years. He seemed convinced he had done nothing inappropriate, but reports in the media revealed that his old society was investigating all the same.

At this point it was more stop-start than a scientific examination. The society had more to think about than hunting down Fingleton's personal investments, which were poorly enough documented. Whether this was just the usual bad housekeeping or something else was hard to tell.

In any event, in early 2010 it became known that the society had completed a review of the ownership of its fifty branches. It had long been rumoured that Fingleton secretly owned some of them. One member of the society, Michael Maughan, executive chairman of the Gowan Group, a business stretching from cars to kitchen brands, had raised the issue at a public meeting in December 2009. As a result a review had been ordered of the society's property portfolio to see whether Fingleton had any personal interests there.

It found that there was simply no evidence that Fingleton had ever owned any of the society's branches. He did own a property next door to the society's branch in Phibsborough, Dublin, which housed a bakery and an Oxfam charity shop, but this was hardly untoward. The society owned other odd assets, like eight houses behind its head office, which it leased to tenants. It also owned an unsold block of sixty-two apartments in Booterstown Wood on the Stillorgan Road, Dublin, which had been built for the society by Brian M. Durkan and Company. But again nothing wrong was uncovered about the society's ownership of these properties.

As the results of this review trickled back to Fingleton, it cannot have pleased him that the society he created now trusted him so little. This fed his grievance against its new owner, the state.

Many of Irish Nationwide's old clients were either falling like dominoes or being reined in by NAMA, which insisted on them curbing their extravagant life-styles. Old clients like Bernard McNamara, Tom McFeely and Larry O'Mahony were heading to England to try to be declared bankrupt. They realised that the game was up. Other favourites, including Seán Dunne and Niall Mellon, were spending more time abroad. They realised that they needed to create new wealth from the rubble of their old fortune.

Fingleton was as caught out as his old golden circle, as personally exposed as his Mickey-Mouse society. The first project to publicly implode for him was a land deal in Co. Cavan, which revealed much of his greed and his stupidity. In 2005, as property in Co. Dublin skyrocketed, the price of land near commuter towns had also surged. Irish Nationwide was making fat profits riding this wave, and Fingleton decided to get in on the act, just as he did the same year in Montenegro. For decades he had dabbled in property speculation and investment on a small scale, and the new deals were a step upwards in risk.

In Co. Cavan, Fingleton teamed up with an old Fianna Fáil pal, Senator Francie O'Brien. A dairy farmer by trade, O'Brien knew the area intimately as a regular land speculator who had often been backed by Irish Nationwide in the past. He had a reputation for popping up unexpectedly in land deals with a higher bid. He was part of the loose inner circle that revolved around Fingleton who didn't need to bother with such things as paperwork or too many questions about their ability to repay borrowings.

Olivia Greene, a former home loan supervisor with Irish Nationwide, knew O'Brien as a regular visitor to head office after he finished his day toiling in the political backwater of the Seanad. 'Francie would always be sitting in reception waiting when he was in,' she recalled. 'He'd meet Michael Fingleton upstairs out of hours. "I have a bit of business to discuss with himself",' she recalled O'Brien saying.

The 'bit of business' had built up over the years as O'Brien dabbled in loans from the society of €7 million to fund various land deals, mainly in Cos. Cavan and Monaghan. It's not surprising that the two men got on, united as they were by a love of being close to the powerful and influential while building up pots of money and plotting how to make more.

O'Brien was a lifelong Fianna Fáil activist. Fingleton was also a fan of what was then Ireland's dominant party, though in a less obvious way, and he had pals too in Fine Gael.

In 1989 O'Brien was made a Fianna Fáil senator, a position he held for the next twenty years. It was a good gig, providing a decent allowance, access to the Dáil bar, and a bit of prestige in his community. It was his reward for his years toiling for the party as a member of Monaghan County Council from 1979 to 2003 and chairman of the council from 1986 to 1987.

Two Monaghan businessmen, Charles McGuinness and Noel Mulligan, were also added in to the consortium. It is not clear why they were needed. Fingleton was then considered a rich man, and he certainly didn't need any additional investors in order to borrow big money. Mulligan ran a small business in Monaghan called Star Lighting Interiors as well as Jono's, a furniture shop. He'd dabbled in property development but was a small enough player. McGuinness was a farmer who also had a background in small and medium enterprise. He ran a mobile phone shop in Monaghan and had an alarm installation business. In 2004 he became briefly famous when his wife, Helen, filmed a large unidentified creature that became known as the 'Border Beast' when it was broadcast on RTE.

In late 2005 Fingleton and his crack team of investors began negotiations with the Wall family for a fifty-acre site at Swellan Upper and Lower outside Cavan. The family had tentatively agreed a deal to sell to a Northern developer, but Fingleton and his pals slid under the wire with a higher bid. At the time it was quite a coup. A price of €11 million was fixed on, and Ulster Bank agreed to fund the purchase. Ulster Bank was then headed by Cormac McCarthy, who is now chief financial officer of Paddy Power, a massive gambling company. His time in Ulster Bank was not dissimilar.

Under McCarthy, Ulster Bank was far bigger and far better managed than Irish Nationwide. But when it came to the basic mistake of failing to spot the property bubble, it made many of the same blunders. It was the principal banker to Fingleton's friend Seán Dunne in his grandiose purchase of a seven-acre site in Ballsbridge, Dublin, for €380 million which Dunne had vainly hoped to turn into an ultra-expensive residential and shopping area.

Ulster Bank had lent billions to other developers to snap up plots of land around the country, and lending another few million to Fingleton and his pals looked like a safe bet. The bank didn't see a large hilly field outside a border town: like Fingleton's grand consortium, it saw a goldmine that could be turned into houses that would be flogged to Ireland's young people.

These were exciting times for Fingleton as he worked on this side deal while busying himself with the serious business of preparing to sell his beloved society. In retrospect, both this and Montenegro were dangerous distractions for Fingleton at a time when he should have been hell-bent on cleaning up Irish Nationwide and getting it sold.

In July 2006 Fingleton et al. borrowed €13.2 million from Ulster Bank. The loan covered the purchase of the site plus a little bit extra to help guide it through the planning process. At the time, four-bedroom semi-detached houses were selling in Co. Cavan for up to €200,000 a pop, creating a huge potential gain from the site once they could get the right planning permission. Fingleton and his cronies decided they could at least double their money even if all they did was get planning permission and then 'flip' the site on another builder. If they held onto it all the way and developed the site themselves they stood to make tens of millions. There was a proviso: the price of houses had to hold up.

Then there was the tricky problem of planning permission. Unfortunately for the consortium, Cavan County Council turned down the first application to build 433 houses on the site. It felt that the roads in the area could not sustain that level of traffic. It was a hitch that Fingleton hadn't considered. And the delay would lead to a financial catastrophe as the 'impossible' began to happen: property tanked.

In June 2008 things were rough, and Ulster Bank agreed an interest roll-up facility with the four men. This bought them more time while they hoped things would pick up again. It also took their borrowings to €13½ million. Ulster Bank gave them the extra facility on the condition that they sell part of the site to Bennett's Construction, a building firm, to reduce their level of debt. But, as the financial crisis unfolded, this deal fell through. The consortium realised they were stuck with their fields.

As their advisers drew up a fresh proposal for the site, it must have begun to dawn on Fingleton that he was on the wrong side of a property bubble that he had so ably and greedily helped create. He and his cronies had no choice but to plough on and try to get planning permission, even as property prices continued to fall off a cliff.

In July 2009 Fingleton paid €42,875 to Ulster Bank to cover interest on the project, three months after he resigned from the building society. This was the first interest payment in a year on their loan. In November

2009 Ulster Bank moved Fingleton's loan into its internal 'bad bank', such was its poor quality. This unit took a much harder line, as Ulster's parent, Royal Bank of Scotland, had by now been bailed out by the British taxpayer. It began to threaten the investors to try to get its money back.

Three further payments—for €26,811, €34,842 and €34,769—were forthcoming to the bank, covering interest up to the end of November 2009. Then Ulster Bank really began to get worried. The money simply stopped. In December 2009 it wrote to Fingleton and his partners, asking for arrears of interest to be paid and for the investors to show how they intended to repay the loan in its entirety.

On the last day of 2009, with the property market in free fall, Fingleton and his fellow-investors got planning permission for an 82-bedroom nursing home. It was better than nothing but hardly enough to repay a loan of more than €13 million. In any event, the investors hadn't got the money to build a nursing home. Instead Ulster Bank was breathing down their necks looking for more repayments.

Suddenly, Fingleton's field of dreams died. By 2010, local auctioneers valued the site at €15,000 an acre, or €750,000 in total. This was one-fifteenth of its purchase price of approximately €220,000 an acre.

The prospects for the site were bleak. The Department of the Environment, asleep during the boom, suddenly realised that the country had a huge oversupply of houses at various stages of construction. In Co. Cavan alone it counted 147 ghost estates. This was a big surplus, which would mean that Fingleton and his friends had little prospect of ever selling any houses on their site, even if they could afford to build them.

At the beginning of March 2010 Ulster Bank was owed €13.535 million, with arrears standing at €285,000. On 3 March the bank wrote to all four borrowers, asking for net worth statements and tax returns. It also demanded again a repayment proposal from the men. It wasn't happy with what it got back.

On 23 March, Fingleton sent Ulster Bank a handwritten statement of net worth. He said his most valuable asset was a stake in a development site in Kotor, Montenegro. He valued this at €4 million. Next was his family home and nearby land in Shankill, Co. Dublin, which was worth €3 million. Ulster Bank wasn't happy about this asset when it discovered that Fingleton had put his interest in it into his wife's name in October 2009. This made it less clear to the bank whether it could take control of this asset. Fingleton also said he owned four apartments in the Mespil complex in Ballsbridge that he had acquired so controversially decades earlier. These were worth €1.2 million, according to Fingleton. He also owned a house in Leopardstown, Co. Dublin, worth €950,000, and a retail property in Phibsborough worth €900,000. He also had a cool million in cash—the exact amount of his much-disputed bonus.

Furthermore, he said he had 'initiated legal proceedings to recover €10 million plus held in trust by a third party from actual earned and received profits in relation to a major Northside development.' This was a reference to a case Fingleton had begun a few days before Christmas 2009 against his former friend Gerry Gannon. He claimed he had put £75,000 into a huge project Gannon planned in Clongriffin, Co. Dublin, some time in the 1990s, and this entitled him to a quarter share in it. Gannon disputed this and denied there was a deal. It was all a long way from when the two men were so close that Fingleton picked out an antique silver fruit bowl as a wedding present for his old pal's daughter in 2005.

(It was also curious. Was this a one-off deal, or had there been other little-known agreements between Fingleton and his clients down the years that had never emerged? This was an area that would later be investigated.)

In answer to Ulster Bank's final demand, Fingleton said he had not yet prepared or submitted a tax return for 2009, but 'my income for 2009 was in excess of €400,000.'

The bank was not impressed. Fingleton had assets, but they were mainly in the form of property and therefore hard to value in a falling market. His assets, the bank said later that year, were 'significantly less than was previously understood.'

But what really shocked Ulster Bank was that there was no mention in Fingleton's note of his pension, which had only recently been valued at €27 million. Its absence was a 'considerable surprise' to the bank. In April 2010 it wrote to Fingleton explicitly demanding that he disclose 'all pension fund assets and liabilities, equitable interests in properties or companies held directly, indirectly or in beneficial trust for you, and deposit accounts held within or outside the jurisdiction.' Fingleton, however, was not prepared to tell the bank how much his pension was worth, or to include it in the list of assets he was prepared to hand over to repay his borrowings.

By the summer of 2010 Ulster Bank felt it had no choice but to began legal proceedings, and it applied to have its case fast-tracked in the

Commercial Court that November for full hearing. In mid-October 2010 it began a High Court action to recover €13.65 million from Fingleton, O'Brien, McGuinness and Mulligan.

The case came before Mr Justice Peter Kelly, a famously straight-talking judge who had become de facto chief undertaker for the former stars of Ireland's boom, who were appearing regularly in front of him as their house of cards collapsed.

In an affidavit a manager at Ulster Bank Group Centre, Ted Mahon, outlined the sorry sequence of events. Ulster Bank admitted it had never asked for such basic information as statements of the investors' affairs at the time of granting a loan of more than €10 million. Instead, it admitted, it simply relied on Fingleton's 'perceived wealth'. It said it believed him to be a 'man of substantial means,' and even though he was not previously a client it felt it could trust him because of who he was. The bank was 'at all times very conscious' that Fingleton was a 'particularly well-known person in business and financial circles.'

Ted Mahon, the court heard, had seen Irish Nationwide's annual report in April 2009, which revealed that Fingleton had a pension fund of €27.6 million. Up to April and May 2010, when relations broke down, this gave his bank 'great comfort.' However, he said, Fingleton was refusing to give up his pension.

Mr Justice Kelly described it as 'extraordinary' that Fingleton had omitted his pension from his list of assets and liabilities. Fingleton's pension 'eclipsed' all his other assets, and he could not understand why it wasn't included

A statement of affairs for Francis O'Brien also emerged, which showed a gap of some €12.8 million between his assets and liabilities.

Mr Justice Kelly refused an application by all four investors for a stay on registration and execution of the judgement, which they sought in the light of continuing negotiations with the bank and in the hope that planning permission might enhance the value of the land. He said he was not required to address the bank's stupidity in entering into such a large loan with someone about whom it knew nothing except that his name appeared regularly in newspapers.

Fingleton, however, continued to insist that the deal could be got back on track. He said he had recently spoken to the head of the Penney's chain, Arthur Ryan, who had 'expressed a strong interest' in the Cavan field, and he insisted that Tesco also might be interested in the site.

On 1 November, Ulster Bank secured a judgement against Fingleton and his partners over their unpaid loans. The judgement placed the ageing Fingleton in desperate financial straits. He still had millions, but he was running out of wriggle room.

Within a few months of the decision Francie O'Brien would announce that he had decided not to seek re-election to the Seanad. After so many decades wandering the corridors of power, he was bowing out. The decision, he insisted, had 'absolutely nothing to do with the ongoing controversy over bank borrowings for investment during the boom years.'

———

As 2010 ended, Irish Nationwide again picked up its pursuit of Fingleton's bonus. On 8 December, Danny Kitchen sent Fingleton a copy of Irish Nationwide's report on his pension and pay. The report, he said, was about to be made public by being handed over to the Committee of Public Accounts. 'As you have clearly and publicly stated that the reason for not returning the 2008 bonus was that this report was not made available to you, I hope that providing it to you will remove the last obstacle to repayment and that the society may expect to receive the amount to which you committed.' Fingleton did not reply.

A week later, on 15 December, the chief financial officer of Irish Nationwide, John McGloughlin, wrote to Fingleton. It was a no-nonsense letter, reflecting his management style. Unlike the more refined Kitchen, he pulled no punches in demanding that Fingleton repay what the society's new regime believed were improper expenses. He told Fingleton that the society had discovered that on 2 December 2008 he had written to the IRFU asking for six ten-year tickets, to be sent to his home and not to the society. 'These tickets are the sole property of the society,' McGloughlin said. He gave Fingleton two options: pay for the tickets he had used and return the remainder, or buy them outright. The cost of the tickets from 2 December 2008 until their expiry in 2014 was €42,900.

McGloughlin also demanded that Fingleton reimburse the society for the £2,373.58 for his two-night stay in the Dorchester Hotel, London, in May 2009. This trip by Fingleton and his wife had taken place after he had resigned from the society.

It went on and on. McGloughlin demanded that Fingleton repay his dental fees of €12,180 run up in 2008 in the Blackrock Clinic. 'The society should not have paid these amounts on your behalf due to the level of health care paid to you by the society,' McGloughlin explained. He also sent him a long list of other expenses that the society wanted clarified or repaid. In total, he identified €73,524 in expenses that the society wanted repaid.

Fingleton did not get around to replying for several months. On 1 February 2011 he replied to McGloughlin and addressed each of his points in turn.

After Michael Walsh had 'suddenly' resigned on 13 February 2009, Fingleton said, Terry Cooney had been appointed acting chairman. Fingleton had been due to retire on 28 February, but Cooney asked him to stay on because of Walsh's departure.

> Mr Cooney was to say the least anxious that I stay on and I had a number of conversations with him on the matter. In the course of those conversations the question of the availability of tickets post retirement arose. He told me I could have as many tickets as I wanted provided I agreed to remain with the Society beyond my retirement date. I said that was a deal and agreed to stay on beyond my contract date.

It was a bizarre explanation. If it was true it provided a shocking insight into Fingleton's priorities in his final weeks with Irish Nationwide. As the society crashed around their ears, Fingleton and his old pal Cooney had time to worry about rugby tickets.

Fingleton then said that, despite having had the tickets for more than a year, he had never actually used them. Either they arrived too late, he complained, or he wasn't around to enjoy them because of 'unforeseen circumstances.'

After making his excuses, Fingleton saw no reason to repay the society for any tickets over the previous year; but, he said magnanimously, 'I am pleased to let the society have all the tickets for the current series.'

Having kicked the tickets issue to touch, he turned to his dental costs. He said that for the previous twenty-five years the society had covered all his medical and dental expenses. 'Fortunately I never had a sick day since I joined the society in 1971. Indeed I believe the dental costs were the first claim of any substance I made.' He said he only did so because he was advised that the treatment was not covered by the the VHI.

'On a separate matter my wife was also covered for all medical health costs as well,' he continued. In June 2008, Fingleton said, his wife had flown to America for 'emergency surgery,' which had cost €35,000. After prolonged negotiation, which continued after his retirement, the VHI agreed to pay only €14,000 of her bills. 'I believe I would be entitled to claim for the difference from the Society but have not done so,' Fingleton said. As a result, he seemed to suggest, the society was evens with him.

Fingleton then explained his rather expensive stay in the Dorchester Hotel, paid for by the society even after he had left it. 'Sometime before my retirement I had arranged to go to London to visit our principal borrowers to reassure them that the new management would be fully accessible to them in relation to their business relationships with the society etc.' He said he decided the best time to do this was at the annual company dinner of Laing O'Rourke, the massive London-Irish construction group headed by Ray O'Rourke. Fingleton said he had spoken to O'Rourke and suggested that Gary McCollum might attend in his place. 'He was insistent that he wanted me there and nobody else,' Fingleton said. He had convinced O'Rourke to do a deal with the society, which earned it a fee of €2 million, so he felt compelled to go. 'This visit while technically after my retirement date was clearly related to Society business and not a personal unrelated matter.' He said he was 'genuinely shocked' at the cost of his stay, as he usually got a room for only £300 a night there. Again he made no offer to repay the cost of the trip.

Finally, in a brief riposte, he brushed aside McGloughlin's other concerns about his expenses, from his green fees at the K Club to thousands spent on chauffeurs.

All expenditure itemised was incurred for the promotion of the business of the Society and for the development and enhancement of customer relationships.

In relation to the last item on the schedule [his going-away watch] this expenditure was not initiated or authorised by me and I had no involvement in it whatsoever.

I trust this sets out my position in relation to the claims made in your letter.

It was a bravura performance. Despite his protestation that he was keeping his €1 million bonus on a point of principle, and that he was entitled to all his expenses, it was not hard to conclude also that Fingleton needed every penny he had.

———

Fingleton was annoyed by these letters from his old society, but his real concern was with his own well-being as yet another horrible year drew to a close. Within a year, what he had described in his statement of affairs as his most valuable asset, a stake in the leisure resort in Montenegro, would look very shaky.

The first public sign of trouble emerged on 15 September 2011 when Fingleton was forced to ring the Employment Appeals Tribunal and say he was unable to turn up that day. He was due to appear in an unfair dismissal case being taken against him by Brendan Beggan, his former Monaghan branch manager. Fingleton told the chairperson of the tribunal he was 'eager' to attend that day to testify against his former friend but that he was unable to as it coincided with a court appearance in eastern Europe.

The case he was referring to related to Montenegro, where Fingleton had fallen out badly with another old friend, Louis Maguire. Their dream of creating a luxury resort there was rapidly falling apart. The Montenegrin property boom had turned to bust, and values had fallen sharply. The city council in Kotor had publicly expressed its frustration at the lack of progress on the Hotel Fjord, which it had hoped would help to build a tourist industry there. By the end of November 2011 the authorities had placed Fingleton and Maguire's New Fjord Developments in receivership during a closed court hearing in the capital city, Podgorica.

The accounts of New Fjord Developments had been frozen after an unnamed creditor who was owed more than €70,000 petitioned the court for the company to be placed in receivership. The company also owed money to the city council in Kotor, which was claiming that it was owed unpaid property taxes. A creditors' meeting had been called for 29 December, and a special court hearing was set for the following February. It was a royal mess.

Worse, Maguire's company United European Partners Montenegro was suing Fingleton for €6½ million. Maguire blamed Fingleton for the project's woes and accused him in court documents of 'corporate negligence'. The company claimed that one of the reasons the development was in trouble was that Fingleton had failed to explain the origins of the €5½ million he had used for the purchase of the hotel. Fingleton has not publicly explained why the company saw the origins of his money as an issue.

In January 2012, Dearbháil McDonald reported in the *Irish Independent* that Fingleton had moved €500,000—half the cash savings he had disclosed to Ulster Bank—into an offshore account four days after he was hit with a €13.6 million debt order by the bank. It was moved into his account at the Atlas Mont Bank in Podgorica on 5 November 2010. Then, the *Independent* reported, on 21 January 2011 he had emptied this account by moving €480,000 out of Montenegro into the account of his son Michael Fingleton junior in Barclays Bank, London. The same day he transferred another €128,498 from a separate account in Montenegro to his son's London account. This was transferred out of New Fjord Developments.

Inspectors from Montenegro's Authority for the Prevention of Money Laundering and Terrorist Financing had picked up the cash movements during a routine inspection after New Fjord Developments was forced into bankruptcy by its creditors the previous year.

The purpose of the transfer of €500,000 was described as 'foreign investment', but the inspectors say in their report that it has not been confirmed that Fingleton in a personal—as opposed to a corporate—capacity has invested in property in Montenegro.

The inspectors have queried the transfer of €128,498 from New Fjord accounts to Michael Fingleton junior's account, stating that it was 'without a clear basis.' They said that Fingleton's son had no 'commercial relationship' with New Fjord Developments, and appeared concerned that Fingleton had nonetheless moved money there.

Late the night before the *Independent* went to press, Fingleton sent a text message to McDonald.

. . . I am unable to comment on matters before the Courts in Montenegro. You will simply compound the enormous Libel already perpetrated which my Lawyers advise me is the most blatant they have ever encountered. I would respectably [*sic*] advise you to await the outcome of the case. When the case is finalised I and my Lawyers will have a lot to say.

In objections submitted in Podgorica in response to the inspectors' report, Fingleton said that he and his son were not the subject of any official investigation into their private accounts. They were innocent men being wrongfully persecuted—just like back home.

It was hard to know what to make of it all. Fingleton's personal finances, like his society, appeared to have slipped into a bizarre twilight zone, where nothing was as it seemed.

Whatever was happening in Montenegro, Fingleton had clearly decided to get what money he had left there out. Self-preservation was now his primary concern. His dream of relaxing his bones in the new Hotel Fjord was now as distant as his hopes of a quiet retirement as a multi-millionaire.

| FINGERS

A t 9 a.m. on 12 December 2011 Michael Fingleton arrived at Davitt House in Adelaide Road, Dublin. Wearing his trademark fedora, the septuagenarian was ninety minutes early so as to avoid photographers.

He was at the offices of the Employment Appeals Tribunal to testify against an old friend, Brendan Beggan. The former manager of the Monaghan branch was suing Irish Nationwide for wrongful dismissal. Beggan had fallen out badly with Fingleton in a prolonged dispute over his failure to repay his personal loans. In July 2009, four months after Fingleton resigned, Beggan was sacked.

As with Alex Tarbett so many years before, Fingleton was prepared to turn against someone he had once enjoyed socialising with but now perceived to have stepped out of line. He was not intimidated by Beggan, who retained his powerful build from his years on the football field.

Beggan was accompanied into the tribunal by his partner, Olivia Greene. He stared hard at his old boss, but neither man said a word.

At 10:40 a.m. the tribunal began in a room unaccustomed to being filled with journalists eager to hear what might be said in a rare public appearance by Fingleton. It heard that Beggan had begun borrowing from the society in 1999. It was tiny stuff compared with the kind of deals the society was doing with its favoured developers at the time; and, unlike some of them, Beggan was on the hook for all his debts.

In 2002 Beggan had decided to dabble in development by buying a small site. He borrowed €1½ million and built three houses. His borrowings were now many multiples of his income, but this did not bother his employers. In 2004 he sold the houses for €800,000, and his solicitor told him there was not enough money left over to repay his loans to the society. He was in trouble.

The following year Beggan claimed he had met Fingleton to tell him about his problems. He said the two men came to an agreement that he would be given time to repay his debts.

Fingleton's version of events was rather different. He denied he had ever had an agreement with Beggan. Instead he said the society had decided to investigate Beggan when it realised his loans were 'excessive.' In particular, Fingleton said, the society was annoyed that he had sold properties and not used the money to pay off his debts. (It was richly ironic to hear Fingleton complain about excessive borrowing and deals allegedly being done behind his back.)

Fingleton denied 'actively encouraging' members of the staff to get into property by borrowing big multiples of their income. He insisted that the decision by Beggan's partner, Olivia Greene, to give evidence in a High Court case in 2007 in favour of the action of the former manager Brian Fitzgibbon against Irish Nationwide was not connected to its decision to sack him. Revenge had nothing to do with it.

Beggan disagreed and maintained that his relations with Fingleton became 'extremely frosty' after Greene's testimony. He said he believed this was the real reason he was sacked. He was now taking an unfair dismissal case because he believed he had been singled out because his partner had crossed Fingleton.

Fingleton appeared as a witness in Beggan's case on 12 December 2011. He had been following reports in the media and was not pleased at what had been said. At a hearing earlier that year Greene had claimed that Fingleton ran Irish Nationwide like a 'personal bank.' Angrily, Fingleton said Greene's comments were 'slander' and denied that he issued loans at his own discretion.

> I want to refute in the strongest possible terms the claim that I ran Irish Nationwide as a personal bank. That is an absolute slander. I worked under the policy of the society as laid down by the board. In relation to the claim that I gave loans to some customers and they didn't have to pay them back, that is a totally outrageous accusation.

Afterwards Fingleton tried to leave the tribunal by the staff door. Confronted by a mob of journalists and cameras, he was forced to turn abruptly into a consultation room. For fifteen minutes he waited there; then, at 12:30 p.m., he put on his trademark black hat and headed out at a fast pace.

Journalists shouted out questions as he left. Would he repay his €1 million bonus? Would he return his €11,500 watch? Fingleton just ignored them. As he got into his car, Beggan roared at him that he 'wouldn't get away with it all.' Fingleton remained stonily silent as he made it into the front passenger seat of the car.

Beggan lost his unfair dismissal case in January 2013. But his action was still significant; for the first time, Fingleton had been publicly questioned on how he ran the building society—not by a politician, not by a regulator, but by a former employee.

————

Three years had now passed since the state's disastrous decision to guarantee Irish Nationwide. The public knew by then that the size of the bill it was being asked to pay was €5.4 billion, but little enough else. It had little idea of the true extent of the rottenness it was now being extorted to tighten its belt to pay for.

The state had produced two hefty reports on 31 May 2010 into its banking crisis. They were erudite and succinct big-picture explanations of events, prepared in the context of carrying out a much deeper investigation into Irish banking that was expected to take place soon after their publication.

The first of these reports was prepared by Patrick Honohan, the academic turned governor of the Central Bank. It is called *The Irish Banking Crisis: Regulatory and Financial Stability Policy, 2003–2008*. Incredibly, Michael Walsh, chairman of Irish Nationwide, is acknowledged in the report among seven insiders who were owed a 'special debt of gratitude' from Honohan for his 'extensive time' spent helping with the preparation of the report. It was as if Walsh had not spent almost a decade giving Michael Fingleton credibility by remaining year after year as chairman of the society. The opportunity to grill Walsh about his total failure as a chairman was missed. Rather than being held publicly to account by the governor of the Central Bank, his thoughts were not publicly recorded.

Honohan's report was nonetheless a good overview of what went wrong with Irish Nationwide, doubtless with any gaps filled in by Walsh. It was not, however, a proper investigation that would explain to the public who was responsible. In its 177 pages the report never mentions Michael Fingleton, or any other banker, by name. Nor does it criticise in

any detail the people in the Financial Regulator's office and in politics
who facilitated him. Honohan, a talented and essentially decent man,
did not see pointing fingers as part of his job. But on page 17 of the
report there is an intriguing footnote.

> The central management figure in INBS was seen as an overly
> dominating figure that needed to be surrounded by a stronger
> governance structure.
>   While it was understood by all that he was politically well-
> connected, the failure to resolve the issue is not attributed by anyone
> involved to his having a privileged status. While unconscious factors
> may have been at work, FR [Financial Regulator] management and
> directors agree that there is no evidence of political representations
> being made on his behalf aimed at influencing regulatory decisions.

The fact that none of the insiders interviewed by Honohan admitted
that there had been political interference to protect or aid Fingleton
down the years was hardly proof that nothing had occurred. Fingleton's
relationship with those in the corridors of political power was simply not
investigated. He had spent decades making political donations, paying
for political golf outings, dining with politicians in fancy restaurants,
offering politicians free tickets to Croke Park. Irish Nationwide also
directly subsidised political parties. In 2007, for example, it made three
substantial political donations: €5,000 to the Progressive Democrats,
€5,000 to Fine Gael, and €7,500 to the SDLP. In February 2008 it paid
€2,500 to Fianna Fáil for a table at its spring fund-raiser at Leopardstown
race course, which was attended by all its political bigwigs. This was
in the interregnum when Bertie Ahern was preparing to step down as
Taoiseach, to be replaced by Brian Cowen. The society almost certainly
made many other donations over the decades, but there has been no
thorough investigation of these financial links. It would take a phone
call from the government to order one.

At board meetings too Fingleton would on occasion drop the name
of a government minister he had met on the golf course. Politicians were
his friends, his associates and his clients. The society had lent millions to
politicians and their families and associates down the years.

On the night of the bank guarantee at least ten members of the Dáil
had borrowings from the building society, according to a list of 'PEP' or

politically exposed people who had borrowed from the society. Some of the loans down the years to politicians or people connected to them were given on generous terms, sometimes with little regard for paperwork or the creditworthiness of the borrower.

In May 2011 the society's new chief executive, Gerry McGinn, had acknowledged that the society had reviewed its loans to politicians. 'I have not come across a loan made to a public representative where there were special favours done [beyond Fingleton's remit],' he said. 'There was nothing untoward in loans being given on slightly generous terms.' McGinn said the type of loans enjoyed by this elite included loans that were interest-only or had capital repayment holidays. Fingleton had extraordinary powers to lend however he liked, so that saying he had not gone beyond his remit meant little. No information was given on whether or there were clusters of loans in particular areas, or to the families of politicians.

Fingleton was amazingly close to the levers of power. At the same time he was somehow untouchable for decades at the top of his accident-ridden and scandal-ridden society. The possibility that these two facts might be related has never been investigated publicly. The answer to why Fingleton gave favourable loans to such people as politicians has never been given, because the question has not really been asked. There was little political will to dig deeper into the society's relations with politicians.

The clearest example of this lackadaisical approach to investigating the society's links to politics could be seen on the wall of the private members' bar in Leinster House. A picture of a beaming Fingleton sponsoring the Oireachtas golf team hung in the bar for twenty years, showing politicians from the Progressive Democrats, Fine Gael and Fianna Fáil clamouring around him. As politicians relaxed over a pint after a long day working out new ways to cut back public spending, up on the wall behind them all through the financial crisis hung a photograph of Michael Fingleton. Nobody even thought of taking the picture down until April 2011, when Pearse Doherty, the recently elected Sinn Féin TD for Donegal South-West, called for it to be 'taken down from its perch and placed in the dustbin of history once and for all.'

Ireland's second report into its banking crisis was published on 31 May 2010 by the German banking economist Klaus Regling and a former deputy director of the International Monetary Fund, Max Watson. Their report was called *A Preliminary Report on the Sources of Ireland's Banking Crisis.* This report again names nobody. Regling and Watson interviewed Fingleton in private, along with other senior figures from the society. According to well-placed sources, Fingleton was unrepentant when interviewed and defended all his actions. The public were denied the opportunity to hear his testimony for themselves. Even though everybody was paying for it with ever greater austerity, Fingleton's views were kept secret.

It was a farce and a disgrace that Fingleton's right to privacy on what had become a very public matter outweighed the public's right to know. Yet again the powerful were off the hook.

Regling and Watson's report concludes that the banking crisis had 'global influences, yet it was in crucial ways "home-made".' They state that it was 'not clear' that serious failings of corporate governance were 'limited' to Anglo Irish Bank.

> It seems important to identify how such very serious governance failures were initiated; how and why internal checks and balances failed in restraining the management of certain banks; whether there were failures of auditorial vigilance; whether supervisors knew of the events (and if not, why not); and why the response of supervisors was not more forceful.

They called for an investigation into 'breakdowns in risk management approaches and in some cases the unwarranted or excessive overriding of internal guidelines.'

> It should be established how and why internal checks and balances failed; whether supervisors perceived the risks; and why the response of supervisors was not more forceful.
>
> Both strands of the reassessment suggested above—policy review and formal investigation—now need to be pursued rapidly. This is important in order to identify lessons for policy in the future. It is also crucial in order to 'clear the air,' and thus bring public debate on the Irish banking crisis to closure.

They called for a full banking inquiry to be 'pursued rapidly.'

On foot of these two banking reports the leader of Fine Gael, Enda Kenny, tabled a motion of no confidence in the Taoiseach, Brian Cowen. Kenny, who feared his own leadership heave, was anxious to position himself as a man tough on rogue bankers who was keen to hold people to account. The motion failed, and Cowen hung on.

It was only later, in January 2011, that Cowen finally resigned in the wake of *The FitzPatrick Tapes*, which revealed that he had been in repeated contact with Seán FitzPatrick, chairman of Anglo Irish Bank, during the thick of the financial crisis. They had discussed, among other things, how the country's richest man had taken a disastrous €2½ billion punt on Anglo Irish. This was the very thing neither of Ireland's two official reports chose to investigate: the interface between politics and banking.

After Kenny became Taoiseach in March 2011 he blustered about holding a banking inquiry. But for some reason, as the months stretched into years, it never got anywhere. A proper investigation into how men like Fingleton had cost the taxpayer €5.4 billion kept fizzling out. There was little political rush to find out Fingleton's secrets.

On 19 April 2011 the new Minister for Finance, Michael Noonan, published yet another report, this time by the Finnish banking expert Peter Nyberg, called *Misjudging Risk: Causes of the Systemic Banking Crisis in Ireland*. The report had been completed in March but was delayed until after the general election that threw Fianna Fáil out of power and replaced it with a coalition of Fine Gael and the Labour Party.

This third report found that Irish Nationwide's business model was 'unique', as it was 'concentrated primarily on speculative site finance, which proved initially to be very profitable in a rising property market. The model was risky, however, and risk mitigation primarily involved selecting trusted and previously successful customers.' Lending in the society (as also in Anglo Irish) had 'proceeded with insufficient checks and balances during the period.'

Irish Nationwide's situation was made worse by its reliance on wholesale funding to fuel its crazed lending. 'As wholesale funding tends to be much more volatile than customer deposits, [Anglo Irish and Irish Nationwide] were particularly vulnerable to any doubts regarding their own solvency or that of their borrowers.' Nyberg holds back, however, from really explaining how it was that this funding became the opiate that allowed men like Fingleton to go mad.

It would have been a brave argument to make. Europe was by then really worried about whether the euro itself would survive. It needed Ireland to carry the can for its broken banks. Any suggestion of making bond-holders pay for their stupidity in backing rogues like Fingleton would have had a knock-on effect that would have driven up the cost of raising money in the bond market for all European banks. Nyberg said:

> At INBS, a number of essential, independent functions either did not effectively exist or were seriously under-resourced. The problems in Anglo and INBS in particular, were not hidden but were in plain sight of the FR [Financial Regulator] and the CB [Central Bank].
>
> INBS's expansion into development lending was clearly documented and the governance problems in the bank were widely known by the authorities.

The issues were 'repeatedly' raised but with 'only modest results.'

> While the poor state of loan documentation in INBS and insufficiency of collateral in both would have required closer inspection, such information was readily available to the FR. Had they considered it necessary or appropriate, there was sufficient information to have allowed the authorities to take more decisive action than was the case.

There it was. In black and white, Nyberg concluded that Irish Nationwide could have been stopped.

Surely now, with three reports in the bag, a full banking investigation would begin at once? At first it seemed that it might. Enda Kenny said after the publication of Nyberg's report that after ten years of Fianna Fáil it was finally time 'to hold persons, who by reckless greed and whatever else, lack of oversight, went off the rails completely, and the taxpayer has to pay.' The Minister for Finance, Michael Noonan, said it was important that justice had not only to be done but to be seen to be done. 'I think it would be proper that those who are personally culpable would be brought before an Oireachtas committee and would answer for what they have done or indeed for their omissions.'

Byron Georgiou, a member of the Financial Crisis Inquiry Commission that produced a report on the American crisis and who has represented investors in Enron and WorldCom, told Tom Lyons in the *Sunday Times* that he was flabbergasted at the slow pace and the anonymity of Ireland's banking investigations. 'It serves a public purpose to identify individuals who were responsible and to identify institutions that failed in their mission, both in the private sector and the public sector. Unless we do that we run a serious risk of it occurring again in our lifetime. That would be a terrible tragedy.' He said he could not understand why the Nyberg commission did not carry out its interviews with bankers, regulators, civil servants and politicians in public. America's inquiry had publicly interviewed Alan Greenspan, former head of the Federal Reserve System (central bank), Hank Paulson, former Secretary of the Treasury, and senior bankers from Goldman Sachs, Bank of America and Morgan Stanley, among many others, as well as publishing thousands of documents.

It seems to me when we have so many people unemployed, so many people who have lost their homes, so many at risk of losing their homes, so many people whose mortgages are well in excess of the value of the property today, so many people who have lost their retirement savings . . . they are entitled to have a glimpse into what happened.

The fact that Ireland had granted a blanket taxpayer bail-out to banks like Irish Nationwide, he said, made this even more pressing here than in America. He could think of no legal reason for keeping Nyberg's 120 interviews and 200,000 documents secret.

Why shouldn't [the public] get it now? I don't understand the argument that bankers who at the risk of losing their entire franchise begged the Irish taxpayers to bail them out, how they should have standing to object when the taxpayers want a window into what happened so they can avoid this happening to their children and their grandchildren.

The principal actors in Ireland's economic collapse, such as Michael Fingleton, by asking the public to pick up the bill for their mistakes had 'lost their right to privacy,' Georgiou believed.

However, there was a legal hitch before an effective inquiry could take place.

———

In November 2001 thirty-six gardaí successfully challenged an Oireachtas inquiry into the shooting dead of John Carthy in Abbeylara, Co. Longford. In its judgement the court found that such inquiries had not got the power to make findings of fact or expressions of opinion adverse to the good name or reputation of citizens. Enda Kenny decided to hold a referendum to change the constitution to ensure that an Oireachtas committee would have the power to hold bankers to account. 'The clarity of the advice given to the Government by the Attorney-General,' he said, 'means I have no intention of going down a road in which the Oireachtas literally would be laughed out of court by attempting to pursue something that it cannot do because of the inadequacy of its powers.'

The referendum was set for October. It would have allowed reports into Irish Nationwide, such as the Ernst and Young report, to finally see the light of day. Fingleton had had a six-month reprieve, but now it appeared that things were going in the right direction.

Days before the referendum was due to be voted on, eight former attorney-generals wrote a public letter that warned that granting these powers to politicians would seriously weaken the rights of individuals to their good name. Among the signatories were Dermot Gleeson, former chairman of AIB; Paul Gallagher, who had advised the state on the night of the guarantee; and Peter Sutherland, chairman of Goldman Sachs, which had advised Irish Nationwide. The independent presidential candidate Mary Davis, a former director of a subsidiary of Bank of Ireland, also came out against it. 'I have real concerns that this change— if approved—will undermine and dilute the rights of every citizen of this state,' she said.

The Minister for Justice, Alan Shatter, was quick to call their concerns 'nonsense' and 'simply wrong.' However, it was too late. The public were justifiably deeply distrustful of politicians, and 53 per cent of them voted against the measure on 30 October 2011. An incredible opportunity to expose bankers like Fingleton and the people who facilitated their costly recklessness was lost. The special powers of the Oireachtas, if used correctly, could have introduced a new level of transparency and accountability into public life.

The Committee of Public Accounts, after the three reports, tried to hold an investigation, but because of legal concerns as well as political infighting it kept being put off. Years went by without any answers to the many questions posed by Irish Nationwide.

In November 2012 the *Irish Times* reported that 'the promised
Oireachtas inquiry into the State's banking crisis is unlikely to begin until
early 2014 at the earliest, according to an indicative time limit prepared
for the Oireachtas Public Accounts Committee.' Despite the outrageous
cost to the public of the banking collapse, and that of Irish Nationwide
in particular, the public were still none the wiser about their worst bank.

———

Irish bankers were not the only ones enjoying anonymity and
unaccountability for their actions. The really big winners were the hedge
funds. They too not only enjoyed being nameless and unanswerable to
anyone in Ireland but also enjoyed mega-profits as the Irish taxpayer
poured the country's wealth into Irish Nationwide's black hole.

It didn't have to be this way. In March 2011, for example, Irish
Nationwide announced that it planned to buy back two outstanding
lower-tier bonds at 20 per cent of par or face value. The offer was
voluntary, but almost unanimously all the holders of the bonds, which
had a face value of €250 million, signed up. At a stroke, Irish Nationwide
had saved the taxpayer €200 million by doing what the public were told
was impossible: it burned some bond-holders.

It was the very thing Europe was preventing the society doing with
its other big bond-holders, who remained protected by the government
guarantee.

The hedge funds included Millhouse, the investment vehicle owned
by Roman Abramovich. Millhouse had clubbed together with other
funds to try to sue the society in London and force it to pay out in full.
They argued in court that Irish Nationwide was not a special case, like
Anglo Irish Bank, but should be considered more like AIB, where even
lowly bond-holders were being covered in full.

Even lowly Irish Nationwide bond-holders, they argued, should not
have to take a hit for Ireland's handling of the society, which 'ultimately
had fallen victim to the government's policies that allowed for the
creation of a real estate bubble and its simultaneous failure to properly
supervise the bank's management.'

They lost their case, however, when the courts decided that Anglo
Irish and Irish Nationwide should be treated in the same way. This left

them no real choice but to sell out. Even at 20 cents in the euro some of the bond-holders still made money, as they had bought them in some cases for even less than that. The new management of Irish Nationwide had taken on a Russian oligarch and won.

BNP Paribas, the French investment bank, advised Irish Nationwide's new management team on how to burn its bond-holders, for a hefty fee. The same bank had accompanied Michael Fingleton and Stan Purcell down the years when they raised the money in the first place from German and French bond-holders, who threw billions at the two men with little regard for how badly they would lend it.

In 2010 Irish Nationwide's new management had done an extensive investor road-show in order to get to know their bond-holders. It was in part intended to let them know that the society intended to burn a relatively tiny number of subordinated bond-holders. BNP Paribas had organised the tour to Paris and Frankfurt, Europe's financial powerhouses, without whose money Irish Nationwide would never have been able to do what it did to Ireland. 'A lot of German banks attended these meetings, but they weren't that worried,' a well-placed source said. 'They had already greatly reduced their exposure to the society or even entirely sold out at that stage by selling on their bonds at a discount to various hedge funds.'

'The government would not let the society burn the bondholders,' a capital markets source said. 'Europe was calling the shots. The Germans were strongly opposed to any burning and wouldn't let the society do anything.' Another capital markets source said:

A lot of money was there to be made. The big German and French banks were desperate to sell Irish Nationwide's bonds as they were continually downgraded. They got out and others got in as Irish Nationwide's senior bonds were sold off at 50c to 60c in the euro and even less. Hedge funds and private equity guys were prepared to take on the risk by buying at this level. They figured they might take a minor hit but that Europe wouldn't let the Irish government burn them entirely. They made a total killing when the society was made pay out on most of its bonds at 100c in the euro.

The management of Irish Nationwide and the government knew that billions were being transferred from the ordinary citizens to hedge funds in London, Geneva and New York. 'BNP handled things, the cheque went into a clearing system and was then distributed on the various funds,' an informed source said. 'You couldn't see who was making the money as a result. A lot of people more than hit their bonuses. The Irish taxpayer will be paying for many years.'

As the government cut back on spending on health and other services, billions were transferred from the Irish citizen to these hedge funds, which were often domiciled for tax purposes in the Caribbean or Switzerland. It was possibly the greatest transfer of wealth from the many to the few in recent history.

In December 2012 Debt Justice Action, a lobbying group, applied to the Guinness Book of Records to have Ireland's banking bail-out recognised as the world's most expensive bank bail-out. It was the decision to take the hit for Europe by paying off the bond-holders in full that ensured that we were a shoo-in for the prize.

———

Behind the scenes, things were moving slowly but steadily against Michael Fingleton and his former cronies. Accountability was still some way off, but at least things were beginning to go in the right direction.

Irish Nationwide was in crisis. Its priority was trying to stabilise the society and get back what it could for the taxpayer, so its new management had few resources to put into inherited problems. There were other priorities to deal with.

On 10 February 2011 Anglo Irish Bank applied to the High Court to be allowed merge with Irish Nationwide, subject to approval by the European Union. A merger and gradual winding down of both banks had been a condition of the agreement between the government and the €85 billion EU ECB IMF bail-out.

Mike Aynsley, the chief executive of Anglo Irish, led this complex merger of Ireland's two zombie banks. 'It is a necessary step in enabling the possibility of a wider restructure of the banking sector to happen,' he said.

As part of this process Irish Nationwide's remaining €3.6 billion in deposits held by 160,000 customers was transferred to Irish Life and Permanent. Safely among these deposit-holders were the very members who had cheered on Fingleton's recklessness and shouted down rebels like Brendan Burgess. They were happy now to shelter behind the state guarantee, which protected their deposits, which might have been wiped out if the society had been allowed to collapse.

With most of Irish Nationwide's large property loans now in NAMA, there was little enough left. Aynsley and his management took over what he termed in a press briefing 'Ireland's answer to sub-prime': a rump €2 billion residential mortgage book and some small commercial deals. In communication with Brussels around this time, Aynsley said the society planned to try to clean up this loan book before flogging it in 2015 at an estimated loss of between €220 and €330 million.

The merger of Anglo Irish and Irish Nationwide would take 'a couple of months,' Aynsley said on 31 March 2011, announcing Anglo Irish Bank's last set of results before its merger. Anglo Irish made a loss of €17.7 billion in 2010, the biggest loss in a single year in Irish corporate history. But as Anglo Irish was ten times the size of Irish Nationwide, pound for pound the society was still the worst bank in Ireland.

Aynsley said he believed the merged entity could be used to manage or warehouse any toxic loans that had not gone into NAMA but still needed to be dumped off the balance sheets of the four surviving banks. 'We could end up being like the Borg, and we will assimilate what we are given and do the best job we can managing it,' he said.

On 20 April 2011 the Anglo Irish Bank sign was ceremonially taken down from its head office in St Stephen's Green in front of a crowd of photographers. It was placed for safekeeping in the bank's now-empty vaults, with Aynsley hinting that some day it might go into a museum. And it did.

Irish Nationwide's signs were treated less reverentially. They were torn down and thrown into skips in the months preceding the merger. The only sign of Irish Nationwide that remained was a slight shadow along the front of its building where the outline of its old name could vaguely be made out.

In mid-June a deadline was set for the merger of the two failed institutions. 'The two organisations are working towards the July 1st date for the merger on a very open and co-operative basis, which is pleasing,' Aynsley said. It was now more or less official that Aynsley would become chief executive of the combined bank, with the chairman of Anglo Irish, Alan Dukes, taking up the same role in the still-unnamed new institution.

On Thursday 30 June 2011 what was effectually the final board meeting of Irish Nationwide was held on the seventh floor of its head office. The board had been firefighting for two years and were exhausted from the strain.

Danny Kitchen, the chairman, thanked his board. He did not intend to seek a position on the combined entities' new board but instead planned to return to the private sector. Gerry McGinn, the chief executive, was also planning to return to his home in the North. In September he would take on a new job as head of First Trust, the Northern Ireland arm of AIB. This left John McGloughlin as the most senior executive left in Irish Nationwide. Roger McGreal, an expert in banking, credit and risk who had proved a rock of common sense around the boardroom table, was later invited by Alan Dukes to join the board of the combined entity.

This final meeting was primarily concerned with ensuring that the merger went smoothly, but in some ways it was also a reflective one. Among the items on the agenda was a report prepared for the Department of Finance on the outstanding issues relating to the society. Along with the Ernst and Young report on unusual lending and a broader McCann Fitzgerald report on failings of corporate governance, this was now the third report delivered to the Department of Finance. It covered much of the ground of the two earlier reports and updated the department on more recent developments.

The department, however, was still not prepared to release any of these reports publicly, because, it said, it feared their release would 'prejudice or impair' potential court proceedings. This now seemed to be on the cards.

A division had been set up inside the Central Bank, headed by Peter Oakes, its new director of enforcement since October 2010, that was concentrating very hard on Irish Nationwide. Oakes, a native of Australia, had previously founded Compliance Ireland, a consultancy that specialised in advising financial institutions on corporate governance, compliance and risk. He faced a mountainous task trying to clean up the financial services industry, which had been so neglected by his predecessors. Besides Irish Nationwide there were many other issues to deal with, not least the failed Anglo Irish Bank and Quinn Insurance, one of the country's biggest insurance companies, which had been put into administration because it was insolvent.

Oakes and his team, however, were being updated regularly on each fresh revelation unearthed inside Irish Nationwide. The final version of

Ernst and Young's report had been sent to the Central Bank, along with the report by McCann Fitzgerald into the society's failings of corporate governance. Other files and issues were also sent up the line as they were uncovered.

The contents of some of these reports were so serious that they were referred to the Gardaí, the Minister for Finance admitted in response to a Dáil question. This explained in part, he said, why he was unable to publish the reports. It was still hard to know, however, when and whether any action would be taken, as the issues were complex and the rules unclear. In any event, Michael Fingleton and everybody else involved in the society denied all wrongdoing.

After reviewing these files and reports the governor of the Central Bank and the new Financial Regulator, Matthew Elderfield, determined that the Central Bank would begin preparing its own case against Irish Nationwide and its former senior figures. Given the scale of the losses incurred by the society and the extent of the wrongdoing, however, a relatively small number of personnel had been allocated to the investigations. The entire financial system had been hugely neglected, so the Central Bank's investigation teams were constantly moving from crisis to crisis. There was much to clean up. The Financial Regulator actively fined wrongdoers and even shut down some investment firms in an unyielding manner like never before.

The Central Bank was keen to improve the dismal quality of Irish banking, and it had introduced new regulations and standards of fitness and probity to ensure that bankers still in place who had made serious mistakes in the past were held to account. This had little effect on Irish Nationwide at first, as most senior figures had by then departed. However, on 6 November 2011 Tom Lyons reported in the *Sunday Times* that the Central Bank planned to assess Michael Walsh to decide if he was a fit and proper person to act as a director of International Investment and Underwriting, Dermot Desmond's financial investment company. This was an extension of its earlier investigations that applied only to individuals who had held senior posts in either Anglo Irish or Irish Nationwide at the time of the government guarantee in September 2008 and who were now in posts in other firms it regulated.

Finally, it seemed, Walsh would be questioned about his actions, or lack of them, while chairman of the society if he wanted to stay on the board of International Investment and Underwriting, which was regulated by the Central Bank. His responses would be heard behind closed doors, but it was better than nothing.

The day after the newspaper report Walsh resigned from International Investment and Underwriting; this meant he no longer faced being questioned. He remains today a close adviser to Desmond and an important figure behind the scenes in Irish financial circles. He sits on the board of two of Desmond's companies. One of these is QED Equity, a low-profile investment firm that has thrived during the global banking bust. It states on its web site that it has restructured $45 billion worth of 'risk assets' since 2007. It is an unlimited company, owned by two other companies based in the Isle of Man, making it impossible to tell how exactly it made its money during the global financial crisis.

Walsh also sits on the board of Daon, a biometric identity company founded by Desmond that includes on its board Tom Ridge, former first secretary of the US Department of Homeland Security. In December 2012 Desmond thanked Walsh by name for his help in establishing the International Financial Services Centre in Dublin when the financier was given an award by *Business and Finance* at a gala dinner attended by Ireland's business leaders.

The Central Bank is not finished, however, with Walsh and others in the society. In July 2012 Tom Lyons reported in the *Sunday Independent* that it was preparing a case against the society's former senior executives and board members. Its investigation has identified about forty instances in which the building society may have broken the banking rules. The Central Bank's focus was on unorthodox lending to developers. Among the cases it is examining are large loans granted to developers without approval by the credit committee, millions given to developers for unclear purposes, and major loans given without proper board supervision. It is expected to draw on expert witnesses who will criticise the processes operating in the society and seek to assign responsibility for its failings to its executives and board.

While Fingleton was granted extraordinary powers by his board over the decades, the Central Bank hopes to prove that this did not mean he had the power to act without any supervision from his board or to do absolutely anything.

By July 2012 the Central Bank was in written communication with the individuals it was investigating. Before responding, Fingleton asked for an assurance that his legal costs would be picked up by the state. Stan Purcell, the society's secretary and long-standing finance director, is being questioned about the society's practices and processes, especially as he is a link between the board and executives.

Wrongdoing, if proved, could lead to fines of up to €500,000 for Fingleton, Walsh and others. Other sanctions that might be imposed on individuals involved in the society include disqualification for a number of years from the management of a regulated financial service provider.

The extent of any sanction will depend on various factors being examined by the Central Bank, including whether the society or individuals acted in what its procedures term a 'deliberate, dishonest, or reckless way.' It will also examine the 'general compliance history' of the society and whether it had 'previously been requested to take remedial action.' A full formal inquiry will begin in 2013 when the Central Bank has finished gathering its evidence. All individuals questioned in this process have denied any wrongdoing.

———

Meanwhile the slow death of Irish Nationwide continued. Having exhausted all other options, a decision had been made to wind down the society, and the government and the European Commission decided that the cheapest way to do this was to merge it with the other zombie bank, Anglo Irish Bank.

On 1 July 2011 all the assets and liabilities remaining in Irish Nationwide were officially moved to Anglo Irish. The merged banks would later be renamed the Irish Bank Resolution Corporation. John McGloughlin was in day-to-day charge of the society, reporting to Mike Aynsley. The IBRC was now a pure asset-recovery bank, given a deadline, in agreement with the European Commission, of 2020 for winding itself down. Irish Nationwide is no more.

———

Having cleared out his files just before his departure, Michael Fingleton was also anxious to turn his back on his past. He emptied most of his accounts in the society in October 2010 and moved more than €790,000 offshore in a number of different transactions. The society delayed the transfer while it sought confirmation from the Gardaí that there was no reason to block him from doing so. None was given, and there was nothing to be done but let the money go.

In February 2011 Fingleton moved the remaining balance in his account to Permanent TSB, ending, he hoped, all involvement with his old society.

On 2 August 2011 Aynsley wrote to Fingleton, telling him the bank was 'reviewing and considering various legacy matters' relating to Irish Nationwide. As part of this process, he said the bank wanted him to finally repay his €1 million bonus, as promised in March 2009. He said he had reviewed Fingleton's reasons for not returning it and his contractual entitlements to the bonus.

> It is certain that in the absence of state support to INBS from 2008, there would have been no prospect of INBS surviving nor would funds have been available for any such payment to you. In that context, such a payment was inappropriate.
>
> In light of the above, as group chief executive and on behalf of the Irish taxpayer, who continues to bear a significant burden as a result of the failure of certain Irish financial institutions including INBS, I am calling on you to make good your commitment [to return the bonus] at a time when it is crucial that the costs to the taxpayer be minimised.

Aynsley also told Fingleton to return his going-away gift of a watch valued at €11,500.

> You received this in April 2009 at a time when it was clear that inbs along with the rest of the Irish banking system was highly distressed. It is surprising that you accepted a gift of this magnitude, and particularly at a time when INBS was the beneficiary of a government guarantee . . . I would ask you to return it so that we may realise sales proceeds and recoup some value for the taxpayer.

On 10 September 2011 Fingleton wrote back to Aynsley.

Dear Mr Aynsley,
    I believe it is now opportune, timely and necessary to respond to your letter of the 2nd ultimo [2 August] and to the media campaign conducted by you and your chairman in particular to your allegations

that I received a retirement gift of a watch from the Irish Nationwide Building Society in a manner that was inappropriate and improper.

I am somewhat surprised that INBS having spent very substantial sums of money on consultants reports, enquiries and investigations that you do not have the facts in relation to this matter. With the few people involved who were all in situ until relatively recently it should not have taken more than five minutes to do so.

I wish to categorically state that I was not presented with any retirement gift by the society. The facts are as follows. On Friday 30th April at 5pm I ceased to be CEO of INBS. I agreed afterwards to attend a small drinks reception in the board room comprising a cross section of management and long serving staff. In the course of the reception I was presented with a gift 'on behalf of the management and staff.' I accepted it on that basis with some considerable reluctance. It was only good manners to accept the gift as presented. I had no idea what it was or its value. I also wish to make it clear that I had no prior knowledge of the intended presentation and I had no hand, act or part in its acquisition or selection.

In relation to the so-called 'bonus' of €1m (less tax of €410K paid to the Revenue Commissioners) I wish once again to refer you to my letters of the 25th September and 21st October 2009 to the society which clearly and comprehensively sets out my position. This position has been deliberately ignored by the former chairman and the CEO of INBS in their public statements in the interim period. For the purpose of clarity I am once again compelled to set it out once more.

I entered an agreement with the Government at the highest levels to which the Minister for Finance was a party. I agreed to repay the net sum of €590K to the Society subject to certain undertakings and commitments agreed by the government. The terms of the agreement (which was confidential at their request) was as set out in my letter of the 25th September 2009. Because of the confidentiality element in the agreement I did not advert to it in my public statement of intent. This agreement shortly afterwards was reneged on by the subsequent actions of the Minister for Finance and because of this I was released from any obligations I had to pay the society the sum concerned.

There was, as has now been acknowledged, no legal obligation on me to repay anything. I simply agreed to voluntarily do so in good faith and for the benefit of the government. The Attorney General informed the Minister of the legality of my contract and subsequent legal opinion confirmed this. CIROC [the Covered Institutions Remuneration Oversight Committee] was indeed forced to change its stated position on this and acknowledge that it was a legal and binding contract and nothing to do with the Government Guarantee scheme.

The simple fact of the matter is that I was prepared to honour my agreement but the government failed to honour theirs. For a government and particularly a minister for finance to renege on an agreement which was effectively a contract and which was for their political benefit is reprehensible. Fortunately I have two independent witnesses who were involved in negotiations with the government side, who are prepared to fully confirm the facts as stated by me. I have also contemporaneous notes of the discussions.

In conclusion I never had any legal obligation to repay any of the funds received and because of the government's breach of my agreement with them I have no obligation either now or in the future to do so. They had their opportunity but blew it for whatever reasons.

This clearly sets out the factual position in relation to the matters raised as they concern me. I expect an appropriate response from the bank to set the record straight.

Yours sincerely,
Michael P. Fingleton

Seventeen days later Aynsley replied. He said he had considered Fingleton's letter 'carefully' and concluded that 'your responses are not satisfactory.'

You indicated with regard to the expensive watch that was presented to you on your retirement, that it was given to you on behalf of the management and staff of the society, and you seem to imply that on that basis you are entitled to keep it. I can confirm that the watch was not provided on behalf of the management and staff. It was paid for by the Society, and a copy of the receipt against which the Society's disbursement was made can be provided to you if you wish to see it. I repeat therefore the request to return this item to the bank so that it can be disposed of for the benefit of the taxpayer.

With regard to what you say about the bonus of €1m paid to you after the government guarantee had to be introduced and at a time when there was no doubt at all as to the devastating condition in which the Society found itself as a result of your years of leadership, the response you provide is simply not an answer to the request I made of you. You are yourself choosing to ignore the agreement you reached with the Minister for Finance to repay the bonus and you seem to think that your doing so is justified by asserting a failure of the Minister for Finance to honour the agreement he reached with you that there would be, as you put it, 'closure' in relation to your bonus and pension (a concession to you that I am advised was not provided.) Even if the Minister had agreed such a concession and even if the Minister, by giving public instructions to the government appointed directors of the society to carry out investigations into these two matters, would have breached it, this would have nothing to do with the request I made of you which expressly was not concerned with contractual niceties.

The request I made of you was to invite you to behave in a decent, proper and honourable way by recognising that the payment of the bonus should never have been paid to or accepted by you in the circumstances concerned. Without the state rescue, the Society would definitely have failed, with catastrophic consequences, and the payment of your bonus whether contractually due or not, could not have been met. Not only this, you must surely recognise the inappropriateness of your receiving a bonus of €1m at a time when it was already abundantly clear that dire consequences were flowing to this State and its citizens as a result of the extraordinary losses arising from the reckless decisions made during your stewardship of the Society.

It is also apparent to me that expenses were claimed by you during (and even after) your tenure at the Society that were inappropriate. I have seen John McGloughlin's letter to you of 30 March 2011 in reply to your letter of 1 February 2011 and I understand that you have not replied to it. That letter deals with two expense items, €12,180 incurred for your dental work at the Blackrock Clinic and £2,373 incurred in relation to a 2 night stay at the Dorchester Hotel in London for you and Eileen Fingleton that occurred after you ceased to be employed by the society. These certainly appear to have been claimed inappropriately and you have provided unacceptable and unsupportable explanations. There are others totalling €73,524 that I consider equally suspect where you have not provided either adequate explanation and/or documentation to evidence the legitimacy of the item as a company expense. It is not at all acceptable for you to simply state that costs were incurred reasonably on behalf of the society without providing verifiable details, including the reason and nature of the expense, receipts and other supporting documentation. The other expense that I consider suspect are included in the attached document and I again ask you to behave in a decent, proper and honourable way by refunding these amounts without delay.

I think it is plain that you should deal with each of the above matters by returning the watch to the bank, by providing full repayment of the bonus and by reimbursing the above inappropriate expense claims and you ought to get on with doing so without further ado.

Yours sincerely,

A. M. R. (Mike) Aynsley

The letter was a clear warning shot. Aynsley was determined to finally achieve what the late Minister for Finance, Brian Lenihan, had wondered if he could ever achieve: he was going to try to get Fingleton. But first he had to determine if there was a case.

———

On 28 March 2012 journalists filled one side of the boardroom table in the sparkling head office of the IBRC, which had once been home to the wealth management division of Anglo Irish Bank. After announcing that the IBRC had lost €873 million in 2011, as against €17 billion in 2010, Aynsley was asked by the media about Fingleton. He had prepared his response.

The IBRC, Aynsley said, had initiated two sets of proceedings against former senior figures in the society. The first was against Michael Fingleton, and the second was against five others: Michael Walsh, Stan Purcell, Con Power, Terry Cooney and David Brophy. Aynsley described the actions as 'protective plenary summonses' against the men, to 'signal a potential series of actions to come.' The actions were undertaken to avoid problems with the statute of limitations, which blocks certain legal actions after six years.

Aynsley was guarded in what he revealed of the nature of the bank's case. He said that in general the bank was required to pursue individuals believed to have breached regulatory and contractual obligations or fiduciary duties. Any action that was being taken was taken with the full backing of the Minister for Finance. 'We just don't charge off and do this: the minister has now provided his approval to commence these proceedings,' he said.

The IBRC's approach to taking legal action was deliberately wide-ranging, as it was still sifting through the society's loan files and other records, which had been poorly kept. It was hard to know whether particular items had gone missing, had ever existed or had even been destroyed. Equally it was not clear who would be prepared to co-operate with any investigation into the society.

The only former senior figure in the society prepared to comment on this or any other matter on the record in relation to pending investigations was Con Power. He was shocked to be included among those named by Aynsley. More than anybody on the society's board, he had tried to take on Fingleton and improve the society's treatment of its small borrowers. He was the only one prepared to meet distressed borrowers, and he had at all times pushed hard for reforms. Now his name was being sullied by being associated with Fingleton, a man he tried hard to contain. Brendan Burgess, critic-in-chief of Fingleton's regime, believed it was totally wrong that Power had been dragged into the Irish Nationwide debacle. He believed Power had been the only board member prepared to work with him on trying to take on Fingleton's dominant leadership.

Power obtained legal advice immediately. The prognosis was good. He had resigned from the board on 23 February 2006, so technically he was outside the statute of limitations, and his legal advisers felt he could not be sued. Power, however, was determined to clear his name.

He had behaved honourably as a director and had twice—on 1 October 2002 and 5 December 2005—tried to resign from the board in frustration at Fingleton's leadership. The Financial Regulator, Dr Liam O'Reilly, had urged Power both times to stay on as a non-executive director. O'Reilly, Power said, told him in 2002 that the Central Bank was 'relying' on him and Michael Walsh to act as a 'counterbalance to the dominance of the managing director within the limits of our capacity as non-executive directors.'

In December 2005 Power had again threatened to resign, because the society was dragging its heels about expanding its board. O'Reilly had told him to hang on a bit longer, and, he said, the Central Bank would back him on this matter. O'Reilly retired as Financial Regulator later that month, and the board of Irish Nationwide was not changed until after it was too late.

The fact that he had stayed on the board only so long because the Financial Regulator himself had urged him to, and that now his name was appearing in the papers as being linked to Fingleton's, was a source of great hurt to Power. Nonetheless, rather than kicking up a stink he instructed his solicitor to write to the IBRC saying he would like to meet them. This was arranged in the second half of 2012, and a meeting was held that lasted several hours.

Power explained his role and his many efforts to challenge Fingleton and improve Irish Nationwide on many different fronts. At the end of the meeting Power agreed to help the bank in any way it asked. Finally the IBRC had a boardroom insider prepared to speak up. Power wanted to do the right thing rather than slip away on a technicality.

At lower and middle ranks, meanwhile, the IBRC gathered other potential witnesses who had either left the society or continued to work there under the IBRC umbrella and who were prepared to help. These people had carried out what paperwork there was; they had witnessed important decisions. The situation was not entirely hopeless.

The IBRC, like the Central Bank, began to seek out banking experts to review its files and determine whether, as it suspected, there had been unusual and repeated breaches by Fingleton, and possibly others, of their obligations to monitor Irish Nationwide and ensure that it was run correctly.

As each file was dusted off and reviewed it became clear that failures in loan procedures and approvals were not confined to a few loans. Errors, corner-cutting and bizarre decision-making were endemic. Unorthodox lending was as much the rule as the exception. These failures, which Fingleton as managing director ultimately was responsible for, compounded the scale of the losses inside Irish Nationwide. Too often the society found that it was on the back foot relative to its bigger borrowers, who were insulated from the problems associated with their loans. Non-recourse borrowing that was limited only to the special-purpose vehicle set up to do an individual deal ensured that when a deal went bad it was the taxpayer who ultimately took the hit. Wealthy borrowers could simply walk away from the problems they helped create.

The IBRC, however, needed to prove more than just stupid deals, like those made by every other Irish bank: it wanted to prove that Irish Nationwide under Fingleton had made many loans that simply would not have been possible had the proper procedures existed. For example, it had lent large sums to some borrowers without investigating whether they had any ability to repay. Functioning credit committees should have stopped this type of lending.

Worryingly for Fingleton, for his close executives and for the society's former board, it was quite clear from the KPMG reports in 2000 and 2005, as well as from other correspondence with the Central Bank, that it was no secret that the society was not working properly. Along with the pay and power of being involved with Irish Nationwide, the IBRC planned to argue that there should also have been responsibilities at the executive level and board level to ensure that the correct procedures were operating. Fingleton had a duty as managing director, being paid millions per year to ensure that the correct controls and procedures were adopted. His failure to remedy these matters opened up the possibility of the IBRC suing him for failing to address these failings and deficiencies.

As the IBRC kept digging deeper, it began to consider whether it could prove that Fingleton was negligent not only in general but in relation to particular loans. The Ernst and Young report, and subsequent findings, provided plenty of ammunition.

Broadly, the evidence Ernst and Young discovered in relation to a number of big clients showed, among other things, a general lack of processes and control, unsubstantiated draw-downs of loans, multi-million consultancy fees that had not been vouched for, loans being allowed to get bigger than sanctioned, money paid out for things that were not in the original facility letter, money being used to settle rows that had not been approved by anyone other than verbally by Fingleton, a loan granted to one company that was actually spent by another group company, making it hard for the society to get the money back, loans being declared non-recourse, conflicts of interest, and loans being given with security that had already had a charge from another bank.

There was ample evidence, even though the IBRC's plenary summons went back only as far as April 2006. Unorthodox activities at the society stretched back many more years than that, but nothing could be done about it.

The IBRC also appointed forensic accountants to pick through Fingleton's pension and other personal investments down the years. Fingleton had in effect managed his own pension fund and increased it to an incredible €27 million. What exactly had he invested in to create such incredible returns? Were there any undeclared conflicts of interest among his investments?

He also had large amounts of cash in his bank account. Where did it all come from, and what did he spend this money on? While there is no suggestion that Fingleton engaged in any wrongdoing in relation to his personal fortune, these were the type of questions that the IBRC was asking the staff to look into. Having formerly regarded Fingleton as an unchallengeable feudal chieftain, his old staff were being asked to question everything he ever did.

Besides investigating whether Fingleton had behaved correctly with his investments, an additional reason for examining his wealth was to try to determine what fortune he had left. The bank had to decide before beginning any legal action whether he had sufficient assets to pay any potential damages.

There was also the elusive issue of Fingleton's bonus. In contractual terms, the IBRC knew it had little chance of recovering the €1 million. The legal advice the bank received from senior counsel was pretty clear on this. Instead it decided to try a new approach. It planned to argue that the bonus would never have been offered or granted if the extent of Fingleton's wrongdoing had been disclosed to the board. Fingleton was in a fiduciary position as managing director of a financial institution. His special powers did not give him the right to do anything he liked: he had a duty to disclose any major action to his board.

If the bank could prove he had known about problem loans or had made significant bad decisions without informing his board, it could argue that his contract would not have been extended and he would therefore not have been eligible for his bonus.

Fingleton was an executive director and so had a duty to act with skill and diligence in the performance of his role. He had to act in the best interests of the society and in a proper way. He also had a duty to ensure that any conflicts of interest had been authorised by the society, and that he made no secret profits.

The society was in the business of giving loans, and it had been caught out by a property bubble, so inevitably many of these loans had gone bad. It wasn't enough to show that the society had lost a lot of money because it got the property market wrong: the real challenge was to show that not enough prudence and care had been taken in giving out loans in the first place and in monitoring them over time by Fingleton, his executives and his board.

————

As 2013 began, it finally looked as if Michael Fingleton was going to be made explain just what had happened with Irish Nationwide and how it had ended up costing the taxpayer €5.4 billion.

The economist Colm McCarthy commented in the *Sunday Independent* in December 2012 that the cost of bailing out the society, if laid out in one-dollar bills laid end to end, would stretch to the moon and back one-and-a-half times. But still the public didn't know what had happened. The bill for Irish Nationwide had been paid by Ireland, but nobody—more than four years after the bank guarantee—had been held responsible.

Early in the morning of 7 February 2013, emergency legislation was rushed through the Oireachtas to allow the immediate liquidation of Irish Bank Resolution Corporation. Michael Fingleton's Irish Nationwide was finally being killed off by Ireland's politicians, along with its zombie sister, Anglo Irish Bank. Many of the same politicians in Ireland's two biggest parties, who voted in favour of this new legislation, had sat in the Dáil for decades. In 2006 they had voted through the legislation required for Irish Nationwide to be sold, in a move which Fingleton believed would bag him millions after he had spent the previous years fattening up the society, recklessly.

But that was in the past. No politician, regulator or civil servant wanted to remember, in 2013, that it was they who had allowed Michael Fingleton to run riot.